ILLINOIS

LAND AND LIFE IN THE PRAIRIE STATE

Edited by
onald E. Nelson

Illinois Geographical Society

KENDALL/HUNT PUBLISHING COMPANY
2460 Kerper Boulevard, Dubuque, Iowa 52001

Contents

Foreword

Few states are able to boast of a geographical textbook written entirely by geography scholars from within the borders of that state. With the publication of *Illinois: Land and Life in the Prairie State,* Illinois now has that distinction.

In 1973 the Illinois Geographical Society initiated a project to prepare a textbook that could be used in teaching the geography of Illinois. The plan was to produce a book that might assist a wide variety of scholars and students in increasing their awareness of geographic characteristics of Illinois. The task of compiling and editing the book was accepted by Ronald Nelson. Under his astute guidance, the manuscript was prepared and assembled into a readable, comprehensive, and scholarly volume. He and his eight coauthors—Irving Cutler, Alden Cutshall, Arlin Fentem, Robert Koepke, Albert Larson, Dalias Price, Martin Reinemann, and Siim Sööt—can take pride in their fulfillment of the project's goals.

In behalf of the Illinois Geographical Society, I wish to thank the editor and authors for their efforts in making possible the publication of *Illinois: Land and Life in the Prairie State.* Through their generosity, all royalties from the book will be assigned to the Society to help support its future educational and professional endeavors. Also, Kendall/Hunt Publishing Company deserves our gratitude for their cooperation in publishing this volume.

Charles Womack, President
Illinois Geographical Society
Lake Land College

Preface

This book attempts to further the reader's understanding of Illinois in three ways. First, it contributes to an awareness of the state's landscape variety by emphasizing geographical patterns of environmental and human phenomena. Second, it illustrates the intimate relationships between human populations and their habitat in the state. Third, it traces the development of these landscapes and relationships through time in order to determine how the state's present land and life came to be. To supplement the written descriptions and analyses, well over a hundred maps are included in the book.

We have adopted a broad scope, and our search of the past for origins of present conditions encompasses not only the human history but also the geologic history of Illinois. For the reader to acquire a reasonably thorough understanding of the state, an effort has been made to support the extensive coverage with adequate detail. To examine an area as large and complex as Illinois in a single volume necessitates the abbreviated treatment of some topics and the omission of others, however. A list of selected readings at the end of each chapter is provided to guide the reader who is interested in obtaining additional or more specialized information.

In planning the book's organization, consideration was given to a variety of alternatives. It was eventually decided that a series of topical chapters, each covering the state as a whole, followed by a regional chapter on each of the two most populated segments of Illinois (the Chicago metropolitan area and the Metro East area) was the most promising organization for maximum utility of the book. Although the chapters complement one another and collectively provide a relatively complete survey of the state, each is capable of being used independently by a reader interested only in the topic or region it covers.

Although the book should benefit anyone interested in the geography and history of Illinois, we anticipate that its primary use will be as a student textbook. The need for an up-to-date text for courses on Illinois geography has been acute over several decades; in order to provide students with reading assignments, instructors have been forced to rely upon diverse journal articles, bulletins, and pamphlets that are inconvenient to assemble and often fail to incorporate a geographic perspective. In history and other social science disciplines, textbooks have been more generally available. While *Illinois: Land and Life in the Prairie State* has been written by geographers primarily to meet the needs of students in their own discipline, care has been taken to make it an attractive alternative text for use in the social sciences generally.

The finished book has evolved from an Illinois Geographical Society project initiated in 1973 to provide instructors with current materials on the geography of Illinois for classroom use. Nine geographers, all of whom have acquired intimate familiarity with the state through years of teaching and research activities, were organized into a writing team to draft chapters for the book. Each author agreed to contribute his services without financial reward so that royalties from the book can be assigned to the Illinois Geographical Society to support the organization's future educational and professional activities.

Although we have made every effort to avoid errors and inaccuracies, it would be rare for a book of this magnitude to appear in an initial edition without flaws. The editor welcomes correspondence from readers who are willing to report shortcomings or offer constructive criticism so that subsequent editions may be a more perfect product.

Ronald E. Nelson

Acknowledgments

In addition to the authors, several individuals have assisted in the preparation of this book and deserve to have their efforts acknowledged. Joyce Tikalsky and Nancy Nocek provided both editorial and clerical assistance, and Patty Crick and Cindy Jorgensen did much of the typing. Most of the original maps were drafted in the Western Illinois University Cartographic Laboratory by Scott Miner and his assistants, particularly Steve Jennings. Preliminary bibliographical material was assembled by Burton Kessler, and assistance with the index was provided by Steve Hughes. Others who contributed to the book will go unnamed, but they have our sincere thanks.

Chapter One

AN INTRODUCTION TO THE PRAIRIE STATE

Ronald E. Nelson
Western Illinois University

The person who is only casually acquainted with Illinois may tend to associate the state with the legend of Abraham Lincoln, whose restored home village of New Salem and the state capital of Springfield where he practiced law and became a national political figure have become favored attractions among tourists. Others may be inclined to link the state with the seemingly endless fields of corn and other crops now occupying the vast grasslands that posed such a difficult habitat for nineteenth century pioneer settlers and gave Illinois its nickname—the Prairie State. In the minds of those who are politically sensitive, Illinois is likely to be closely linked with the political machine of Chicago's late Mayor Richard J. Daley. The inadequacies of such tendencies to stereotype the state should become apparent to readers as they progress through this book; Illinois is a complex entity that defies easy characterization.

As perceived by most Illinoisans, the state is divided into two segments—the Chicago Metropolitan Area and "Downstate"—and the inhabitants of each tend to be suspicious of the other area. The Chicago Metropolitan Area, of course, contains the state's greatest industrial complex and urban agglomeration; its inhabitants represent about 62 percent of Illinois' total population. Although Downstate Illinois encompasses numerous smaller cities, it is fundamentally an agricultural region of enormous productivity. The massive output of its farmers enables Illinois to be one of the country's leading states in agricultural income. Nevertheless, agriculture is far less important than manufacturing in the state's economy, and the wealth of Illinois is concentrated in the Chicago Metropolitan Area.

In terms of area, Illinois is not distinctive; with about 56,400 square miles, it ranks only 24th among the 50 states. At its maximum

1

Figure 1-1. New Salem, where young Abraham Lincoln lived and worked, is now a popular attraction among tourists. The village has been meticulously restored to reflect the nature of pioneer life in central Illinois during the mid-nineteenth century. (Courtesy Illinois Office of Tourism.)

breadth from the Mississippi River near Quincy to the boundary with Indiana, the distance is barely over 200 miles. On the other hand, the north-south axis from Cairo at the confluence of the Ohio and Mississippi rivers to the Wisconsin boundary is considerably greater—about 380 miles. As a consequence of this pronounced elongation (involving over 5° of latitude), there are significant climatic differences between southern and northern Illinois. Winters are distinctly milder and the growing season begins about a month earlier in the southern part of the state than in the north.

In addition to such climatic variations, other environmental variety contributes to the diversity of the Illinois landscape. Fairly rugged and scenic terrain, with a local relief of several hundred feet, exists in the unglaciated ("driftless") areas of the state: the Shawnee Hills south of Carbondale; the Galena area in the far northwest; and part of the western margin, especially Calhoun

County. Although the remainder of the state is a glaciated plain with low relief, it contains several distinctive features including the lake plain on which Chicago was built; floodplains along the major rivers; and glacial moraines, particularly in northern and central Illinois. The extensive prairie grasses and occasional marshes and swamps that once were distinctive elements of the northern and central Illinois environment are now gone, however. In converting these areas into productive croplands, man has plowed under virtually all of the prairie grasses and has dug drainage ditches and installed tile networks to carry away excess water. Despite being cut over extensively, the forests of southern Illinois have survived to a greater degree. A large part of the timberland in that part of the state is now contained in the Shawnee National Forest.

Although what is now Illinois was virtually a wilderness with only a few thousand people at the beginning of the nineteenth

Figure 1-2. A portion of downtown Chicago. The wealth of Illinois is markedly concentrated in the city and its suburbs. (Courtesy Illinois Office of Tourism.)

Figure 1-3. Near Bishop Hill in southern Henry County, this is one of the few remaining areas of natural prairie in Illinois. Big bluestem and little bluestem were the dominant grasses of the Illinois prairie. (Photo by Ronald E. Nelson.)

century, subsequent development and growth has been spectacular. In 1970 Illinois contained 11,113,976 inhabitants, ranking fifth in population after California, New York, Texas, and Pennsylvania. Eighty-three percent of the 1970 population resided in urban areas, including 3,369,357 in Chicago alone. Although only a small community of 30,000 people in 1850, Chicago acquired more than 1.5 million inhabitants and became the nation's second largest city before the end of the nineteenth century. Illinois' second largest concentration of urban population is "Metro East"—the Illinois portion of the St. Louis Metropolitan Area. Like Chicago, the development of Metro East was based on the availability of water and land transportation, heavy industry, and the processing of agricultural commodities.

As a result of its development over the past century and a half, Illinois is now a leader in many areas of endeavor and serves as the key midwestern state. In agriculture, Illinois leads all states in the production of corn, soybeans, and a number of minor crops. It is the country's greatest exporter of both agricultural and industrial products. Only New York, California, and Ohio lead Illinois in most measures of manufacturing. If the output of mills in neighboring Gary, Indiana, is included, the Chicago area is the greatest producer of iron and steel in the country. Long noted for its importance as a lake port and railroad center, Chicago's role as a leading transportation center is now enhanced by O'Hare airport—the busiest air transportation facility in the world. Major events and achievements in the development of Illinois are discussed in some detail in the pages and chapters that follow and are included in a chronological list in the appendix.

The Significance of Location

The character of Illinois is to a great extent a reflection of its location. Positioned in the midsection of the country, the state is adjacent not only to Lake Michigan but also to the Mississippi and Ohio rivers (Fig. 1-4). In earlier times, these waterways served as routes for explorers and pioneer settlers to reach Illinois and they provided a means for early farmers to ship grain and livestock products to market. This excellent access to water transportation, now involving huge barge tows on the rivers and even ocean vessels on the Great Lakes, has enabled Illinois to become a leading exporter of a variety of agricultural and industrial products. In addition, relatively inexpensive water transportation has facilitated the assembly of such bulky industrial raw materials as iron ore for Chicago area steel mills and petroleum for southwestern Illinois oil refineries. Chicago, now the leading port city on the Great Lakes, has had its accessibility by ocean vessels enhanced with completion of the St. Lawrence Seaway in 1959.

Partly because of marketing advantages associated with its central location within the country, Illinois has developed into a leading industrial and commercial state. Numerous firms involved in manufacturing and marketing a variety of products such as steel, construction equipment, agricultural machinery, electrical appliances, foodstuffs, and alcoholic beverages have chosen to locate in Illinois because of the state's situational advantages. Central location was also a major factor in the establishment of the nation's leading mail-order firms, notably Sears, Roebuck and Company, Montgomery Ward, and J.C. Penney, in Chicago.

Illinois is positioned in a part of the North American continent that was covered by

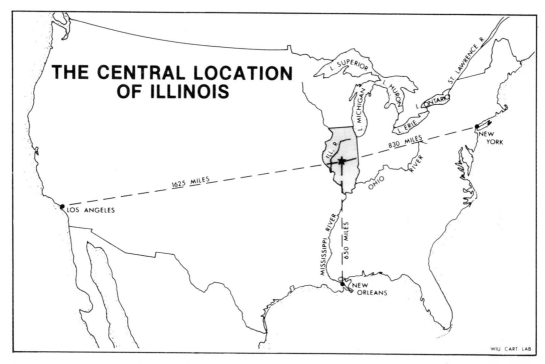

Figure 1-4. Direct access to major rivers and the Great Lakes and central location within the United States have been major advantages in the development of Illinois.

Figure 1-5. At twilight, a barge tow makes its way south on the Mississippi River beneath a bridge near Savanna, Illinois. (Courtesy Illinois Office of Tourism.)

shallow seas during the geologic period known as the Paleozoic. Formed on the bottom of these ancient water bodies were the layers of sedimentary rock that now exist beneath the surface of most of Illinois and are exposed at the surface in a few areas, particularly in the southern and northern extremities of the state. Contained within these sedimentary strata are the major mineral resources of Illinois, notably bituminous coal and petroleum. During a much more recent geologic period—the Pleistocene, which began between one and two million years ago—four enormous continental glaciers formed in Canada around the margins of Hudson Bay. These ice sheets, each separated in time by a warmer and drier interglacial period, advanced outward from their source regions and eventually covered parts of northern United States. At least two of the Pleistocene glaciers covered large segments of Illinois, the margin of one reaching as far south as Giant City State Park near Carbondale. As a result of being located within the glaciated area of North America, most of Illinois was covered by a blanket of glacial debris as the ice melted and had its surface form and drainage pattern altered by the advance and subsequent melting of the ice sheets. Rough terrain in Illinois today is mostly restricted to small areas in the northwestern corner and the far southern parts of the state that escaped glaciation.

Because Illinois occupies a middle latitude position in the interior of a large landmass, its climate involves four distinct seasons, a large annual temperature range, and moderate amounts of precipitation. Maximum summer temperatures are consistently high and occasionally exceed 100°F, while in winter the thermometer may plunge to sub-zero readings. The moderately long growing season (ranging from about 200 days in the far south to 160 days in the north) and the moderately abundant precipitation (varying from an average of 45 inches in the south to 34 inches near the Wisconsin border) are nearly ideal for most middle latitude crops. As throughout eastern United States, tropical air masses from the Gulf of Mexico provide most of the moisture that falls as precipitation in Illinois. Dry and relatively cool conditions occur when polar air masses from Canada migrate across Illinois. Its position between the Gulf and Canada therefore allows Illinois to experience the alternating passage of tropical and polar air masses and the consequence of frequent weather changes.

Settlement and Early Development

More than 300 years have passed since the land of Illinois was first observed by European explorers (Louis Jolliet and Jacques Marquette in 1673) and, of course, several centuries earlier Indian civilizations flourished in portions of the Illinois and middle Mississippi River valleys. The first permanent European settlements in what is now Illinois were French forts and small villages (Cahokia, Kaskaskia, Fort de Chartres, Prairie du Rocher) founded at the turn of the eighteenth century along the Mississippi River in the southwest. Although these French communities were the most significant white settlements in Illinois before 1800, they never attained a population of more than a few hundred. Not until several years after Illinois became a state in 1818 did the number of settlers and degree of land development reach a substantial level. In 1810, the year of the first census enumeration in Illinois Territory, the number of inhabitants was only 12,282 (Table 1-1).

Table 1-1. Population of Illinois, 1810-1970.

Year	Population	Percent Increase
1810*	12,282	
1820	55,162	349.5
1830	157,445	185.2
1840	476,183	202.4
1850	851,470	78.8
1860	1,711,951	101.1
1870	2,539,891	48.4
1880	3,077,871	21.2
1890	3,826,352	24.3
1900	4,821,550	26.0
1910	5,638,591	16.9
1920	6,485,280	15.0
1930	7,630,654	17.7
1940	7,897,241	3.5
1950	8,712,176	10.3
1960	10,081,158	15.7
1970	11,113,976	10.2

*Illinois Territory.

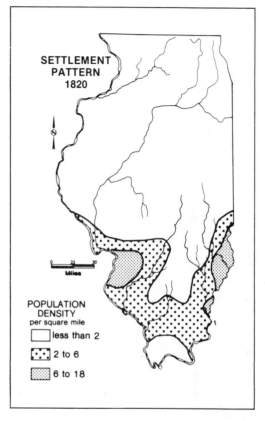

Figure 1-6. Settlement pattern, 1820. (Adapted from a map in Harlan H. Barrows, *Geography of the Middle Illinois Valley*, 1910.)

Following the War of 1812 there occurred expansion of settlement in wooded southern Illinois, and by 1820 the settled area containing at least two people per square mile extended completely across the southern part of the state from the Mississippi to the Wabash River (Fig. 1-6). The northward push of settlers by this time also resulted in a population density of at least two people per square mile in the Wabash Valley, the Mississippi Valley to a point about 50 miles north of the mouth of the Illinois River, the Big Muddy Valley, and the lower valley of the Kaskaskia.

The frontier was largely in central Illinois by 1830 when the population of the state totaled 55,162. The Sangamon country and the southern part of the Military Tract in western Illinois were settled rapidly during the 1820s. In addition, a detached nucleus of settlement, the Galena Lead District in the northwestern corner of the state, had become established by this time. All of these areas as well as the valley of the Illinois River to a point about midway between its mouth and Lake Michigan had attained at least two people per square mile by 1830 (Fig. 1-7). Illinois numbered 157,445 inhabitants in 1830, an increase over the 1820 figure of nearly three fold.

Although a complex of factors influenced the areal pattern of settlement in Illinois up

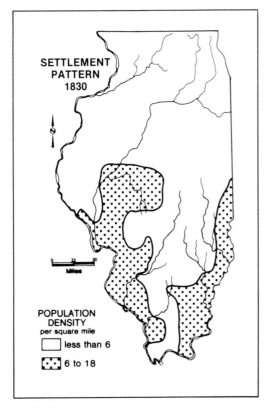

Figure 1-7. Settlement pattern, 1830. (Adapted from a map in Harlan H. Barrows, *Geography of the Middle Illinois Valley,* 1910.)

to the 1830s, most authorities are in agreement that accessibility was of greatest importance. The Ohio River, the paramount route to the West during these early decades of settlement, led to southern Illinois; the northern part of the state, in contrast, was distinctly isolated prior to the 1830s. In addition to accessibility, the early settlement pattern was influenced by the opening of lead deposits in the Galena area and the tendency of pioneers to locate in or close to timber. The settlers who reached Illinois prior to the 1830s were predominantly from the Upland South and tended to have a greater aversion for the prairies of the central and northern parts of the state than did their successors. The need

for timber to provide material for such pioneering necessities as shelter, fuel, and fencing was critical, and the prairies were notorious for their poor drainage, seasonal fires, and isolation.[1] It is clear that all but a few of the early settlers located in or near timbered areas.

The delay in the settlement of northern Illinois was not entirely because of its inaccessibility and domination by prairie, however. Not until after the infamous Black Hawk War in 1832 did white settlers feel that the Indian threat was eliminated. (In reality, the Indians did not pose a significant threat to nineteenth century pioneers in Illinois because they were few in number and their civilizations had seriously deteriorated by that time.) Also, early pioneers found the acquisition of land titles difficult because the government was tardy in establishing land offices in northern Illinois and often the choicest tracts had been obtained relatively early by land speculators. Many early pioneers, by necessity or choice, became squatters and improved land that they did not legally own.

The vast expansion of the settled area and the great increase in population in Illinois during the 1830s and 1840s was facilitated by the opening up of transportation routes to the northern part of the state, particularly the establishment of steamboat service on the Great Lakes; accelerated sales of public lands; and the development of a steel plow to ease the task of breaking the tough prairie sod. In 1840 the population reached 476,183 and by 1850 Illinois could claim 851,470 inhabitants. Between 1830 and 1850 only two areas failed to surpass a density of six people per square mile, one northwest and the other southeast of the Illinois Valley (Figs. 1-8 and 1-9). The largest of these two areas, the Grand Prairie of eastern Illinois, was the most nearly woodless, poorly drained, and inaccessible part of the state. Frontier condi-

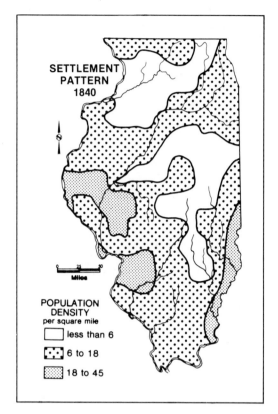

Figure 1-8. Settlement pattern, 1840. (Adapted from a map in Harlan H. Barrows, *Geography of the Middle Illinois Valley,* 1910.)

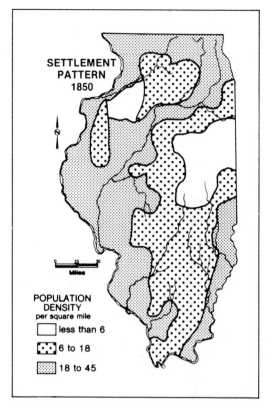

Figure 1-9. Settlement pattern, 1850. (Adapted from a map in Harlan H. Barrows, *Geography of the Middle Illinois Valley,* 1910.)

tions persisted here into the decade of the 1850s, longer than in any other part of the state.

The settlement of northern Illinois was conducted largely by pioneers from northeastern United States and foreign immigrants. Most of them travelled westward by way of the Great Lakes, landing at Chicago and subsequently fanning out over the northern prairies. Douglas McManis has found that they were inclined to place a higher evaluation on the prairie and were more willing to venture out onto the grasslands than their earlier counterparts from the Upland South.[2] Numerous placenames and many cultural institutions in

Chicago and other parts of northern Illinois today clearly reflect the "Yankee" and foreign origin of the area's earliest settlers.

The development of Illinois during the 1850s was highlighted by transportation improvements, particularly the construction of railroads; the development of Chicago as the state's premier urban center; final organization of the state's 102 countries (Fig. 1-10); and the passing of frontier conditions. Chicago was incorporated in 1833 and by 1850 its population had grown to about 30,000. Founded on the shore of Lake Michigan, the young and bustling city was joined with the Illinois River by the Illinois and Michigan Canal in 1848. Its role as the dominant

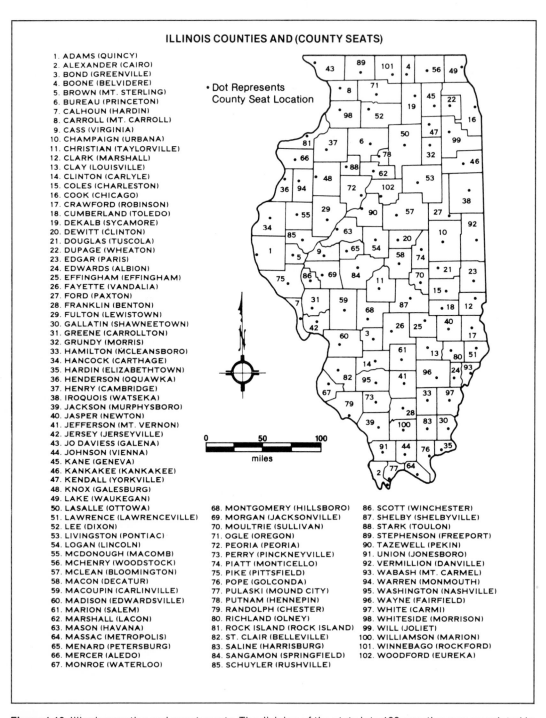

ILLINOIS COUNTIES AND (COUNTY SEATS)

1. ADAMS (QUINCY)
2. ALEXANDER (CAIRO)
3. BOND (GREENVILLE)
4. BOONE (BELVIDERE)
5. BROWN (MT. STERLING)
6. BUREAU (PRINCETON)
7. CALHOUN (HARDIN)
8. CARROLL (MT. CARROLL)
9. CASS (VIRGINIA)
10. CHAMPAIGN (URBANA)
11. CHRISTIAN (TAYLORVILLE)
12. CLARK (MARSHALL)
13. CLAY (LOUISVILLE)
14. CLINTON (CARLYLE)
15. COLES (CHARLESTON)
16. COOK (CHICAGO)
17. CRAWFORD (ROBINSON)
18. CUMBERLAND (TOLEDO)
19. DEKALB (SYCAMORE)
20. DEWITT (CLINTON)
21. DOUGLAS (TUSCOLA)
22. DUPAGE (WHEATON)
23. EDGAR (PARIS)
24. EDWARDS (ALBION)
25. EFFINGHAM (EFFINGHAM)
26. FAYETTE (VANDALIA)
27. FORD (PAXTON)
28. FRANKLIN (BENTON)
29. FULTON (LEWISTOWN)
30. GALLATIN (SHAWNEETOWN)
31. GREENE (CARROLLTON)
32. GRUNDY (MORRIS)
33. HAMILTON (MCLEANSBORO)
34. HANCOCK (CARTHAGE)
35. HARDIN (ELIZABETHTOWN)
36. HENDERSON (OQUAWKA)
37. HENRY (CAMBRIDGE)
38. IROQUOIS (WATSEKA)
39. JACKSON (MURPHYSBORO)
40. JASPER (NEWTON)
41. JEFFERSON (MT. VERNON)
42. JERSEY (JERSEYVILLE)
43. JO DAVIESS (GALENA)
44. JOHNSON (VIENNA)
45. KANE (GENEVA)
46. KANKAKEE (KANKAKEE)
47. KENDALL (YORKVILLE)
48. KNOX (GALESBURG)
49. LAKE (WAUKEGAN)
50. LASALLE (OTTOWA)
51. LAWRENCE (LAWRENCEVILLE)
52. LEE (DIXON)
53. LIVINGSTON (PONTIAC)
54. LOGAN (LINCOLN)
55. MCDONOUGH (MACOMB)
56. MCHENRY (WOODSTOCK)
57. MCLEAN (BLOOMINGTON)
58. MACON (DECATUR)
59. MACOUPIN (CARLINVILLE)
60. MADISON (EDWARDSVILLE)
61. MARION (SALEM)
62. MARSHALL (LACON)
63. MASON (HAVANA)
64. MASSAC (METROPOLIS)
65. MENARD (PETERSBURG)
66. MERCER (ALEDO)
67. MONROE (WATERLOO)
68. MONTGOMERY (HILLSBORO)
69. MORGAN (JACKSONVILLE)
70. MOULTRIE (SULLIVAN)
71. OGLE (OREGON)
72. PEORIA (PEORIA)
73. PERRY (PINCKNEYVILLE)
74. PIATT (MONTICELLO)
75. PIKE (PITTSFIELD)
76. POPE (GOLCONDA)
77. PULASKI (MOUND CITY)
78. PUTNAM (HENNEPIN)
79. RANDOLPH (CHESTER)
80. RICHLAND (OLNEY)
81. ROCK ISLAND (ROCK ISLAND)
82. ST. CLAIR (BELLEVILLE)
83. SALINE (HARRISBURG)
84. SANGAMON (SPRINGFIELD)
85. SCHUYLER (RUSHVILLE)
86. SCOTT (WINCHESTER)
87. SHELBY (SHELBYVILLE)
88. STARK (TOULON)
89. STEPHENSON (FREEPORT)
90. TAZEWELL (PEKIN)
91. UNION (JONESBORO)
92. VERMILLION (DANVILLE)
93. WABASH (MT. CARMEL)
94. WARREN (MONMOUTH)
95. WASHINGTON (NASHVILLE)
96. WAYNE (FAIRFIELD)
97. WHITE (CARMI)
98. WHITESIDE (MORRISON)
99. WILL (JOLIET)
100. WILLIAMSON (MARION)
101. WINNEBAGO (ROCKFORD)
102. WOODFORD (EUREKA)

• Dot Represents
County Seat Location

0   50   100
miles

Figure 1-10. Illinois counties and county seats. The division of the state into 102 counties was completed in 1859. Only nineteen counties had been organized 40 years earlier.

transportation center of the midcontinent was firmly established by 1855 when it became the focus of 10 railroad trunk lines. The railroads linked Chicago with the rapidly developing farm lands of northern Illinois and the markets of the East, resulting in the city's role as a major agricultural processing and distribution center. The building of the enormous Chicago stockyards reflects that function. The railroads also gave access to previously isolated prairies and provided a means of importing wood products in areas where timber was scarce. The last remaining major unoccupied areas of Illinois were thereby settled and frontier conditions were superceded on the eve of the Civil War. In 1860 the federal census recorded 1,711,951 inhabitants of Illinois.

The disposal of the public domain in Illinois was carried out primarily by two means: (1) cash sales of land at government land offices in various parts of the state and (2) land bounties awarded to the enlisted noncommissioned veterans (or their heirs) of the War of 1812 in the Military Tract located between the Mississippi and Illinois rivers (Table 1-2). Cash sales, usually for $1.25 per acre, was the dominant means, accounting for over half the land converted to private ownership in the state. The other methods of disposal of land, of which railroad grants and swamp and saline land grants were the most important, involved relatively small acreage. Homesteading was insignificant in Illinois, as nearly all the land was entered prior to the passage of the first homestead law in 1862. The chronology of land sales in Illinois (Table 1-3) closely paralleled that in the country as a whole during the period between the War of 1812 and the Civil War. Sales reached their highest levels immediately preceding the economic crises of 1819, 1837, and 1857. It has been pointed out that the upward trends in land sales were closely associated with speculation and increases in business activity.[3] Maximum annual land sales in both the state and the nation occurred in 1836, a year of widespread speculation and prosperity. Following the depression of 1837, on the other hand, the decade of the 1840s was a time of tight money and modest land sales in Illinois. Improvements in economic conditions were accompanied by increases in sales in the early 1850s, but

Table 1-2. Disposal of Federal Land in Illinois.

Method of Disposal	Percent of Total Area
Cash Sales	56.1
Military Bounties	26.9
Homesteads	0.1
Miscellaneous	0.7
State Grants:	
Swamp and Saline Lands	4.5
Educational Grants	2.9
Internal and River Improvements and Public Buildings	1.5
Railroad Construction Grants	7.3
	100.0

Source: Adapted from Allan G. Bogue, *From Prairie to Corn Belt: Farming on the Illinois and Iowa Prairies in the Nineteenth Century* (Chicago: University of Chicago Press, 1963), p. 30. Bogue acknowledges that these statistics are approximations but is of the opinion that they are reasonably accurate.

Table 1-3. Public Land Sales in Illinois
(in thousands of dollars).

Year	Amount	Year	Amount
1814	168	1838	983
1815	53	1839	1,421
1816	207	1840	492
1817	572	1841	440
1818	1,491	1842	544
1819	611	1843	520
1820	87	1844	616
1821	64	1845	611
1822	335	1846	600
1823	76	1847	615
1824	58	1848	374
1825	82	1849	319
1826	110	1850	313
1827	81	1851	421
1828	121	1852	492
1829	282	1853	1,218
1830	402	1854	1,562
1831	420	1855	897
1832	261	1856	473
1833	381	1857	155
1834	440	1858	12
1835	2,688	1859	12
1836	4,003	1860	. . . . .
1837	1,271		

Source: Adapted from Vernon Carstensen (ed.), *The Public Lands* (Madison: University of Wisconsin Press, 1963), pp. 234-5.

by the middle of that decade relatively little land remained for purchase in Illinois.

Among the various methods of disposal of public land in Illinois, the awarding of military bounty lands was second only to cash sales. Following the War of 1812, lands in western Illinois were surveyed and designated as the Military Tract (Fig. 1-11). From October, 1817, through January, 1819, the War Department issued patents to veterans for over 2.8 million acres in the Military Tract, according to calculations by Theodore Carlson.[4] An individual holding a patent was allowed to draw by lot a quarter section (160 acres) in the Military Tract. The great majority of the veterans holding rights to bounty lands decided to sell or trade those rights rather than become actual settlers, however. In this way, large segments of the Military Tract were acquired for a low price by eastern speculators.

With the prairies finally conquered and the Civil War terminated, the following decades brought rapid growth and development interrupted by temporary economic problems and outbreaks of worker dissatisfaction in Illinois. The availability of jobs, particularly in railroad construction and new factories, brought waves of European immigrants to the state. During each decade between 1870 and 1900, the population grew by more than 20 percent—a rate of increase not exceeded since (Table 1-1). As farmers improved the land and acquired pieces of horse-drawn machinery, their increased production led to a surplus of agricultural commodities. As a consequence, the prices of farm products declined and agriculture experienced a depression that culminated in the Populist Revolt as the century drew to a close. Stimulated by the Civil War, manufacturing grew at a phenomenal rate during succeeding decades. Between 1870 and 1890 the number of employees in manufacturing increased from 82,979 to 312,198 and the net value of manufactured products grew from $78,020,595 to $379,621,191.[5] Worker dissatisfaction with low wages, however, led to the formation of labor organizations and outbreaks of violence, most notably the Haymaker Riot in Chicago. Perhaps the most significant accomplishment in Illinois immediately following the Civil War was construction of the railroad net. By 1893 every point of land in the state was less than 20 miles from a railroad and 85 percent of the land was within four miles of a track.[6]

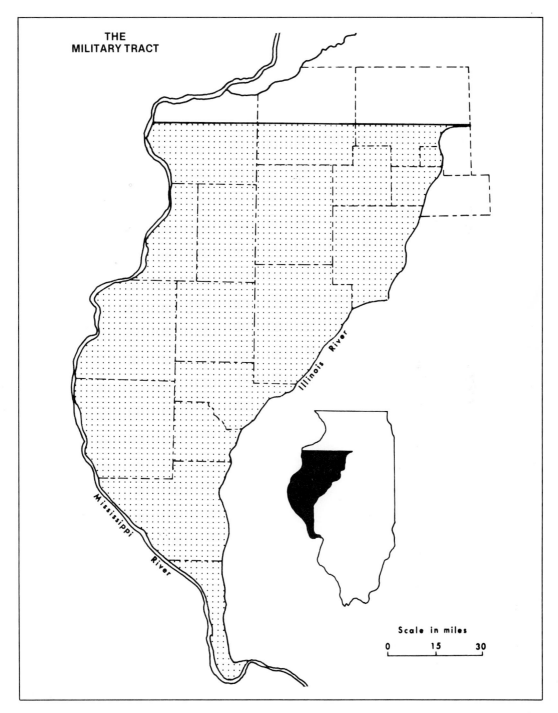

THE MILITARY TRACT

Illinois River

Mississippi River

Scale in miles

0   15   30

Figure 1-11. The Military Tract. The federal government granted land bounties totalling nearly 3 million acres between the Illinois and Mississippi rivers to veterans of the War of 1812.

From the end of the Civil War to the beginning of the twentieth century, Illinois made the transition from a predominantly rural and agricultural state to one in which a majority of the people lived in urban places and engaged in nonfarm occupations. With transportation improvement brought on by the boom in railroad construction, with rapid industrial growth, and with the surge of immigration to swell population numbers, small towns and villages became bustling cities in a matter of only a few years. Chicago recovered from its most famous disaster, the fire of 1871 that left nearly 100,000 people homeless, and attained a population of over one and a half million by the end of the century. Despite a high rate of population growth for the state as a whole, predominantly rural counties began losing population in the 1870s; by 1900 only 45.7 percent of the state's 4.8 million inhabitants were classified as rural. Although Illinois would continue to be one of the country's leading agricultural states, an urban-industrial way of life had moved to the forefront by the beginning of the new century.

Illinois in the Twentieth Century

In terms of population and most areas of endeavor, Illinois has continued to experience growth and development during the twentieth century. Such national emergencies as the Great Depression of the 1930s and two world wars—and to a lesser degree the conflicts in Korea and Viet Nam—have caused irregularities in these trends, however. After entering the century on an economic upswing, Illinois responded to demands created by World War I with an enormous increase in production on its farms and in its factories. Between 1917 and

1918 Illinois farmers increased their wheat production by 100 percent and that critical food grain temporarily displaced corn as the state's leading crop.[7] Heavy industries were quickly converted to produce munitions and weapons for the war; in 1918 one-third of the state's industrial output was to fulfill direct war contracts.[8] Upon successful completion of "the war to end all wars," optimism and prosperity prevailed until they were replaced by the stock market crash, bank closures, and widespread unemployment of the depression. In 1933, 1.5 million Illinoisans were without gainful employment. As the state and the nation struggled through this period of economic collapse, the jobless and poor formed enormous food lines in the cities and farmers resorted to burning their grain for fuel. The depression persisted until World War II again created demands for food and factory products to aid the Allies and support the soldiers. Illinois farmers responded with new production records and the state's factories accounted for about one-tenth of the national war production between 1940 and 1943.[9] In addition, scientists at the University of Chicago succeeded in establishing the first controlled atomic reaction to make possible the atomic bombs that ended the war in Japan.

Although the high rates of population growth of the nineteenth century have not been maintained, the number of Illinois inhabitants has increased with each decade of the twentieth century (Table 1-1). The lowest rate of demographic growth for any decade in the state's history (3.5 percent) occurred during the depression years between 1930 and 1940; however, it was followed by a post-World War II acceleration in immigration and "baby boom" that placed heavy strain on educational facilities during the 1950s and 1960s. Natural population in-

Figure 1-12. In order to accommodate burgeoning enrollments during the 1960s, colleges and universities found it necessary to erect large student dormitories such as these on the campus of Western Illinois University. (Courtesy Donald W. Griffin.)

crease continued to be heavily supplemented by European immigration during the early years of this century, but in more recent time blacks from the South have comprised the largest group of people relocating in Illinois. Blacks were first attracted to Illinois on a significant scale by World War I labor shortages in the industrial cities, particularly East St. Louis and Chicago. Between 1910 and 1920 the black population of Chicago more than doubled; blacks accounted for 10 percent of the city's population in 1950, 14 percent in 1960, and nearly 33 percent in 1970. Illinois now has approximately 1.5 million black inhabitants, more than any state other than New York.

Throughout the twentieth century the urban population of Illinois has exceeded the number of people in rural areas. Mechaniza-

tion of agriculture has greatly reduced the need for farm workers, while a growing number of jobs in industry and services has attracted people to urban centers. Consequently, predominantly rural counties have suffered an absolute population decrease. Population loss was experienced by 56 counties between 1900 and 1910, 63 counties between 1920 and 1930, and 49 counties between 1960 and 1970. On the other hand, urban population has increased from 54.3 percent of the state's total in 1900 to 82.9 percent in 1970. There were 64 Illinois cities with 25,000 or more inhabitants in 1970, 33 of which were in the two counties of Cook and DuPage (Fig. 1-13). This concentration in Cook and DuPage counties reflects the rapid growth of suburbs in the vicinity of Chicago. The population of suburban Cook

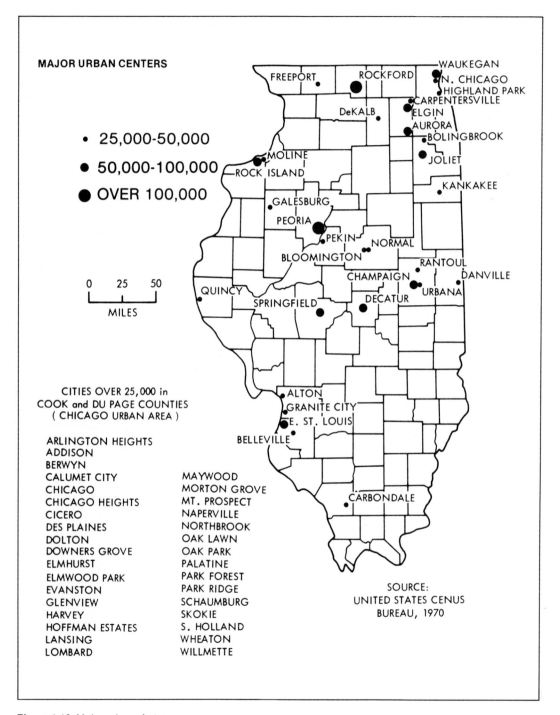

MAJOR URBAN CENTERS

WAUKEGAN
FREEPORT   ROCKFORD   N. CHICAGO
                        HIGHLAND PARK
            DeKALB   CARPENTERSVILLE
                        ELGIN
                        AURORA
                        BOLINGBROOK
        MOLINE   JOLIET
    ROCK ISLAND
                        KANKAKEE
        GALESBURG
        PEORIA
                PEKIN   NORMAL
        BLOOMINGTON
                        RANTOUL
                CHAMPAIGN   DANVILLE
    QUINCY   DECATUR URBANA
        SPRINGFIELD

- 25,000-50,000

● 50,000-100,000

● OVER 100,000

0   25   50
MILES

ALTON
GRANITE CITY
E. ST. LOUIS
BELLEVILLE

CARBONDALE

CITIES OVER 25,000 in
COOK and DU PAGE COUNTIES
(CHICAGO URBAN AREA)

ARLINGTON HEIGHTS
ADDISON
BERWYN
CALUMET CITY   MAYWOOD
CHICAGO   MORTON GROVE
CHICAGO HEIGHTS   MT. PROSPECT
CICERO   NAPERVILLE
DES PLAINES   NORTHBROOK
DOLTON   OAK LAWN
DOWNERS GROVE   OAK PARK
ELMHURST   PALATINE
ELMWOOD PARK   PARK FOREST
EVANSTON   PARK RIDGE
GLENVIEW   SCHAUMBURG
HARVEY   SKOKIE
HOFFMAN ESTATES   S. HOLLAND
LANSING   WHEATON
LOMBARD   WILLMETTE

SOURCE:
UNITED STATES CENUS
BUREAU, 1970

Figure 1-13. Major urban centers.

County increased by 34.6 percent and that of DuPage County grew by 56.9 percent between 1960 and 1970.

Although farming now requires the labor of less than 4 percent of the state's people, it remains one of the major sectors of the Illinois economy. Almost $4.6 billion worth of agricultural commodities were sold by Illinois farmers in 1974, including $3.1 billion in crops and $1.4 billion in livestock and poultry. To attain such high levels of production, farmers have invested not only their labor but also vast amounts of capital in land, buildings, machinery, fuel, seed, and chemical fertilizers and pesticides. Their production expenses in 1974 totaled $2.8 billion. Choice farmland in the state now is priced at approximately $4,000 an acre and tens of thousands of dollars worth of machinery is necessary to operate a successful grain farm. The staggering costs of farming has caused operators of small holdings to find second jobs or sell their land to neighbors who are attempting to strengthen the viability of their farms by acquiring additional acreage. Through consolidation of land holdings, Illinois farms now average 250 acres in size and grain farms commonly are two to three hundred acres larger.

With extensive mechanization, technological developments, and changing economic conditions, Illinois farming has drastically changed in character during the twentieth century. Horses have been replaced by tractors, and consequently oats, which were needed to feed the horse population in the past, are no longer a major crop. The better profit prospects and less rigid labor requirements in grain farming have stimulated an increasing number of farmers to abandon the rearing of livestock and concentrate on the production of cash grain crops, primarily corn and soybeans. In areas of expanding cash grain farming, therefore, fences and

barns have been demolished and animal manure has been replaced as a fertilizer by such chemical products as nitrogen and anhydrous ammonia. Virtually all grain crops are now raised from commercially produced hybrid seeds, first developed in the 1930s. Even the traditional practice of crop rotation to maintain soil fertility is being abandoned as consistently high yields are now ensured by the use of hybrid seeds and commercial fertilizers.

The symbiotic relationship established between the state's farms and factories during the nineteenth century has continued to the present. Most early manufacturing in Illinois involved the processing of grain and livestock and the production of tools, fencing, wagons, machinery, and implements for sale to farmers. Moline, Kewanee, Peoria, and Chicago became important centers of the farm implement and machinery industry, and East St. Louis and Chicago acquired a national reputation for their livestock slaughtering and meat packing functions. As late as the World War I years, meat packing was the leading Illinois industry in terms of value of product. The famous Chicago stockyards were closed in 1971, but nearby Joliet has helped fill the void as a meat processing center and Decatur has joined the list of industrial centers with a speciality related to agriculture—the processing of soybeans.

Although its developmental record includes some temporary reversals, particularly a sharp reduction in output and employment during the depression of the 1930s, manufacturing has been the dominant sector of the Illinois economy during the twentieth century. Recovery from the depression and the attainment of new production records accompanied World War II and the immediate postwar years when demands ran high for consumer goods, most of which were unavailable or extremely scarce during the conflict. By 1974 the value added by manufacture exceeded $29 billion and more than 1,300,000 people were employed in manufacturing in Illinois. Manufacturing now accounts for almost 30 percent of the gross state product.

Significant changes in the emphasis and geographical pattern of manufacturing have occurred in the state over the past several decades. Durable goods have become the most important group of products manufactured in Illinois factories. Primary metals, fabricated metal products, machinery, and electrical equipment and supplies presently account for about half of both the value added by manufacture and total manufacturing employment in the state. The greatest concentration of Illinois manufacturing traditionally has been in Chicago, but the city's dominance is declining. Between 1947 and 1973 manufacturing employment in Chicago dropped from 56 to 32 percent of the total for the state. Factories, like people, have been migrating from the city to the suburbs. The counties of Cook, DuPage, Kane, McHenry, and Will that form the Chicago Standard Metropolitan Statistical Area (SMSA) contain almost 70 percent of the total employment in Illinois manufacturing. The proportion in each of the seven other SMSAs in the state is less than 5 percent.

With a maturely developed and diversified economy involving both industrial and agricultural productivity of high national rank, Illinois is the wealthiest midwestern state and among the most affluent in the country. The current gross state product is approximately $95 billion, and the per capita personal income for 1970 in Illinois was $4,502—nearly $600 above the national average. Measured in terms of median family income, the Chicago suburbs of Wilmette ($21,757), Highland Park ($20,726), and Northbrook ($19,992) were among the country's five wealthiest cities above 25,000 population in 1970. Poverty nevertheless remains a persistent problem in parts of the state, particularly in some inner city neighborhoods and rural southern Illinois counties. In 1970 more than one-fifth of the families in Pulaski, Alexander, Pope, Hardin, and Hamilton counties had subpoverty incomes. Welfare programs for the poor constitute one of the heaviest burdens for the state's taxpayers.

The remainder of the twentieth century seems likely to hold a number of challenges as well as opportunity for Illinoisans. The nation's greatest remaining deposits of bituminous coal are contained within the boundaries of the state, and a revival of the depressed Illinois coal mining industry seems imminent as petroleum supplies dwindle. Illinois coal has a high sulphur content, however, and its increased use as a fuel may add to existing air pollution problems. Environmental deterioration in such forms as air and water pollution, soil erosion, and disturbance of the land's natural surfaces has been a detrimental result of the state's industrial and agricultural development. To reverse these trends and undertake necessary measures to improve the quality of the environment can be expected to require new technology, the expenditure of vast sums of money, and at least slower rates of economic growth in the future. Another necessity for the years ahead is increased effort to eliminate racial and ethnic frictions, a particularly critical problem in Chicago, East St. Louis, and other cities where diversified populations must live and work in close contact with one another. Legislation will need to be supplemented by personal commitments to understanding, compassion, compromise, and even sacrifice in order for people of all races and ethnic backgrounds to enjoy a peaceful and fulfilling future.

Figure 1-14. Strip mining coal in Fulton County, Illinois. Although an economical means of producing coal, strip mining has been a major cause of environmental deterioration in the state. (Courtesy Donald W. Griffin.)

Notes

1. Carl O. Sauer, *Geography of the Upper Illinois Valley and History of Development,* Bulletin No. 27 (Urbana: Illinois State Geological Survey, 1916), p. 155.
2. Douglas R. McManis, *The Initial Evaluation and Utilization of the Illinois Prairies, 1815-1840,* Department of Geography Research Paper No. 94 (Chicago: University of Chicago, 1964), p. 92.
3. Vernon Carstensen, ed. *The Public Lands* (Madison: University of Wisconsin Press, 1963), p. 238.
4. Theodore L. Carlson, *The Illinois Military Tract: A Study in Land Occupation, Utilization and Tenure,* Vol. XXXII of *Illinois Studies in the Social Sciences* (Urbana: University of Illinois Press, 1951), p. 7.
5. Theodore Calvin Pease and Marguerite Jenison Pease, *The Story of Illinois* 3rd ed. (Chicago: University of Chicago Press, 1965), p. 188.
6. Ibid., p. 193.
7. Ibid., pp. 231-232.
8. Robert P. Howard, *Illinois: A History of the Prairie State* (Grand Rapids, Mich.: William B. Eerdmans Publishing Co., 1972), p. 444.
9. Pease and Pease, *Story of Illinois,* p. 251.

Selected References

Barrows, Harlan H. *Geography of the Middle Illinois Valley.* Bulletin No. 15. Urbana: Illinois State Geological Survey, 1910.

Boggess, Arthur C. *The Settlement of Illinois, 1776-1830.* Chicago: Chicago Historical Society, 1908.

Bogue, Allan G. *From Prairie to Corn Belt: Farming on the Illinois and Iowa Prairies in the Nineteenth Century.* Chicago: University of Chicago Press, 1963.

Carlson, Theodore L. *The Illinois Military Tract: A Study in Land Occupation, Utilization and Tenure.* Vol. XXXII of *Illinois Studies in the Social Sciences.* Urbana: University of Illinois Press, 1951.

Cutshall, Alden. "Illinois in Its Sesquicentennial Year." *Bulletin of the Illinois Geographical Society,* XI (June, 1969), 4-9.

Garland, J.H. *The North American Midwest, A Regional Geography.* New York: John Wiley & Sons, 1955.

Howard, Robert P. *Illinois: A History of the Prairie State.* Grand Rapids, Mich.: William B. Eerdmans Publishing Co., 1972.

McManis, Douglas R. *The Initial Evaluation and Utilization of the Illinois Prairies, 1815-1840.* Research Paper No. 94. Chicago: University of Chicago Department of Geography, 1964.

Pease, Theodore C. *The Frontier State, 1818-1848.* Chicago: A.C. McClurg and Co., 1922.

Pease, Theodore Calvin, and Pease, Marguerite Jenison. *The Story of Illinois.* 3rd ed. Chicago: University of Chicago Press, 1965.

Poggi, Edith Muriel. *The Prairie Province of Illinois.* Vol. XIX of *Illinois Studies in the Social Sciences.* Urbana: University of Illinois Press, 1934.

Pooley, William V. *The Settlement of Illinois from 1830 to 1850. Bulletin of the University of Wisconsin,* No. 220. (History Series, I.) Madison: University of Wisconsin, 1908.

Ridgely, D.C. *Geography of Illinois.* Chicago: University of Chicago Press, 1921.

Sauer, Carl O. *Geography of the Upper Illinois Valley and History of Development.* Bulletin No. 27. Urbana: Illinois State Geological Survey, 1916.

Walton, Clyde F., ed. *An Illinois Reader.* DeKalb: Northern Illinois University Press, 1970.

Chapter Two

THE PHYSICAL ENVIRONMENT

Arlin D. Fentem
Western Illinois University

The Illinois that exists today has been evolving since the dawn of earth history. The advent of man into the middle Mississippi region happened only a few thousand years ago; since that time, the physical landscape has both shaped the nature of man's activities and has itself been altered by his presence. Geographers describe and try to understand the differences from place to place in human institutions, economies, and works and their interrelations with physical environments. The subject of this chapter is the physical world that was here before man invaded, the changes that resulted from his coming, and the importance of physical environments for present-day human activities.

Physical environment is such a general term that it does not mean much until it is broken down and specified. It includes the shapes and forms of the earth's surface (landforms) and the earth materials which compose it; conditions and patterns of drainage; climate and its changes during man's occupation; natural vegetation and its evolution during the same period; soils; and, finally, the minerals which have been useful to man. All of these components, as we have become increasingly aware, are interrelated; none can be entirely separated from the others. For example, each combination of surface form, earth materials, drainage conditions, and climate produces a different natural vegetation, which in turn has been continuously altered by man, and the same sets of environmental conditions have produced present variation in soils.

We might simply describe and map all these elements, but true understanding needs more than that; it requires that we look for answers to the questions *Why?* and *How?* as well as *What?* The key to geographical interpretation is the map, which shows the variation from place to place in an element such as landform or vegetation. In this chapter, we will also rely a great deal on another perspective, that of changes in mapped distributions through time, in order to understand the evolution of the present landscape. Finally, this chapter will be different from those in most textbooks, which tell what is known and omit discussion of that which is not. The events that have transpired on the landscape of what we now call Illinois have been very complicated, and we are not at all sure, sometimes, of our interpretations. Some distributions (shown on maps) will be presented as problems; e.g., why was central Illinois covered with tall grass instead of trees? The various explanations of scientists who have worked on the problem will be outlined so that the reader may judge which interpretation seems most plausible and best supported by evidence.

The Shape and Composition of the Land Surface[1]

To a visitor from Colorado or New England, Illinois seems monotonously flat and lacking in interest; nevertheless, the state has areas of unusual scenic beauty, and its subtle differences in form and materials have important consequences in the uses of the land and in the prosperity of its people.

Bedrock

One of the most important controls bringing about these differences is the bedrock which lies just below a thin "skin" of unconsolidated (loosely compacted) materials. Figure 2-1 shows how the major rock types are arranged in and near the state. In the pages to follow, each of the rock types will be described, with particular reference to qualities important for shaping the surface and for utility to man.

Almost all the rocks which appear at the surface are made of materials that were deposited in or along the shores of successive oceans during the Paleozoic geological epoch, which began about 600 million years ago and ended about 230 million years

before the present. The exceptions are rocks of Cretaceous age (about 100 million years old), which occupy small areas in west central Illinois and in the extreme south (Fig. 2-2). These rocks are very similar to the older Pennsylvanian sedimentary rocks which surround them and which range in age from 300 to 280 million years. In both cases, soft and easily broken (friable) shales predominate, although there are occasional layers and lenslike bodies of sandstone. Shales were originally laid down at the bottoms of small seas and shallow lakes as mud or clay. The sandstone bodies and layers mark the courses of ancient streams or the sites of beaches and deltas at the margins of lakes and seas which expanded, shrank, and sometimes disappeared as the multimillion year prehistory of the Pennsylvanian unfolded. The shales and weak sandstones of both Cretaceous and Pennsylvanian age weather and erode very easily when exposed to the atmosphere and running water. Areas floored by such rocks often become lowland plains with a thick mantle of weathered material over the bedrock.

The Pennsylvanian rocks also contain two major economic resources—bituminous coal and petroleum. Coal is organic in origin; it was formed from remains of the profuse tropical vegetation that grew and was subsequently preserved in Pennsylvanian swamps. There are more than 30 well-defined layers or beds of coal below the surface of this region, and seven of these have been extensively mined. Less well understood are the petroleum deposits, now greatly depleted, which have been found in the Pennsylvanian rocks. While petroleum is also organic in origin, it has often migrated from its source to rock layers of other ages. While more than half the oil that has been produced in Illinois was pumped from Pennsylvanian rocks, it does not follow that so great a proportion originated there.

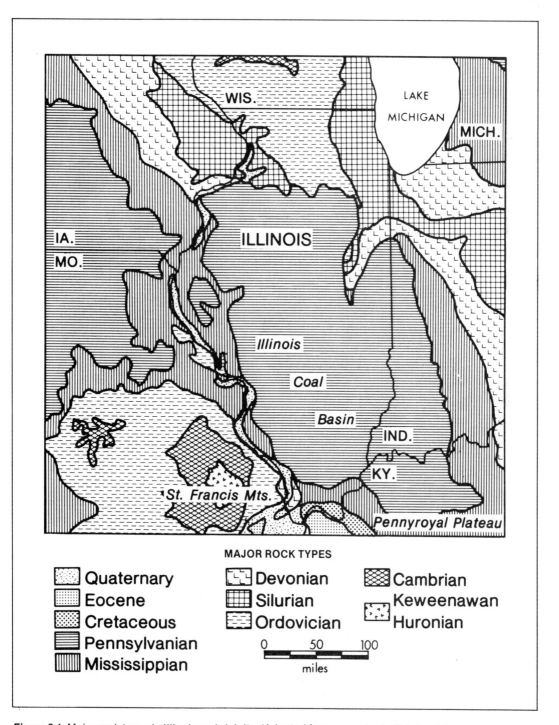

Figure 2-1. Major rock types in Illinois and vicinity. (Adapted from a map by A. K. Lobeck.)

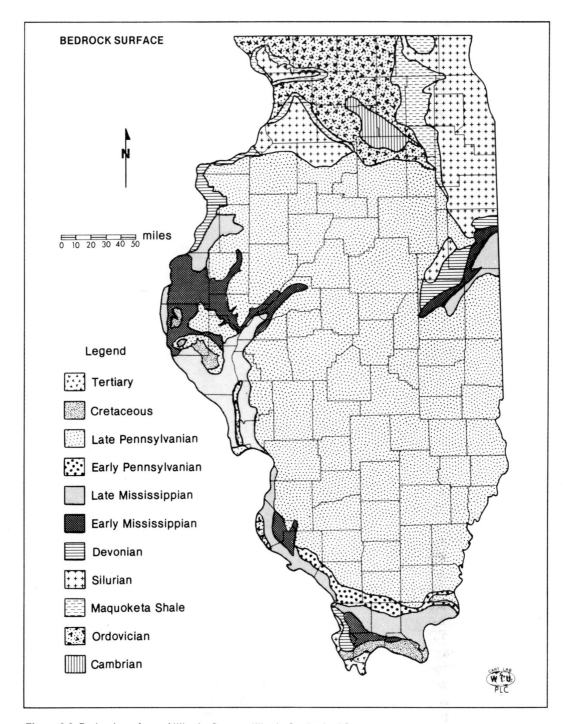

Figure 2-2. Bedrock surface of Illinois. Source: Illinois Geological Survey.

Surrounding the Pennsylvanian rocks just described are those which were deposited at the very beginning of that geological epoch. These consist of thick and strong (massive) sandstones which resist both weathering and erosion and thus tend to stand as rugged ridges when they are surrounded by weaker rocks. Sandstone consists mostly of the mineral silicon (quartz), a very hard substance that does not readily form a deep soil and that contains few of the minerals needed for the growth of most crops. In Illinois, this rock outcrops along a quite narrow band in the extreme south.

Succeeding these sandstones outward from a center near Centralia, are the oldest of the Mississippian rocks ($\pm$ 350 to $\pm$ 300 million years old). This geological era was one during which deep, warm, and quiet seas usually covered the Midwest. The rocks which formed when the seas were present are made up, for the most part, of lime (calcium carbonate, $CaCo_3$), and consist mostly of the "skeletal" remains of small, often near-microscopic, marine plants and animals. They are easily cut by saws, make excellent building stone, and are a convenient source of lime used in making quicklime, dentrifices, face powder, and agricultural fertilizers. These "pure" limestones are easily weathered and eroded, and they are alkaline rather than acidic. They frequently produce lowland plains and often are responsible for "karst" topography. Pure limestones are so easily dissolved by water that the seepage of rainfall downward through fissures in the rock and along bedding planes (where one "layer" or "bed" of rock succeeds another) often results in caverns. When these underground rooms and passages become extensive, their roofs often collapse; the result is a "dimpled" surface whose funnel-shaped depressions may contain small, nearly round lakes. The Pennyroyal "Plateau" (Fig. 2-1) has such a karst landscape. Note that this

particular formation is scarcely present in Illinois, but is widespread in Kentucky. The best-developed karst landscape in Illinois is in southern Calhoun County, north of St. Louis.

Among the uppermost Mississippian rock layers is still another massive sandstone closely resembling the oldest of the Pennsylvanian rocks described above. Like those formations, it is represented by a narrow band in the extreme south, parallel to its neighbor (not shown on Fig. 2-2).

Much of the rest of the state is floored by late Mississippian limestones (Fig. 2-2). Although some of these are relatively "pure," the greater number include other minerals as well. The most significant of these minerals is magnesium; when a great deal of it is present, the rock is called dolomite. Dolomite is quite resistant to weathering and erosion, not easily dissolved, and likely to produce either a high plain or a range of low hills. Few of the rocks in this area are true dolomites; they are best described as "dolomitic limestones," with characteristics intermediate between dolomites and the pure limestones described earlier.

The only areas of Illinois not yet described are in the far north. Most of the surface here is underlain by a dolomite (Niagara) of Silurian age. Because it has so much magnesium, it has resisted erosion. In the northwest it makes a pronounced ridge along which runs US Route 20, and outside the state it is responsible for the Door Peninsula (northeast of Green Bay, Wisconsin), for Mantoulin Island, and for the escarpment that forms Niagara Falls. Just below the Niagara formation (and outward toward the northern boundary of Illinois) is a thick layer of very weak shale, called the Maquoketa (for a town in Iowa) or New Richmond (for a town in Indiana). It has the same characteristics that predominate in

Figure 2-3. Niagara dolomite caps the crest of a mound in the driftless region of northwestern Illinois. (Photo by Arlin D. Fentem.)

Cretaceous areas. In southern Wisconsin, the shale is succeeded northward by Galena-Platteville dolomites of Ordovician age, a layer of very weak sandstone (the St. Peters), still another dolomite (the lower Magnesian limestones), and finally by a great expanse and thickness of early Paleozoic (Cambrian) sandstones.

Below all these Paleozoic rocks is the Precambrian "basement"—the complex (usually very hard), metamorphic (changed), crystalline (recrystallized by heat and pressure) rocks whose surface (if we were to strip away all the layered Paleozoic sediments) would form a gently undulating plain over the interior of the United States. These rocks (and that surface) are indeed exposed in northeastern Minnesota, northern Wisconsin, and over much of southern and eastern Canada.

Development of Bedrock Geography

Bedrock geography may be a term which falls strangely on the ear, because the study of the earth's mineral crust is usually the province of geology. But geographers are concerned with the patterns of distribution on the earth's surface, and as they explain and interpret these patterns, they are inevitably involved with sister sciences whose subject is the thing or event which makes the pattern.

Figure 2-2 clearly shows a regular, concentric pattern which indicates the operation of general processes. Spatial patterns develop through time, and in the paragraphs to follow, we will trace that development, beginning with the situation at the dawn of the Paleozoic (ca. 600 million years ago). The processes that took place during that immense span can be generalized as (1) sedimentation—the deposition of sediments in or at the edge of water bodies; (2) warping—the gentle bending of the earth's crust into shallow basins scores or hundreds of miles across and separated by equally broad swells or domes; and (3) erosion—the stripping away of much of the accumulated sediment by running water to produce a near-uniform plain. While this division is useful for understanding, it should be remembered that these processes overlapped to a considerable degree.

Figure 2-4 shows the geological column for Illinois—the sequence and timing of the sedimentations which built up the layers of rock we have been describing. We do not know how long these depositions continued nor how thick the deposits eventually became. With but one exception, the upper layers—if they were ever present—have been eroded away and washed into the sea. The exception consists of the Cretaceous sediments which lie unconformably (that is, with missing layers in between) upon much older sediments (Fig. 2-2).

At the same time that the sediments were accumulating upon the Precambrian basement (and perhaps continuing afterward), the earth's crust was bending very gently and slowly to form the broad, shallow basins shown in Figure 2-5. The thickness of the sediments in the basins (geosynclines) naturally became much greater than those deposited on domes (geanticlines). The two western domes (the Ozark and the Wisconsin) are separated by a "sag" in the Precambrian rocks and that a similar depression separates the upwarpings in Ontario and in Kentucky-Tennessee. Between these two major axes are two broad, shallow basins, one of which is deepest in Michigan and the other whose lowest point is in southeastern Illinois. Similarly, the two basins are separated by a broad swell called the Kankakee Arch.

The last step in understanding the general concentric arrangement of bedrock types in Illinois is to consider the effects of long- continued erosion. To aid in visualizing the relations among sedimentation, warping, and erosion, Figure 2-6 has been prepared. The end result of erosion on a stable landscape is to bring about a nearly horizontal surface. Since the rock layers are *not* horizontal, but slope gently downward into the basins, the *erosional* surface slices across the *bedrock* surface. Note that the youngest surface rocks are at the centers of the simple and idealized basin shown in Figure 2-6, while the oldest appear near the centers of the domes. (The Precambrian basement rocks peep through the sediments in the Ozarks, in north central Wisconsin, and in Ontario).

In the real world, of course, perfectly geometric features almost never occur, and the midwestern geanticlines and geosynclines are not truly circular. It is worthwhile to compare the surface bedrock map (Fig. 2-2) with the cross-sections shown in Figure 2-6 and in Figure 2-7 until you can see, in your mind's eye, the three-dimensional image that relates the vertical and horizontal views. The bedrock map reveals that not only were the downwarped basins not circular, but also that the warping and bending were accompanied by some wrinkling of the crust, and sometimes even by breakages or faults. The wrinkles (called anticlines when they are sharply upward) duplicate, in their results, what occurs on a large scale with the geanticlines.

The more important of these structures may be seen on Figure 2-8, where the surface as it would exist on top of one of the rock layers is shown. The most significant anticline from an economic point of view is the LaSalle, because it formed a "trap" roofed

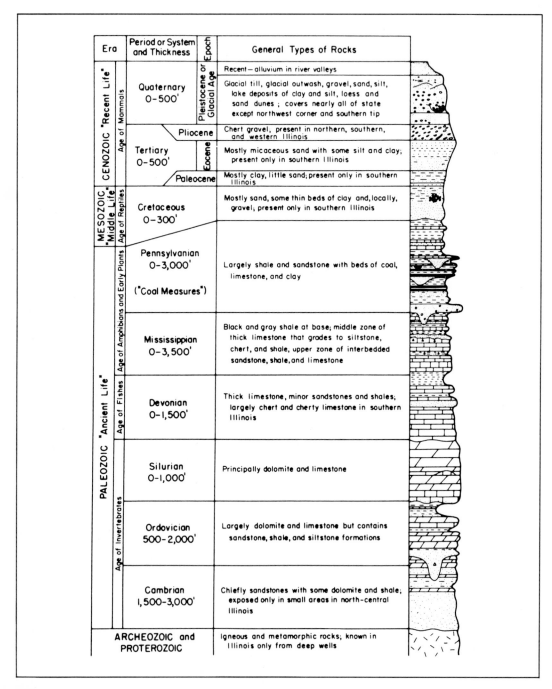

Era	Period or System and Thickness	Epoch	General Types of Rocks
CENOZOIC "Recent Life" / Age of Mammals	Quaternary 0–500'	Pleistocene or Glacial Age	Recent—alluvium in river valleys
			Glacial till, glacial outwash, gravel, sand, silt, lake deposits of clay and silt, loess and sand dunes ; covers nearly all of state except northwest corner and southern tip
		Pliocene	Chert gravel; present in northern, southern, and western Illinois
	Tertiary 0–500'	Eocene	Mostly micaceous sand with some silt and clay; present only in southern Illinois
		Paleocene	Mostly clay, little sand; present only in southern Illinois
MESOZOIC "Middle Life" / Age of Reptiles	Cretaceous 0–300'		Mostly sand, some thin beds of clay and, locally, gravel; present only in southern Illinois
PALEOZOIC "Ancient Life" / Age of Amphibians and Early Plants	Pennsylvanian 0–3,000' ("Coal Measures")		Largely shale and sandstone with beds of coal, limestone, and clay
Age of Fishes	Mississippian 0–3,500'		Black and gray shale at base; middle zone of thick limestone that grades to siltstone, chert, and shale, upper zone of interbedded sandstone, shale, and limestone
	Devonian 0–1,500'		Thick limestone, minor sandstones and shales; largely chert and cherty limestone in southern Illinois
Age of Invertebrates	Silurian 0–1,000'		Principally dolomite and limestone
	Ordovician 500–2,000'		Largely dolomite and limestone but contains sandstone, shale, and siltstone formations
	Cambrian 1,500–3,000'		Chiefly sandstones with some dolomite and shale; exposed only in small areas in north-central Illinois
ARCHEOZOIC and PROTEROZOIC			Igneous and metamorphic rocks; known in Illinois only from deep wells

Figure 2-4. Geologic column for Illinois. (From *Guide to Rocks and Minerals of Illinois*, Illinois State Geological Survey, Urbana, 1959.)

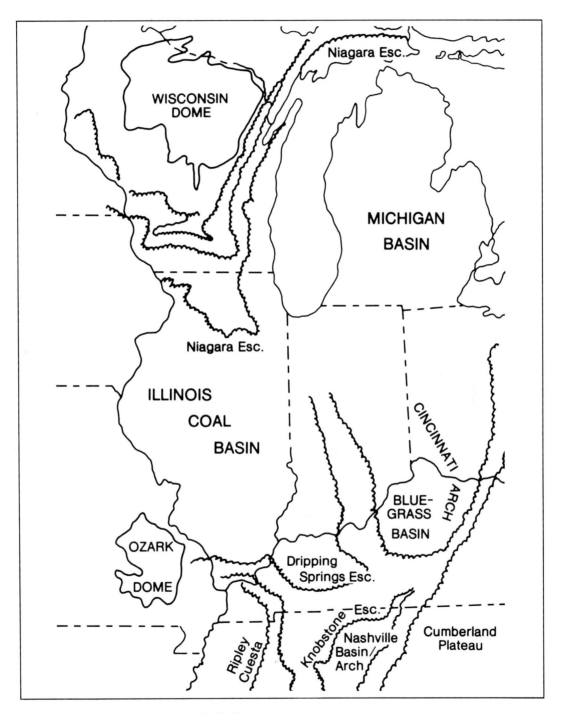

Figure 2-5. Basins and domes in the Middle West.

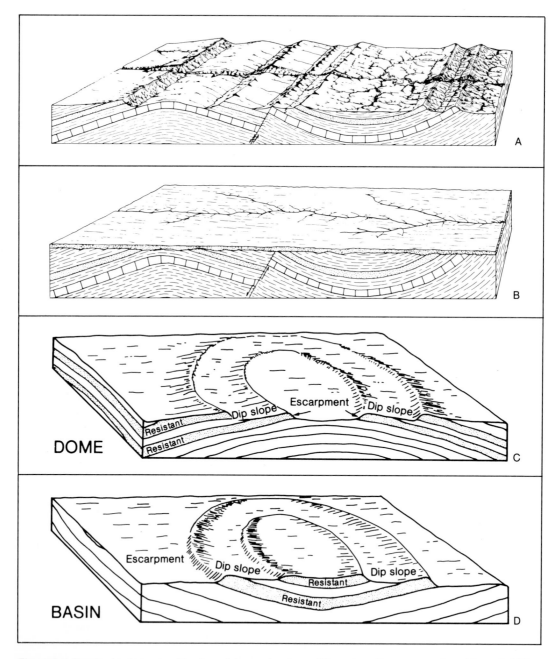

Figure 2-6. Erosion landscapes of basin and dome structures. (Upper two diagrams are from Victor C. Miller, *Photogeology,* McGraw-Hill Book Co., Inc., New York, 1961 and lower two are from V. Finch, G. Trewartha, A. Robinson, and E. Hammond, *Physical Elements of Geography* (4th ed.), McGraw-Hill Book Co., Inc., New York, 1957, with permission.)

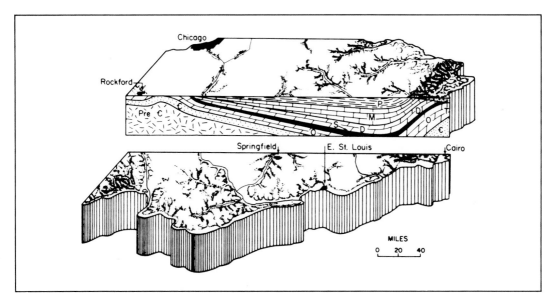

Figure 2-7. Geologic profile of Illinois. (From *Guide to the Geologic Map of Illinois,* Illinois State Geological Survey, Urbana, 1961.)

by nonpermeable shale, which confined petroleum deposits to a narrow band. Almost all the oil found in Illinois before 1935 came from this structure. It had little effect on topography, however, because the younger rocks that were exposed by its erosion were almost identical to those which surround it. Dashed lines mark the crest of the Du Quoin and other anticlines which produced a great deal of oil after the mid-1930s.

A very large monocline in the vicinity of the Illinois River in west central Illinois also has had important consequences. In this case, nearly horizontal dolomitic limestones (Mississippian) and shales plunge suddenly into the Illinois Coal Basin (eastward) at a rather steep angle. The results are: (1) the flat-lying bedrock (the western Illinois Platform) may have helped to preserve an upland plain, and (2) the coal measures in the Pennsylvanian rocks stayed near the surface

and can be easily reached by strip mining over a large area. Since the Illinois River provides an inexpensive means of sending coal to the large Chicago market, Fulton, Peoria, and Knox counties have become important for strip coal mining.

More dramatically, the faults named the Sandwich, the Savanna, and the Cap Au Gris provide sudden contrasts in either or both bedrock and topography. Not only did the earth's crust fracture along these lines, but segments of it slipped vertically relative to each other, sometimes for hundreds of feet. Thus, what is accomplished by gently tilted bedrock over hundreds of miles can be duplicated in a few thousand feet. This can be seen on the bedrock map, where Ordovician sediments are found side by side with those of Cambrian age along the Sandwich fault. Figure 2-6B shows how such a condition comes about.

Folding and faulting have produced the

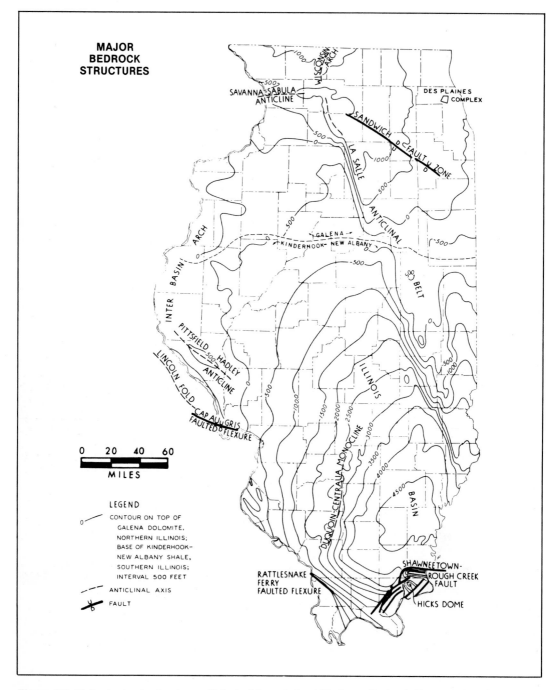

Figure 2-8. Major bedrock structures. (Adapted from Leland Horberg, *Bedrock Topography of Illinois*, Illinois State Geological Survey, Urbana, 1950.)

beautiful scenery in Calhoun County and at Pere Marquette State Park, north of St. Louis. Here Mississippian and Ordovician bedrock are brought together at the surface to make contrasts in landform scenery, including the karst topography of the southern tip of the county. Palisades Park, north of Savanna, owes its vertical rock walls to both folding and faulting which placed a weak shale at the level of the Ice Age Mississippi with dolomitic (Ordovician) limestone above. As the weak shales were eroded, the massive limestone blocks they supported came tumbling down to form the cliffs which are the park's attraction. A number of closely spaced faults in the southeast have altered

that scenery as well. There is still a great deal of instability in the crust of the midwestern earth, and earth tremors are relatively frequent. Within historic time, a massive movement and quake produced Reelfoot Lake in west Tennessee.

The Shape of the Bedrock Surface

The previous discussion has brought the development of landforms in Illinois to the condition that seems likely to have existed sometime in the Tertiary—a condition similar to that idealized in Figure 2-6B. Just as natural large-scale patterns are seldom geometric, broad surfaces have never been

Figure 2-9. The Cap au Gris fault in Calhoun County separates forested ridges from the dimpled karst topography on Mississippian limestones in the upper portion of the photograph. (Photo by Arlin D. Fentem.)

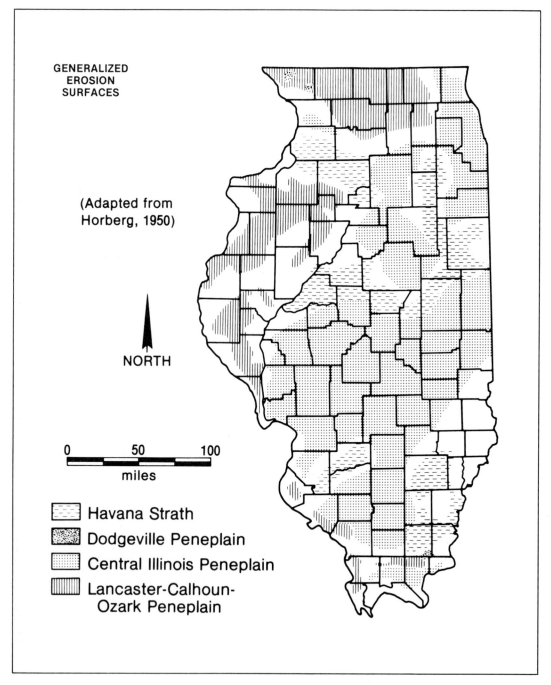

GENERALIZED
EROSION
SURFACES

(Adapted from
Horberg, 1950)

NORTH

0   50   100
miles

Havana Strath
Dodgeville Peneplain
Central Illinois Peneplain
Lancaster-Calhoun-
Ozark Peneplain

Figure 2-10. Generalized erosion surfaces. (Adapted from Leland Horberg, *Bedrock Topography of Illinois,* Illinois State Geological Survey, Urbana, 1950.)

perfectly flat; nevertheless, that condition (called a peneplain when it results from erosion) was probably approximated at that time. In order for such a condition to be maintained, the earth's surface must remain stable. If the level of the sea into which streams flow is lowered, or if the land is uplifted above the sea, the streams will flow more swiftly and begin to cut new valleys.

It is at this juncture that the differences in the erodibility of the bedrock types becomes important. The softer rocks (especially the Pennsylvanian shales and weak sandstones) are rather quickly attacked and carried away as sediments to the sea. The more resistant rocks (the massive sandstones near the contact between the Mississippian and Pennsylvanian systems and the dolomites of Silurian and Ordovician age) tend to remain as upland belts (as idealized in Fig. 2-6). Fairly recent uplift and renewed erosion have produced the "cuestaform" hilly belts found in the extreme south and northwest of the state. The Shawnee Hills is the name given to the two belts of sandstone, the Pennsylvanian (Dripping Springs) and Knobstone escarpments, as they cross southern Illinois. The Silurian outcrop in the northwest is made of Niagaran dolomite and is called the Niagara Escarpment.

One further aspect of the bedrock surface requires attention, for it appears that there are four roughly defined levels of elevation in the state. On Figure 2-10 their relative locations are shown. Each level may be a remnant of a peneplain as shown in Figure 2-6B. To suggest how such an arrangement might have come about, we will describe the series of repeated events which have been posed as an explanation, beginning with the oldest and outermost surface, the Dodgeville.

The development of peneplains is closely related to the pattern of drainage which existed before the Ice Ages (Fig. 2-11). At that time, the Mississippi River followed roughly the route of the present Illinois River and was joined near present Beardstown by a very large river which we can think of as the ancestral Ohio. When we remember that peneplanation requires a long period of stability in the earth's crust, it is not surprising that the process was interrupted more than once before it could be completed. After an uplift of the land relative to the sea, the major rivers of that time would gain renewed strength and begin cutting new valleys in the flat surface. As the valleys become deeper, however, the energy of their streams diminishes, and finally there is no further downcutting; the master streams then begin to widen the floors of their valleys. At the same time, new tributaries begin to form and erosion advances upstream or "headward" (toward the heads of the stream) until they too can no longer cut downward; consequently, they begin to widen their own valleys. The peneplain comes into being as the widening valleys approach each other and coalesce (come together) to form a new and lower surface.

Just such a surface, the Dodgeville, appears to have developed throughout the Midwest. Subsequently, however, there was a renewed uplift, a rejuvenation of streams, and the development of a new surface (the Lancaster)—again working its way outward from the juncture (confluence) of the major streams. This cycle embraced all of Illinois, but outside the state, the Dodgeville surface—a gently rolling plain—still exists and the tributaries are still deepening their narrow valleys.

In similar manner, the development of the Lancaster surface was interrupted by still another uplift and surface (the Central Il-

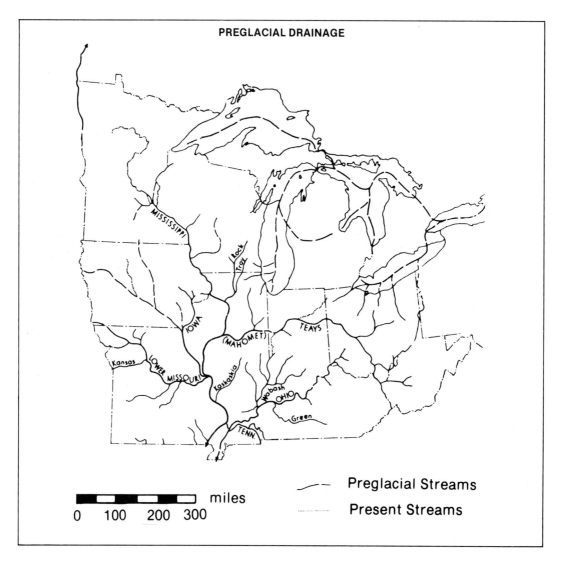

Figure 2-11. Preglacial drainage. (Adapted from Leland Horberg, *Bedrock Topography of Illinois,* Illinois State Geological Survey, Urbana, 1950.)

linois Peneplain) which developed quite rapidly because the Pennsylvanian rocks there were so weak. There are two smaller "patches" of a still lower surface (called strath lowlands) southeast of the Quad Cities and near Havana; these two erosional surfaces may be of quite recent date. Finally, the valley floors of the streams in the southern third of the state, such as the Kaskaskia and the Big Muddy, are so wide and flat that they, too, may have developed during this fourth, and last, erosional cycle. The idea of peneplanation in the Midwest is rejected by some geomorphologists, who think that the "four story" topography is more related to the resistance of rocks than

Figure 2-12. A tributary of the Pecatonia River incises the peneplain surface of the Rock River Hills. (Photo by Arlin D. Fentem.)

to erosional cycles as described. These dissenters would say that the widespread upland surface in western Illinois is there because the rocks are hard (dolomitic) and horizontal.

A million or two years ago, Illinois would have looked much as southwestern Wisconsin does now. Its terrain would have been much rougher than it now is, and flat or nearly flat land would have been relatively rare. Although its finer features have been obliterated, and its drainage pattern only approximates the present one, today's surface is much influenced by both rock types and the preglacial topography, as we shall presently see.

The Pleistocene

Although the glacial epoch occupied only a very small fraction of geological time, its rèsults for present landforms are very great—partly because of its recency. There

has been but little time since the last ice advances—a few thousands of years—and glacial features are still much in evidence. It is now widely believed, indeed, that the Ice Age has not ended and that all of human civilization belongs to a brief interval between major ice advances.

More than 90 percent of Illinois was overridden by glaciers during the past 100,000 years, and the last of the glacial ice was still present in the northeast less than 15,000 years before the present.[2] Earlier glaciations, reaching back to more than a million years ago, have had their most obvious manifestations wiped out by time or by later ice invasions. We will first indicate what the general effects have been, and then point out differences that result either from the manner of glaciation or the length of time which has elapsed since glaciation occurred. Figure 2-13 shows the most important stages and substages in the glaciation of the state, as well as the currently used names. From time

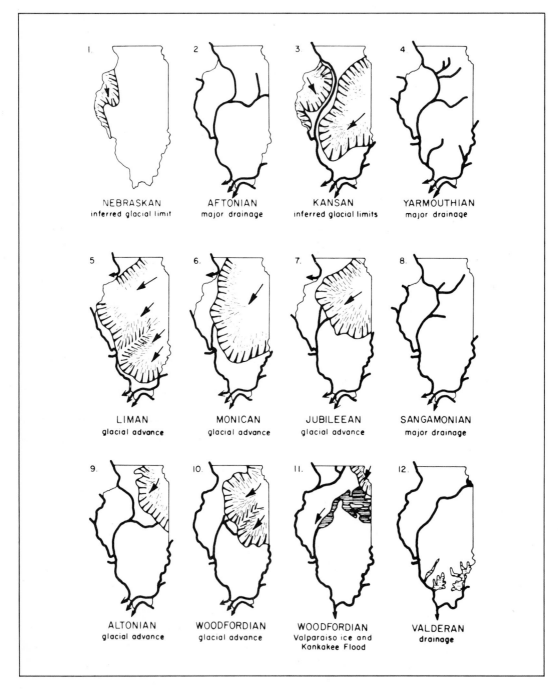

Figure 2-13. Glacial stages and drainage in Illinois. (From H. B. Willman and J. C. Frye, *Pleistocene Stratigraphy of Illinois,* Illinois State Geological Survey, Urbana, 1970.)

to time it will be necessary to refer back to this map-table in order to clarify the discussion to follow. Figure 2-14 is a summary which shows the distributions of the last ice sheets to cover each area of the state.

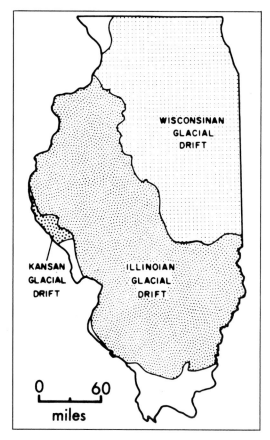

Figure 2-14. Glacial drift in Illinois. (From *Guide to the Geologic Map of Illinois,* Illinois State Geological Survey, Urbana, 1961.)

The initial effect of glaciation was to add to, rework, and redistribute the regolith (unconsolidated earth materials overlying the bedrock). Whether by the weight and passage of the ice itself, or by the vast amounts of running water from melting ice, these earth materials filled in valleys and formed a

new surface even higher than the crests of the bedrock hills. This new surface was much smoother than the terrain it replaced, and was virtually free of stream valleys.

Differences from place to place in the present glaciated surfaces depends upon three factors: (1) the thickness of the unconsolidated materials (called *drift* when they are of glacial origin); (2) differences in the behavior of the ice itself at different periods; and (3) the length of time since the ice sheets retreated. The last of these is particularly important, because the drift is so easily eroded that even a few thousands of years witness a great deal of erosion and alteration of the landscape.

Types of Drift Covered Surfaces

Figure 2-15 depicts the major types of drift-covered surfaces to be found in the state and the accompanying diagrams indicate the relations between and among thickness, age, and original drift characteristics. After distinguishing between driftless and drift-covered areas, the most important distinction is between thin and thick drift within the portions of the state once covered by Illinoisan but not by Wisconsinan ice sheets. The *upland* of the thindrift areas in the north central and south central regions of the state appear little different than they would have had glaciation not occurred; nevertheless, hills have been smoothed and rounded and slopes are longer and more gentle than they otherwise would be. In the south central region, much of the original glacial material is now collected in the valleys of streams and this helps to account for their very wide and very flat floors.

Within the areas covered by thick Illinoisan drift, the original surface was—unlike those of most regions of glacial

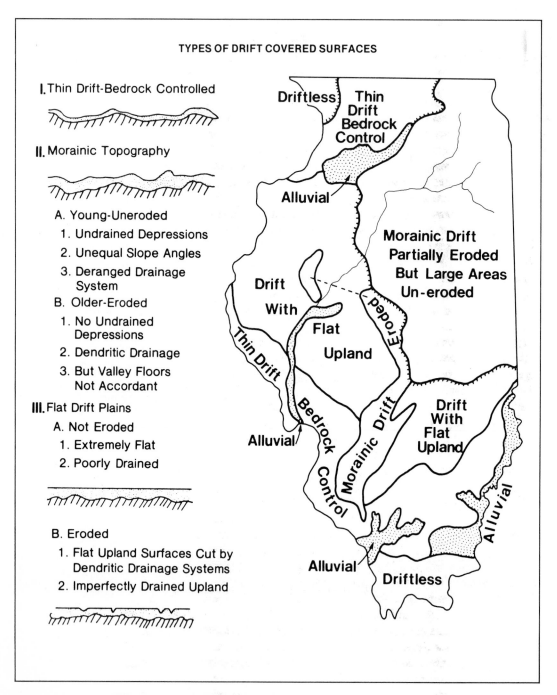

Figure 2-15. Types of drift covered surfaces. (Adapted from P. MacClintock, *Physiographic Divisions of the Area Covered by the Illinoisan Driftsheet in Southern Illinois,* Illinois State Geological Survey, Urbana, 1939.)

deposition—exceptionally flat. No one is quite sure of the reasons for this flatness, but two explanations have been suggested. Ice movement during the Illinoisan glaciation was from northeast to southwest (Fig. 2-13). In the thick-drift regions, the Illinoisan ice was building and flowing across rocks which were mostly shales; the clayey drift that resulted may have been plastic enough to be flattened by the weight of overlying ice.

It is more likely that the flatness was related to the manner in which the ice retreated after the Monican advance (Fig. 2-13). Ordinarily, glacial retreats are halting and interrupted by readvances. During periods when the ice margin is nearly stationary, the ice continues to flow, carrying with it earth materials. Melting at the margin removes the ice there and results in the accumulation of the earth materials in long hummocky ridges that mark the stationary edge of the ice. These low ridges are called moraines—end moraines when they mark the furthest advance in a glacial period and recessional moraines when they mark pauses during a glacial retreat. It is possible that the Monican retreat resulted from an abrupt climatic change which was not reversed, and that the ice wastage and retreat was rapid and nearly uninterrupted. If that were true, recessional moraines would be nearly absent. Furthermore, a rapid retreat would have produced an enormous amount of extremely turbid (dirty) water; sediments might have been deposited from these waters over wide areas and helped to smooth the land surface.

Figure 2-16. Headward erosion by postglacial streams on the flat upland of the Galesburg Plain. (Photo by Arlin D. Fentem.)

Even when recessional moraines are rather abundant on the Illinoisan Drift Plains, as they are, for example, east and northeast of St. Louis, they are not very prominent because erosion has subdued them during the long period (more than 100,000 years) since their formation.

During the long period since the Illinoisan ice sheets last retreated, a great deal of the originally flat surface has been destroyed and converted into an extensive system of stream valleys. Nevertheless, there are broad areas of that flat surface still present on the Illinoisan Drift Plains, and even when valleys are quite close to each other, the narrow divides between them are almost perfectly flat.

The shapes of the land on the Wisconsinan drift surface are in rather sharp contrast to those of the Illinoisan plain. Curving parallel moraines are the most conspicuous features (Fig. 2-17). These broad belts of low hills are often thousands of yards across and extend for many scores of miles. In the south where the drift is oldest, there has been time enough to establish a fairly well integrated drainage system, and there were no natural lakes when Europeans first arrived. However, rainwater is removed from the lowlands between the moraines very sluggishly, and many areas were wet or covered with standing water during much of the year. Vast temporary lakes developed after heavy rains.

To some observers, the southern part of the Wisconsinan glaciated area seems quite flat; nevertheless, even the areas between the morainic ridges usually have a very gently rolling surface as compared with the extreme flatness of the *upland* surface on the Illinoisan plain. Another difference between the two regions is the vertical location of the flattest land. It is the *lowest* land between

moraines which has most of the flat land in the Wisconsinan areas of thick drift; it is the *highest* areas between stream valleys which embrace most of the flat land in the Illinoisan areas of thick drift.

The northern and northeastern reaches of the Wisconsinan drift have landforms that are distinctive because ice retreats and advances were even more frequent and because the latest of these occurred little more than 12,000 years ago. High morainic ridges are quite close to each other. The stream drainage system has not had time to develop completely, and there were, therefore, numerous lakes, swamps, and peat bogs when Europeans first saw the area.

As the ice retreated from northeastern Illinois, huge volumes of meltwater accumulated in the Great Lakes; the concentric moraines of northeastern Illinois served as temporary dams, impounding the waters of an expanded Great Lakes system which spilled over into the areas between the moraines and made huge shallow lakes (Fig. 2-17). These lake bottoms accumulated sediments and became low and very flat plains. Most of the land where Chicago now stands was covered by the enlarged Lake Michigan.

One of the most spectacular events toward the end of the Wisconsinan glaciation was the Kankakee torrent. Meltwater escaping from an ice tongue occupying what is now Lake Michigan, and from still further east (glacial Lake Erie), spilled into Illinois from the east along a path south of Lake Michigan, forming temporary lakes: Watseka, Wauponsee, Pontiac, and Ottawa. After breaching the moraine near Marseilles, Illinois, the flood was directed westward, toward the present sharp bend in the Illinois River at Hennepin. The upper Illinois River was entrenched (cut downward) during this

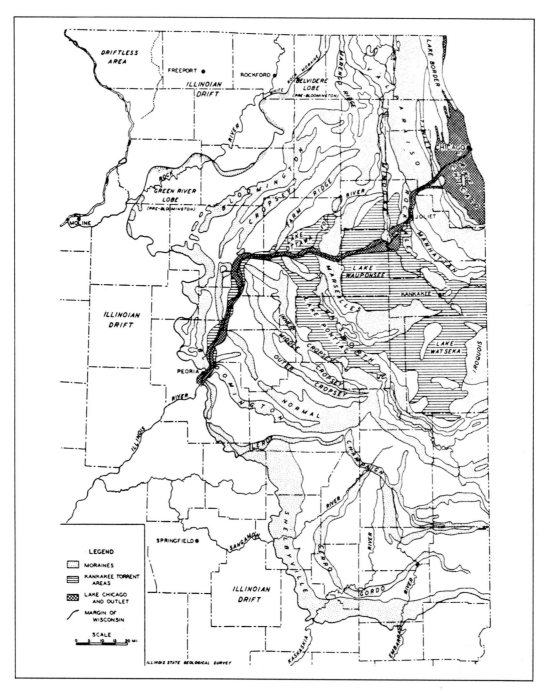

Figure 2-17. Wisconsinan glacial features in Illinois. (From M. M. Leighton, George E. Ekblaw, and Leland Horberg, *Physiographic Divisions of Illinois,* Illinois State Geological Survey, Urbana, 1948.)

Figure 2-18. Undulating surface of the Cerro Gordo Moraine near Champaign-Urbana. (Photo by Arlin D. Fentem.)

Figure 2-19. Forested moraine behind an outwash plain in McHenry County (Wheaton Morainal Country). (Photo by Arlin D. Fentem.)

flood. Downstream from Hennepin, the gigantic flood of water deposited great quantities of sediment in the valley itself. And because the waters were so high, the tributary streams were backed up in their valleys as temporary slackwater lakes where still more deposition took place. Finally, as the course of the flood across the lake floors became more concentrated and the currents more swift, huge sand and gravel bars were formed.

Outwash and Valley Trains

As we have just seen in the case of the Kankakee Flood, the effects of Pleistocene glaciation on landforms are not limited to the areas covered by the ice sheets. In the following paragraphs, large areas of the state whose landforms have been partly shaped by outwash and valley train will be identified. "Outwash" is the general term used to identify material carried away from ice margins by moving meltwater. "Valley trains" occur when the meltwaters become concentrated along valleys and deposit the earth materials they hold in suspension along those valleys. The surface of areas covered with outwash is, of course, generally quite flat immediately after deposition, as all water lain deposits are.

Two areas which received large quantities of outwashed materials were the Havana Strath Lowland above Beardstown, and the Green River Lowland south and east of Rock Island and Moline. Portions of both areas were covered by water from time to time and became lake bottoms, but much of their character can be attributed to the vast amounts of earth materials washed into them from melting glaciers. On occasion, the deposited material consisted of fine sands. Before vegetation became firmly established on the sands, strong westerly winds whipped them into migrating sand dunes. Although these dunes are now stabilized, their shapes reveal to us their origin thousands of years ago.

Much of the meltwater escaped down the Wabash River Valley and thence through the Ohio or the Cache River gap (an earlier path for the Ohio River parallel to and north of its present course). So much valley train was deposited in the Wabash and Ohio valleys that it dammed the mouths of the tributary streams in Illinois and converted them into lakes, further widening and flattening those valley floors (Fig. 2-15).

Drainage Changes

Figure 2-20 represents the bedrock surface below the glacial drift as envisioned by Leland Horberg after detailed reading of hundreds of well logs.[3] Although a number of refinements have been made in charting buried bedrock valleys since Horberg's monumental investigation, the valley systems which are shown by dashed lines give an essentially accurate picture of the drainageways that were present before glaciation but have since been abandoned and filled with glacial drift. The buried valleys are themselves of great interest because they often serve as sources of groundwater. Sand and gravel deposits (usually old valley trains) found in these buried valleys can contain a large amount of water, and this water can move freely through the buried alluvium into shallow wells which penetrate it.

There are also important landform results of drainage diversions. New valleys—those formed since the Late Pleistocene—were entrenched during short periods of time and are therefore deep in relation to their width, while preexisting valleys usually have bluffs which are quite far from each other. Preex-

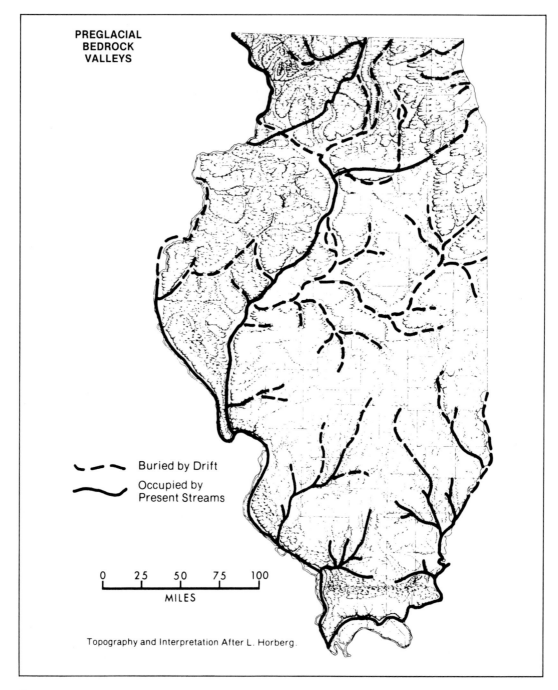

**PREGLACIAL
BEDROCK
VALLEYS**

Buried by Drift

Occupied by
Present Streams

0   25   50   75   100
MILES

Topography and Interpretation After L. Horberg.

Figure 2-20. Preglacial bedrock valleys. (Adapted from Leland Horberg, *Bedrock Topography of Illinois,* Illinois State Geological Survey, Urbana, 1950.)

isting valleys that are still present, but whose streams were permanently diverted to other courses by the later ice invasions, may provide convenient pathways for railways or for canals. New valleys, forced into their present courses by ice invasions, make it easier to build bridges and dams; earlier, they were fordable, and hence helped to direct the paths of early settlement and commerce. The "ford" in the town name *Rockford* reveals the early significance attached to a rock-bottom ford on the Rock River; it helped to develop one of the state's leading cities.

In some areas of Illinois, local stream drainage changes are the most important geomorphological (landform developmental) events which have occurred; in others, these diversions have had far-reaching consequences for the present human geography. Some of the most important effects will be described below.

By far the most significant change was the permanent diversion of the Ancient Mississippi. Until about 20,000 years ago that river flowed from a point south of Savanna to the present big bend in the Illinois River at Hennepin through what is today called Meredosia Channel. That great valley, once 300 feet deeper than at present, became the route of the Hennepin or Illinois-Mississippi Canal. Although the canal has not been used for commerce for a long time, its right-of-way, locks, and bridges are visible history. Furthermore, a Chicago-Upper Illinois River-Hennepin Canal-Upper Mississippi Waterway to Dubuque and beyond is often proposed. Such a route, feasible from an engineering standpoint, would of course divert Mississippi River commerce eastward to the southern end of Lake Michigan. The economic effects on Mississippi River cities such as St. Louis and Memphis would be profound.

Eastward from the Hennepin bend on the Illinois the valley is new (cut during the Kankakee Flood); southward from there, the river is an underfit stream, flowing through a wide floodplain. The old (formerly Mississippi) and new valleys together unite the Great Lakes System (via the Cal-Sag Waterway and the Des Plaines and Chicago River tributaries) with the Gulf of Mexico. This canalized river route—the Illinois and Michigan Canal—is the only connection between the Great Lakes-St. Lawrence and Mississippi systems. This fact helps to explain why Illinois—despite its location in the heart of Mid-America—is usually foremost among the states in foreign trade.

Vast tonnages of grain and soybeans leave Illinois via Chicago on Lake Michigan and New Orleans on the Gulf by this route. Coal from southern Illinois, petroleum and sulphur from east Texas and Mexico, copper and tin from Bolivia and Chile, and alumina (from the Caribbean and northern South America via Gulf Coast processors) are among the products which pass along this route and help to determine the industrial character of the Calumet region of Chicago and the Metro East area opposite St. Louis. The worldwide markets of the earthmoving equipment industry (Caterpillar and LeTourneau-Westinghouse) at Peoria are brought closer by this waterway. The Port of Chicago, developed around Lake Calumet and connected with the main waterway by the canalized Calumet River, is the place where foreign flag vessels meet domestic barges in Illinois.

Since the river flows in a new valley above Hennepin, the scenery of the upper Illinois valley is quite different and includes the picturesque bluffs at Starved Rock. Since the valley narrows abruptly above the bend, barge sizes must be changed at that point.

Figure 2-21. The Illinois River upstream from its sharp bend at Hennepin is narrow and occupies a postglacial valley. (Photo by Arlin D. Fentem.)

Another stretch of young and strikingly different valley occurs along the Mississippi downstream from the point where the river was finally diverted into its present course by the Woodfordian ice advance (Fig. 2-13). As the ice advanced from the east, it successively closed off the channels which could accommodate the waters flowing southeastward through the Meredosia Channel. Finally, at present Cordova, the rising waters spilled over southwestward and cut a narrow gorge (Cordova Gorge) to Rapid City. The river here is quite narrow, and before locks and dams were built this stretch was marked by swift water. A similar reach occurs upstream from Keokuk, Iowa, and marks the site of a major power dam—the only one in the environs of the state.

As may be seen on Figure 2-20, a part of the upper Rock River occupies a new (and therefore scenic) valley between Grand Detour and Byron, and there is a similar narrows in the Illinois River below Peoria.

Surface Drainage Conditions

Except for the farmers who must directly contend with environmental conditions in making a living, most citizens are only intermittently aware that the natural conditions of drainage in Illinois are so poor that in the past they posed a serious problem in using the land. The poor drainage has been over-

Figure 2-22. The first locks on the upper Illinois River were constructed at Lockport, thus uniting the Great Lakes and the Mississippi Waterways for barge traffic. (Photo by Arlin D. Fentem.)

come or controlled only through great efforts and huge capital expenditures. The flooding of flatlands along stream courses is common to almost all regions with humid climates, but in Illinois most of the uplands suffered poor drainage as well. For the most part, sluggish and incomplete drainage resulted from the recent glaciations.

No matter what the shape of a land surface at a given time in earth history, natural processes will produce, within a relatively brief period (scores or hundreds of thousands of years), a drainage system competent to remove quickly all the precipitation from the surface and convey it to the seas. Glaciation, however, is a catastrophic process which not only obliterates the preexisting system, but also deposits earth materials in a topsy-turvy fashion and frequently results in slopes that converge in depressions lacking outlets. All the present natural lakes in Illinois are in the northeast, from whence the glacial ice most recently retreated. Although glaciated upland surfaces in Illinois were sometimes very near to being flat, there are undulations almost everywhere. In addition, the floors of former glacial lakes were flattened by the accumulation of sediments, as were the valley trains adjacent to the southern rivers and in the Havana and Green River strath lowlands.

The conditions of drainage encountered by early settlers were influenced by both the land types just described and by the length of time since glaciation. Floodplain, valley train, and lake basin drainage is accom-

Figure 2-23. Typical drift surface and glacial lake on the Wisconsinan Till Plain of the Wheaton Morainal Country. (Photo by Arlin D. Fentem.)

plished by engineering on a large scale. It requires surveys by civil engineers, the digging of an artificial system of drainage ditches, and the building of levees for deflecting floodwaters to man-constructed basins and channels where they can be contained. In Illinois, however, the poor drainage of the recently glaciated uplands was a problem encountered and solved by individual farmers and groups of neighbors. And it was a problem with which they were at first ill-prepared to cope.

Two regions of the state, in particular, had to attack the drainage problem early: the west central area of thick Illinoisan drift, and the Wisconsinan drift region in the east central part of the state. In both instances, a high proportion of the land was useless until drained. While the northeast embraced large fractions of poorly drained land that included numerous lakes and bogs, these were relatively small and fragmented; the slopes of the closely spaced moraines, as well as sandy expanses (with rapid under drainage), provided early sites for farming. Southern Illinois, despite its thin drift, also had limitations imposed by poor drainage, but these were brought about, in large measure, by soil characteristics that prevented water from percolating downward.

In the west, poor drainage was more easily ameliorated than in the east. Here the unusual flatness of the Illinoisan drift surface was frequently interrupted by the ramifying tributaries of a stream system which had been developing for perhaps 100,000 years. The solution turned out to be the installation of tiles made from fired clay. Most

Figure 2-24. A common sight on the Bloomington Plain near Mt. Pulaski—standing water after spring rains. (Photo by Arlin D. Fentem.)

Figure 2-25. Corn damaged by standing water in Coles County. (Photo by Arlin D. Fentem.)

farmers in the region initially were un-familiar with their use, and tiles were not at first readily available. Also, digging a mile of ditches and installing thousands of tiles to drain a forty-acre plot was no picnic. Never-theless, the fact that there was usually near at hand a gully heading the natural drainage system made the projects feasible. In effect, the natural system was completed by a man-made underground system. If we could "X-ray" western Illinois, we would see that nearly all the flat upland is now tiled.

In the "Prairie Province" of east-central Illinois, the low-lying stretches between the great moraines were, during the wettest part of the year, little better than marshes. There are early travellers' accounts of standing water stretching almost unbroken for miles

in spring. The younger drainage system here is much less complete, and the shallow val-leys much further apart than in the west. The heads of all the rivers draining the region focus—and their tributaries radiate—from a point north of Champaign-Urbana. Tiling and hand-dug ditches would not suf-fice, neither could drainage be undertaken by individuals without vast wealth or large acreages of land. Illinois, unlike Indiana and Ohio, did not pass enabling legislation pro-viding for public surveyors or for compacts organizing drainage districts. The effects on settlement and agricultural development were profound. Poorer settlers tended to be excluded because they could not afford the large expenditures necessary to make farms profitable; one large farmer devised a ditching plow drawn by 65 oxen! Landownership plots became unusually large while tenant farming and pioneering went hand in hand. Settlement was doubtless impeded and delayed. The land was not completely brought into production until this century—partly because of these circumstances, and also because the marshlands bred mosquitoes which in turn subjected the pioneers to frequent bouts with "the ague," as malaria was then called.

Landform Regions

Having surveyed the distribution and development of the various aspects of landform, we will now turn to a regional description summarizing the relations among the elements which give particular character to places.[4] On Figure 2-26, boundaries have been drawn about areas which have similar landform characteristics. A classification of the regions themselves should help to make the differences and similarities among regions more clear (Fig. 2-27).

Since the driftless areas have escaped the most dramatic effects of Pleistocene events, they have the fewest complications in their developmental histories and are probably the most scenic parts of the state because their angular features have not been obscured by glacial erosion and deposition. Both the Driftless Region (a name generally used to describe the adjacent unglaciated portions of Illinois, Iowa, Minnesota, and Wisconsin) and the Shawnee Hills are beautiful, if not very productive.

The greatest local relief (difference in elevation between the highest and lowest points in small rectangular areas from five to eight miles on a side) in the state occurs in the *Driftless Area* where the Mississippi cuts through the Niagara Escarpment, that low

and nearly continuous range of hills that dominates the region and marks the outcrop of Niagaran dolomite. The north-facing slopes of the hills generally drop quite sharply for a hundred feet or so and are then gently concave until they pass through the underlying shale and reach the Galena-Platteville dolomitic limestone, a beautiful buff-colored stone which has been used in the construction of attractive old houses and country schools in the area. On the southwestern "backslopes," elevations decline much more slowly, but these gentle slopes are interrupted by narrow valleys that deepen with increasing distance from the crest of the escarpment. It must not be thought that the escarpment is a sharply defined feature; in fact, it is quite "ragged" and extends bold promontories toward the north. Considerable fragments have also become detached from the retreating face of the escarpment and stand as buttes or "mounds" on the gently undulating (Lancaster) plain which stretches northward far into Wisconsin. Some of these picturesque hills are many tens of miles away from the escarpment itself and bear names such as Scales Mound and Charles Mound in Illinois, Sinsinawa Mound in Iowa, and Belmont, Platte, and Blue Mounds in Wisconsin. They are exceptionally scenic and interesting, and afford magnificent views from their flattish crests.

Finally, the latest cycle of erosion has cut deep and narrow valleys into the Ordovician rocks of the Lancaster Peneplain, which are themselves quite attractive. One of these, Apple River, steeper and deeper than most because of its youth (waters in a tributary of the Rock River were impounded behind an advancing ice dam in the vicinity of Stockton, Illinois, and spilled over into the Mississippi drainage during the Pleistocene),

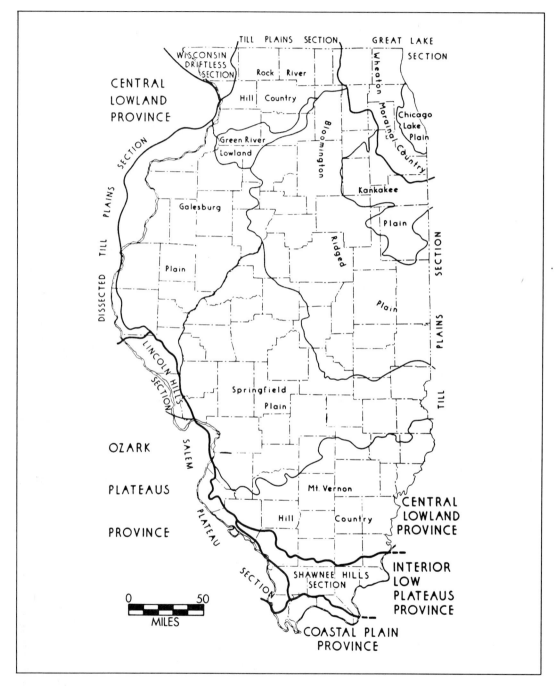

Figure 2-26. Landform regions of Illinois. (From M. M. Leighton, George E. Ekblaw, and Leland Horberg, *Physiographic Divisions of Illinois,* Illinois State Geological Survey, Urbana, 1948.)

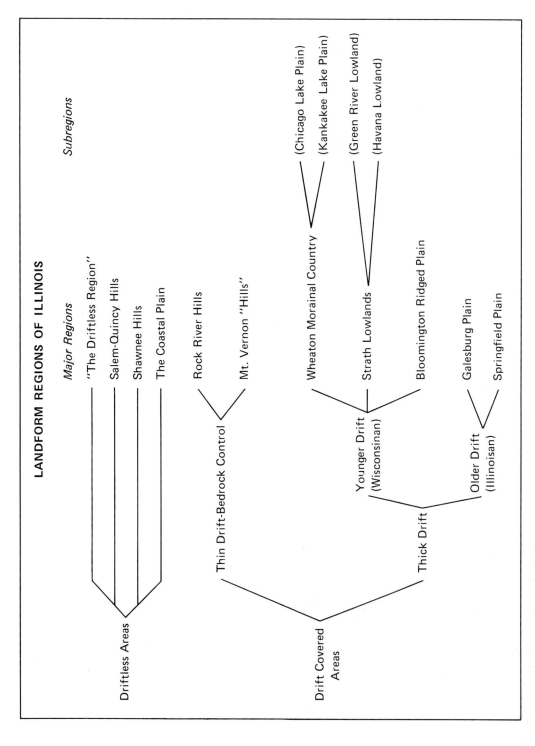

Figure 2-27. Classification of the landform regions of Illinois.

Figure 2-28. Outliers of the Niagara Escarpment, called "mounds," rise above the Lancaster surface. (Photo by Arlin D. Fentem.)

Figure 2-29. A view along the Niagara Escarpment showing a peninsula of that cuesta in profile. (Photo by Arlin D. Fentem.)

Figure 2-30. A youthful stream, Apple River, exposes Ordovician limestone in its valley sides. The valley is a rare interruption in the undulating peneplain. (Photo by Arlin D. Fentem.)

has become a tourist attraction. One of its branches has become a state park, while the other is being developed as a private venture. The wide floodplains of these streams in their lower courses have developed, to a large extent, since man came upon the scene, cleared and cultivated the hills, and initiated lead mining. Galena River was once wide and deep enough to allow steamboats to dock bow-to-shore at the town of Galena; now their passage alone could not be accommodated.

The *Shawnee Hills* may be even more impressive in their natural scenery. Like the Driftless Region, this area is traversed by a bold and prominent escarpment with elevations exceeding 800 feet and with precipitous slopes on its outfacing (southern) flank. Magnificent views are to be seen from secondary roads which follow the crest. Near the

western end a prominent hill, Bald Knob, not unlike the mounds of the northwestern corner of the state, rises more than 200 feet higher; its even crest may be, like those of the northern mounds, a remnant of the oldest (Dodgeville) erosional surface.

Southward from their highest elevations, the Shawnee Hills descend like a series of giant stairsteps (each step marking the outcrop of a gently inclined and resistant rock stratum) to the floodplain now occupied by Cache River and the Ohio River, which surrounds—like a sea about an island—the low and gently rounded Cretaceous Hills. South of Carbondale, Giant City State Park has been created about house-sized sandstone blocks piled topsy-turvy along the foot of the escarpment. When the Illinoisan ice advanced from the north—moving upwards along the backslope of the Pennsylvanian

Figure 2-31. Bald Knob, the highest point in southern Illinois, rises above the general crest of the Shawnee Hills. (Photo by Fred C. Caspall.)

Escarpment, its melt waters were impounded by the higher elevations there, creating a great "head" of water that was then forced, through fissures and along bedding planes in the rock, to escape along the escarpment face, which to this day is often called the Dripping Springs escarpment. Soft shales just below the massive sandstones were by that means removed from beneath, and the sandstone blocks slid and toppled into their present positions. Local faulting, such as that which helped produce Grand Tower, are responsible for still other impressive scenic features in the Shawnee Hills region.

Along the western extremity of the state there are narrow uplands also lacking glacial features and bordered on one or more margins by the bluffs of the major rivers, the Illinois and the Mississippi. This *Salem Upland-Quincy Hills* region is essentially a relatively narrow ribbon of gently undulating, limestone supported, and highly

elevated plain that extends ridges to the west (in the north) and both east and west (in the south) in a herringbone pattern. These ridges are separated from each other by short but steep reentrants and terminate on the floodplains. The ribbon of upland (the Lancaster Peneplain) broadens to the north in Pike and Adams counties and narrows to hundreds of yards in the south between the two rivers before ending abruptly at the Cap Au Gris fault. Southward from there the hummocky karst topography described earlier occupies part of Calhoun County.

Two landform regions of the state have features only partially subdued by glaciation. Despite the similarity of their genesis, they are quite different in appearance. The *Rock River Hills* are very much like what the Driftless Region would be without the Niagara Escarpment, which "peeks" through the drift only occasionally in the extreme west. The region consists, in its major aspect, of a

Figure 2-32. Huge blocks of sandstone at the base of the Shawnee Hills, the result of "sapping" by the movement of water underground. (Photo by Fred C. Caspall.)

broad and gently undulating plain, which is thought by some to represent the Lancaster erosional surface. A thin layer of drift modulates, but does not obscure, its erosional origin. Occasionally, there are small patches of exceptionally flat upland which probably mark the sites of former glacial lakes. The region's scenic beauty is provided by the stream valleys which interrupt the surface. Tributaries of the Rock River, chiefly the Pecatonica, have cut valleys up to 250 feet deep. Because the rock is hard, the valleys are narrow and have steep and prominent sides.

The *Mount Vernon Hill Country,* on the other hand, has almost no relief features of note and only rarely does local relief reach as high as 100 feet. There are three reasons for this contrast with the Rock River Hills. First, the surface is but little higher than the master streams (the Mississippi, the Ohio, and the Wabash) so that valleys were deepened but little and only very slowly. This situation allows valleys to become exceptionally wide, even as they are incised. Second, the weak rocks and the veneer of glacial drift were soft and easily eroded—still another reason for the extreme width of the valleys. Third, the valleys have probably been filled with a great amount of outwash during glacial melting. Perhaps half the total surface, then, consists of the nearly featureless flats along the water courses. Between these wide floodplains, the very low and gently sloping hills are usually no higher than the tallest trees. The effect on the traveller is one of great monotony. Here and there, especially northeastward from St. Louis, there are subdued remnants of Illinoisan moraines, but these too rise only a hundred feet or so above the gently sloping uplands. In the Wabash Valley, the valley train was so voluminous that it obliterated

Figure 2-33. Man-made terraces control erosion on the limestone topography of the Quincy (Lincoln) Hills. (Photo by Arlin D. Fentem.)

the upland over large areas, leaving only occasional islandlike hills to protrude through the glacial-fluvial materials.

Having experienced similar histories, the *Galesburg Plain* and *Springfield Plain* are quite similar in their geomorphic landscapes. Both have thick Illinoisan drift and are characterized by a high proportion of unusually flat land. In both cases, the flat land is located at the upper end of the elevation range; small and scattered moraine remnants stand on top of the high flats in both regions, and both have dendritic (treelike) stream systems that are actively reducing the high flats to sloping land.

Despite these many similarities, there are grounds for distinguishing between the two. The differences are in local relief and in the forms of the stream valleys. The valleys of the Galesburg Plain are deeper by 60 or 80 feet (Spoon River and Crooked Creek valleys are about 160 feet deep in their middle courses). These valleys also have steeper

sides and narrower floodplains than does, for example, the Sangamon valley of the Springfield Plain. When we recall that western Illinois has a higher surface and one floored by stronger (mostly Mississippian) rocks, these differences are expectable. In order for the stream valleys of the Galesburg Plain to approach their base levels, they have had to deepen more quickly, while erosion acting on the valley sides has been operating for the same length of time. And valley sides that expose dolomites will retreat more slowly than will those which develop largely on shales.

The Galesburg Plain has two other minor characteristics which lend some distinction. The first of these is a large area of exceptionally straight and parallel valleys; the second consists of a sprinkling of small, shallow, and roundish basins. The Buffalo Hart (now called the Table Grove) and Mendon moraines shown on Figure 2-34 appear to mark a stage in the retreat of the Illinoisan

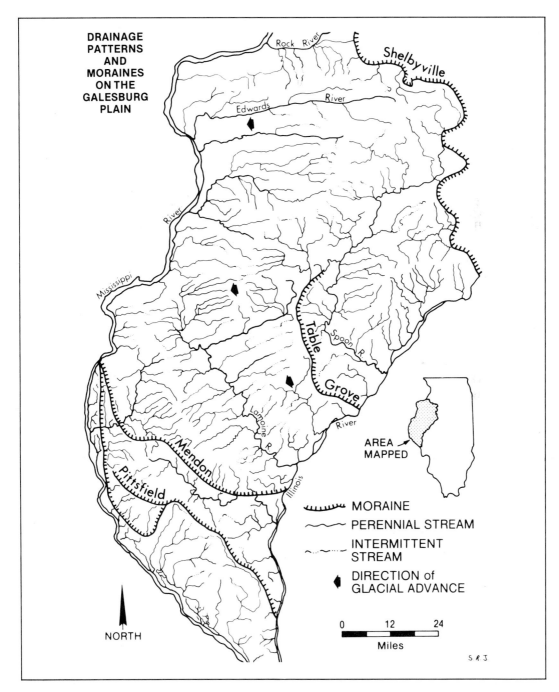

DRAINAGE PATTERNS AND MORAINES ON THE GALESBURG PLAIN

Rock River

Shelbyville

Edwards River

River

Mississippi

Table

Spoon R.

Grove

Lomoine R.

River

Mendon

Illinois

Pittsfield

AREA MAPPED

〰〰〰 MORAINE

——— PERENNIAL STREAM

········· INTERMITTENT STREAM

◆ DIRECTION of GLACIAL ADVANCE

0   12   24
Miles

NORTH

S R J

Figure 2-34. Drainage patterns and moraines on the Galesburg Plain. (Adapted from Fred Caspall, ''Parallel Drainage in West-Central Illinois,'' Western Illinois University, Macomb, 1965.)

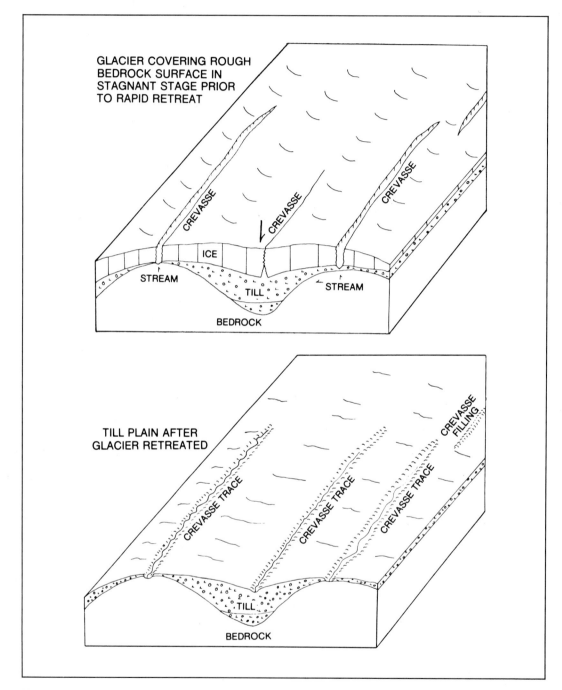

Figure 2-35. Postulated development of parallel drainage in western Illinois. (Adapted from Fred Caspall, "Parallel Drainage in West-Central Illinois," Western Illinois University, Macomb, 1965.)

ice sheet during which the thickness of the ice was unusually small and the melting continuous and rapid. Geographer Fred Caspall has demonstrated that the surface in this region bears remarkably straight and parallel low ridges and alluvial (water lain) deposits trending northeast-southwest at right angles to the ice margin.[5] He postulates that these "traces" on the land originated as crevasses in the ice itself and that these crevasses collected and channeled the melting waters. How these crevasses might have developed is shown on Figure 2-35. The inconspicuous corrugations might well have directed the courses of streams as they developed and thus account for the straight and parallel stream valleys (trellis drainage) that characterize the area (Fig. 2-34). Scattered shallow depressions in this same region are thought to mark the sites where icebergs ran aground. Deposition of sediments from glacial meltwater might have built the surrounding plain a little higher. It is possible also that these depressions, which would have become shallow lakes and marshes later on, could have attracted grazing animals, probably buffalo, and that their trampling and destruction of vegetation exposed the basins to wind erosion.

As has been previously described, the areas covered by thick Wisconsinan drift—the *Bloomington Ridged Plain* and the *Wheaton Morainal Country*—owe their peculiar character to the recency of their glaciation and to the manner in which the glacial materials were deposited. Both areas have a distinctive pattern of curving low ridges (the moraines), a gently undulating surface, and somewhat sketchy and incomplete drainage systems. On the Bloomington Plain local relief is everywhere low and there are no deep valleys to lend interest to a somewhat monotonous landscape. Early explorers, impressed in part by the near

absence of trees, often likened its appearance to the sea. (Those who live there may be compensated for the dearth of scenic excitement by their knowledge that most rural square miles had a value of well over a million dollars in 1975.) The bolder and more closely spaced moraines of the Wheaton Morainal Country provide a more exciting and varied natural landscape. Not only are the ridges steeper on their flanks, but their crests are sometimes broken by conical knolls and sharp depressions (kames and kettles). The courses of the major streams have been directed by the curving ridges so that the lowlands between them have become stream valleys as well. Since the drift was topsy-turvy to begin with, and because the time elapsed since deposition has been so short, the area is dotted by small lakes, marshes, and bogs. The materials that make up the drift include a great deal of sand and gravel, and this too helps to vary the natural environment; within short distances, areas that are low, flat, and wet alternate with those that are high, steep, and dry.

Two lowlands within the area covered by the Wisconsinan ice, the *Kankakee Lake Plain* and *Chicago Lake Plain,* are the beds of former lakes. They are very flat, lower than surrounding regions, and are almost devoid of stream valleys. Among the most conspicuous relief features are railroad embankments and other man-made features. Nevertheless, some variety is imparted by differences in materials, as well as by fluctuations in Pleistocene lake levels and by the Kankakee Flood, an event described earlier.

The deposition of silts and sands in Glacial Lake Kankakee subdued the already smooth surface of the Kankakee Plain. Part of the area was modified by the flowage of a vast amount of water across the plain toward the end of the brief period during which all the interconnected lakes were being lowered

Figure 2-36. From the air, the absence of stream valleys on the Bloomington Ridged Plain is shown by rectangular fields and nearly 100 percent cultivation. (Photo by Arlin D. Fentem.)

Figure 2-37. "Swell and swale" topography typical of young drift surfaces. (Photo by Arlin D. Fentem.)

after the breaching of the Marseilles Moraine. The swiftly moving water transported sands and gravels, which were deposited as gigantic bars as the torrent finally ebbed. As seen from above, the pattern of bars resembles that which might be seen on the bottom of a washtub after extremely dirty water has been drained from it by "pulling a plug" at one edge.

The Chicago Lake Plain is varied by two kinds of features—beach ridges (gently curving and parallel sandy ridges) that mark former beaches, and remnants of moraines that now stand as "islands" above the former lake bottom. One of these, Blue Island, is the site of the town with the same name. As in the Kankakee Plain, the materials of the lake floor range from fine clays to

sands and gravels. Both the bogs in the lower areas and the sands were ideal for producing vegetables, and before these foods were imported from great distances, truck farming was an important industry here. The beach ridges, because they were dry, helped determine early routes of travel and continue to be used as major thoroughfares today.

There are two additional landform regions that, like the lake plains, are lower in elevation than their environs and also lack stream valleys—the *Green River Lowland* and the *Havana Strath Lowland*. The similarities of their features are matched by similarities in their origins. Both have flattish bedrock floors and both have accumulated huge amounts of glacial-fluvial materials (outwash) that contain fairly large quantities of

Figure 2-38. The Cal-Sag Channel, the canalized route of one branch of the Kankakee Torrent, skirts the southern end of a moraine remnant called Blue Island. On the site of Blue Island is the modern city with that name. (Photo by Arlin D. Fentem.)

sand. Viewed from the prominent Bloomington Moraine the Green River Lowland appears to be almost featureless. Green River itself has been so modified that it resembles a system of drainage ditches more than it does a natural stream. From the floor of the basin the imposing wall of the bounding moraine stretches along the southeastern horizon and from this vantage point one becomes aware of small "hills," a few tens of feet high, and may note that their southern slopes have frequently been chosen as sites for farmsteads. In the far west, these features sometimes coalesce into fairly extensive tracts of low hills that resemble giant waves. They are in fact former sand dunes whose migrations across the lowland ceased when vegetation became established on them. Their soils are so poor and excessively drained that they are almost useless for crops and are usually relegated to scrub timber or poor pasturage. The hills are favored for building because they make possible the avoidance of wet basements and muddy feedlots that prevail elsewhere. Irrigation is practiced to some extent on the sandier areas. The sand hills disappear to the east where extensive peat bogs once existed, and in the narrow panhandle some of the best soils in the state are devoted to seed corn, asparagus, and sweet corn. The Havana Strath is much smaller, but very similar in its alternation of sandy relict dunes and intervening flats. Here the accumulation of coarse drift between the Wisconsin terminal moraine and the Illinois River is so great that it can contain a huge amount of easily accessible ground water, some of which is now used to irrigate about 160 farms in the area.

The Climate of Illinois

To consider the climate of a single state comprising only a tiny fragment of a continent is to risk loss of perspective and comprehensive understanding of variable and changing atmospheric patterns. For the global atmosphere is a restless unitary system; nothing occurs within it that does not ramify throughout the system and hence affect all areas of the earth. The word *climate,* itself, refers to an average of all the meteorological events that occur in the atmosphere over an area throughout a period of years. When it is remembered that a single day at a midwestern town may have a temperature range greater than the average difference between the coldest and warmest months at Springfield or Chicago, it may be seen that the generalization we call climate is capable of obscuring as much as it reveals. And the climate for one year may be quite different from that of the next. For these reasons, the discussion of Illinois climate will begin with the presentation of climatic norms, and then go on to a consideration of dynamic (changing) conditions in the atmosphere that have brought them about.

Temperature and precipitation, the primary ingredients of climate, both vary markedly over Illinois, not only because the state is almost 400 miles (or six degrees of latitude) from its northern border to its southern tip, but also because of its situation in relation to air masses and fronts (boundaries between air masses), to major storm tracks which move along the fronts, and to the Caribbean Sea and the Gulf of Mexico—the sources of most atmospheric moisture in Illinois.

Temperature

Two maps in Figure 2-39 show the seasonal distributions of temperature over the state, while the third map in the series relates those to the most significant measure for crop growth—the growing season. For so small a state, the differences between the northern and southern extremities are truly

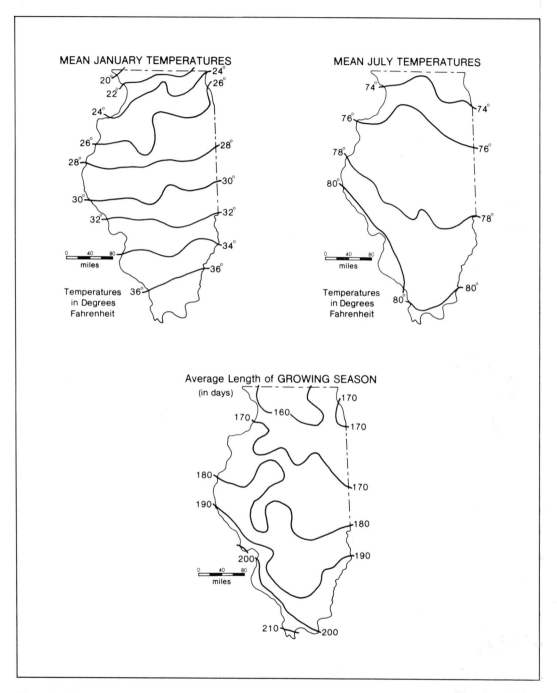

Figure 2-39. Temperatures and growing season. (Adapted from *Water Resources and Climate,* Section I of the *Atlas of Illinois Resources,* Illinois Department of Registration and Education, Springfield, 1958.)

remarkable. As suggested by Figure 2-40, heating bills are probably more than twice as high at Rockford as at Cairo. Equally as significant for human needs and use, the range in the growing season made the northern quarter of the state very risky for growing corn (before hybridized seeds and grain dryers) while permitting cotton to be grown at the foot of the Pennsylvanian escarpment in the south. The types of agriculture practiced—from dairying in the north to "plantation" cotton in the south— were begun, at least in part, in response to these climatic differences.

Two conditions, "continentality" and relatively high latitudes, combine to bring about great ranges of temperature for locations in the interiors of large land masses.

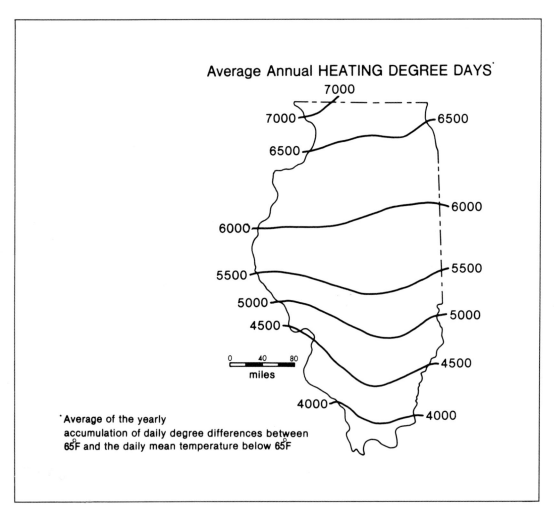

Figure 2-40. Heating degree days. (Adapted from *Water Resources and Climate,* Section I of the *Atlas of Illinois Resources,* Illinois Department of Registration and Education, Springfield, 1958.)

Continentality refers to the fact that land heats more rapidly than the seas when it is receiving more solar energy than it is radiating to outer space (during the summer half-year) and cools more rapidly when incoming energy is less than that lost at the outer edge of the atmosphere. The higher the latitude (distance north or south of the equator), the greater the seasonal difference in the length of day and in the angle at which the sun's rays meet the earth's surface. Since both direct rays and long days increase the energy received from the sun, colder winters and relatively hotter summers accompany increasing latitude. The high annual ranges of temperature in Illinois between the averages of the coldest and warmest months (from 43 °F in the south to 55 °F in the northwest) are thus shared with the interior of the country generally. The higher ranges in the northwest result from both its higher latitude and (especially) from its greater distance from the moderating influence of the sea.

Comparison of the maps in Figure 2-39 and reference to Table 2-1, however, shows that there are still other important controls of temperature differences. The *difference* in annual temperature range from north to south is mostly the result of differences in the winter temperature. Although both maps use an interval of two degrees F between isotherms (lines connecting points with equal temperatures), there are twice as many of

these lines on the January map as on the one for July. The rates of change (temperature gradient) are − 1 °F per 66 miles northward at the height of summer and − 1 °F per 26 miles in midwinter. A part of this discrepancy may be attributed to the effects of latitude; in July the day length at Rockford is about a half-hour longer than at Cairo, but in January the sun is above the horizon at Cairo for the longer time. The more important reasons for the steeper winter gradient, however, are connected with another control of climate—air masses and the fronts that exist between them. The air mass source regions affecting Illinois are shown on Figure 2-41. Most of the weather we experience is associated with the polar continental (cP) and tropical maritime (mT) air masses and the interactions between them that take place when they are in contact over or near Illinois.

Fronts are boundaries between air masses. During the First World War it was discovered that when air masses with different humidities and temperatures meet, they resist mixing and tend to maintain their internal characteristics just as two spreading blobs of gelatin on a glass plate would do when they met. Both polar and tropical air masses are "fed" from above by air settling from high in the atmosphere and the volumes of descending air are constantly changing; therefore, one of the two air masses in

Table 2-1. Selected Climatic Statistics for Rockford, Springfield, and Cairo, Illinois.

City	Summer Precip.	Winter Precip.	Jan. Temp.	July Temp.	Annual Range	Days with Snow	Days with Snow Cover	Days of Growing Season
Rockford	11.4″	5.8″	21°F.	73°F.	52°F.	34	80	160
Springfield	9.9″	6.3″	27°F.	76°F.	49°F.	20	40	188
Cairo	9.9″	10.5″	36°F.	79°F.	43°F.	10	20	210

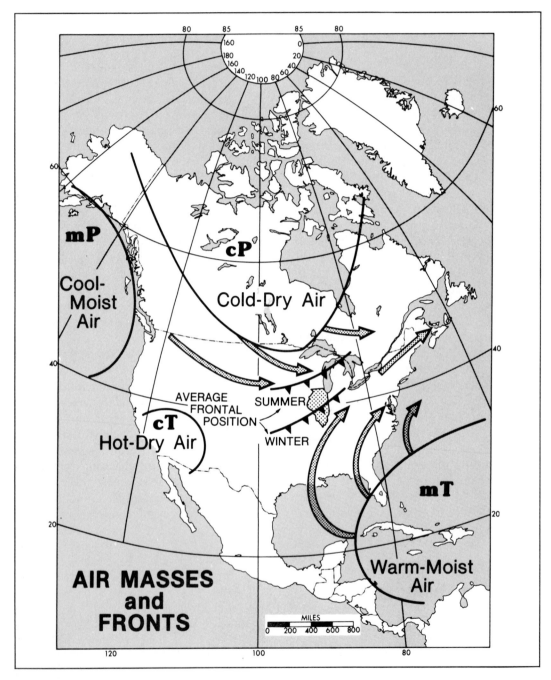

Figure 2-41. Air masses and fronts. (Adapted from Robert E. Gabler (ed.), *A Handbook for Geography Teachers,* National Council for Geographic Education, Normal, Illinois, 1966.)

contact is usually advancing at the expense of the other. To meteorologists, the analogy with shifting battle fronts in Europe seemed clear, and the boundaries were dubbed "fronts" for that reason.

On Figure 2-41 the positions of the polar front are approximated for both summer and winter, and this feature of the map illustrates why the winter temperature gradient is so steep. Quite often, the front in winter divides Illinois so that the cold and dry polar air lies over the north and warm moist tropical air over the south. The streamlines which approximate the directions of air movement are another indication of the same situation—the air streams in the two air masses are indeed "advancing" against each other.

To visitors from other climes, one of the most surprising (and distressing) features of the Midwestern winter is the rapid day to day alternations in temperature and moisture characteristics that result from the to-and-fro migration of the polar front. The immediate cause of these abrupt changes is the passage of cyclonic storms along the front. When the continent is viewed from a few hundred miles in space (as is done by sensors in artificial satellites) the polar front boundary appears as a line. One way to conceive a cyclone is as a wave travelling along this boundary—just as a "wave" travels along a loosely suspended rope when it is sharply shaken at one end. A typical wave is several hundred miles from trough to crest (south to north) and even wider in its east-west dimension. In winter, the crest (northerly apex) of a typical wave (cyclone) might progress from Denver to New England in about three days. And during that three days, the people of Peoria might experience one cold and cloudy day as the storm approached, a rapid rise in temperature as the "warm front" of the

wave passed the city, a day of unusually high temperatures, and, finally, what we call a "cold wave" as the "back side" of the wave passed by and placed central Illinois behind the "cold front" and again in the polar air mass. (See Fig. 2-42.)

It frequently happens that the bulge of cold dry air behind an advancing cold front has so much strength that it advances more rapidly than the leading (warm) front. The wave may become so steepened that a huge "bud" of the polar air mass bursts through the front as a great, roughly circular dome of extremely cold and dry air occupying much or all of the eastern United States. These buds or domes are called anticyclones and bring with them bright, sunny, and extremely cold weather. Recalling the analogy with military movements, such an event is similar to a massive "breakthrough" by the "forces of the north" which begins as a major flanking movement on the "right" while giving up ground on the "left."

One final explanation for the steeper winter temperature gradient may be understood by referring to Figure 2-43 and Table 2-1. These illustrations reveal that the number of days with significant snowfall increases more rapidly with distance northward in the "top" half of the state than in the south (the isolines are more closely spaced from about the latitude of Peoria northward), and that the number of days with snow on the ground is distributed in much the same way. The effect is to make the northern part of the state colder than it otherwise would be. The sunshine which penetrates the earth's atmosphere and reaches the surface includes a high proportion of short-wave lengths (in the violet and ultraviolet range of the visible light spectrum). When the surface which receives the light is dark, most of the solar energy is "ab-

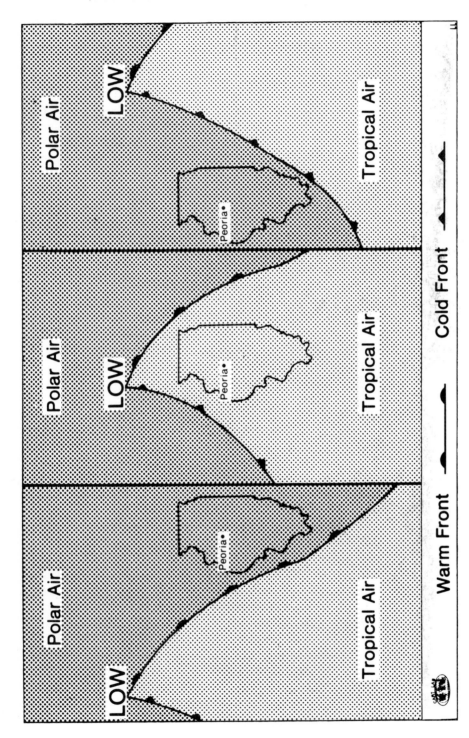

Figure 2-42. Cyclonic progression.

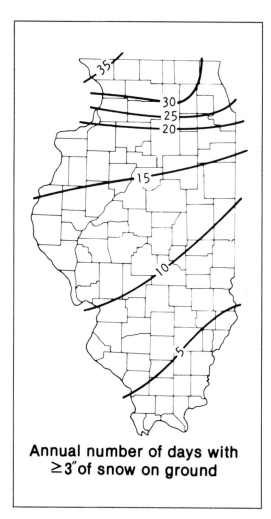

Annual number of days with ≥3″ of snow on ground

Figure 2-43. Significant snow cover. (Adapted from Stanley A. Changnon, Jr., *Climatology of Severe Winter Storms in Illinois,* Bulletin 53, Illinois State Water Survey, Urbana, 1969.)

sorbed" and is converted to heat. The warm earth surface radiates energy just as the sun does (although at much lower levels), but in this case the energy is transmitted outward through the atmosphere by much longer waves. These waves cannot pass through the atmosphere without being absorbed by the molecules which make up the gases in the air (especially water "gas" and carbon dioxide) and by pollutants such as dust and smoke particles. This uninterrupted passage of incoming radiation, its absorption at the surface, its conversion to long-wave radiation, and its eventual "entrapment" is called the "greenhouse effect." (In greenhouses, the glass panes greatly reinforce the effect of the atmosphere itself.) When snow covers the ground, however, the incoming solar radiation is reflected rather than absorbed. This is the reason that snow appears "white;" it is "returning" all the light that it receives. When a surface appears black, it is absorbing all the energy. The reradiated long waves are invisible, although some of them will register on specially prepared (infrared) photographic films. The short waves of energy reflected from the snow-covered surface pass as easily through the atmosphere (without warming it) as they did on their inward journey, and are lost to space. Thus, on a great many days each winter (twice as many at Rockford as at Springfield), the sun is heating the atmosphere much more efficiently in the south than in the north—even on days when the amount of solar energy received is the same.

Precipitation

Figure 2-44 and Table 2-1 show seasonal and annual distributions of precipitation over Illinois. Although there is considerable variation from place to place, the decrease in precipitation northward is compensated somewhat by decreased evapotranspiration. Because different crops have greatly different water requirements, it is never possible to say that any region has an optimum supply of moisture. Corn and soybeans, however, dominate the field crop agriculture of the state to an unusual degree, partly because of their suitability to Illinois' soils. If every year were an average year, the distribution of pre-

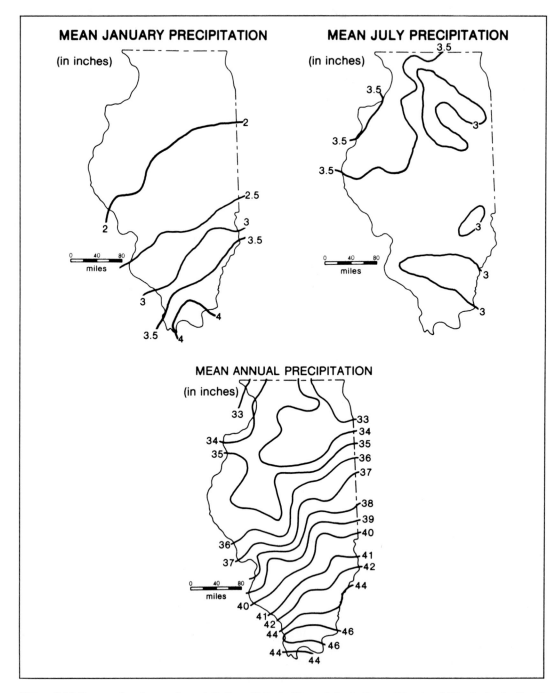

Figure 2-44. Seasonal and annual precipitation. (Adapted from John L. Page, *Climate of Illinois,* Agricultural Experiment Station Bulletin 532, University of Illinois, Urbana, 1949.)

cipitation in time and space would be close to ideal for these crops. Indeed, the suitability of the physical environment for farming is matched by few places on earth. Most of the environmental difficulties experienced by Illinois agriculturists occur during occasional drought years, or because rains fall at inopportune periods during the growing season.

The decrease northward in annual precipitation is entirely the result of the steep gradient during winter (Fig. 2-44); the summer rains are actually a little greater along the northern border. Both the winter and summer patterns are best understood in relation to the general circulation of the earth's atmosphere and to the polar fronts which help to produce the contrast in seasonal temperature gradients already described.

On an average day, the atmosphere over Illinois contains about two trillion gallons of atmospheric moisture and approximately 5 percent of that falls as precipitation. An even lesser amount is contributed by the surface of Illinois to the atmosphere through evaporation and the transpiration of water vapor by vegetation. Most atmospheric moisture, including even that in the interiors of continents, is evaporated from the seas. Because Illinois is situated so far eastward in North America, air transported from the mT source region over the Atlantic and the Gulf of Mexico supplies a high proportion of its atmospheric moisture.

The probability of precipitation for a particular place depends in part upon whether or not Atlantic-Gulf air is present. The United States is situated in the Polar Westerlies, a latitudinal zone in which prevailing winds, both at the surface and aloft, are from westerly points. The energy which drives the Westerlies (which are but one component of the planetary wind system) is

the steep gradient in temperature northward. As the foregoing discussion of temperature gradients points out, this gradient is much less steep in the summer hemisphere, and the Westerlies are therefore much weaker then. Consequently, continentality—the heating of air over continents—tends to make summers a great deal hotter than average for given latitudes. Gases expand when heated and become less dense; air during the summer, therefore, tends to drift into the interior of the continent from the (relatively) cooler seas. At the same time, the Westerlies, along with the other planetary winds, shift northward. The result is (on average) a slow drift of warm, moist air up the Mississippi Valley and overspreading Illinois. The surface Polar Front boundary between polar and tropical air masses in summer is usually located north of Illinois. In winter, on the other hand, the Polar Front frequently bisects the state, so that the prevalence of the moisture-rich air mass is much greater at Carbondale than at Rockford.

Almost all precipitation is brought about by cooling large volumes of the atmosphere; cooling *of this kind,* in turn, is almost always a consequence of great vertical displacements. Although air may be cooled in other ways, temperature drops which produce thick clouds result from the expansion of parcels of air when they are lifted from near the surface (where they are compressed by the entire weight of the overlying atmosphere) to higher levels (where the weight and densities are less). If upward-moving air is cooled to a critical temperature—the "dew point"—the condensation of water vapor into water droplets begins, clouds form, and precipitation may result. One of the "triggers" of upward-moving columns of air is the heating that takes place at the base of the atmosphere by radiation from the earth's surface on hot summer days. When moist tropical air overspreads the state, as it does in summer, air mass thunderstorms may occur in one place about as well as in another, which is one reason why summer precipitation varies so little over the state.

The waves (cyclones) along the Polar Front, which are so important in understanding the changeability in temperature, are also closely connected to precipitation patterns. While a detailed explanation of cyclonic precipitation is beyond the scope of this text, the following discussion is intended to draw a general picture of the processes involved and to relate them to the planetary circulation. The great stream of air flowing from west to east in these latitudes may be thought of as a fluid moving in a gigantic

"river" at speeds which increase with altitude. For reasons too involved to discuss here, this stream of air circles the North Pole in a series of huge waves so that its path across the continent curves gently. One of these waves is shown over North America as it was mapped in December of 1951 (Fig. 2-45). The speed of this river of air is greater at some places than at others, and is greatest over places where the temperature gradient (which supplies the energy) is also greatest. That location is, of course, the Polar Front—especially in winter when the air arriving from Canada may be well below 0 °F. This narrow zone of very high velocities in the stratosphere has been named the Polar Jet Stream (Fig. 2-46).

Within the Polar Jet Stream, the surface

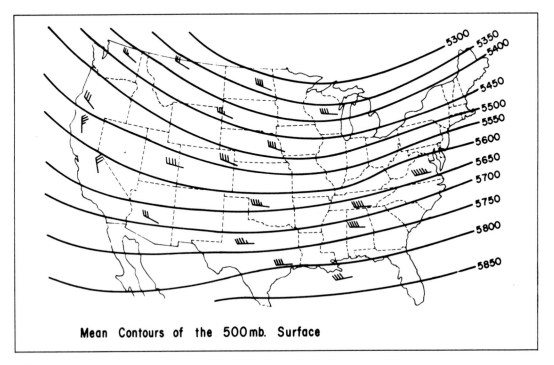

Mean Contours of the 500 mb. Surface

Figure 2-45. A wave over the United States. (Jay R. Harmon, *Tropospheric Waves, Jet Streams, and United States Weather Patterns* (Washington, D.C.: Association of American Geographers, Resource Papers for College Geography, No. 11), 1971, p. 31. Reprinted by permission.)

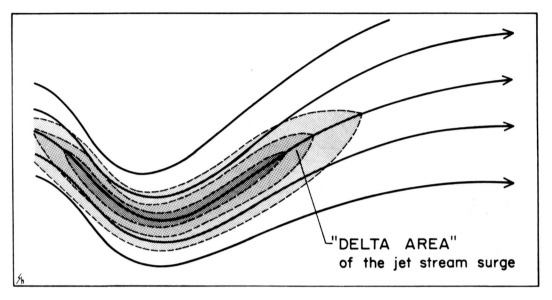

"DELTA AREA"
of the jet stream surge

Figure 2-46. A segment of the polar jet stream. (Jay R. Harmon, *Topospheric Waves, Jet Streams, and United States Weather Patterns* (Washington, D.C.: Association of American Geographers, Resource Papers for College Geography, No. 11), 1971, p. 12. Reprinted by permission.)

cyclones interact with the upper air waves to produce surges of greater wind speed that travel through the long waves. Air moving southeastward along the stream lines is compressed as it changes direction (following the wave form) to the east, subsides (sinks) in the atmosphere, and tends to bring with it an outbreak of polar continental (cP) air. As the air passing through the surge turns northeastward, its velocity slows and the air begins to spread out (diverge), creating lower density and favoring the movement of air upward from the surface (Fig. 2-46).

In the earlier description of cyclones, the movement of air at the surface was described as currents advancing against the fronts. This *convergence* of air toward the crest of the cyclonic wave is greatly accelerated if a Polar Jet Stream surge is passing over the surface front, because the zone ahead of the speed surge produces divergence at upper levels to make "room" for converging and

rising air within the cyclone. The horizontal picture of surface winds and fronts presented earlier is accurate, but a cyclone may also be conceived as a huge, rotating mass of air with strong upward movement. In many ways it resembles the eddies that form in strongly-moving (and especially) curving streams of water. Both the waves at upper levels and the counterclockwise circulation of air near the surface in cyclonic storms results in part from the rotation of the earth, from frictional or "shear" effects as streams of air encounter each other, and from turbulence caused by irregularities in the earth's surface. In the United States, the chief source of surface modification on air streams and frontal positions is the Rocky Mountains.

The development of waves (cyclones) on the Polar Front is thus seen to be closely related to the path of the Polar Jet Stream, and the Jet Stream is sometimes said to

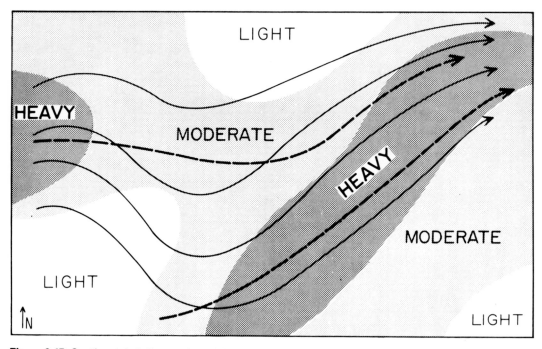

Figure 2-47. Continental air flow and precipitation. (Jay R. Harmon, *Tropospheric Waves, Jet Streams, and United States Weather Patterns* (Washington, D.C.: Association of American Geographers, Resource Papers for College Geography, No. 11), 1971, p. 16. Reprinted by permission.)

"guide" the cyclones in their courses across the continent. There is considerable stability in the large wave pattern at high altitudes over the United States. This persistence of the Jet Stream position, and therefore of "preferred" storm tracks, helps to explain why similar weather patterns often continue for days or weeks (say drought over the Northern Plains and violent storms and heavy rain in the Ohio Valley). When the upper air waves shift their positions, the persistent weather patterns are then broken and replaced by others. Long-range weather forecasting is grounded in attempts to assess probable upper air wave patterns and Jet Stream locations.

Most winter precipitation occurs with the passage of cyclonic storms. We have seen

that, in a general way, this is true because huge volumes of air are being lifted toward regions within the upper atmosphere where density is becoming less through expansion (divergence) ahead of Jet Stream surges. *Within* the moving cyclone, some regions receive more precipitation than others. When other conditions are equal, maximum precipitation occurs near the center where convergence and lifting is greatest. The other major controls are the fronts themselves. Since the warm and cold air masses have quite different densities, boundaries between them are maintained both at the surface and aloft. The advancing cold air mass to the west often travels more rapidly than the storm itself (the back of the wave is steepening). When this happens, the warm, moist mT air is forced upward vigorously and precipitation tends to be heavier (though shorter-lived) just ahead of, along, and immediately behind the cold front.

The heavy concentration of winter precipitation in the southern part of the state may be understood in relation to cyclone tracks. Ordinarily, a semipermanent long wave in the upper atmosphere loops far southward over the United States, with the Jet Stream imbedded in it. A favored zone for the development of cyclonic storms is just east of the Rockies, because the mountains are so high and so continuous that they tend to maintain the boundaries between polar maritime (Pacific) air to the west and polar continental and/or tropical maritime air to the east.

Cyclones developing in southern Colorado and southward to Texas tend to follow the southward-looping Jet Stream to the middle of the continent and then to turn sharply to the northeast (recurve) so that the centers of the cyclonic eddies then move up the Ohio Valley, often passing through southern Illinois in a northeasterly direction (Fig. 2-48). It is just after the recurving takes place, as the cyclones turn toward the northeast, that the Jet Stream surges are likely to intensify and to overtake the cyclone (Fig. 2-46). This interaction intensifies the storm and increases precipitation. Seventy percent of severe winter season storms in Illinois are "Texas Track" cyclones, both because of their great intensities and because their centers passed through or near Illinois. In

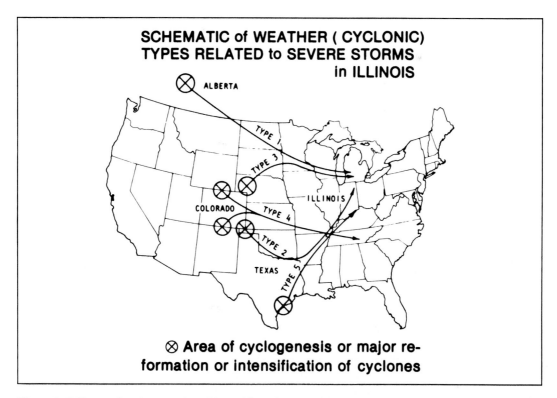

Figure 2-48. Types of cyclone tracks. (Adapted from Stanley A. Changnon, Jr., *Climatology of Severe Winter Storms in Illinois,* Bulletin 53, Illinois State Water Survey, Urbana, 1969.)

summer, on the other hand, the centers of lows usually pass well north of the Wisconsin border so that cyclonic precipitation is no longer concentrated in the southern part of the state.

One further mechanism for inducing precipitation which favors southern Illinois is orographic lifting. Only in the extreme south is there a terrain barrier to the movement of surface air currents, the Shawnee Hills. While the escarpment crest is only a few hundreds of feet above the surrounding countryside, it appears to trigger a slight increase in rainfall.

Climatic "Insults" and Climatic Change

Unusual events and periods in the environmental system are more significant to man and to the environmental complex itself than their short-lived character seems to indicate. Man designs a cultural baggage—house types, space-heating systems, transportation facilities, cropping regimes, etc.—that copes rather well with usual conditions, but he and his constructions suffer severe damage when unusual weather produces floods, strong winds, ice glazing, deep snows, rainless periods during the growing season, or wet fields at planting time. One storm may produce more erosion than results from all the others during a year; thus, even the shape of the land surface may have been largely sculpted during catastrophic weather events. Nine years in ten might have enough rainfall to support a forest vegetation, but episodic droughts might prevent young trees from ever being established.

Tornadoes have been the most destructive to human life of all storm types and have killed more than a thousand people in Illinois since 1916. They almost always occur along with violent thunderstorms which themselves may be widespread and cause

Figure 2-49. Damage from a 1942 tornado in Urbana, Illinois. (Photo by Alden Cutshall.)

much damage. The probability of tornadoes at any point in Illinois is less than that in seven other states, but Illinois ranks first in the number of tornado-caused deaths and second, after Oklahoma, in property damage for the period 1916-69.[6] Tornado damage is usually limited to a very small area (less than four square miles, on average). Nearly 1,600 years would pass before every area of the state experienced a tornado passage if the 1916-69 frequency were maintained. It is common for news reporters to refer to "tornado alley" and to give the impression that there is a zone of high danger in the state (Fig. 2-50), but the near random distribution shown by Figure 2-51 indicates that a longer record will be necessary before the calculation of probabilities at points will mean very much. More than two-thirds of tornado-caused deaths occurred on either May 26, 1917 or March 18, 1925. The average length of tornado tracks on the ground in Illinois is less than 14 miles and the average diameter 185 yards; the killer tornadoes of 1917 (101 deaths) and 1925 (603 fatalities) were continuously on the ground for 283 miles (188 in Illinois) and 219 miles respectively, and reached maximum diam-

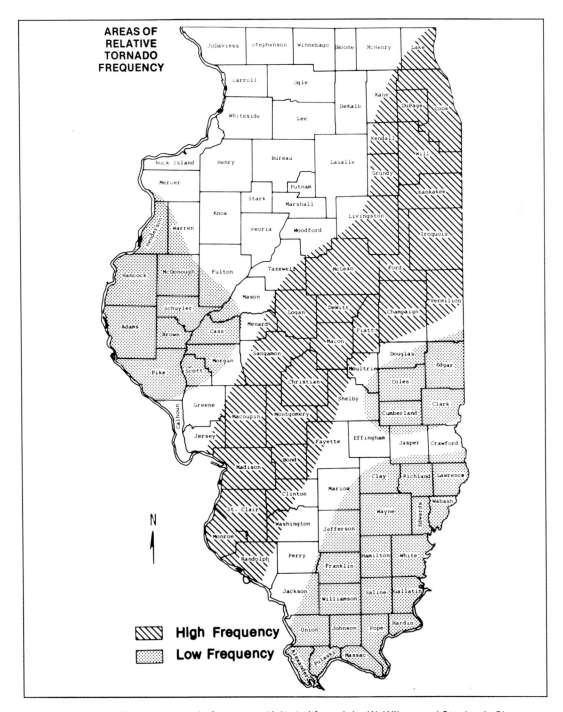

Figure 2-50. Areas of relative tornado frequency. (Adapted from John W. Wilson and Stanley A. Changnon, Jr., *Illinois Tornadoes,* Circular 103, Illinois State Water Survey, Urbana, 1971.)

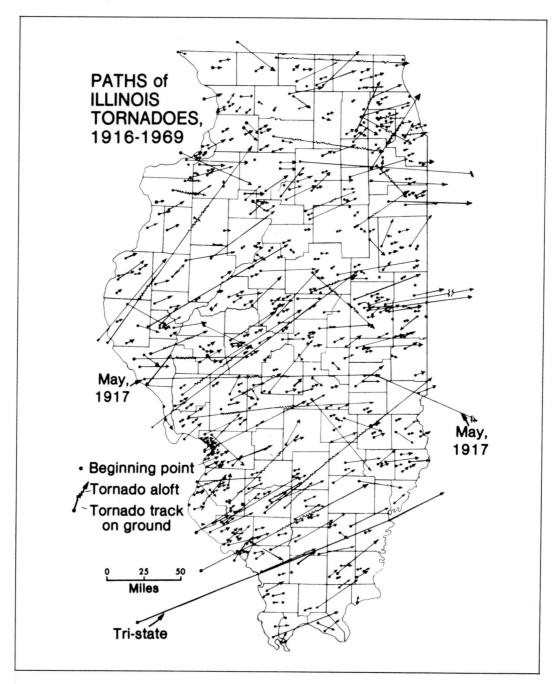

Figure 2-51. Paths of Illinois tornadoes, 1916–1969. (Adapted from John W. Wilson and Stanley A. Changnon, Jr., *Illinois Tornadoes,* Circular 103, Illinois State Water Survey, Urbana, 1971.)

eters of 0.5 and 1.0 miles. The 1925 storm, the Tri-State Tornado, is by far the worst tornado on record anywhere.

A tornado is a violently-rotating funnel of air which descends from a thunderstorm cloud to the ground. The greater the violence of thunderstorms, the greater the probability that they will spawn tornadoes. Most midwestern tornadoes develop in squall lines—series of thunderstorms ahead of, along, or just behind a cold front—in well-developed cyclones. The same conditions in the upper atmosphere, a speed surge through the Jet Stream, that favors intense cyclones also increases the likelihood of tornadoes. Another element favoring tornadoes is warm and moist air, because thunderstorms are more frequent and more intense when there is a great deal of water vapor present. When water gas condenses, great quantities of heat energy are released. The heating of air in rain clouds causes it to expand and to continue its upward movement; once condensation occurs, cloud development tends to be self-sustaining. Spring is the favored season for tornadoes in Illinois because it offers the most favorable *combination* of cyclone development *and* abundance of warm and moist air masses. In summer, tropical maritime (mT) air is abundant but frontal activity diminishes. A secondary tornado maximum occurs in the fall as conditions favorable for cyclogenesis intensify. Finally, in winter, cyclones increase in frequency and intensity but tornadoes are relatively rare because the presence of mT air is less frequent and its moisture content much lower.

Tornadoes are so dramatic and so frightening in their violence that a great deal of effort has been devoted to their forecasting. Radar can sometimes detect their characteristic "hook" shapes, but more often echoes from heavy rain areas obscure them. About all that forecasters can do is to warn the public when there are conditions favorable to tornado development approaching a region. Once an intense squall line or single storm has been identified on radar screens, radio and TV announcements warning of the approach of the storms can be broadcast. This "tornado warning" can be supplemented by tornado alerts, which are reports of ground sightings of tornadoes or funnel clouds. If possible, the alert is accompanied by an announcement of the direction of movement. Most tornadoes move in directions close to northeast, so that a sighting alone can be more useful if one keeps a map of the local area available.

There is some promise for another warning system based upon sferics, the excess of electrical activity within thunderstorms having funnel clouds. Tornado-breeding thunderstorms seem to have almost continuous lightning (10-100 flashes per second) at a center high in the cloud that can be detected by radio receivers tuned to 150 kilohertz. So far, the necessary combinations of radar detectors (for the thunderstorms), receivers, and direction-finders have not been developed into a remote warning network. Meanwhile, Newton Weller has suggested that home television sets may be used to detect the approach of sferics accompanying a tornado.[7] A set in good working order is tuned to Channel 13 and the brightness adjusted downward to the threshold of picture visibility, or black; the channel selector is then turned to Channel 2. On the dark screen, lightning appears as flashes. If the picture (or the black screen) begins to brighten and remains so, a tornado within 20 miles is indicated. It should be emphasized that this method is still experimental and that the absence of screen brightening does not guarantee the absence of nearby tornadoes.

Severe winter storms cause far greater economic loss than do tornadoes and nearly as many directly-caused deaths. Indirect losses are probably several times greater than measurable property damage and death tolls imply. The best record of indirect losses for a single storm was assembled for one which crossed northern Illinois on January 26-27, 1967. Reported physical property damages totaled nearly $22 million and indirect economic loss was calculated to be $174 million. Automobile accidents due to ice and snow, transportation tie-ups which closed or reduced the efficiencies of businesses and public institutions, heart attacks that resulted from overexertion, and the costs of

rescue operations and snow removal all contributed to the death toll of 56 and economic losses of nearly $200 million.

Between 1900 and 1960, 293 winter storms either produced at least six inches of snow at some point in Illinois or caused glazing (icing) conditions to be reported by 10 percent or more of Weather Bureau substations. Eleven others caused property damage, deaths, or injuries. Colorado-Texas Track cyclones moving northeastward toward the lower Great Lakes constitute more than two-thirds of these storms. The typical severe storm moves in a direction 30° south (to the right) of northeast and maximum snowfalls occur in an elongated (3:1) core about 75 miles north and closely parallel to the path followed by the cyclone center. A model (generalization) developed from the 304

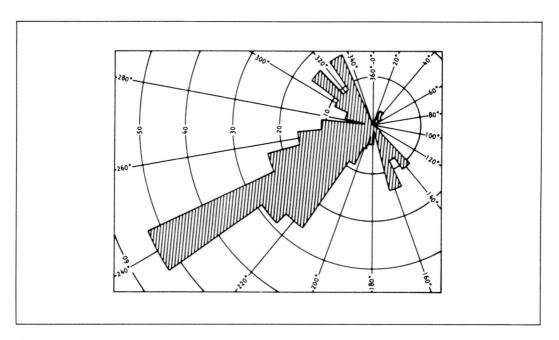

Figure 2-52. Direction of storm movement across Illinois sorted by number per 10-degree interval. (From Stanley A. Changnon, Jr., *Climatology of Severe Winter Storms in Illinois,* Bulletin 53, Illinois State Water Survey, Urbana, 1969.)

storms indicates snowfalls of more than six inches in an area 156 miles by 52 miles (about 8,000 square miles or 15 percent of the state's area). Locally heavy snowfall may be anticipated when a fairly strong easterly wind is blowing as snowfall begins. If the wind direction is maintained for several hours or very slowly backs toward the northeast, the storm center is likely to pass not far south of the observer and to place him in the core of heaviest snowfall.

During the past 20 years it has become apparent that "spells" of weather are typical of our climate. "January thaws" and October's "bright blue weather" are not just figments of our imaginations, and weather events do not occur in a random fashion with respect to time. There really are recurring cycles of drought and sequences of wet years. Climatologists and meteorologists have determined that each persistent weather type is associated with an equally persistent pattern of upper air circulation, and they have developed some insights into what conditions may affect the planetary wind system during both long and short runs of time. For example, recent droughts south of the Sahara in Africa and in India seemed to be signaled by a sudden increase in the amount of the north polar area covered by ice and snow (as seen on satellite photography). The increase in the meridional (from equator to pole) temperature gradient that resulted may have supplied more energy to the system and altered the pattern of flows within it.

Returning to this theme serves as a reminder that the climate of the past (or future) 10 years could be quite different than that of the past 100, and that the climate of Illinois a few centuries or millenia ago might have been distinctly warmer and drier or cooler and wetter than now. Soils, vegetation, wild animals, and the life style of

prehistoric man in the Midwest may have been greatly influenced by former climes. In particular, neither the natural vegetation nor the soils of the state are congruent with the present climate; it may be that they are relics of earlier and different meteorological conditions.

Native Vegetation

Of all the unusual features encountered by the explorers and settlers of the Midwest, none so excited their curiosity or posed so many practical problems as did the Prairie Peninsula (Fig. 2-53). This vast sea of tall grasses, extending as a wedge from the eastern boundary of the arid Great Plains, stretched all the way past the tip of Lake Michigan into present Indiana and had outliers as far as western New York State. To the scientific mind, which had learned to associate grasslands with dry climates, these tall and coarse grasses were not only different from those found elsewhere, but were also a puzzle because they grew in humid environments which seemed clearly capable of supporting dense forests. To the agriculturalist, the prairies were both boon and bane, although at first encounter the difficulties they imposed far outweighed the blessings that would later become evident.

Since only vestiges of the original prairie remain, it might seem that the grassland could be dismissed with only a cursory examination in this chapter. Its original distribution, however, is closely tied to other elements of the physical environment, and its presence influenced both agricultural settlement and the types of farming which developed. Its most important consequence was to make soils much more productive than they otherwise would have been. The very extensive systems of fine roots which

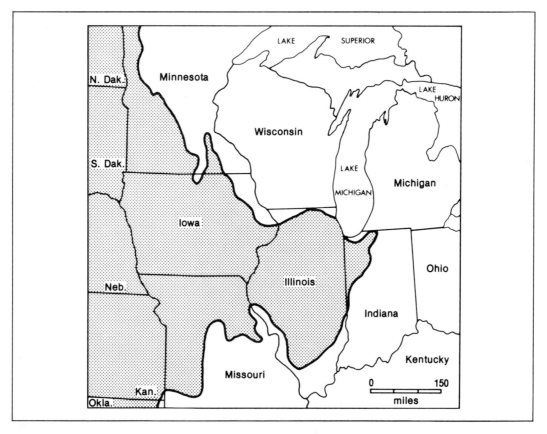

Figure 2-53. The Prairie Peninsula. (Adapted from H. E. Wright, Jr., "History of the Prairie Peninsula," in Robert E. Bergstrom (ed.), *The Quaternary of Illinois,* Special Publication 14, University of Illinois College of Agriculture, Urbana, 1968.)

characterized the prairie grasses were readily incorporated into the upper soil horizons as decayed organic matter (humus). This material imparts the characteristic dark color to prairie soils, improves their tilth by clumping together the smallest of particles, and reduces the rate at which mineral plant foods are dissolved and carried downward by rainwater.

The pioneer settlers on the prairie were the products, both in Europe and in America, of woodland environments, and had developed an appropriate technology and system for making woodlands productive. Their en-counter with the grassland forced a pause in the tide of settlement, which first skirted the prairie margins and eventually reached its core in the heart of the Grand Prairie about a generation late. This delay, and the technologies and tenure systems developed in the interim, resulted in the distinctive agricultural landscapes to be described in a later chapter.

The earliest settlers were handicapped in a number of ways. At the time, most of them did not have the steel moldboard plow invented by John Deere at Grand Detour and put into mass production about 1847 at

Moline. The tough sod of the prairie plains could not be turned over effectively by the cast iron plowshares then available. Poor drainage and prairie soils were usually associated, and the combined capital expenses of sod breaking, ditching, and tiling were beyond the financial resources of most. It was also harder to find wood for fuel and housing, particularly on the wide expanses of the Grand Prairie in eastern Illinois. Even "navigation" could be a problem. James Caird, a Scots traveller, essayed a journey from Springfield to Decatur in 1858 and has left this description:

> . . . we stood across the great plain which stretched out before us. The horses struck without hesitation into the long coarse grass, through which they pushed on with very little inconvenience, although it was in many places higher than their heads. It was not thick, and parted easily before them; then sweeping under the bottom of our waggon it rose in a continuous wave behind us as we passed along. The surface of the ground was firm and smooth. We had fixed our eye on a grove of timber on the horizon as our guide, and drove on for about an hour in a straight line, as we believed, towards it. But stopping now and then to look at the soil and the vegetation, we found that the grove had disappeared. Without knowing it we must have got into a hollow, so we pressed on. But after two hours' steady driving we could see nothing but the long grass and the endless prairie, which seemed to rise slightly all round us. I advised the driver to fix his eye upon a cloud right ahead of us, the day being calm, and to drive straight for it. Proceeding thus, in about half an hour we again caught sight of the grove, still very distant, and the smart young American driver "owned up" that he had lost his way.[8]

Finally, the wet prairie was accurately associated in the popular mind with hazards to health, which were thought to be caused by "miasmas"—noxious vapors believed to be included in the night mists which developed over the poorly-drained hollows of the plain. The chills and fevers of "ague," as they called the disease, are now known to have been caused by mosquito-borne malaria.

Grasslands and Woodlands

The species making up the tall grass prairie can be seen today only in abandoned pastures, in unkempt cemeteries, along rural roads and railroad rights of way, or in nature preserves. Fortunately, the native vegetation patterns can be reconstructed with a high degree of accuracy. In the case of the Grand Prairie, some lands were not plowed until about 1900, and interviews with original settlers could be conducted as late as 1920. Surveyor's notes made during the original rectangular surveys prescribed by the Northwest Ordinance (1787) may also be consulted.

The map of vegetation prepared by R.C. Anderson in 1970 (Fig. 2-54) shows the fragmented nature of the grassland distribution. Except in the extreme northeast and the far south, the grassland dominated in most areas, but it was broken wherever the land was sloping. When it is remembered that flat land prevails throughout most of the state, and that most sloping land is found on the valley sides of streams which are actively invading the higher tracts of flat land, the dendritic pattern of the forested areas becomes understandable. In eastern Illinois, the crescentic moraines also bore forests on their steeper slopes. Flat land and grassland, then, usually occurred together; the major exceptions were the floodplains of streams, where mixed hardwood forests occupied large tracts. Upland forests, which occur in better drained situations, were usually composed of mixed oaks and hickories in the northern part of the state. In the south, however, the variety of deciduous trees increased dramatically and included even spe-

PRAIRIES

0   40

miles

Figure 2-54. Illinois prairies at time of settlement (1810–1820). Based on original land survey records. (Adapted from R. C. Anderson, "Prairies in the Prairie State," *Transactions of the Illinois Academy of Science*, 63 (1970).

cies usually associated with the southern United States, such as tupelo (black gum), red gum, and cypress.

Figure 2-54 also reveals what at first seems surprising: The most coherent and unbroken tracts of prairie occur, not in the west closest to the steppes of the dry plains states, but east of the Illinois River near the tip of the peninsula. This seeming paradox is explained by the general absence of well-defined valleys in the Bloomington Ridged

Plain; since the Wisconsinan ice retreated only a short time ago, there has not been time enough to develop a well-defined drainage pattern.

Explanations for the Prairie

The observation that prairie grasses were associated with areas that had slow and incomplete surface drainage led to the first hypothesis advanced to explain the climatically anomalous prairie. As more information was gathered, it became evident that some gently sloping land with good surface drainage also had a grass cover; this was particularly true of the "grey prairie" south of the Shelbyville moraine in southern Illinois. In these cases, however, there was a drainage problem of a different sort, this time brought about by "tight" or impermeable subsoils which did not permit soil water to percolate downward more than a few feet. At the same time, flat floodplains nearby might support woodlands if underdrainage was adequate. E.N. Transeau observed that areas with tight subsoils (pans) were alternately saturated (during rainy periods) and then quickly dried out (during droughts) because the reservoir of moisture above the pan was so small.[9] Fluctuations in the water table were, in his view, the condition which inhibited the development of woodlands in the prairie wedge.

The geographer Carl O. Sauer is the best-known spokesman for the "fire hypothesis."[10] Pointing out that the separation of woody and herbaceous plants coincides with changes in terrain, he concluded that the pattern is best explained by fire. Prairie fires might have been caused deliberately by man as a means of "herding" game animals into traps, set by man accidentally, or ignited by lightning. The incidence of fires, he thought, was greater on plains than in broken country, and consequently the scarps and hills provided a refuge for trees. The fire hypothesis is intimately bound up in a scholarly controversy concerning the invasion of the Midwest by man after his crossing of the Pleistocene land bridge from Asia in the vicinity of the present Bering Strait. The effects of invading hunters upon prehistoric vegetation and animal life are yet to be sorted out.

Additional evidence supporting the fire hypothesis has been developed in response to still another explanation most effectively presented by John Borchert in 1950.[11] Borchert believed the prairie wedge to be a response to a distinctive climate which existed in the prehistoric past and that some elements of the distinctive grassland climate still persist. After collecting a wide range of climatic data for the area east of the Rockies, he concluded that the Peninsula was characterized by low winter rainfall and snowfall as compared to areas northeast (in the case of snowfall and snow cover) and southeast (in the case of rainfall). Borchert, and later Reid Bryson, also pointed out that the mean positions of "preferred" storm tracks in winter closely coincided with either the northeastern or southeastern borders of the grassland. Since persistent weather patterns are generated by equally persistent airstream patterns, Borchert then examined the climates that characterized the occasional drought years in the Midwest and discovered that the departures from normal years (during droughts) in summer rain, temperature, relative humidity, and sunshine, when mapped, produced geographic patterns similar to that of the prairie wedge.

One might guess that even an occasional drought year might inhibit the invasion of forest species. Reasoning that drought years might have been more frequent in the past and might even have been "normal" during some period after glaciation, Borchert then examined the climatology of drought years

in more detail, giving particular attention to the behavior of the westerly airstreams across the continent. Two conclusions emerged: (1) the axis of the prairie wedge coincides with the greatest average transport of air eastward from the base of the Rocky Mountains; and (2) the transport of Rocky Mountain air is greater during drought years, and during those same years, cyclone tracks are displaced away from the grassland. Rocky Mountain air, because of its long trajectory over land and because it has lost moisture in being lifted over the western Cordillera, is a poor source of atmospheric moisture as compared with the mT air that has been displaced southeastward. Deprived of both moisture and the cyclonic triggers of precipitation, the grassland might develop a distinctive, and drier, climate. Such a climate could result from an increase in the strength of the Westerlies. Indeed, a change in the average curvature or location of the long waves in the atmospheric circulation could have profound effects in the distribution of heat and moisture over the continent. Did such a climate exist in the past, and did it "create" the prairie wedge? At the time of Borchert's examination, there existed a widespread consensus that the period from 7,000 years to about 4,000 years before the present was both warm and dry, not only on the Great Plains, but also in Europe, and that a cooler and wetter regime began to set in after the latter date.

Evidence for past vegetations and climates comes from a variety of sources, which include counts of plant fossils, pollens, and seeds preserved in bogs. Appropriate sites are few in number (as are the scholars to examine them); pollens are blown great distances and dating is sometimes difficult. For all these reasons, the data are insufficient for reaching final conclusions. More recently, another method of investigation, opalphytolith analysis, has been developed. These studies are based upon the fact that the roots of both grasses and woody plants accumulate silica (opal), which is extremely resistant to chemical decay and, therefore, remains in soils indefinitely. The grasses accumulate opal at a much more rapid rate than do woodland plants. The organic remains can be dated by radiocarbon techniques, and it is therefore possible to estimate the length of periods a given soil was developing under one or the other plant community. Some recent data developed from additional sites and from opalphytolith studies cast considerable doubt on the hypothesis of a warm dry postglacial interval (the Altithermal) and have given more

credence to the fire hypothesis. We will let the fire group have the last word.

John Alford and Fred Caspall have assembled evidence that the Altithermal may not have existed at all, and they have presented another train of evidence supporting fire as the cause of prairie grasslands.[12] Alford and Caspall select three tree species—pin oak, red maple, and eastern red cedar—which grow very well in both poorly-drained and very dry situations and which are also highly vulnerable to fire. Red cedar, in particular, is very easily ignited and consumed by fire. The distributions of the three species do not seem to reflect exclusions from the prairie for climatic reasons. The present rapid colonization of the prairie

Figure 2-55. Rare survivors of trees planted in rows along the highways of east-central Illinois during the drought years of the 1930s. (Photo by Arlin D. Fentem.)

Figure 2-56. Fire susceptible red cedar invades native big bluestem grasses in Hancock County (Galesburg Plain). (Photo by Arlin D. Fentem.)

by the red cedar, now that it is protected by man from fire, suggests that it was only fire which produced the prairies.

Formal attempts to explain the Prairie Peninsula were begun more than 50 years ago. It is evident that not only is this riddle unsolved, but that a host of others, all reflecting the complex interaction of environmental elements with each other and with man have arisen. Problems have been introduced, both here and in the section on climate, which are as yet unsolved and which must be left "up in the air." This has been done deliberately, because it is honest and because the brief summaries of research presented both illustrate the methods scholars use to solve problems and suggest directions in which the search for truth might be pointed. In particular, these problems il-

lustrate that research requires the mutual support of workers in many different fields of knowledge. Geographers often "put together" different sets of information through the compilation of maps, and this approach is especially useful in showing ways in which these data might be related to each other. This "geographic" approach is very appropriate for environmental studies.

Soils

Few residents of Illinois any longer have direct contact with the soil. Only about 100,000 live on farms and the number who actually till the soil is far less; more than 80 percent of the state's vast agricultural output in 1974 was produced by farmers who, together with their families, could easily be accommodated within a metropolitan area the size of Springfield. Nevertheless, the quality of these soils—and the maintenance of their fertility—remains as vital as ever. Illinois soils are among the most productive in the world and produce vast surpluses of feedgrains and soybeans for the rest of the nation and for export. The "agribusiness" which the soil supports dwarfs the 5 billion dollar value of direct farm sales.

The soil occupies a distinctive niche within the total environmental complex. Not only does it express in its character the interaction of all other physical elements, but in it are rooted, ultimately, all forms of terrestrial life. Since man develops his most intimate contact with the earth's surface through the medium of soils, he has lavished far greater attention to their changing character from place to place than he has to the other elements of the natural world. More than 10,000 soil series have been recognized and mapped in the United States alone, and many shades of difference within the series themselves are recognized in detailed county mapping.

Ordinarily, the soil develops from a parent material—such as bedrock, glacial drift, alluvial sands, or windblown silts—over very long periods of time. The interrelations of slope, exposure to wind and sun, temperature, moisture, natural vegetation, and parent materials are expressed in weathering (physical and chemical) and biological processes within the soil body itself. In a humid lowland environment such as that of Illinois, the soil may be conceived as a continuous "blanket" of varying thickness and includes any materials that support plant life. Describing and subdividing this layer are rather difficult tasks because the soil extends in all three dimensions and because its character varies in all directions.

The purpose of this introduction to Illinois soils is to understand the broad regional differences in soil character and quality as responses to natural processes. In order to do this effectively, it is necessary (1) to identify the characteristics which affect utility, (2) to have a basic understanding of the processes which produce differences in soil character, and (3) to describe the methods by which the broad regional variations are generalized (summarized) from the complex mosaic of "soilscapes" that are typically found within even small territories.

Soil Characteristics

If a soil unit is undisturbed for a sufficiently long time it usually becomes arranged vertically into three major (and some minor) horizons, each one roughly parallel with the soil surface. One of the important reasons for horizon development is the vertical transfer of materials from place to place within the unit induced by gravity, capillary action, and biological activity. The upper, or A horizon, has the most active population of organisms, is therefore marked by an accumulation of dark organic matter, and has usually lost some of its soluble materials and smallest particles through movement downward into the B horizon. This horizon, in turn, is marked by the accumulation of materials from above, usually by stronger (often reddish) color, and frequently by distinctive prismatic or blocky structure. Finally, the C horizon consists of the weathered rock material from which the upper two horizons have been formed. When we describe soils in relation to their utility, we are most often describing the A horizon, for it is in this zone that field crops are seeded and very largely grow. It is often true, however, that the other two horizons influence, both directly and indirectly, the vigor of plant growth.

An elemental soil characteristic is texture, the mix of particle sizes that results when a soil sample is totally disaggregated and dispersed in a liquid. The range may include quite large objects, but most particles are less than 5 millimeters in diameter; the largest are designated as sand, the middle range as silt, and the finest as clay. Mixtures of all sizes are called loams. The selective diffusion of the finer (clay-sized) particles downward is called eluviation and increases the density of the B horizon (which is then said to be illuviated). The transfer of minerals in solution from the A horizon is called leaching, and these minerals often reappear as salts in the B horizon. Both processes tend to result in horizontal layers (called pans) that either greatly retard or totally impede the percolation of water, with unfortunate results for crop production because soils with pans are alternately waterlogged after rains or excessively dry during rainless episodes. (Available stored soil moisture is limited to the shallow zone above the pan.)

A very obvious soil characteristic is structure, or the arrangement of particles into aggregates or clumps that are usually separated from each other by air or water-filled pore-spaces. Structure is observed most often as tilth or "handling consistence," the "feel" of soil between the fingers and its resistance to crushing. Anything which "clumps" particles together "improves" structure because it affords more passages for water and air, increases infiltration and percolation of water, and "crushes" into more friendly seedbeds. Aggregation is aided by an abundance of calcium and humus, or decomposed organic matter. These often combine into a gluey substance which aggregates the fine particles.

Organic matter at the surface and humus at greater depths are present in most Illinois soils; however, it tends to be much more abundant in areas that were naturally covered by grass. Here the extremely dense fine-root system of grasses is protected from direct exposure to the weather elements and decomposes beneath the surface. When humus is abundant, leaching, eluviation, and pan formation are slowed or stopped, while tilth, fertility, and resistance to drought and waterlogging are improved.

The processes that form the A horizon are largely subtractive; fine particles are carried downward and minerals are taken into solution and percolated into the B horizon. The effectiveness of this latter process (leaching) depends not only upon the amount of rainfall and the texture and structure, but also upon soil acidity. If soil water percolating downward is acidic, it takes minerals into solution much more effectively. The results for the human use of soil are two: (1) minerals that serve as plant foods are carried downward beneath the reach of cultivated plants, and (2) the soil acidity itself hinders most plant growth. Finally, the more acidic a soil is, the more acidic it tends to become. Calcium, a very common mineral element (and one easily obtained from limestone), is quite alkaline and helps to maintain a balance between extremes of alkalinity and acidity in soils. But calcium is also very easily dissolved, and thus removed, which makes soil water even more acidic and calcium depletion even more effective.

When we review the processes that form soils in humid areas like Illinois, we may note with some surprise that (with the exception of humus formation) they all seem to produce soils with lower potential for crop growth the longer they operate. Although this is a greatly simplified version of soil formation, it is generally accurate and it provides the key to understanding broad regional differences in Illinois soil quality. It applies, of course, only to areas where soil formation has been in progress for thousands of years, and not to those areas that receive periodic deep deposits of materials through flooding or that have very rapid erosion or very poor drainage.

Illinois and the central Midwest have soils of quite exceptional fertility for four reasons, the most important of which are their parent materials and their youth. Glacial drift and wind deposited dust (loess) predominate as parent materials, so that the long process of developing soils through the weathering of bedrock is replaced by the alteration of materials that have already been finely divided and have been subjected to so many alterations and so much mixing that they are likely to provide the "raw materials" for a wide range of soil elements. The short time Illinois soils have been in place under conditions similar to the present means that the most negative results of soil development are still far in the future. The areas covered by the prairie have more humus, less leaching, and better structure than otherwise would have been the case; in effect, the aging of soils under prairie vegetation was retarded. Finally, the soils with the very highest fertility—grassland soils in semiarid climates—suffer from moisture deficiencies that do not plague Illinois agriculture.

Loess, Time, and Fertility

One of the most important insights into the geography of Illinois soils was acquired by Guy D. Smith in the late 1930s, when he discovered that the parent material for a high proportion of upland soils was entirely or in part a thin blanket (sometimes more than one) of windblown dust, which had been laid down over the entire state before, during, and after the Wisconsinan glaciation.[13] The identified loess sheets range in age from the Sangamon (post-Illinoisan) interglacial to the Peorian (ca. 20,000 B.P.),

and loess is probably still accumulating. As a parent material, it is quite youthful and rich in desirable minerals.

To understand the processes that have taken place in the loessial parent materials through time and how these produced a major proportion of present soils, we will begin by describing the soils that would exist in an area soon after it had been blanketed by several feet of Peorian loess. Even though no soil development had taken place, the parent material itself would be highly productive of crops. One of several reasons for high fertility is the mineral composition of fresh loess, which includes a variety of plant nutrients and a very high content of calcium carbonate (more than 40 percent by weight). The high $CaCO_3$ ratio in turn helps produce a desirable pH (a measure of alkalinity). Secondly, thick and freshly deposited loess contains a mixture of particle sizes, most of which are in the desirable silt-sized range. The irregular shapes of these particles results in an arrangement (structure) that provides an abundance of pore space and hence rapid infiltration of water and excellent tilth. Finally, since no horizons have developed, the pans which often impede underdrainage in mature soils are missing and when topsoil is lost by erosion, the soils beneath are equally as productive as those lost.

The map of loess thickness (Fig. 2-57) and the graphs in Figures 2-58 and 2-59 that show changes in the present character of loess from one place to another reflect both differences in the original materials and modification following deposition. The pattern in Figure 2-57 seems to indicate that the sources of the windblown dust were river valleys, valley trains, outwash deposits, and the beds of former lakes. The uplands southeastward from major river valleys, from the Havana Strath, and from the Green

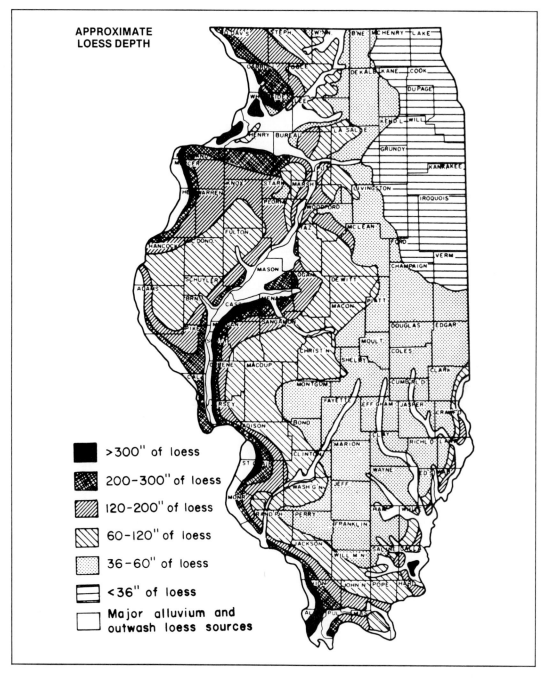

Figure 2-57. Approximate loess depth on level, uneroded topography. (Adapted from J. B. Fehrenbacker, et al., in Robert E. Bergstrom (ed.), *The Quaternary of Illinois*, Special Publication 14, University of Illinois College of Agriculture, Urbana, 1968.)

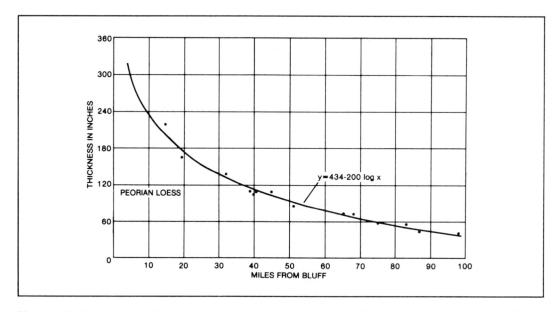

Figure 2-58. Relationship of loess thickness and distance from bluff. (Adapted from Guy D. Smith, *Illinois Loess—Variations in Its Properties and Distribution: A Pedologic Interpretation,* Agricultural Experiment Station Bulletin 490, University of Illinois, Urbana, 1942.)

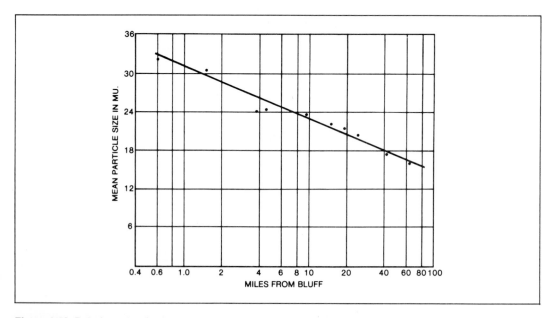

Figure 2-59. Relationship of loess particle size and distance from bluff. (Adapted from Guy D. Smith, *Illinois Loess—Variations in Its Properties and Distribution: A Pedologic Interpretation,* Agricultural Experiment Station Bulletin 490, University of Illinois, Urbana, 1942.)

Figure 2-60. A brook cuts deeply into thick loess between the Illinois and Mississippi rivers in the Illinois Peninsula. (Photo by Arlin D. Fentem.)

River Lowland all have very thick accumulations. Even more interesting is the area of shallow deposits centering in Western Illinois—downwind from a narrows on the Mississippi caused by an Ice Age stream diversion. (This "narrows" was chosen as the site for a major power dam at Keokuk in 1918.) It is very likely that most of the loess came from such nearby areas, that it was largely deposited in winter, and that the immediate sources were those broad expanses where abundant glacial meltwater was present and deposition was occuring in summer. During the ensuing winter, the meltwaters must have ebbed, exposing large areas without vegetation and therefore very subject to wind erosion. The graphs showing decreases in loess thickness and particle size with increasing distance from bluffs all imply the accuracy of this reconstruction of events and hint at a close relation with soil quality.

It was earlier suggested that there is a tendency for soils in Illinois to deteriorate with age; it is important to realize, however, that soils age much more rapidly in some situations than in others. In the areas with several feet of loess accumulation, the process has been slow indeed; hence, the calcium content remains virtually the same as it was in the beginning. It is probable that water from the rains of summers succeeding those dusty winters ten and twenty thousands of years ago was quickly saturated with "lime" and thus was incompetent to leach calcium from the annual deposit. In fresh roadside cuts near river bluffs today, small nodules of marl (calcium carbonate) can be seen.

Figure 2-61. Cultivation has resulted in the removal of several feet of easily eroded loess surrounding a fenced pasture near Bluffs in the Illinois Valley. (Photo by Arlin D. Fentem.)

Further downwind, some leaching of calcium occurred during the season of deposition, and still further away from loess sources, all the calcium has been removed. At the same time, the decline in average particle size together with more acidic soil water and more active leaching leads to increasing illuviation and precipitation of minerals in the B horizon. The areas shown on Figure 2-62 as having "hardpan and claypan soils" are those from which A horizons have lost virtually all their calcium. Locally, these soils are called "crayfish soils" in recognition of the high perched water tables which provide a favorable environment for these crustaceans. Geographers call them "grey prairie" soils because of the bleached appearance of the uppermost horizon which, in newer and fresher soils further north, is characteristically very dark-colored. A vegetation of prairie grasses appears to retard leaching, but not to halt it.

Glacial Drift, Time, and Fertility

Once it is accepted that the passage of time is an important element in soil formation, it is not surprising that *in general* young glacial drift—specifically that of Wisconsinan Age—is quite fertile, even when loess deposits are thin. An important feature of the relationships among loess, drift, and modern soils is not apparent on the generalized map of loess depth in Figure 2-57. Loess thins abruptly at the margin of the Wisconsinan glacial drift margin. Fertility is probably higher on the younger drift, both because the younger drift (unleached and only slightly eroded) is productive and because the loess, while thin, accumulated at a rapid rate and therefore retained its calcium. Earlier accumulations were obliterated by advancing ice.

Generally, transitions from highly productive to infertile soils are gentle and may be

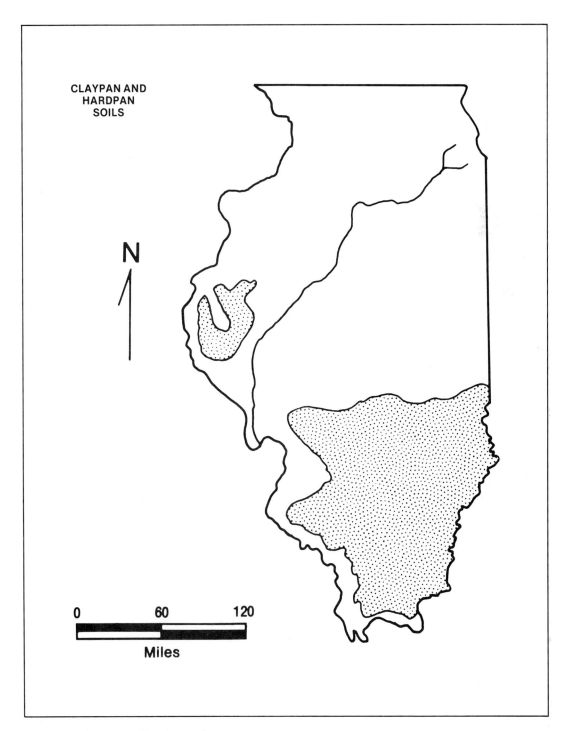

Figure 2-62. Claypan and hardpan soils.

disturbed somewhat by local conditions such as topography. One very dramatic contrast, however, is found where the southern boundary of younger drift (at the Shelbyville Moraine) abuts against the claypans developed from thin loess overlying thin Illinoisan drift. The tier of counties north of the boundary produces twice the value of agricultural products as does the row just south of the moraine.

The Distribution of Soil Fertility

Almost any rural landscape in Illinois presents a complicated mosaic of soil types that contrast sharply with each other in fertility. Such a landscape is shown on Figure 2-63, which represents an area in the transition zone between the highly productive soils of western Illinois and the grey prairie of the southern counties. The information shown here is just the kind that someone bidding on a farm in Montgomery County needs, but only eight of the 35 soil series found in the county and of the 375 that occur in the state are present in the sample area. Clearly, some way of examining soil qualities in a more general way (and mapping them at smaller scales) is needed.

The means for such analyses are provided

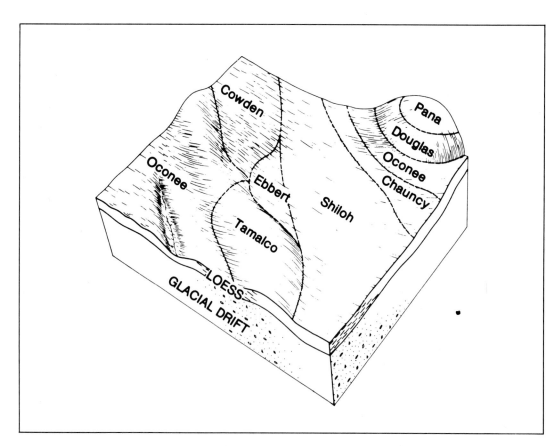

Figure 2-63. Generalized landscape of soil types. (Adapted from C. E. Downey and R. T. Odell, *Soil Survey of Montgomery County, Illinois,* U.S. Government Printing Office, Washington, 1969.)

by soil sample information collected by the U.S. Soil Conservation Service for its *Water and Soil Conservation Needs Inventory.*[12] On average, these data provide a 2 percent random sample by county, and they can be extrapolated so as to make estimates of the total distribution of soil series in each county. A second step in arriving at estimates of soil productivity by county is to consult yield records for each soil series, a painstaking task that has been completed for a ten-year period. The yield records come from farms that have had soil samples taken and whose operators report management practices. It is thus possible to determine, for a particular soil, the yield of each of the major crops under high, medium, and low levels of management. In compiling the data from which Figure 2-64 was made, Paul Mausel used only corn yields expected under a "high level of management."[14] Detailed study, however, showed that in general the variation in yields among the major crops by soil series was very similar.

The effects of topography are clearly seen in the low yields in the Shawnee Hills and in the Driftless Area in the extreme northwest, as well as along the Illinois River. The southerly portion of the Wisconsinan Till Plain, where the drift is old enough for reasonably good surface drainage, young enough to have escaped excessive leaching, and remote enough from major streams to have avoided deep dissection, has the best soils. The rapid transition from this peak to much lower productivity southward testifies to the importance of fresh and unleached materials as young drift and rapidly accumulated loess is succeeded by thin loess. The differences from place to place in total agricultural production are even greater than those in "theoretical corn yields" because counties with unproductive cropland usually have much greater proportions of pasture, woods, and wastelands.

Soil Regions

If we were to pinpoint a particular spot on Figure 2-64 and try to predict the productivity of a field from the average productivity of all fields in the county where it is located, we might make a very bad guess. If we take the further step of grouping counties and portions of counties into regions of similar soils associations, we will be even further from the reality of individual fields. Nevertheless, it is as important for understanding to see the larger picture as it is to distinguish between counties and among individual plots of land. Soils regions, such as those appearing on Figure 2-65, help to simplify the great complexity revealed by detailed soils study.

Modern soil scientists, in developing the soil classification system now used in the United States, recognized ten orders into which any soil sample in the world could be placed. Five of these orders are present in Illinois. By applying the principles of the 7th Approximation (as the comprehensive system is named), the five orders may be subdivided into 47 suborders worldwide, further broken down into great groups numbering 206), subgroups, families, and—ultimately—the soil series (of which there are approximately 10,000). Detailed examination by Paul Mausel revealed that 65 subgroups were represented in the state, but that only 34 of these made up as much as 3 percent of any of selected representative counties.[15] The final step in regionalization was to examine soil maps at various scales in order to draw boundaries that enclosed associations of subgroup soils in particular areas of the state (Fig. 2-65).

Although areal classification of this kind furthers our understanding of the natural world, the practical interests of most people are focused upon the capabilities of soils for producing crops. For that reason, the soil productivity data amassed by the Soil Con-

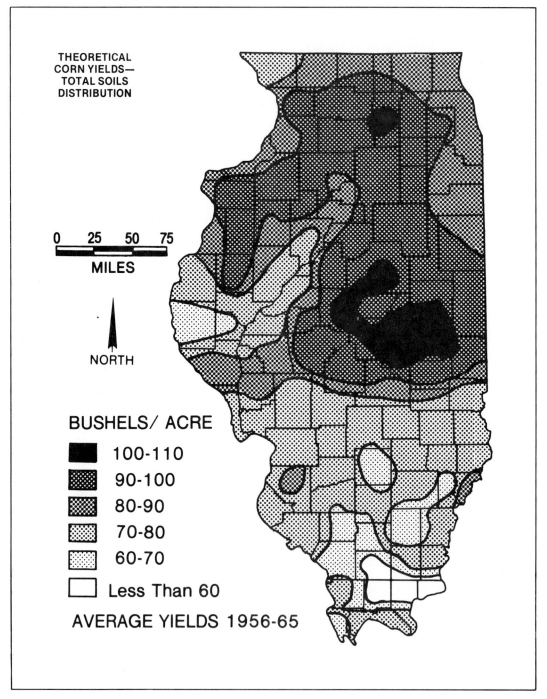

Figure 2-64. Theoretical corn yields—total soils distribution. (Reproduced by permission from *The Professional Geographer* of the Association of American Geographers, Volume 23, 1970, P. W. Mausel.)

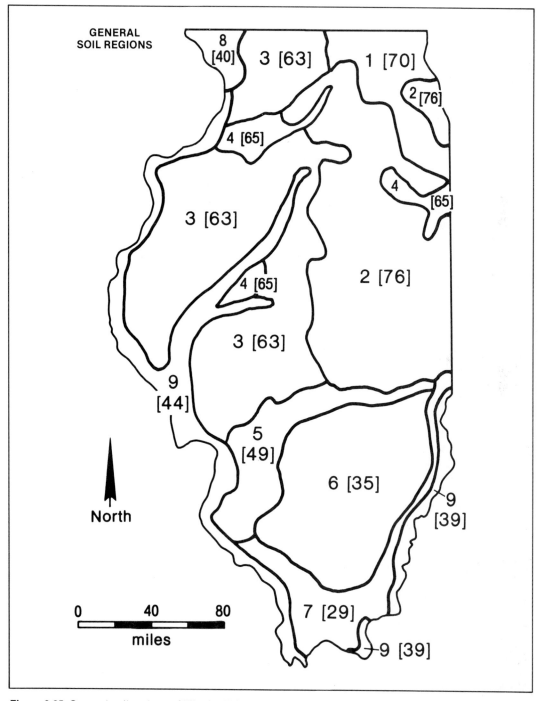

Figure 2-65. General soil regions of Illinois. (Adapted from Paul W. Mausel, "General Subgroup Soil Regions of Illinois," *Bulletin of the Illinois Geographical Society* 11 (June 1969).

servation Service were again consulted by Dr. Mausel in assigning productivity levels to the subgroups (as he had already done in estimating county productivities). Since the proportion of each region that is covered by each subgroup can be measured, it is possible to estimate productivity ranges for each region. The bracketed figures shown within each region on the map are very general estimates of the differences in expected yields of the major crops under *low* levels of management. The numbers are index numbers only and should not be translated into yields as measured by bushels or some other unit. The low level management index has been chosen in the hope that it will better reflect natural productivity. The disparities in productivity among regions are much less when high level management indexes are used. (This could mean that technological and other man-created inputs are becoming more important in determining returns from varied soil resources.)

The soils of an area reflect the interactions of the other physical environmental elements; therefore, the general soils regions delineated on Figure 2-65 may also be thought of as environmental regions. Region 1, in the northeast, embraces much variety because of the recency and complexity of glacial events there. Closely spaced clayey moraines with steep slopes are bordered by aprons of sandy outwash and alternate with old lake plains and bogs. Despite the unpromising nature of some of the parent materials and the near absence of loess, the fertility of these soils is generally quite high, both because of their youth (ca. 12,000 years) and because natural prairies were widespread. The crests of the morainic ridges are sometimes forested and often pastured; in recent decades they have been attractive to exurbanites seeking rural homesites with prospects overlooking the pleasantly rolling countryside.

Most of Cook County is included in another region because its relief is lower, its parent materials are more uniformly derived from outwash and old lake sediments, and its native vegetation was more consistently made up of prairie grasses. The remainder of region 2 is essentially the older part of the Wisconsinan Till Plain where moraines are broad, widely spaced, and gently sloping. Since stream dissection is minimal, slopes are almost everywhere gentle. Add to these favorable auspices a virtually unbroken prairie and the advantages of youth, and the very high natural fertility is readily accounted for. The rather thin loess blanket accumulated quickly; recently it has been suggested that organic matter and loess might have accumulated simultaneously in this region. The great thickness of the dark (organically stained) horizon in the Brunizem soils might have resulted from development upward as well as downward.

Region 3 is the domain of relatively thick Illinoisan Till overlain by thick loess. The most favored areas are the broad interfluves between streams which had the advantages of nearly flat surfaces, fresh and nearly unleached loess, and prairie vegetation. The best of these soils compare favorably with those in the region just described; however, the greater age of parent materials, the thinning of loess near the southeastern margins of the region, and—most of all—the greater proportion of forested and steep slopes resulting from 70,000 years of stream erosion creates a greater range, and lower overall level, of potential productivity.

Smaller areas like those set aside as region 4 are incorporated within the regions just discussed; the Green River Lowland, Havana Strath, and Kankakee Lake Plain, however, are large enough for separate consideration. All three areas have a high proportion of sandy and medium-textured parent material deposited by glacial meltwater as outwash or lake sediments; all were predominately flat and were largely covered by prairie. In general, fertility is quite high, but some of the coarser materials are subject to drought, especially where sands were blown into dunes; still other areas require ditch drains. Ground water for irrigation is sometimes easily accessible, and supplemental irrigation is used successfully to produce grains, potatoes (Green River Lowland and Havana Strath), and green beans (Havana Strath).

Region 5 is transitional between the two major soil orders in Illinois as the result of increasing dissection of the surface and the thinning of the loess blanket. The soils here are more leached and their B horizons are usually characterized by clay accumulations.

Region 6 has the least productive soils to be found on essentially flat surfaces; even the best of the soils here are lacking in organic matter, are droughty, excessively wet during rainy episodes, and acidic. Soybeans—better adapted to survive drought than corn and capable of maturation even when planting is delayed into summer by waterlogging—have made these soils more useful since their introduction during World War II. This region is the only one where soybean acreage exceeds that of corn.

The low productivity of region 7, on the other hand, is attributable to steep slopes and forest vegetation as well as to the passage of time and warm, wet climates. Region 8, The Driftless Region, is likewise characterized by steep slopes. Finally, the

Figure 2-66. A relict dune in the Havanna Strath Lowland; in the past the dune migrated southeastward and buried the thick A-horizon of a soil rich in humus (foreground). (Photo by Arlin D. Fentem.)

areas along the major streams are most difficult to describe because they embrace great extremes—from extensive areas of floodplain now reclaimed and exceptionally fertile to excessively sandy areas elsewhere, and from thin soils on the upper slopes of valley sides to deep accumulations of productive loess on flattish but narrow interfluves. Problems of drainage, flooding, weed control (weed seeds arrive with floodwater), and erosion all help to limit usefulness, although some areas of floodplain are exceptionally productive.

Conclusion

•This survey of Illinois' physical environment has been comprehensive, but it has viewed the state at some far remove. In effect, we have seldom been closer to our subject than we might have been from one of our orbiting satellites. If we were to observe a county as closely as we have the state, we would find that the same level of complexity exists there. Still closer examination brings us to landscapes we may see in their entirety with our own eyes. Between the county scale and our own backyard, we can make our observations with the aid of aerial photographs or topographic maps at scales ranging from 1 inch:1 mile to 1 inch:2,000 feet.[15] Field trip leaflets describing and interpreting more than a hundred local physical situations are available from the Illinois Department of Registration and Education. Few activities are more interesting or rewarding than applying the knowledge and principles of earth science to the study of our home territories.

Notes

1. Most of the information about landforms has been gleaned from publications of the Illinois State Geological Survey, which have been comprehensively compiled and indexed in H.B. Willman, Jack A. Simon, Betty M. Lynch, and Virginia A. Langenheim, *Bibliography and Index of Illinois Geology through 1965,* Bulletin 92 (Urbana: Illinois State Geological Survey, 1968).

2. The most comprehensive survey of ice age events and consequences in Illinois is in H.B. Willman and J.C. Frye, *Pleistocene Stratigraphy of Illinois,* Bulletin 94 (Urbana: Illinois State Geological Survey, 1970).

3. The pioneering work of Leland Horberg is the most important source of knowledge about the bedrock surface. See his *Bedrock Topography of Illinois,* Bulletin 73 (Urbana: Illinois State Geological Survey, 1950).

4. The landform regions described are based on M.M. Leighton, George E. Ekblaw, and Leland Horberg, *Physiographic Divisions of Illinois,* Report of Investigations No. 129 (Urbana: Illinois State Geological Survey, 1948).

5. Fred Caspall, "Parallel Drainage in West-Central Illinois" (M.S. thesis, Western Illinois University, 1965).

6. John W. Wilson and Stanley A. Changnon, Jr., *Illinois Tornadoes,* Circular 103 (Urbana: Illinois State Water Survey, 1971), p. 4.

7. The Weller method of detection is explained in W.G. Biggs and P.J. Waite, "Can TV Really Detect Tornadoes?" *Weatherwise* 23 (1970), pp. 120-124.

8. Sir James Caird, "1858: A Birdseye View of Illinois, Prairie Farming, and the State Capital," in *Prairie State,* ed. Paul M. Angle (Chicago: University of Chicago Press, 1968), p. 325.

9. Edgar N. Transeau, "The Prairie Peninsula," *Ecology* 16 (1935), pp. 423-437.

10. Carl O. Sauer, "A Geographic Sketch of Early Man in America," *Geographical Review* 34 (1944), pp. 529-573.

11. John Borchert, "Climate of the North American Grassland," *Annals of the Association of American Geographers* 40 (1950), pp. 1-44.

12. John J. Alford and Fred C. Caspall, "Topography and Fire as Factors in the Origin of the Prairie Peninsula" (Paper delivered at the Annual Meeting of the Il-

linois Academy of Science, Peoria, Spring 1971).
13. Guy D. Smith, *Illinois Loess—Variations in Its Properties and Distribution: A Pedologic Interpretation,* Agricultural Experiment Station Bulletin 490 (Urbana: University of Illinois, 1942).
14. Paul W. Mausel, "Soil Quality in Illinois—An Example of a Soils Geography Resource Analysis," *The Professional Geographer* 23 (1971), pp. 127-136.
15. Paul W. Mausel, "General Subgroup Soil Regions of Illinois," *Bulletin of the Illinois Geographical Society* 11 (1969), pp. 70-81.

Selected References

Aldrich, S.R. *Illinois Field Crops and Soils.* Cooperative Extension Service Circular 901. Urbana: University of Illinois, 1965.

Anderson, R.C. "Prairies in the Prairie State." *Transactions of the Illinois Academy of Science,* 63 (1970), 214-221.

Barber, S.A. "A Classification of Landforms— Illinois." Master's Thesis, Western Illinois University, 1969.

Bergstrom, Robert E., ed. *The Quaternary of Illinois.* Special Publication 14. Urbana: University of Illinois College of Agriculture, 1968.

Bier, V.A. *Landforms of Illinois* (map). Urbana: Illinois State Geological Survey, 1956.

Borchert, John. "Climate of the North American Grassland." *Annals of the Association of American Geographers,* 40 (1950), 1-44.

Caspall, Fred. "Parallel Drainage in West-Central Illinois." Master's Thesis, Western Illinois University, 1965.

Changnon, Stanley A., Jr. *Climatology of Severe Winter Storms in Illinois.* Bulletin 53. Urbana: Illinois State Water Survey, 1969.

Fehrenbacher, J.B.; Waler, G.O.; and Wascher, H.L. *Soils of Illinois.* Agricultural Experiment Station Bulletin 725. Urbana: University of Illinois College of Agriculture, 1967.

Guide to the Geologic Map of Illinois. Educational Series 7. Urbana: Illinois State Geological Survey, 1961.

Horberg, Leland. *Bedrock Topography of Illinois.* Bulletin No. 73. Urbana: Illinois State Geological Survey, 1950.

Leighton, M.M., and Brophy, T.A. "Illinoisan Glaciation in Illinois." *Journal of Geology,* 69 (1961), 1-31.

Leighton, M.M.; Ekblaw, George E.; and Horberg, Leland. *Physiographic Divisions of Illinois.* Report of Investigations No. 129. Urbana: Illinois State Geological Survey, 1948.

MacClintock, P. *Physiographic Divisions of the Area Covered by the Illinoisan Driftsheet in Southern Illinois.* Report of Investigations No. 19. Urbana: Illinois State Geological Survey, 1939.

Mausel, Paul. "General Subgroup Soil Regions of Illinois." *Bulletin of the Illinois Geographical Society,* 11 (June 1969), 70-78.

_____. "Soil Quality in Illinois—An Example of a Soils Geography Resource Analysis." *The Professional Geographer,* 23 (April 1970), 127-136.

Page, John L. *Climate of Illinois.* Agricultural Experiment Station Bulletin 532. Urbana: University of Illinois, 1949.

Piskin, Kimal, and Bergstrom, Robert E. *Glacial Drift in Illinois: Thickness and Character.* Circular 416. Urbana: Illinois State Geological Survey, 1967.

Smith, Guy D. *Illinois Loess—Variations in Its Properties and Distribution: A Pedologic Interpretation.* Agricultural Experiment Station Bulletin 490. Urbana: University of Illinois, 1942.

Transeau, Edgar N. "The Prairie Peninsula." *Ecology,* XVI (July 1935), 423-437.

Willman, H.B., and Frye, J.C. *Pleistocene Stratigraphy of Illinois.* Bulletin No. 94. Urbana: Illinois State Geological Survey, 1970.

Wilson, John W., and Changnon, Stanley A., Jr. *Illinois Tornadoes.* Circular 103. Urbana: Illinois State Water Survey, 1971.

Chapter Three

HISTORICAL GEOGRAPHY

Alden Cutshall
University of Illinois at Chicago Circle

Over a century and a half ago—in 1818—Illinois became the nation's twenty-first state and began making history. Over the years it has attained a position of leadership in agriculture. By 1860 the Prairie State was the leading producer of corn, wheat, and oats. Today Illinois leads the nation in corn again (having lost the leadership to Iowa for a period of years), soybeans, Swiss cheese, onion sets, red clover seed, pumpkins, and horseradish. It is one of the world's great centers of industrial production, its factories fueled in part by the state's coal and petroleum resources. In the heartland of America, it is a crossroads state, and its major city has become the world's foremost rail center, a leading center for highway transportation, and the greatest inland seaport. O'Hare airport is the world's busiest airfield. Illinois is the foremost exporting state, accounting for 8.3 billion dollars or nearly 10 percent of the nation's 1974 total export trade.[1] The state has come a long way since the first perma-

nent settlement at Shawneetown in 1809, and since the capital was moved upon attaining statehood from French-flavored Kaskaskia to more centrally situated Vandalia.

Figure 3-1. Old state capitol building in Vandalia. The seat of government was transferred from Kaskaskia to more centrally located Vandalia in 1820 and eventually to Springfield in 1839. (Photo by Ronald E. Nelson.)

The Indian Era

Even before there was a State of Illinois or an Illinois Territory, what is now Illinois was Indian land, with many different tribes or groups at different times and places within the area. Early Illinois Indians lived with the environment, not against it. Their ancient village sites are widely distributed. There are ashes of burned-out camp fires along the bases of bluffs and outlines of long-gone settlements once enclosed with palisades. Their crudely drawn pictures and rough carvings have been found on several rock outcrops, but only a few are left, normally beneath a protecting rocky ledge. Most of those that remain are only faded fragments, generally splotches of a single color. There are rounded stone pits or more irregular depressions where the Indians pounded corn or other food products. Bone needles suggest the manner in which they made their clothes. Remains of camp refuse and piles of flint chips indicate where they made weapons or implements. Illinois, from Chicago to Cairo, is rich in prehistoric Indian lore.

Most striking of the early Indian remains are the mounds, more than 10,000 of them constructed by prehistoric people in Illinois. And most striking of the mounds are those at Cahokia where there are over 100 on the site of an early Indian city. The largest one, Monk's Mound, is said to be the largest prehistoric earthen construction in the world.

A dense Indian population once lived in the American Bottoms, that broad flood plain area to the east of the Mississippi River from Alton to Chester. This was one segment of a prehistoric culture that flourished along several midwestern rivers (Mississippi, Illinois, Wabash, Ohio, and Tennessee). A string of "towns," possible satellites of Cahokia, extended upstream along the Illinois Valley, and others downstream as far as Memphis. Ninety percent of the mounds probably were used as burial places. Dickson Mounds, south of Peoria, was a major burial ground and is now a state museum. It was of the same age and culture as Cahokia, and probably was a satellite of its larger southern neighbor. Recent archaeological explorations at the Koster site (Kampsville) have unearthed remains of twelve successive Indian settlements, the oldest dated 8,500 years ago.[2]

According to archaeological finds, the Cahokia site was first inhabited about 700 A.D. The city of Cahokia covered about six square miles and had a peak population of between 30 and 40 thousand. It was primarily an urban area; the residential section was quite extensive. Houses were arranged along what appear to have been streets or around open plazas. The inhabitants hunted, fished, gathered wild plant foods, and practiced gardening. The main agricultural fields were probably outside the city. These people were dependent upon a well-developed agricultural system with corn, beans, and squash the principal cultivated crops.

Only a culture that relied on the growing of plants for food could have supplied the apparently large population and comparatively permanent settlements of these people. The type of culture helps to explain the flood plain or alluvial terrace location of their settlements; these sites offered a more fertile, more friable soil than that which existed on the nearby uplands.

For reasons that are most unclear, the prehistoric Cahokian culture came to an end about the time Columbus reached the New World. A gradual decline in population began around 1300 A.D. and by 1500 A.D. the site had been abandoned. Around 1300 A.D. there was a climatic change throughout much of the southern part of the United States. This may have adversely affected the food supply and made it increasingly difficult to feed the large population. Other contributing factors may have been the depletion of natural resources in the surrounding woodland areas, revolution, disease, and war. Possibly the number of people simply increased to the point of overpopulation with respect to the available resource base. Whatever the cause or causes of abandonment, Cahokia represented the highest achievement of prehistoric Indian civilization north of Mexico, and it represents but one of several vanished civilizations that peopled parts of Illinois prior to the time of recorded history.

At the time of white man's penetration into the Illinois region he found many groups of Indians within the area. During the eighteenth century the Potawatomi, the Kickapoo (a portion of the Piankeshaws), and the Illini tribes lived within the present limits of Illinois. Early accounts of the Indian population indicate that tribes of the Miami family inhabited most of the lower Wabash Valley. At that time these people occupied much of the present basins of the Wabash, Maumee, and Miami rivers to the east of Illinois, and at a slightly later date were as far west as Peoria. The Shawnee had come northward from their more southern habitat and occupied the area at the junction of the Wabash and the Ohio as well as downstream from this confluence to the Mississippi. The friendliness of the Shawnee in this area, holding the key position with respect to river transportation, probably contributed much to encourage and foster the early settlement of whites in southern Illinois and adjacent Indiana.

Other names of Indians that appear in early history are the Kaskaskia (primary along the Mississippi), the Ottawa, and Chipewa. The Potawatomi lived around the shores of Lake Michigan, but penetrated well beyond the lake area. In the northern protion of present Illinois were the Winnebago, Fox,

Sauk (Sacs), and Iroquois. Both the Fox and Sauk roamed the forested hills of the Driftless Area in large numbers prior to 1800 and normally lived by collecting, farming, and hunting; in later years some of them shifted to lead mining. (The Galena area was listed as the nation's principal lead mining region in the early 1800s, although the first mining there by white men occurred in the 1820s. Apparently lead was extracted in the vicinity by Indians as much as a century earlier.)[3] Whatever the group of Indians, however, their life-style was attuned to the environment.

In many ways the Illinois Valley can be considered the core area of Indian occupation in the 1700-1800 period of time. The owners of that valley at the time of statehood were the Illini, or Iliniwek, who may have occupied much of the present state's area in the seventeenth century. They were essentially prairie Indians and lived largely by the chase. The vast areas of prairie grass and the wooded areas along the rivers and streams apparently harbored abundant animal life to supply their needs. Their dependence on game forced them to move widely on hunting trips. Consequently, they did not build permanent homes. The "towns" of the Illini were clusters of wigwams. Their social institutions were primitive. At this period in history they were quite willing to have white man live in their midst. They are the people who gave their name to a river, a state, and a university football team. They had been the largest tribe in the Illinois Valley region, and at one time were probably the strongest tribe in the midcontinent. Their chief food was maize (corn), but they also cultivated beans, squash, and other vegetables. Apparently the debilitation of their society was a result of several factors. In random order, some of them were wars with the Iroquois; the sudden introduction of gun powder and iron into a stone age culture, and its attendent change in the life-style; the use of English rum and French brandy, as the Indian had no inherited resistance to alcohol; and his susceptability to the white man's diseases of measles, small pox, and tuberculosis. In most cases, the arrival of the European was followed by a decrease in Indian population and a weakening and debilitation of Indian society.

The Illini have been described as handsome, brave, tall, strong, fast, proud, and affable. They were also called idle, jealous, dissolute, and thievish. Perhaps all the adjectives were applicable, not only to the Illini but to other tribes of the area as well.[4]

The Sequence of Early Settlement

The early history of modern Illinois is one of European conquest, at least in a general way. Initially, the activities of the English and the Dutch were confined to the Atlantic coast; the Spanish concentrated on Florida, the Southwest, and the West Indies; and the French were most interested in the St. Lawrence Valley. The English had difficulty in penetrating deeply into the interior, partly because of the ferocity of the Indians, especially the Iroquois. The Spanish focus was southward; they were much more interested in the gold of Mexico and Peru than in the less spectacular resources of interior North America. French explorers and fur traders were the first white men to visit what is now the American Midwest, but they did not come as settlers to develop the country.

Specifically, the first white men to penetrate the heart of the American continent were a priest and a mapmaker. Father Jacques Marquette, a French Jesuit missionary came to New France in 1666. He studied the Indian languages and worked among the Ottawa tribes of the Upper Great Lakes. Louis Jolliet (Jolliet), a French-Canadian fur trader and mapmaker, met Marquette at Sault Sainte Marie in 1669. Four years later the two men led the historic expedition from Green Bay up the Fox (Wisconsin Fox) and down the Wisconsin rivers to the "great river of the west," the Mississippi. They continued downstream well to the south of present-day Memphis until they were convinced that the river led to the Gulf of Mexico. The small party then returned north, ascended the Illinois and Des Plaines and portaged across the low, swampy continental divide into the Chicago drainage basin, following approximately the alignment of the old Illinois and Michigan Canal and present Chicago Sanitary and Ship Canal. Thus, they became the first explorers to cross the present state of Illinois and to see its entire western border.

This expedition, together with the one by Robert Cavelier, Sieur de La Salle, almost a decade later, laid the foundation for a series of forts and fur trading posts between Detroit and New Orleans. La Salle was a woodsman with many friends among the Indians, a convincing conversationalist, and an international promoter—a truly unusual combination of talents. He envisioned the economic potential of the great Middle West and proposed to establish a large colony of fur traders and farmers in the heart of the Mississippi Valley. As a result of his vision, and his ability to persuade people and raise funds in France, a number of French forts and settlements was established. Fort Crevecoeur, constructed on the bluffs above the river near Peoria in 1680, was the first in Illinois. In 1682, Fort St. Louis on the three-fourths acre top of a sandstone promatory that later came to be known as Starved Rock, was established as the principal French stronghold in Illinois. Both were destroyed, and a new Fort St. Louis and

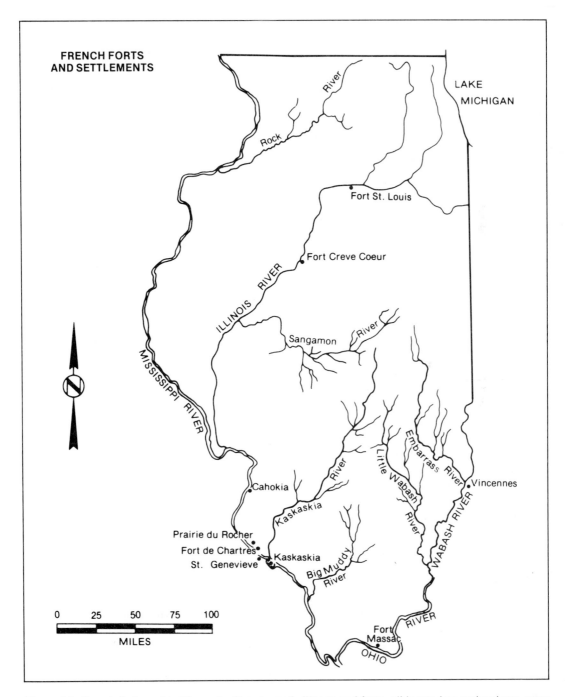

FRENCH FORTS AND SETTLEMENTS

LAKE MICHIGAN

Rock River

Fort St. Louis

Fort Creve Coeur

ILLINOIS RIVER

Sangamon River

MISSISSIPPI RIVER

Embarrass River

Cahokia

Kaskaskia River

Little Wabash River

WABASH RIVER

Vincennes

Prairie du Rocher

Fort de Chartres

St. Genevieve

Kaskaskia

Big Muddy River

Fort Massac

OHIO RIVER

0   25   50   75   100

MILES

Figure 3-2. French forts and settlements. These small villages and forts, all located on major rivers, were the earliest European settlements in Illinois and vicinity.

Figure 3-3. Fort de Chartres was one of the early eighteenth century French strongholds on the Mississippi River in southwestern Illinois. The restored gate of the fort is pictured here. (Photo by Ronald E. Nelson.)

Figure 3-4. Inside the wall of Fort de Chartres, today only the foundations remain of the barracks buildings. In the right center of the photo is the fort's powder house. (Photo by Ronald E. Nelson.)

French settlement on Lake Peoria (a wide portion of the Illinois River) was established in 1791. It existed until the War of 1812. A Catholic mission was built at Cahokia in the America Bottoms in 1699, and Kaskaskia was established four years later. Prairie du Rocher, in present Monroe County, was settled in 1723 and nearby Fort de Chartres was begun soon afterward. Vincennes, Indiana, established as a fur trading post in 1680 with a fort and mission added in 1702, and St. Genevieve, across the river from Kaskaskia in Missouri, were part of this series of early French forts and settlements in the Midwest, and by their position, immediately across the Wabash and the Mississippi respectively, had some impact upon early development in Illinois.

A few of the early French may have been itinerent fur traders and trappers, but generally they lived in compact villages, whether by habit, or for protection, or both. The French villages were representative of ones in France and differed notably from settlements in the English colonies. The Catholic Church was the center of village life and the priest the most influential citizen. One-story houses, usually with wide verandas, lined narrow streets. Except for shopkeepers or more wealthy traders, each man farmed a narrow strip of land aligned at right angles to the riverbank and grazed his animals in a common pasture. In general, the villagers have been described as gay, carefree people who enjoyed dancing and card playing to a degree unthought of in early New England. The original French settlements were a dependency of Canada, but in 1717 were placed under the government of Louisiana. This political alignment to the south, although generally weak and lax, partially helps to explain the *de facto* slavery that existed in Illinois until the Civil War.

By the Treaty of Paris in 1763, title to the Illinois country passed from France to England, but it was a full two years before Great Britian actually occupied the territory. English military occupation was never substantial. Their civil government was minimal. The French settlements continued a rather placid existence in the heart of official British territory, and their customs, tradi-

tions, and practices remained as outposts of French culture under a British flag.

The colony of Virginia claimed this Illinois country under its colonial charter granted by the King of England. Patrick Henry, as the first governor of the new Commonwealth of Virginia, commissioned George Rogers Clark to attack Kaskaskia. Clark, then a lieutenant colonel in the militia, had organized the defense against the Indians in Kentucky, which was then a county of Virginia. Clark assembled some

Figure 3-5. The home of Pierre Menard, an early political leader and businessman, reflects French architectural characteristics introduced into the eighteenth century villages of southwestern Illinois. (Photo by Ronald E. Nelson.)

175 men and trained them on an island near the falls of the Ohio River, the present site of Louisville. From this location they floated down the Ohio in keelboats to Fort Massac, a former French fort that was abandoned by the British. From there Clark marched first northward, then westward to capture Kaskaskia from its landward side without a shot on July 4, 1778. The other French settlements in Illinois, as well as British Fort Sackville at Vincennes, then came into possession of the Virginia forces without a struggle. On December 9, 1778, Virginia created the county of Illinois, a vast area with indefinite boundaries that extended from the Ohio and Mississippi northward to Canada.

At this time the settlements along the Mississippi had about three-fourths of the non-Indian population of the entire area. Kaskaskia, with 500 white persons and about the same number of slaves, was the largest community. Cahokia's population was about 300 whites and 80 blacks. The other villages were on their way to abandonment or had already ceased to exist. The population of Illinois had actually decreased between 1763 and 1778. French patriotic sentiment had been high, and many families abandoned their homes and moved to St. Genevieve or St. Louis, the latter having become a major French fur trading center, rather than live under English rule. This strong anti-British feeling probably helps to explain the lack of resistance to Clark's small, impoverished force at Kaskaskia and Vincennes.

The British, however, had recaptured Fort Sackville at Vincennes in the early winter of 1778-79. This left Clark at Kaskaskia in a rather vulnerable military situation. Upon learning that the French settlers at Vincennes would welcome the Americans he embarked upon a bold, almost irrational move of ma-

jor strategic significance. In the middle of winter (February) and at the time when rivers were flooded, he marched 140 miles across Illinois with 170 Virginia militia and French volunteers to attack and capture Vincennes. The last 60 miles took eight days, much of that time wading in the ice-cold waters of the flooded bottoms of the Little Wabash and its eastern tributaries, and then skirting the lower Embarrass and crossing the Wabash to the south of Vincennes. It was truly one of the boldest, and probably one of the most courageous campaigns in early American history.

By the close of the Revolutionary War settlers were pressing beyond the limits of the original colonies, and Illinois was considered a desirable place for settlement. Some of Clark's soldiers returned to their eastern homes, then came back to the area to establish themselves in the timbered woodlands of southern Illinois. Other pioneers came, mainly from the southeastern states. Their Anglo-Saxon ancestors had crossed the Atlantic from the British Isles or Germany to settle in Virginia, the Carolinas, or Georgia. Later generations had spread into Tennessee and Kentucky. Then, after more time had passed, they moved northward and into southern Indiana, southern Illinois, and eastern Missouri. Those from the middle Atlantic States who came down the Ohio had basically the same backgrounds, with their intermediate ancestral stops in western Pennsylvania, Ohio, and possibly Indiana. As early as 1790 several communities had been established in the area of present Randolph, Monroe, and St. Clair counties, on or near the fertile flood plain along the Mississippi and in the general proximity of the older French settlements. This immigration was the real beginning of settlement by English-speaking peoples and the introduction of English culture. The French culture then ceased to be dominant and gradually declined, preserved today only at Prairie du Rocher.

Whereas the French had lived among the Indians and oftentimes associated with them, the English-speaking settlers viewed the Indians as an inferior race and as people who hindered the welfare of the newcomers and handicapped the progress and development of the area. Obviously, this attitude brought the races into conflict. A running warfare continued until the end of the War of 1812 when the pioneers essentially came into control of the areas immediately around their settlements.

In this period, immigrants began to populate other sections of the state. The Ohio River was the principal east-west artery. Settlers came down the Ohio, then up one of its tributaries or up the Mississippi and later the Kaskaskia and Illinois, settling near their place of debarkation. It was not until after 1830 that the Great Lakes route, the second important western water route, was used to any appreciable extent. The location along, or near the streams gave the settler access to some of his basic needs (water, fuel, and shelter), which were usually lacking or difficult to obtain on many of the interstream areas. Wild game was more abundant, too, along the watercourses than in the prairie regions.

After the War of 1812 Fort Dearborn was rebuilt, Fort Armstrong was erected at Rock Island, and Fort Edwards was constructed where Warsaw stands today. But southern Illinois was the first region in the state to be definitely settled, a trend that continued for several years. Old Kaskaskia served not only as the capital of Illinois Territory but as the first state capital as well. At the time of admission to statehood, 1818, most of the population was in the American Bottoms, centered in some half-dozen growing communities. Gallatin county, with 3,200 settlers, was the most populous center in the eastern part of the state. Shawneetown, first settled in 1806 and resettled in 1809, was the first permanent community in that area and was already the chief river port on the eastern side of Illinois. It was the southern anchor of a strip of discontinuous settlement extending northward along the Wabash for about a hundred miles. Other established settlements were Palestine and Carmi on the Wabash, Golconda on the Ohio downstream from Shawneetown, Equality, and Albion. The two occupied areas on the western and eastern sides of Illinois were connected by significant trails with taverns for overnight stops along them, but there were probably less than a half-dozen settlements of any significance within the interior of the then "settled" state of Illinois (really southern Illinois). Carlyle, on the Kaskaskia, probably was the best known among them. Lawrenceville, Fairfield, and Vienna were new in 1818. Salem was founded in 1823 as the halfway station on the Vincennes-St. Louis stagecoach route.

Central and northern Illinois remained essentially a vast wilderness. As late as 1821 there were a few huts downstream from Peoria, but not a single white habitation between Peoria and Chicago. Permanent occupation was not underway in Galena until 1820, although numerous miners had come upstream for the summer season prior to that time.[5] There was no connection between Kinsey's trading post and Fort Dearborn at Chicago and Galena, nor was there any meaningful association between the Chicago area and either Kaskaskia or Shawneetown, the principal settlements in the southwestern and southeastern parts of the state, respectively. Alton was founded in 1814 and Edwardsville in 1815, a northern extension of the earlier settlements along the Mississippi.

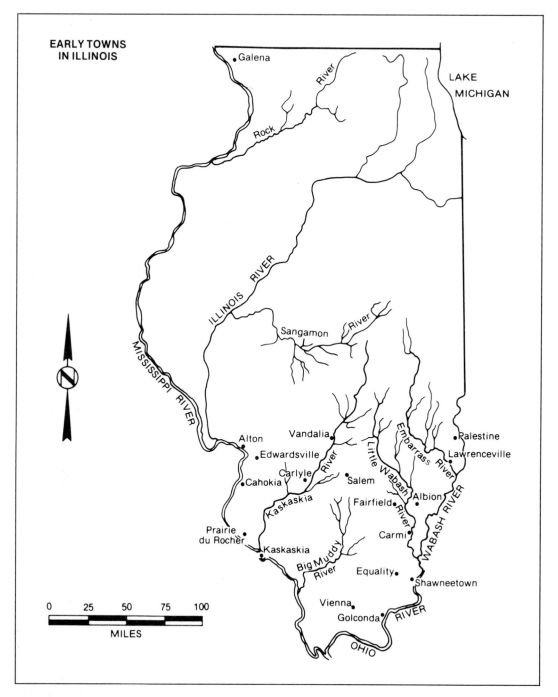

Figure 3-6. Early towns in Illinois. Most of the first towns founded in Illinois were situated in the southern one-third of the state.

Figure 3-7. Shawneetown bank building. This building was constructed when Shawneetown was considered the financial capital of the state. It replaced an earlier log bank building that stood adjacent to the Ohio River. When Shawneetown was moved to higher ground after the disastrous flood of 1937 on the Ohio, this heavy building was the only significant structure left behind in Old Shawneetown. (Photo by Alden Cutshall.)

But there was no Quincy, Decatur, Champaign-Urbana, or Springfield (the first log cabin in Sangamon County was built in 1817). It was known that there was a Grand Prairie extending southward and westward from Lake Michigan to midstate, but descriptions of it were both vague and inaccurate. Illinois in 1818 was really southern Illinois. Shawneetown was the closest approach to a commercial center, primarily because of the importance of the salt springs twelve miles inland. In 1809 it was described as having more business activity than any other place west of Pittsburgh.

Early Political Geography

At the time of admission to statehood Illinois was characterized by many small, pioneer settlements, almost all of them south of a line drawn from Alton via Carlyle to Palestine, and almost all of them along a river or at least a small stream. In 1821 Illinois had only 22 counties, but this number had increased to 56 by 1830;[6] however, the latter number is misleading, as many of those in the central and more northern parts of the state were paper counties, merely organized political units with very few people and no meaningful government. Interestingly, in 1816 Crawford County extended northward to the limits of Illinois Territory, and included the tiny Chicago settlement. As new counties were created and county boundaries changed, Chicago was successively included in Clark, Pike, Fulton, Peoria, and Vermilion counties from 1819 until 1831 when Cook County was formed.

But in 1830, although the stars and stripes waved over the new Fort Dearborn, only about 50 people lived in the village that was destined to become "Hog Butcher of the World," the nation's great freight handler, and the site of the world's busiest airport.

Except for a fortuitous series of circumstances involving geography, slavery, trade, taxes, politics, and historical accident, Chicago would never have been in Illinois at all. The Ordinance of 1787, which established the Northwest Territory, included the stated intention of ultimately creating two states north of a line "drawn through the southerly bend or extreme (southern end) of Lake Michigan" and three states south of that line.

When Ohio filed for statehood in 1803, it prevailed upon Congress to establish its northern boundary five miles north of the 1787 line in order that the mouth of the Maumee River would be included within the state. When Indiana became a state in 1816, it tried to claim territory 25 miles north of the 1787 line, but settled for ten miles which gave it a shoreline on Lake Michigan from Hammond-Whiting to Michigan City. Two years later the initial proposal for the state of Illinois indicated a northern boundary to correspond in latitude with that of Indiana.

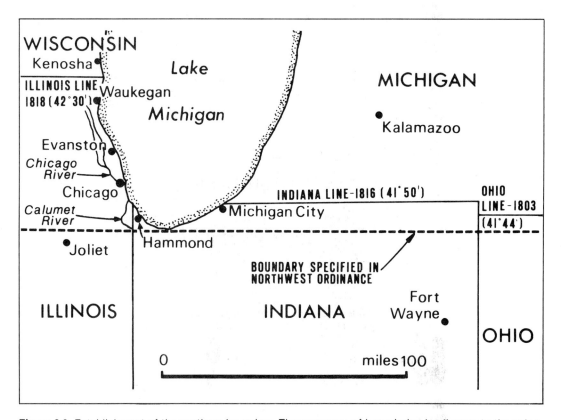

Figure 3-8. Establishment of the northern boundary. The sequence of boundaries leading up to the selection of latitude 42°30′ as the eventual northern boundary of Illinois is indicated on the map.

This would have given the new state possession of the mouth of the Calumet River, but everything north of that line would have eventually become a part of Wisconsin.

Shortly afterward, Illinois' farsighted territorial representative, Nathaniel Pope, proposed an amendment extending Illinois 51 miles farther north to 42° 30′. Whatever the stated reason or reasons, the realistic purpose was to give Illinois access to Lake Michigan through both the Chicago and Calumet Rivers. (It is not assumed that Nathaniel Pope ever envisioned a mighty metropolis developing between and around these two small streams with sandbars and mud flats blocking easy entrance into an infrequently used lake.)

Pope's amendment had little opposition. A precedent for violating the 1787 line had already been established by Ohio and Indiana. The states of the South were unconcerned about the boundary, but wanted Illinois admitted quickly in order to attract migration from the North and hopefully give them a free hand to establish slavery in Missouri. Legislators from the eastern states were convinced by Pope that, without good access to Lake Michigan, Illinois would be linked with the South and might well become a slave state. With his proposed access, he argued, Illinois would be oriented to the East and would become "the keystone to the perpetuity of the nation." Probably, too, the proponents of an envisioned Illinois and Michigan canal, not authorized until 1822, wanted to keep the planned canal enterprise within a single state. In any case, the ultimate loser, Wisconsin, had no one to protest on behalf of what was soon to become the Territory of Wisconsin. (In 1842, a mass meeting was held at Oregon City, now Oregon, and the fourteen counties north of the line designated in the Ordinance of 1787 tried to secede from Illinois, either to form a new territory or to be added to Wisconsin which was then about to become a state. Taxes were believed to have been one motive for this "rebellion."

Obviously the history and politics of Illinois would have been very different without its northernmost fourteen counties, which now represent more than half of the state's population. For example, Illinois would not have gone Republican in 1856 without the vote of these fourteen counties. And, without a Republican administration in Illinois, Abraham Lincoln would not have been nominated for president in 1860. Hence, it may be said that by putting the small settlement of Chicago in Illinois in 1818, Congress did contribute to the perpetuity of the Union in the 1860s, as Nathaniel Pope had so glibly argued almost half a century earlier.

Early Life-Style

Settling the woodlands of southern Illinois was a task of considerable effort. The land usually was cleared of all trees below some definite size, normally those less than fifteen inches in diameter. The larger trees were deadened; that is, they were girdled deeply enough to cause them to die. Occasionally all were cut so that the land was completely cleared. In either case the logs and brush were gathered into heaps for burning. A "logrolling," like house-raisings and barn raisings, was a communal occasion, and in some respects a social gathering as well. The practice of logrolling continued until well past the midcentury, barn raisings sporadically until the World War I years.

Early farmers fenced their cultivated stump fields and turned their livestock loose to forage in the nearby unfenced, wooded areas. Livestock kept in fenced pastures were easy to identify; however, range animals were not, as herds oftentimes combined or stray animals left one herd to join another. Consequently, their owners adopted a system of brands or marks. Early Illinois farmers sometimes used branding irons, a system of identification more commonplace in the western prairies at a later period in history. More often, however, they cropped a portion of the ear, or placed notches or holes in the ear of the animal. By the position of the marks on the top or bottom of the ear, or on the right or left ear, and by the combination of them, a great number of individual identifications were possible. So long as livestock were kept in this semiwild, unsupervised manner, these marks or brands were used and recognized as a legal means of claiming animals or proving ownership. However, it was required that the identifying mark or brand be registered with the county clerk where the owner resided. When stock was traded or sold, the new owner was responsible for changing the marks to indicate the change of ownership. Furthermore, the remarking was done in the presence of two creditable witnesses.

The early farm family was a more-or-less self-sufficient unit. Much of their summer and fall work was in preparation for the winter months. Hay and corn were harvested and stored in some fashion so that the essential animals could be kept through the cold season. Surplus animals were sold to the local slaughter house or livestock buyer sometime during the autumn, at least before Christmas. In addition, some animals were butchered on the farm to supply meat for the family during the winter and even into the early summer months. Most families butchered at least one beef and often several hogs, usually sometime between Thanksgiving and Christmas.

Hog butchering became an almost ritualistic procedure and was an all-day affair for the family, usually with the help of a couple of neighbors or a few close relatives from nearby farms. Actually, the work extended far longer than a single day. Preliminary arrangements required the gathering of a quantity of good, dry wood to heat the water for scalding the animals, and the placement of the wooden scalding barrel in a firm position and leaned or tilted at the proper angle for convenient use on "butchering day." Iron kettles, usually of 30 or 50 gallon size, were assembled at the site, whether from a summer storage place on the farm or borrowed from a neighbor if the family did not possess its own. The kettles were placed on rocks or, more likely, suspended at the proper height from a small log or heavy pole supported by two forked posts set firmly in the ground. Near dusk the night before, the hogs to be butchered were separated from the other animals and placed in a small temporary pen near the butchering site. The kettles were filled with water from the well, stream, or pond either the night before or very early on butchering day, as the fires were lighted at daybreak so the water would be boiling and the work could begin when the help arrived.

The process itself required shooting the animals with a rifle at appropriate intervals or stunning them with a heavy hammer or an axe and immediate "sticking" (cutting of the jugular vein with a long sharp knife); scalding and scraping to remove the hair; cutting the carcass into the hams, shoulders, sidemeat, and other cuts; making of sausage and possibly head cheese from the leaner trimming; and finally rendering of lard from the trimmed fat, the latter process using the same kettles that had contained the hot water earlier in the day. The major work was done in the morning hours. Making sausage and rendering lard were afternoon work, as was the storage of meat in the "smoke-house" or other appropriate places unaccessible to dogs, cats, and rodents. The curing of the better cuts took place at a more leisurely pace a week or more later. Normally, the hams and shoulders were salted or sugar-cured and probably smoked; on the other hand, some of the side pieces were pickled, partly to provide variety of flavor, but more importantly to preserve these cuts for use during the spring and into the summer months.

From settlement until the early 1900s it was the custom of most farm families to preserve and store food for the winter months and to gather wild products when in season. Dried apples and apple sauce were common winter foods. Autumn cider became winter vinegar. Some families dried corn, green beans, and small fruits. Later home canning of domestic fruit and vegetables became popular. Farm families made sauerkraut, having planted late cabbage solely for kraut. They probably owned at least one five- or eight-gallon, glazed, earthen jars solely for this purpose. Also, wild berries, especially blackberries, were gathered and canned for winter pies and cobblers. Hickory nuts and black walnuts, gathered in October, provided the ingredients for nut-cracking on long winter evenings. Persimmons for pudding, wild crab apples and wild plums for preserves, dandelions, plantains, and sheep's sorrel for early spring "greens," and dewberries, elder berries, and wild gooseberries were gathered from the woodlots or fence rows in season. Sassafras roots were dug in March, preferably from the red sassafras, for a delicious, rosy, springtime tea with a delightful odor. Broken twigs of the spicewood bush were used to make a similar drink, but this practice was far less widespread.

After frost, but before the first really hard freeze, the frugal farmer (more likely the farmer's wife) moved the apples, potatoes, turnips, cabbages, celery, pumpkin, and other vegetables into the fruit cellar. If the family did not have a fruit cellar, and most early farm homes did not have cellars, they made an earthen storage hole. This was really a conical or elongated mound on a well-drained portion of the garden area. First a layer of straw, grass, or leaves was placed on the ground. The products to be stored were arranged in a heap or ridge and a thick layer of straw then thrown over and alongside them. The top and sides were then covered with earth eight inches to a foot in thickness. Usually a small drainage ditch was dug around the mound. Boards or planks oftentimes were laid on top or leaned against these mounds as additional protection against the elements. This method of storage would normally keep the product dry and cool and would prevent freezing. It was a rather crude but reasonably effective method of keeping root vegetables and hardy fruits for use throughout the winter months.

The steel kettle used at butchering time was also used in the fall for making apple butter and, usually in the spring, for making soap. The soap was made from animal fat, most often meat fryings, that had been saved during the winter months. Before commercial lye became available, the household collected an alkaline solution for soap making by pouring rainwater over wood ashes, usually in a V-shaped, wooden trough tilted at a low angle to facilitate slow movement of the water through the ashes.

Prior to the Civil War, there was little money in circulation in the more rural sections of the state. Many of the small town shopkeepers sold goods on a year's credit and were paid in crops or livestock during the summer and fall. In a few cases the more affluent merchants in towns along the rivers fattened the livestock on their own farms, operated a seasonal packing house, and shipped pork, beef, and grain to New Orleans by flatboat. On occasion, too, the fattened livestock were shipped by flatboat to downriver markets.

Development of Transportation

Illinois is a crossroads state, with a major hub at Chicago on Lake Michigan and a secondary center at the St. Louis crossing of the Mississippi. The history and development of the state's truly advanced transportation system is the result of many factors, both physical and cultural, and their diverse interrelationships. Relatively flat terrain and easy grades facilitated railway and highway construction. A variety of resources with great potential for trade encouraged investment in transportation. And a culture and economic system based upon exchange necessitated an efficient means of transportation and communication. In little more than a century and a half there developed a vast net of roads, rails, and pipes; a tremendous number of vehicles in all their specialized forms; special route structures; and a variety of specialized terminal service and activities. Facilities evolved from the tavern, wayside inn, stagecoach stop, and obscure railway station to such specialized phenomena as the large grain elevator, piggyback loading dock, and unit train; the ubiquous highway service station and truck stop; the modern motel and fast-food outlet; the pipeline booster-station and oil terminal; the modern airport; and a host of others.

Waterways and Water Commerce

Initially, the movement of people and products was along the waterways. The In-dian canoe, flatboat, keelboat, and steamboat each played a role in the early commerce of the state. Several flatboat loads of coal were shipped from the banks of the Big Muddy River in Jackson County to New Orleans in 1810. But, in general, the flatboat trade was the movement of agricultural products to downriver markets. Flatboats were built and used on the Saline, Kaskaskia, Embarrass, and Little Wabash in southern Illinois; on the Sangamon and Vermilion in the central section; and probably on several other streams as well. However, both the flatboat and keelboat were replaced by steam traffic, the sternwheeler, on the principal rivers during the early years of statehood.

The first steamboat trip down the Ohio and Mississippi to New Orleans occurred in 1811. By 1820, some 70 steamboats were using these rivers. The first steamboat upstream to St. Louis was in 1817, and up the Illinois to Peoria in 1820. Shortly thereafter, steam traffic became commonplace on the major rivers and a few of the lesser ones as well. For years Galena was the most important port north of St. Louis. Later, barge traffic became the dominant feature of commercial water traffic in the state and along its borders.

During the first few decades of the nineteenth century, Illinois faced south in its commercial relations. In fact, over half the state still faced in that direction at the middle of the century,[7] and many river communities continued to do so until the outbreak of the Civil War. In 1845, Shawneetown still had varied trade relations with the South, as did some of the towns along the Mississippi. Palestine, Mt. Carmel, Golconda, Cairo, Quincy, and others sent some grains downstream, but they probably lacked the variety of trade that characterized Shawneetown, Vincennes, Terre Haute, and St.

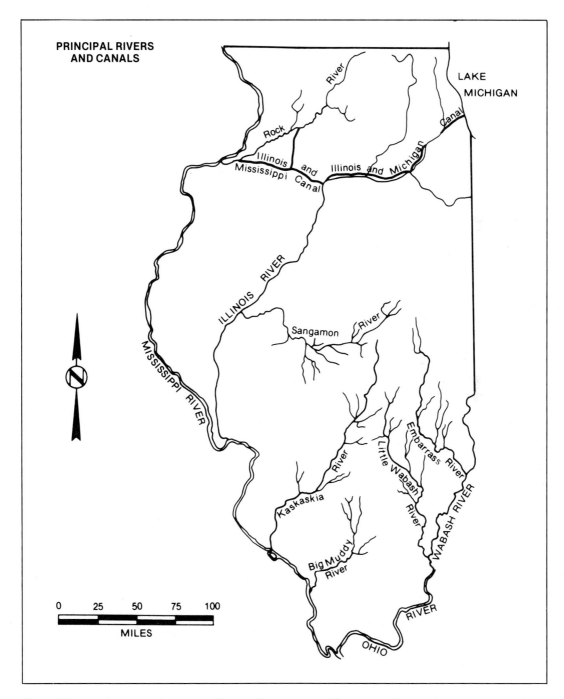

PRINCIPAL RIVERS AND CANALS

Figure 3-9. Principal rivers and canals. The excellent system of internal and bordering waterways has been a major asset for the development of Illinois.

Louis. Some corn, wheat, and flour moved southward to foreign markets, especially after 1845, with wheat and flour in much greater demand than corn. Coffee and other tropical products were transported north by river until the early 1860s.

Flatboat traffic on the Ohio and Mississippi had been surpassed by steam traffic in 1830, and on the Illinois soon after that date, but it continued to form an important part of river commerce for many years. Steamers never penetrated the Wabash or Kaskaskia to any appreciable extent, so produce from those valleys had to be transferred to a steamer or floated on to its destination. As late as 1846, flatboat arrivals at New Orleans numbered 2,792, over 600 of them coming from Indiana and Illinois. Ten years later the number from these two states was reduced to 148, only 12 of them from Illinois.

Early French explorers reportedly suggested the possibility of a canal from the Great Lakes to the Illinois River, and thence a connection via the Mississippi to the Gulf of Mexico. In 1822 the national government granted the state of Illinois a right-of-way for such a route. Officially named the Illinois and Michigan Canal, construction was begun in 1836, but the nationwide depression following the Panic of 1837 delayed its completion until 1848. Although the canal provided safe and cheap transportation, its slowness and other factors caused a general decline in its importance. Particularly significant was its inability to compete successfully with the railroads that were built soon after the completion of the canal.

For a short period, however, the canal was truly a major factor in the economic development of the state. In fact, so great was the canal's role in developing northern Illinois that, of all man-made waterways in North America, only the Erie Canal surpassed it in importance.[8] Grain grown along the Illinois and upper Mississippi rivers could be shipped to market by way of the canal and Great Lakes at less cost than by way of New Orleans. Canal boats exchanged cargoes with river steamers at LaSalle. Peru also prospered, as did Joliet and Lockport. The long, narrow, rounded boats used on the canal carried passengers along with the freight of the season, but supplied neither food nor bedding. On packet boats, which were introduced later, food service was provided. Especially during the deep mud of spring thaws and heavy rains, these improved craft were more reliable and more comfortable than stagecoaches, which had no competition during winter months when the canal was inoperable. Nonetheless, after the early period of prosperity, there was a gradual decrease in the amount of traffic. The canal showed a profit until 1879, and tonnage declined rather consistently after the peak year of 1881.

In 1890 the Chicago Sanitary District undertook construction of a canal, primarily for sanitation purposes rather than transportation, between Chicago and Lockport, where the new canal joined the western segment of the old Illinois-Michigan Canal and the lower Des Plaines River. Opened in 1900, this work provided a waterway with a minimum depth of nine feet for navigation from the South Branch of the Chicago River to Lockport, but from Lockport to Utica there was no adequate means of water transportation. Consequently, the legislative act in 1919 provided a 20 million dollar bond issue for construction of an eight foot channel between the two towns. This proved insufficient to finish the waterway, and in 1930 the federal government completed the project and extended the improvement along the Illinois River to its confluence with the

Mississippi. (The lower Illinois had been canalized, beginning in 1870.) The improved Illinois Waterway was opened in 1933. The Sag Channel, a 24 mile southern arm of the Chicago Sanitary and Ship Canal, was added to connect with the Calumet River and Lake Calumet in 1922. It was subsequently widened and deepened and other improvements have been made during recent years.

The federal government also built, in 1870, the Illinois and Mississippi Canal from Hennepin to the Mississippi near Rock Island. It was little used by 1950 and abandoned by 1970.

The Illinois Waterway, fully opened in 1935, carried a tonnage of 1,700,000 during the remainder of that year. In 1950, the figure was 12 million tons, and more than 24 million in 1960. The opening of the St.

Lawrence Seaway in 1958 greatly stimulated the expansion of the deep water port of Chicago and contributed markedly to increased use of the Illinois Waterway. Today's use of the Waterway consists primarily of barge traffic, with some private pleasure craft. The barges vary in size from 800 to 3,000 tons. They are of various designs to carry dry bulk, liquid bulk, and general cargo. Special barges are used for petroleum products, cement, and alcohol. The largest towboats are 165 by 35 feet and handle a tow of six large barges. With continued growth in population and industry, coupled with a need for a dependable and economical means of transportation, continued increase in traffic on the Illinois Waterway appears to be assured through the remainder of this century.

Figure 3-10. A large barge tow on the Mississippi River. Grain, coal, and petroleum comprise the bulk of the cargo now transported by barges on the Mississippi and its tributaries. (Courtesy Donald W. Griffin.)

Early Railroad Development

In 1850 transportation was still tedious over most of the state. The roads were generally inadequate and, except for the Illinois River and the canal connecting it with Lake Michigan, the really usable waterways were along the margins of the growing state. In all cases, traffic was slow. But the basic framework of a great system of railroads was quickly established between 1850 and 1860 when track mileage in the state was increased from less than 100 miles to almost 2,800 miles. After 1860 the basic framework was filled in with branch lines, competing lines, and shortcut (cut off) lines, until there were more than 12,000 miles of railroad in 1929 and only one of the 102 counties (Calhoun) was without rail service. More recently, the abandonment of unprofitable lines, which began about 1920, and the consolidation of routes has outstripped new construction. Present mileage is approximately 11,000 miles. Illinois owes much of its development into a great agricultural and industrial complex to the extensive railroad facilities within the state.

The state's first railroad, in Morgan County between Meredosia and Morgan City, was 12 miles in length and began service in 1839. A year later it was extended to Jacksonville and, despite financial difficulties, to Springfield by 1842. The trip from Jacksonville to Springfield, 33 1/2 miles, took two hours and eight minutes.[9] This route later became a part of the Wabash System.

The first railroad in northern Illinois was the Galena and Chicago Union, the beginning of the present Northwestern System. Although originally chartered in 1836, work was discontinued during the Panic of 1837 and not renewed for ten years. By the end of 1848 it was completed to the Des Plaines River and brought a load of wheat into downtown Chicago from its terminus ten miles away. Two years later it reached Elgin (via Elmhurst and Wheaton) with a branch south from Turner's Junction (West Chicago) to Batavia and Aurora. It was extended to Belvidere in 1852, to Freeport in 1853, and finally to the Mississippi in 1855. In 1856 it became the first railroad in the West to use telegraph (between Chicago and Freeport). Also in 1856, it purchased two coal burning locomotives, presumably the first ones to be used in Illinois. The Chicago and Galena put into use the standard T-shaped iron rails in 1851. Earlier rails were made of wood, capped with thin strips of iron, the usual practice on frontier lines.

In 1850 Congress passed legislation of truly major significance in the history of Illinois transportation, an act providing for a grant of public lands to the state of Illinois to aid in the construction of a central railroad—the Illinois Central, now Illinois Central Gulf. This railroad, the third in Illinois, was to be built through the interior of the state from a point at or near the junction of the Ohio and Mississippi rivers to the western terminus of the Illinois and Michigan Canal at Peru or LaSalle, then to the extreme northwestern corner of the state (Galena). Another segment was to be built to Chicago from a site near the present city of Centralia. Interestingly, early maps indicate the Centralia-LaSalle-Galena segment as the main line and the Centralia-Chicago route as a branch line. The first train from Calumet (Kensington) reached downtown Chicago in 1852 by way of a wooden trestle. The main line was finished in 1855 and the Chicago branch a year later. With more than 700 miles of track at that time, the Illinois Central Railroad was the longest on the American continent.[10] In fact, it was the longest in the world.

Without question the Illinois Central was of paramount importance to the development of the state. First and foremost, it connected the older southern part of the state with the other center of early development (Galena) and with the newer, fast-growing Chicago region. The railroad, especially the line to Chicago, also traversed extensive prairies which were largely unsettled in 1855. Early travellers along the route were surprised to see so small a portion of the land under cultivation and reported virtually no population except along the larger streams and timber areas, which were generally found together. Probably the construction of the Illinois Central was more important than any other single act in opening up the prairie land of east central Illinois.

Completion of this large mileage of track by a single company within a five-year period during the middle of the nineteenth century was in itself a major achievement, a larger public works project than the digging of the Erie Canal. It was accomplished by simultaneous construction at several points along each line and, at a time of labor shortage, by the recruitment of more than 10,000 men, mostly at New York, New Orleans, and other distant places. Large numbers of Europeans came to America during this period and many of them, especially the Irish, helped to build the Illinois Central Railroad. Many of the Irish workers were recruited directly in Ireland. The practice of assigning an engineer to construct a particular section of track resulted in the identification of that segment of the railroad by the name of the engineer and oftentimes the station on that portion of the track was given his name. For example, Paxton, Gilman, Rantoul, Mattoon, Seidel, and Effingham were stations named for the construction engineer in charge of building the railroad in that particular area.

Although railroad construction continued for more than half a century, the period from 1850 to 1860 was most important for railroad building in Illinois. Among the ma-

jor lines that had their beginnings in this period was the Chicago and Rock Island, which dispatched its first train to Joliet in 1852, and on to Morris, Ottawa, and LaSalle in 1853. It was the first actually to bridge the Mississippi (in 1856). Both the Chicago and Alton (later a part of the Gulf, Mobile, and Alabama) and the Chicago, Burlington, and Quincy were put into operation in the 1850s. Through the Indiana gateway to northern Illinois came two of America's great railroads: from Michigan City in 1852 was a line that later became a part of the New York Central, and from Fort Wayne in 1859 was the forerunner of the Pennsylvania Railroad into Chicago. The Chicago and Milwaukee line, with train service beginning in 1856, helped develop the North Shore and encouraged the growth of Evanston and Lake Forest as college communities. Into Freeport from the north (Beloit) came the Milwaukee in 1859, but its tracks into Chicago were not built until 1872. The Chicago and Great Western was begun in 1854, but was not completed across Illinois until 1887. By 1857, Chicago was the terminus of eleven rail lines, and their direct connections brought to the city immense quantities of pork, beef, and grain. In general, railroad development lagged in southern Illinois, but a line from Vincennes to St. Louis, later a part of the St. Louis-Cincinnati Division of the Baltimore and Ohio, was completed in 1857. The Terre Haute and Alton was finished a year earlier. The Illinois portion of the Atlantic and Mississippi from Terre Haute to Illinoistown (East St. Louis), temporarily blocked by Alton interests, was also completed in the mid-1850s. By 1857, forty-eight railroad projects were either completed or under construction entirely within the state or into Illinois from adjoining states. Almost overnight Illinois became the keystone of the American railway system, and Chicago emerged as the world's greatest

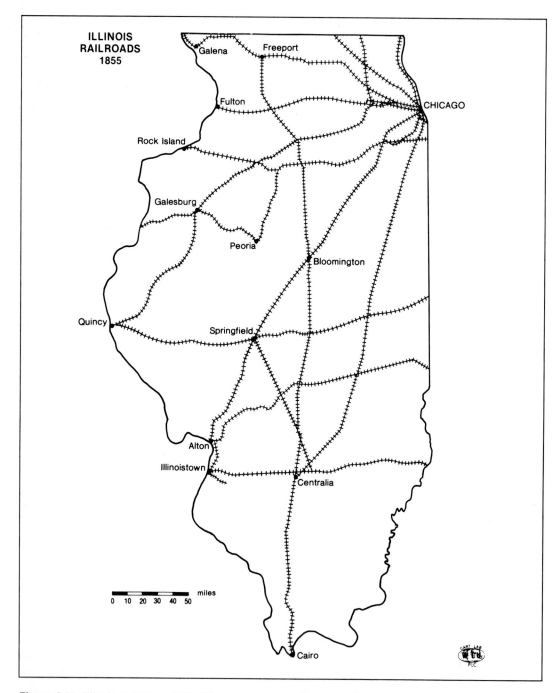

Figure 3-11. Illinois railroads, 1855. The construction of track during the early 1850s soon provided a skeleton network of rail lines. Note that Chicago was already an important rail hub in 1855.

railway center with eleven roads ending in the city.

Geography made it inevitable that Chicago would become a transportation center. Aggressive and farsighted business leaders made the most of natural advantages, as the coming of the railroads helped to make Chicago a great city as well as the greatest railroad center in the world. By 1852 Chicago had rail connections with the East Coast, and in 1869 service was inaugurated with the West Coast. Today some 30-odd lines radiate from the Chicago area, and there are about 8,000 miles of railway trackage in the Chicago terminal district.

Trails, Roads, and Highways

Early American trails tended to follow the buffalo trace or the Indian footpath, which may have been one and the same. The old "Saint Louis Trace," believed to be the first overland trail in Illinois, was originally a buffalo trail for much of the way. Really an extension of the long Wilderness Road from Cumberland Gap, this historic route extended from the falls of the Ohio at Louisville to St. Louis, crossing the Wabash River at Vincennes.[11] This trail, subsequently a stagecoach route, followed an alignment later paralleled by the Baltimore and Ohio Railroad and U.S. Highway 50 in Illinois. The vicinity of old Fort Massac, where the city of Metropolis now stands, was the Ohio River terminus of several paths that extended northward and westward.[12] Other early trails led to salt licks both in southeastern Illinois and a few miles west of Danville.

The Indians used the buffalo trails, but they also had routes of their own making which connected their important villages and centers of population. One such center was in the vicinity of Metropolis, another near

the mouth of the Kaskaskia River, and a third on the Big Vermilion River near Danville.[13] Some native trails were well-beaten footpaths. Others, used less frequently, were faintly visible and difficult to follow without an Indian guide.

Sometime after Kaskaskia and Detroit were founded by the French, an overland trail partially connecting the two settlements was blazed across Illinois to the Great Bend of the Wabash River in Indiana just east of Danville. At modern Georgetown, just south of Danville, it crossed an ancient Indian trail leading southward to Vincennes, thus linking the three most important centers of French influence in interior America. A more important route from Kaskaskia (and St. Louis) to Detroit, however, used the Mississippi and Illinois rivers to a point near Joliet, and then an ill-defined connection eastward to the beach ridges skirting the southern end of Lake Michigan (Sauk Trail),

Figure 3-12. Remnant of a salt kettle along U.S. Route 150, west of Danville. The earliest settlement in this section of the state, in 1827, was associated with the saline waters (salt springs) along Salt Fork of the Vermilion River at this approximate location. (1939 photo by Alden Cutshall.)

from where it extended eastward across Indiana and Michigan. The eastern segments later became more widely known and used as the land route from Chicago to Detroit.

One of the earlier land routes in northern Illinois was Hubbard's Trace, also known as Vincennes Trace. It was basically an extension of the Vincennes-Danville route to the newer Chicago community. The name came from one colorful Chicago pioneer and enterprising Indian trader who set up a series of trading posts across the vast prairie wasteland near the Indiana border. This was the route later followed by the four Chicago men on horses who made an unsuccessful attempt to get a loan from the bank of Shawneetown. In 1834 the state legislature designated it a state road, marked with milestones and terminating in "downtown" Chicago where it became State Street. Wagons of produce, much of it from the Valley of the Wabash, came to Chicago along this route.

Other early roads of the Chicago region that have remained important over the years are Green Bay Road, St. Charles Road, Naperville Road (now Ogden Avenue and U.S. Route 54), Joliet Road (Archer Avenue), and the present Indianapolis Boulevard. Both the Joliet and Naperville Roads were extended to Ottawa at the confluence of the Fox and Illinois rivers. This was the northern segment of the first land route from Chicago to St. Louis. As far as Naperville, this route was identical with the southern stage route from Chicago to Galena, opened in 1834. The earliest impetus toward an overland highway between these two communities, as might be expected, came from Galena rather than Chicago. The first load of lead to Chicago, in 1829, crossed the Rock River at the site of modern Dixon and the Fox River at Plainfield.

The National Road, sometimes called the Cumberland Road, was the first large highway project in Illinois. It was begun in Cumberland, Maryland, in 1811, and subsequently extended through Pennsylvania and the West Virginia panhandle to Wheeling. Shortly before 1830 it was proposed to extend the road westward to connect the capitals of the new states of Ohio, Indiana, and Illinois. (The capital of Illinois had been moved from Kaskaskia to Vandalia, a mere hamlet, in 1820.) The road was completed from Vandalia to Terre Haute in 1836, although the Indianapolis-Terre Haute segment was not finished until 1840. Shortly thereafter the road was extended to St. Louis. It was still known as the National Road when the present system of road numbers was established and it became U.S. 40, now the route of Interstate 70.

The road system of Illinois evolved slowly. Many of the early trails became earthern roads, some of them later stagecoach routes. The principal routes were then improved and became "gravel roads," i.e., all-weather roads, although oftentimes cluttered with chuckholes. The paved highway is a twentieth century development, and coincided somewhat with the increased use of the motor vehicle. In 1914, when state appropriations for hard roads from proceeds of automobile license fees was begun, there was less than one mile of concrete road in Cook County outside of Chicago.[14] Most of the paved highway net of the state was constructed in the 1920s, the result of several successive state bond issues for road construction. The expansion of multilanes, begun in the 1930s, was primarily a post-World War II development. The super highway (limited access and divided pavement) did not become really significant until after 1960.

Historical factors explain much of the highway pattern of the state. In the earlier settled areas many existing roads and highways follow early trails or traces. A few of the main highways inherited these routes and are therefore not oriented to the cardinal points of the compass. But over most of the state, especially in the less rugged areas, a rectangular pattern predominates. The roads are oriented to the lines of the original land survey, a system for surveying the new lands in the west included in the Northwest Ordinance of 1787. Rural roads are commonly spaced at one-mile intervals, following section lines and insuring access to all rural residences. The paved highways built in the 1920s and 1930s are superimposed on this basic rural net and tend to follow this same general pattern.

Along the Road to Greatness

Illinois is woven into the history of America with threads of steel. It took hardy settlers to develop the rolling hills and river bottoms of the southern and western parts of Illinois. It took outcasts and adventurers from the East to see and exploit the possibilities of the lakeside swamplands. It took European money to finance the railroads of Illinois, and European immigrants were needed to build those railroads and man the factories and shops that made the state a major part of the American Manufacturing Belt. Illinois is a great state because of its central position in the midcontinent, its natural endowments, and the foresight and ability of its people over 150 years. It is a crossroads state that has attained a commanding position in agriculture, manufacturing, and transportation.

Over the years Illinois has been noted for leadership, progress, and men of vision. The Morrow plots on the Urbana Campus of the University of Illinois connote leadership in agricultural research for more than a century. John Deere of Grand Detour developed a plow with a steel moldboard that made it possible to turn the matted sod of the Midwestern prairies—the plow that broke the plains and set an agricultural revolution in motion. Cyrus McCormick of Chicago built the reaper to harvest the grain that grew in those fertile prairie soils. Joseph Glidden of DeKalb obtained a patent on barbed wire that permitted fencing the land at moderate cost. Years later, A.E. Staley of Decatur proposed that soybeans be used not only as a forage crop for dairy cattle, but also as an industrial raw material. George Pullman manufactured sleeping cars that made train travel more comfortable; he also built the first completely planned community in Illinois. Elbert Gary of Wheaton became Chairman of the Board of Directors of U.S. Steel and helped to build a city amid the sand dunes of nearby Indiana. William B. Ogden, Chicago's first mayor, talked suburban farmers into joining him in building the city's first railroad. Twenty-one years later, as president of Union Pacific, he drove the golden spike at Promontory, Utah, completing a rail linkup that united the nation. The Chicago-based Illinois Central Railroad developed the first refrigerator car. Richard Sears, an amiable salesman, in the 1890s founded a company that became "the world's largest store." In the 1920s that company operated one of the first commercial radio stations; in the 1930s it marketed the first prefabricated houses; and in the 1970s it built the world's tallest building, the Sears Tower in Chicago. Aaron Montgomery Ward started a mail order business in 1872, but more importantly he fought a decade of court battles to save Chicago's lakefront from commercial development. William Rainey Harper built a major university on the former site of Chicago's first great fair, The World's Columbian Exposition of 1893. Richard J. Daley built McCormick Place on the site of the second great fair, The Century of Progress of 1933-34. Memorial Day was first celebrated in Carbondale, and the idea for the G.I. Bill of Rights at the end of World War II originated in Salem. Gustavus Swift and Philip Armour, along with others, made Chicago the "hog butcher of the world" for many decades, and most of that time East St. Louis was in second position. In 1871, after a fire that left 100,000 homeless, Joseph Medill of the Chicago Tribune said in a now-famous editorial, "Chicago shall rise again." It certainly did. Frank Lloyd Wright received more honors for his works than any other architect of his time. Daniel Burnham exhorted, "Make no little plans." In 1908 he called for developing the Chicago lakefront as a recreation area, for building Wacker Drive in what had been a dirty, smelly wholesale produce area along the Chicago River, and for major traffic arteries radiating from the central city. A practical idealist and activist, Jane Addams, came to Chicago and in 1889 converted the former Hull residence, then used for furniture storage, into a settlement house that became known around the world. These leaders, along with many, many others, helped to make Illinois a great state.

Notes

1. *Chicago Daily News,* 16 June 1975, p. 35.
2. *Chicago Daily News,* 13 January 1975, p. 36.
3. *Illinois Business Review,* 20 (February 1963), p. 3.
4. Robert P. Howard, *Illinois: A History of the Prairie State* (Grand Rapids, Mich.: William B. Eerdmans Publishing Co., 1972), p. 18.
5. Gerald H. Krausse, "Historic Galena: A Study of Urban Change and Development in a Midwestern Mining Town." *Bulletin of the Illinois Geographical Society,* 13 December 1971, p. 7.
6. Randall Parrish, *Historic Illinois: The Romance of the Earlier Days* (Chicago: A.C. McClurg & Co., 1905), p. 296.
7. Henry C. Hubbart, *The Older Middle West: 1840-1880* (New York: Russell & Russell, 1936), p. 76.
8. Howard, *Illinois,* p. 239.
9. *Illinois Business Review,* 5 (May 1948), p. 1.
10. Ibid.
11. Carlton J. Corliss, *Trails to Rails: A Story of Transportation Progress in Illinois* (Chicago: Illinois Central Railroad, 1934), p. 3.
12. Ibid.
13. Ibid., p. 4.
14. *Chicago Daily News,* 12 August 1974, p. 4.

Selected References

Ackerman, William K. *Early Illinois Railroads.* Chicago: Fergus Printing Co., 1884.

Angle, Paul M., ed. *Prairie State: Impressions of Illinois, 1673-1967, by Travelers and Other Observers.* Chicago: University of Chicago Press, 1968.

Allen, John W. *It Happened in Southern Illinois.* Carbondale: Southern Illinois University Press, 1968.

————. *Legends and Lore of Southern Illinois.* Carbondale: Southern Illinois University Press, 1963.

Barrows, Harlan H. *Geography of the Middle Illinois Valley.* Bulletin No. 15. Urbana: Illinois State Geological Survey, 1910.

Beimfohr, John. *Industrial Potential of Southern Illinois.* Carbondale: Southern Illinois University Press, 1952.

Belting, Natalia. *Kaskaskia Under the French Regime.* Urbana: University of Illinois Press, 1948.

Bogart, Ernest L., and Thompson, Charles M. *The Centennial History of Illinois,* vol. 4. *The Industrial State, 1870-1893.* Springfield: The Illinois Centennial Commission, 1920.

Boggess, Arthur C. *The Settlement of Illinois, 1776-1830.* Chicago: Chicago Historical Society, 1908.

Bogue, Allen G. *From Prairie to Corn Belt: Farming on the Illinois and Iowa Prairies in the Nineteenth Century.* Chicago: University of Chicago Press, 1963.

Bogue, Margaret B. *Patterns of the Sod: Land Use and Tenure in the Grand Prairie, 1850-1900.* Springfield: Illinois State Historical Society, 1959.

Brush, Daniel H. *Growing Up with Southern Illinois.* Chicago: Donnelley & Sons Co., 1944.

Buck, Solon J. *Illinois in 1818.* Springfield: The Illinois Centennial Commission, 1917.

Burton, William L. *The Trembling Land: Illinois in the Age of Exploration.* W.I.U. Studies in Illinois History No. 1. Macomb: Western Illinois University, 1966.

Caldwell, Norman. *The French in the Mississippi Valley.* Urbana: University of Illinois Press, 1941.

Carliss, Carlton J. *Trails to Rails: A Story of Transportation Progress in Illinois.* Chicago: Illinois Central Railroad, 1934.

Cutler, Irving. *Chicago: Metropolis of the Mid-Continent.* Chicago: The Geographical Society of Chicago, 1973.

Draine, Edwin H. *Import Traffic of Chicago and its Hinterland.* Research Paper No. 81. Chicago: University of Chicago Department of Geography, 1963.

Ford, Thomas. *History of Illinois.* Chicago: S.C. Griggs and Co., 1854.

Gates, Paul W. *The Illinois Central Railroad and Its Colonization Work.* Cambridge: Harvard University Press, 1934.

Gerhard, Fred. *Illinois As It Is.* Chicago: Keen and Lee, 1857.

Goode, J. Paul. *The Geographic Background of Chicago.* Chicago: University of Chicago Press, 1926.

Hicken, Victor. *The Settlement of Illinois: 1700-1850.* W.I.U. Studies in Illinois History No. 2. Macomb: Western Illinois University, 1966.

Howard, Robert P. *Illinois: A History of the Prairie State.* Grand Rapids: William B. Eerdmans Publishing Co., 1972.

Hubbart, Henry C. *The Older Middle West: 1840-1880.* New York: Russell & Russell, 1936.

Illinois: A Descriptive and Historical Guide. Federal Writers Project. Chicago: A.C. McClurg and Co., 1939.

Krausse, Gerald H. "Historic Galena: A Study of Urban Change and Development in a Midwestern Mining Town." *Bulletin of the Illinois Geographical Society,* XIII (December 1971), 3-19.

Lee, Judson Fiske. "Transportation: A Factor in the Development of Northern Illinois Previous to 1860." *Journal of the Ilinois State Historical Society* (April 1917), 17-85.

McManis, Douglas R. *The Initial Evaluation and Utilization of the Illinois Prairies, 1815-1840.* Research Paper No. 94. Chicago: University of Chicago Department of Geography, 1964.

Mitchell, S. Augustus. *Illinois in 1837.* Philadelphia: Mitchell, 1837.

Moses, John. *Illinois, Historical and Statistical.* Vol. I. Chicago: Fergus Printing Co., 1889.

Parrish, Randall. *Historic Illinois: The Romance of the Earlier Days.* Chicago: A.C. McClurg & Co., 1905.

Pease, Theodore C. *The Frontier State, 1818-1848.* Chicago: A.C. McClurg & Co., 1922.

Pease, Theodore Calvin, and Pease, Margaret Jenison. *The Story of Illinois.* 3rd ed. Chicago: University of Chicago Press, 1965.

Poggi, E. Muriel. *The Prairie Province of Illinois: A Study in Human Adjustment to Natural Environment.* Vol. XIX of *Illinois Studies in the Social Sciences.* Urbana: University of Illinois Press, 1934.

Pooley, William V. *The Settlement of Illinois from 1830 to 1850.* Bulletin of the University of Wisconsin, No. 220 (History Series, I). Madison: University of Wisconsin, 1908.

Putnam, James W. *Illinois and Michigan Canal: A Study in Economic History.* Chicago: Chicago Historical Society, 1917.

Quaife, Milo M. *Chicago's Highways Old and New: From Indian Trail to Motor Road.* Chicago: D.F. Keller & Co., 1923.

Reynolds, John. *The Pioneer History of Illinois.* Chicago: Fergus Printing Co., 1887.

Ridgley, Douglas. *The Geography of Illinois.* Chicago: University of Chicago Press, 1921.

Sauer, Carl O. *Geography of the Upper Illinois Valley and History of Development.* Bulletin No. 27. Urbana: Illinois State Geological Survey, 1916.

Vogel, Virgil J. *Indian Place Names in Illinois.* Springfield: Illinois State Historical Library, 1963.

Weaver, John E. *The North American Prairie.* Lincoln: Johnsen Publishing Co., 1954.

Wheeler, David L. "The Illinois Country, 1673-1696." *Bulletin of the Illinois Geographical Society,* VII (June 1965), 42-47.

Chapter Four

POPULATION AND SOCIAL GEOGRAPHY

Albert Larson and Siim Sööt
University of Illinois at Chicago Circle

Illinois is comprised of two fundamental regions: the six-county Chicago metropolitan area[1] and the remaining 96-county downstate region, which is predominantly agricultural but spotted with an irregular geometry of cities and industrial clusters. Although the downstate region is more extensive, it accounts for only 36 percent of the state's population. Nevertheless, it is impossible to subdivide the state into two regions with a better balance of area and population without fragmenting the Chicago area. This initial dichotomy may prove to be a gross oversimplification, however, as it will be shown that each region is characterized by great diversity. Certainly there are extensive agricultural expanses within the six-county Chicago metropolitan region, as well as numerous other metropolitan areas (Rockford, Springfield, Peoria, Champaign-Urbana, and Bloomington-Normal) scattered throughout the remainder of the state. The dominance of Chicago, however,

will be evident in the analysis of many of the social patterns which distinguish Illinois.

Ultimately, the description of any region leads to a comparison with adjacent regions to contrast internal homogeneity with interregional differences. Generally a region is considered well-defined if its internal variation is less than that found between it and other regions. It would be easy to point to Chicago as a feature of the social landscape which differentiates Illinois from surrounding states and then to reason that the state is truly a unique entity. The great concentration of population and activities in Chicago is the basis for state-level characteristics not found elsewhere in the Midwest. For example, incomes are exceptionally high; in terms of median family income, three of the five wealthiest cities in the United States with populations over 25,000 are found in the Chicago area.[2] Also, the Chicago area is characterized by a concentration of Lithuanian and Polish populations uncommon

Figure 4-1. Both old and new skyscrapers in Chicago are testimony to the city's continuing dominance of the population and economic structure of Illinois. (Courtesy Illinois Office of Tourism.)

elsewhere. Despite such characteristics, if the metropolitan region were deleted from the state and comparisons were made with adjacent states without their respective dominant urban centers, the similarities would be striking.

Although it is not the intent to develop this line of comparison fully, it will suffice to demonstrate the similarities in the populations of these states outside the major cities (Table 4-1). Indeed, Michigan has the largest "downstate" population, while Illinois is only a close third after Indiana. The three states are dotted with important urban centers within their borders. In addition, Indiana and Illinois have major urbanized areas[3] extending into their territories from adjacent states (Chicago and St. Louis, respectively).[4] The table also indicates a general decrease in state population outside the major cities as the distance from Chicago increases. The states closest to Chicago— Michigan, Indiana, and Wisconsin—have the highest levels, while the more distant states are considerably lower. Of course, this pattern would not continue eastward into the more heavily populated Manufacturing Belt. It is interesting to observe that the three states in the United States most similar to each other in areal size are Illinois, Wisconsin, and Iowa. Therefore, it is possible, though not necessarily advisable, to use magnitudes when comparative densities would otherwise be necessary.

This brings us to the question, is Illinois a unique entity? A multifarious list of variables needs to be considered in order to formulate an answer. We have seen some general similarities and differences in comparing Illinois with adjoining states. Suffice it to say that each similarity and difference could be more fully determined, but ultimately the conclusion would most certainly be that the present boundaries of the state are somewhat arbitrary. The Mississippi and Ohio rivers form distinct boundaries, but the linear

Table 4-1. Populations of Illinois and Neighboring States.

State	1970 Population (in thousands)	Area (sq. mi.)	Major SMSA	SMSA Pop. Within State (in thousands)	State Pop. Minus SMSA Population (in thousands)
Illinois	11,113	55,930	Chicago	6,978	4,035
Wisconsin	4,418	54,705	Milwaukee	1,403	3,015
Minnesota	3,804	80,705	Minneapolis-St. Paul	1,813	1,991
Iowa	2,824	56,032	Des Moines	286	2,538
Missouri[a]	4,676	69,138	St. Louis[b]	1,826	2,002
			Kansas City[b]	848	
Kentucky	3,219	39,863	Louisville	695	2,524
Indiana	5,193	36,185	Indianapolis	1,110	4,083
Michigan	8,875	57,019	Detroit	4,199	4,676

[a]Two major SMSAs.

[b]SMSA extends beyond the state boundary.

eastern and northern boundaries have little relation to settlement patterns or topographic relief. Also, it seems illogical for Chicago's eastern city limits to coincide with the Indiana state line. This common boundary has been the basis of numerous problems for state agencies from law enforcement to internal revenue.

Historical Development of Social and Population Patterns

Since the early settlement of Illinois, population growth, redistribution, and in-migration have produced a series of changes in the settlement pattern which reflect a complex of economic, social, and political events. Foremost among these changes in population redistribution has been the growing prominence of Chicago. Concurrently, several other trends in redistribution may be discerned over the last 140 years. An understanding of the historical development of the state's social and population patterns can be facilitated by using the migration of the center of population as a primary reference and decade population change maps as secondary references. A map of these centers of population (Fig. 4-1) suggests a method of identifying meaningful periods in Illinois's history. Though numerous other periodizations are possible, we shall examine an era of growth and settlement (1830-1860) followed by a post-Civil War period (1860-1880), industrialization and immigration (1880-1910), World War I and recovery (1910-1930), depression (1930-1940), and automobile-oriented urbanization (1940-present).

Early Settlement to 1830

Although the earliest European occupation of what came to be Illinois was in the southwest at Kaskaskia, early settlers in the

American period approached from the southeast. Pioneer hunters from the Upland South moved up the watercourses and regarded the open prairie country with the suspicion that was typical of the early nineteenth century. When Illinois became a territory in 1809 and a state in 1818, there was only scant settlement in the central and northern parts of the state (Fig. 4-3). Most of the state had been ceded by Indians during the first two decades of the century, although the last negotiation for Indian land was not until 1833.

At the time Illinois attained statehood, its population was concentrated in both the southeast and southwest. This pattern was still evident in 1830 with the largest concentrations located along the lower Illinois River. Population in southern Illinois was especially sparse in the physically less desirable Shawnee Hills. For the most part, settlement followed the Upland South pattern of individual families taking up forested land along watercourses in relative isolation. Early colony or group settlement from Europe and New England was regarded with suspicion. Attitudes generally followed Jacksonian thinking favoring liberalized land laws and removal of Indians.

Pre-Civil War Settlement, 1830-1860

The fourth decade of the nineteenth century saw both an advance and retreat of settlement in northern Illinois. Beginning about 1830, widespread realization of the value of prairie soil increased settlement. After a hesitant departure from riverine lowlands, it was found that water was available beneath the prairie. In fact, too much water often was an obstacle on the ill-drained flatland. Finding a good plow to break the tough sod also became a pressing need. As settlers experimented with the prairie environment in

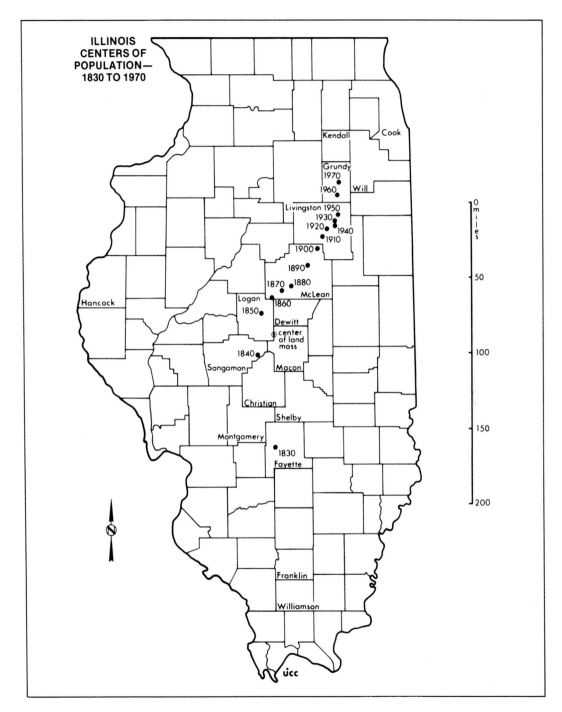

Figure 4-2. Illinois centers of population, 1830 to 1970.

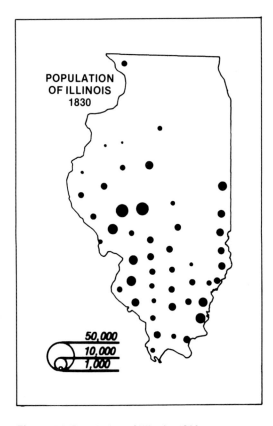

**POPULATION
OF ILLINOIS
1830**

50,000
10,000
1,000

Figure 4-3. Population of Illinois, 1830.

beginning of steam navigation on the Great Lakes in the early 1830s as well as by use of the Erie Canal. Many Easterners moved to the western frontier where they hoped to prosper while maintaining greater control over their immediate economic circumstance. In addition, new settlers came from Europe seeking the same prosperity. The strategically important location of Chicago with reference to Great Lakes transportation led to its early growth, although it came into existence in August of 1810 with only 150 inhabitants.

Land offices were established in the northern part of Illinois in the early 1830s, and a major land boom followed in 1836. Guidebooks circulated in the East proclaimed the ease of farming in the Illinois country. Galena in the far northwest had been established much earlier as a lead mining center. Although most of the mineral was shipped south via the Mississippi, overland connections to the East were forthcoming. This helped to open the agricultural land all across the northern sector. Unfortunately, the land boom, vigorous speculation, and plotting of numerous paper towns led to an economic depression in 1837, which slowed settlement throughout the West. Further settlement after the 1837 depression was spurred by the building of the Illinois and Michigan Canal to connect the Great Lakes and Chicago with the Mississippi system, the appearance of the first railroads, and the building of plank roads.

In 1833 Alton in the southwest was the state's largest city, but increased settlement in the north (Fig. 4-4A) was fast shifting the population balance. By 1845 the largest city was Nauvoo (Hancock County), settled by a colony of Mormons. Other colonies were planted in Illinois, although most settlers arrived singly or in family groups. By 1850 counties in the northern part of the state

northern Illinois, often turning in that direction after a westward journey on the National Road, Indian problems both stemmed the advance and caused a southward retreat. The Winnebago War of 1827 and the later Blackhawk War sent most of the settlers in northern Illinois to areas south of the Illinois River.

After the 1832 Battle of Bad Axe in Wisconsin settled the problems with Blackhawk's Indians, a new group of pioneers, directly from the northern and middle colonies, reached northern and central Illinois. Unlike the restless southern hunter-pioneers, they came to establish permanent roots. There was a general land rush helped by the

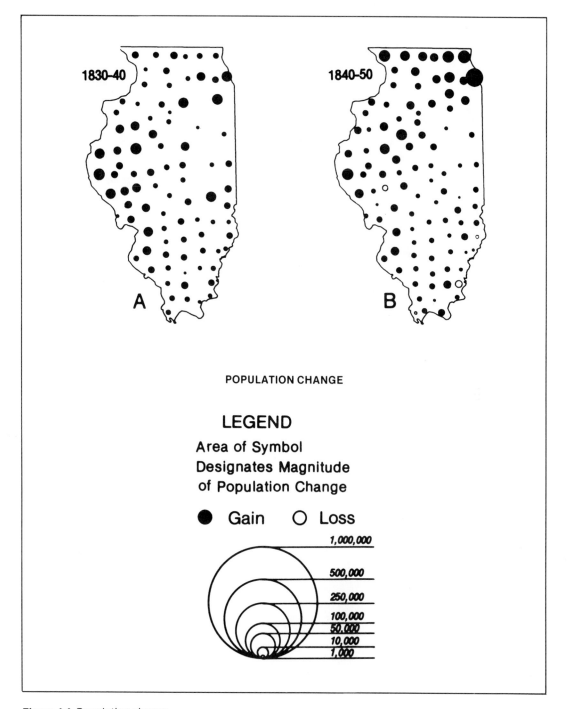

Figure 4-4. Population change.

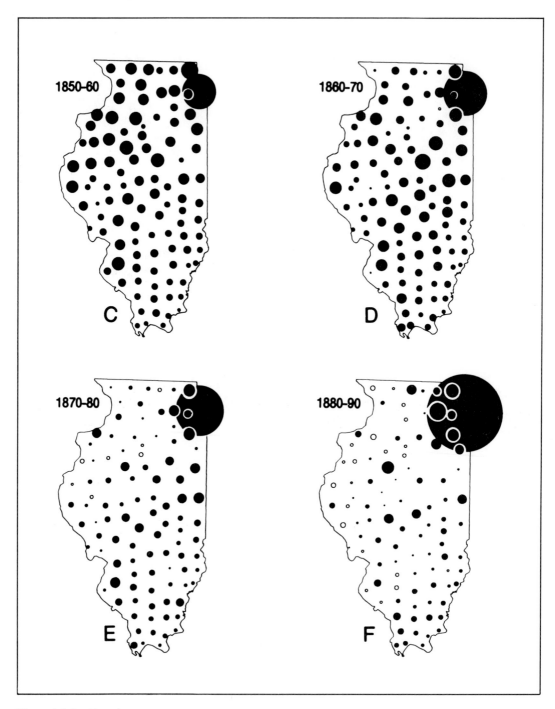

Figure 4-4. Continued.

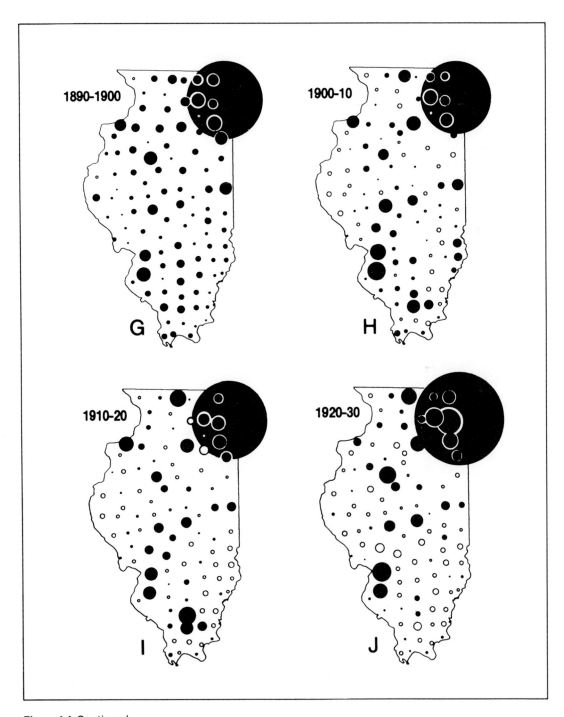

Figure 4-4. Continued.

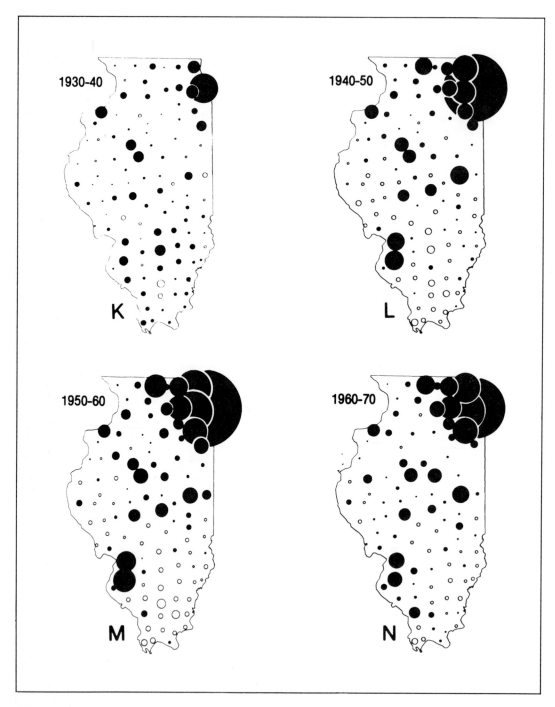

Figure 4-4. Continued.

were growing considerably faster than those in the south, but the growth was not uniform. Especially striking was the contrast between the sizable growth of both the northernmost counties and the Military Tract of west-central Illinois and the very small population increase in the ill-drained Grand Prairie of the east-central section.

With the 1850s, Illinois ceased to be part of the frontier as the leading edge of settlement had disappeared westward. Now, industrialization from the East became established in Illinois, especially in Chicago. A conscious statewide effort to push the growth of Illinois towns and cities, while doing little to aid those of other states, allowed Chicago to attain supremacy in the western part of the United States.[5] For example, Illinoisans supported Alton at the expense of St. Louis; consequently St. Louis was somewhat restricted in its growth, and Chicago benefitted. Continued transporta-

tion improvements both made increased rural settlement feasible and brought to Illinois new settlers who worked as laborers on the construction of new transport facilities. Large numbers of Europeans came to Illinois, many taking up residence in Chicago. Especially numerous in the 1850s were Irish and Germans. By 1860 the recent growth resulted in foreign-born outnumbering the native-born.[6] Not all new settlers stayed in Illinois; some moved farther west, but the newcomers always outnumbered those leaving the state.

In 1857, eleven railroad main lines radiated from Chicago and served in transporting immigrants to unsettled land and collecting produce from developing farms. Chicago's success was assured with the Missouri River crossing at Omaha of the Union Pacific, pointing toward the first transcontinental route and the Illinois city's development into the nation's leading

Figure 4-5. The restored home of Mormon Prophet Joseph Smith on the bank of the Mississippi River in Nauvoo. Although it was the largest city in Illinois in 1845, Nauvoo soon was abandoned by the colony of Mormons following the murder of Smith and the destruction of their temple. (Photo by Ronald E. Nelson.)

railroad center. In the 1850s and 1860s, Chicago's growth was supported not only by immigration but also by its use of raw materials from the Great Lakes area for industrialization.

The real estate boom of the 1830s was duplicated in the 1850s. In 1849, 40 percent of the state was still public land, but within six years almost all the remaining public domain passed to private owners.[7] Still, part of the state remained unoccupied as many thousands of acres were held by speculators. Realizing that woodlots were not a necessity, farmers settled increasingly on the open prairie, especially with the aid of new implements. As the railroads came into ownership of public land, they also entered into the business of selling land. The various lines often employed agents who met newly arriving settlers and promoted sales of their own lands. First wheat, then corn proved to yield well on the prairie; and, as the fertility of thinner soil in southern Illinois began to become evident, emphasis was placed on the better soil in the northern half of the state. Even those counties of the ill-drained Grand Prairie began to grow with construction of the Illinois Central Railroad.

Many towns began as stations on rail lines, and those that prospered grew at the expense of those not so located. The railroads also put long-distance drovers out of business and made Chicago the nation's leading livestock market. The bankers of that city, who supported the market developments, assisted in financing the development of new farm implements as well as new farms. In addition, Chicago established the

Figure 4-6. The remains of a nineteenth century farmer's cabin in Henry County, Illinois. (Photo by Ronald E. Nelson.)

Board of Trade which standardized the grain market and constituted the country's leading lumber market. All of this activity provided many jobs in Chicago, which led to large population growth especially in the 1850s (Fig. 4-4C). Small shops became factories using mass production methods as the Industrial Revolution made itself felt in the midlands of America. The state developed into an economic leader and its combination of agriculture, industry, and transportation engendered attitudes not sympathetic to the South's slave labor cotton economy.

Civil War and Recovery, 1860-1880

At the start of the Civil War, Illinois was suffering the depressed economic conditions affecting most of the United States, but three years of poor crops in Europe and military buying spurred the economy. In addition, many small-town production plants moved to Chicago, contributing to its concentration of trade and industry.[8] The uniform growth of Illinois counties in the 1850s and 1860s changed with the beginning of the 1870s. While the growth of rural counties declined from the previous decade, Cook County more than doubled in size, a rather remarkable event considering the Great Chicago Fire of 1871 and the Panic of 1873. By 1880, Chicago was the nation's fourth largest city.[9]

Following the Civil War, a rural depression led to migration both to newer lands in the West and, even more, to Chicago. Illinois from 1860 to 1890 produced more corn and wheat than any other state.[10] Following 1890, wheat was produced increasingly in the Great Plains, but Illinois and Iowa continued planting ever greater amounts of corn, aggravating the problems of oversupply and lower prices. These conditions resulted in third political parties culminating in the Populist Movement.

European Immigration, Industrialization, and Urbanization, 1880-1910

The period beginning in 1880 was characterized by heavy immigration to Chicago, the state's primary industrial center. Increasingly, the new arrivals came from northern, then eastern and southern Europe. Chicago's industrial power grew with production of Minnesota's iron ore (accessible by lake transportation) and nearby supplies of coal. The rail net brought agricultural produce for processing by the city's growing labor supply drawn from its farming hinterland as well as from Europe. Mechanization on the state's farms released population from the land, often in the richest agricultural counties. Thus, while most of Illinois' downstate counties grew, 31 lost population in the 1880s (Fig. 4-4F).[11] The state's population changed from 69.4 percent rural in 1880 to 55.1 percent rural in 1890.[12] In addition to Chicago, some downstate cities also grew in commercial and industrial importance; several of these were mining centers.

General prosperity returned to the nation beginning about 1900, but even the previous decade was one of economic gain for Chicago and the state of Illinois (Fig. 4-4G). Whereas other more totally agrarian states suffered depressed times, the economic diversity in Illinois coupled with its fortuitous location allowed for economic advancement.[13] The problems faced by farmers, largely brought about by overproduction of crops, culminated in the so-called Populist Revolt, which was especially active in the 1890s. But while some counties in west-central and northwestern Illinois lost population, most of Illinois grew as the changes of the previous decade stabilized. Still, by 1900 Illinois' rural population had dropped to 45.7 percent.[14]

In the face of the depressed conditions of

the early 1890s, Chicago held the Columbian Exposition which, among other things, publicized the city's technological and cultural achievements. In an address given during the exhibition, historian Frederick Jackson Turner pronounced the end of the frontier in America. The effects of that statement have been the subject of much discussion and speculation with regard to further westward movement.

The general prosperity and urban growth of the first decade of the twentieth century was accompanied by population loss in 56 of the 102 Illinois counties. Again, technological improvements in agriculture implements released farm labor (Fig. 4-4H). Much of the wet prairie was drained as drainage districts were formed. Many of the new farms as well as some of those already established were tenant operated. Yellow dent corn and purebred animals became important, bringing more prosperity to the fewer farmers needed to work the land. At the same time the downstate urban and coal mining centers experienced population growth, though considerably more modest than that of Chicago.

World War I and Migration from the South, 1910-1930

Heavy immigrant flow from eastern and southern Europe continued for the first 30 years of the twentieth century. Beginning about 1915, migrants from the American South added to the Illinois population mixture, though not without serious social consequences. Labor shortages during World War I led to the importation of southern blacks. This movement maintained a steadily increasing flow as economic opportunities in Illinois industry constituted a strong pull. (A compilation in 1914 showed important industry in 35 cities of downstate Illinois.[15]) Racial tension, then open racial warfare,

resulted at both Chicago and East St. Louis. Nonetheless, the black population of Chicago more than doubled between 1910 and 1920.

To meet the war effort, very high agricultural and industrial production was needed. This production was realized even though many rural counties continued to lose population. These losses plus Chicago's continued large gains led to the sectionalism which had been building before 1910 and is still in evidence in the 1970s. Downstate feelings, manifesting themselves in Illinois' politics, grew out of a distrust of Chicago and a fear that the city would dominate the rest of the state. Friction between the industrial and ethnically cosmopolitan metropolis and the traditional rural counties became increasingly evident.

Overseas immigration was virtually stopped after the war, but the northward movement of southern blacks continued to increase. The boll weevil had decimated much of the cotton lands of the South, contributing to a surplus of rural labor in that region. With continued industrial growth, especially in Chicago, jobs were available in the North to attract the large labor supply of the South. Chicago's black population rose to 4.1 percent in 1920 and 6.9 percent in 1930.[16] The blacks were squeezed into a definite zone on the south side of the city, one of the factors keeping racial tensions alive.

The decline and demise of small towns in Illinois continued as the means of transport were improved. Electric interurban lines were constructed, beginning about 1900. Towns not served by railroads had suffered, and this trend was accentuated by establishment of the interurbans. With the arrival of the auto and better roads, a new dimension was added, but results were much the same. Passenger railroads and trolleys were used less often. At the same time, the auto en-

Figure 4-7. The main thoroughfare of Roseville, a small town in western Illinois. (Courtesy Donald W. Griffin.)

abled farmers and villagers to travel to larger places where a more extensive array of goods and services was available. The continuing loss of business in small towns hastened their decline. In large urban centers, especially Chicago, the inner city became blighted. Auto transport, just as the street car before it, enabled the working population to commute from suburban residential locations. This sizable suburban growth is suggested in Figure 4-4J.

The increased demand for coal to supply industrial and domestic fuel needs supported population growth in some mining areas during the early part of the century. This is especially evident in extreme south-central Illinois where exploitation of coal deposits in the Marion-Benton area stimulated large increases in population during the decade 1910-1920. On the other hand, the much more modest growth of Franklin County and considerable loss of population in Williamson County in the 1920s (Fig. 4-4J)

reflect the ephemeral nature of mining centers the world over. Both mechanization and the depletion of easily mined deposits were primary factors.

In general, urban Illinoisans enjoyed a high standard of living in the 1920s, but the living standard of farmers did not keep pace with that of urban workers. Thus, 63 counties lost population in the third decade of the twentieth century.

The Depression, 1930-1940

As a consequence of the Great Depression, the migration of Illinois' center of population reversed itself for the only time between 1930 and 1940 (Fig. 4-1). Likewise, Figure 4-4K reflects a reversal of earlier trends. The vast urban growth of the previous decade virtually ceased. In addition, many downstate counties that had suffered a population loss in the 1920s now were the recipients of modest gains, results of a general "back-to-the-farm" movement characteristic of the Depression. In contrast to the previous decade, only 26 counties experienced population losses, and these were generally very small. Illinois population growth, which had been 17.7 percent in the previous decade, was only 3.5 percent in the period 1930-1940. Rural growth actually outpaced urban, 4.6 percent to 3.1 percent.[17]

Unemployment reached approximately 1.5 million during the Depression, and 277,000 families received relief.[18] Immigration was restricted. Chicago lost its economic attractiveness and building construction came to a standstill. Federal relief agencies provided some jobs, followed by the Civil Works Administration, replaced in 1935 by the WPA. For some who lost their city jobs, a return to relatives or friends in a rural location meant at least subsistence and avoiding the degrading aspects of the dole.

Urbanization and Suburbanization, 1940-1970

Although better times began to emerge in the late 1930s, prosperity returned to Illinois as rumors of war stimulated the economy. Domestic war effort requirements found many willing workers. While one million of the state's citizens took an active part in World War II, federal spending in Illinois provided local employment for those who remained on the home front. In some cases labor shortages resulted and the number of blacks migrating northward once again helped fill the need. An estimated 100,000 black Americans moved during World War II to Chicago, where their employment increased from 4.9 percent to 11.7 percent in five years.[19]

Out of the suffering of the Depression, more scientific farming methods emerged. Though the number of farms decreased,

conservation techniques helped develop better farms. Levee and farm drainage districts enabled 88.3 percent of Illinois to be used for cultivation, the largest proportion of tilled land for any state. Illinois farms produced record crops. The state ranked first in soybeans; second in corn, hogs, and cheese; fourth in livestock; and it was an important producer of several other farm commodities. In 1945, thirteen counties in north central Illinois were listed among the leading 100 American counties in value of farm products.[20] That this great production was accompanied by increased mechanization is evident in Figure 4-4L. Many counties, especially in west central and southeast Illinois, lost population in the 1940-1950 decade when a postwar loss of export markets and dwindling prices led to a call for reduced plantings.

The return of peace found Illinois more firmly established than before as a manufacturing state, reversing the back-to-the-farm population movement. While certain Chicago industries lost importance (notably the decentralized meat packing industry), others readily absorbed the skilled and unskilled workers who remained. By 1950, Illinois was fourth in the nation in population, but a strong third in manufacturing. Value added by manufacturing was $6.68 billion, up from $2.1 billion in 1939.[21] Large wartime factories were taken over by corporations in the private sector. The massive growth of Chicago and suburbs, and to a lesser extent, the growth in downstate manufacturing centers is readily apparent in Figure 4-4L. (The growth of Champaign County also reflects the large number of veterans who became students.)

The dominant growth of Cook County and Chicago suburban counties during the 1950s is evident in Figure 4-4M. Jobs in the Chicago area continued to exercise a powerful attraction. The new immigrants were from the American South, Europe, and Latin America. As Chicago's suburbs became the recipients of those who were seeking the good life away from the more crowded and pluralistic city, the new arrivals took up inner city housing of former residents. Population pressure in Latin America, especially Puerto Rico and Mexico, hastened the decision to migrate. In the 1950s, Cook County had more people than the other 101 counties combined. The city of Chicago actually lost population between 1950-1960, but the city's suburbs gained 77 percent in the same period.[22] Elsewhere, growth continued in countries which contained medium to large urban populations and where industrial activity shared in the prosperous American economy.

Those counties which did not share in the urban-oriented job market lost further numbers as the trend toward greater agricultural mechanization continued. Once again, the counties experiencing greatest loss were in the southeast and west-central parts of the state. Beginning in the late 1890s, a county growth pattern emerged which still held in 1960 and continues at the present time. Three major zones of growth are: (1) the northeast, expanding outward from Chicago as population numbers and transportation permit; (2) an east-west axis in central Illinois which splits into two branches toward the west; and (3) the suburban St. Louis area in Illinois. Areas of population loss have been in the aforementioned west-central and southeastern parts of the state. Separating the northeast and central sections of continued growth is an area of population stability. An examination of Figures 4-4G through 4-4N shows that only a few notable exceptions altered the dominant pattern.

By 1970, Illinois ranked fifth in population; third place had been taken by Califor-

nia in 1950 and fourth place by Texas in 1970. The state's population increased 10.2 percent in the 1960s, becoming 82.9 percent urban and 13.6 percent nonwhite in 1970.[23] The rush to suburban fringes in the urban northeast continued in the 1960s, and by 1971 Chicago had more than 180 suburban municipalities. The inner city's inhabitants continued to be black Americans and other recent arrivals. Chicago's black population rose from 10 percent in 1950 and 14 percent in 1960 to 32.7 percent in 1970. Spanish-speaking newcomers constituted 10 to 15 percent of the city's people.[24] Appalachian whites and American Indians were among other minorities in the nation's second largest city. Meanwhile, 40 percent of the population of the second largest United States county lived outside the city of Chicago.[25] The growth went beyond the county, and for the first time since 1920, a majority of Illinoisans in 1970 no longer lived in Cook County. However, those counties showing the greatest increases outside Cook were also in the northeast. Of the state's 19 municipalities over 50,000, seven were in suburban Cook County and four others were in nearby counties. Downstate, the largest growth in the 1960s was again in those counties with sizable cities. Almost one-half of the state's counties (49) again lost population, mostly in areas that had been losing for some time.

In the late 1960s, environmental agencies began to stem the unbridled growth of industry. This constituted another of a growing list of institutions to be financed in the 1970s with a tax base seemingly not large enough. Changes in the 1960s also were associated with the new superhighway system. Whole new suburbs and housing subdivisions were created along the transport arteries, enabling workers to commute greater distances to their jobs. Downstate villages declined, hotels were replaced by motels, and city centers decayed as outlying shopping centers flourished. Nevertheless, Illinois' advantageous location along with its strong balance of agriculture and industry seemingly assures the state's future economic viability.

Present Social and Population Patterns

The following discussion of the present population and social patterns of Illinois is subdivided into five major categories: demographic factors, race and ethnicity, mobility, economy, and population distribution. The interrelationship of these factors is illustrated in Figure 4-8, which implies that ethnic and racial characteristics (together with population distribution) determine, at least in part, the demographic mix and economic makeup of the population. Economic conditions influence mobility rates and, in turn, economically healthy areas attract migrants. On the other hand, since ethnicity and racial status is an inherited trait, it is not determined by any of the other elements of the diagram, with the exception that certain areas attract ethnic and racial minorities. Although other interpretations exist, the illustration depicts the major

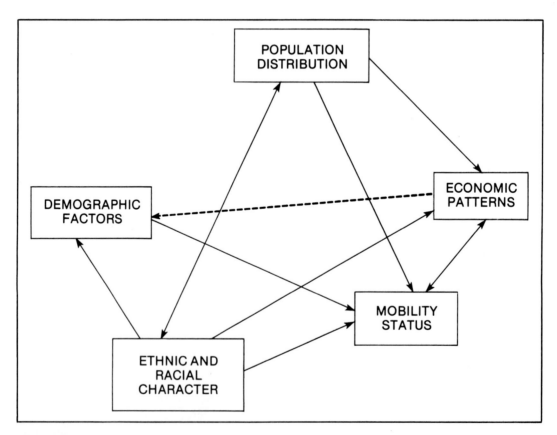

Figure 4-8. The cause-effect relationships among five major aspects of the social and population characteristics of Illinois.

causal interrelationships among the variables.

To better understand the role of the five variables, each will be examined in detail. The sequence of examination will be (1) population distribution, (2) economic patterns, (3) mobility status, (4) ethnic and racial character, and (5) demographic factors.

Population Distribution

As stated previously, the population distribution of Illinois is dominated by Chicago. Indeed, Cook County has had approximately half of the state's population since 1920. As the peripheral urban expansion of Chicago has spread into surrounding counties, however, Cook County's share of the state's population has begun to decline, from 51.8 percent in 1950 to 49.4 percent in 1970.[26] Still, the Chicago SMSA (six-county area) is by far the state's major concentration of population. In fact among all the states, Illinois has the greatest ratio between its largest and second largest cities. Chicago is definitely the prime city of Illinois, dominating the economic, social, and to a lesser degree the political life of the state.

It is important to note, since it is often neglected, that the Illinois segment of the St. Louis SMSA is the state's second largest *urban agglomeration* with a population approximately twice that of the Rockford SMSA (Table 4-2). Although the city of Rockford is the second largest in the state, its SMSA ranks only fourth behind that of Chicago, St. Louis, and Peoria. These four areas head the list of nine recognized by the U.S. Bureau of the Census as metropolitan areas, each with a central city containing a population of at least 50,000. Thus, although LaSalle County's population of 111,409 exceeds that of Macon County

Table 4-2. Population of Standard Metropolitan Statistical Areas Within Illinois.

SMSA	1970 Population
Chicago	6,974,906
St. Louis	536,110
Peoria	341,979
Rockford	271,938
Rock Island-Moline	219,941
Champaign-Urbana	163,281
Springfield	161,335
Decatur	125,010
Bloomington-Normal	104,389

(Bloomington-Normal SMSA), it is not a metropolitan area since the largest cities— Ottawa, Streator, Peru, and LaSalle—do not have populations greater than 50,000 nor do they meet other criteria of proximity.

It is evident that even in agricultural areas of downstate Illinois, most of the population resides in urban centers; in most counties over half of the inhabitants reside in urban communities (Fig. 4-9).[27] For the state as a whole, 83 percent of the population is urban (incorporated places with more than 2,500 inhabitants). Nevertheless, thirteen counties are without communities that qualify for classification as urban, and another nine have populations that are less than 30 percent urban. On the other end of the scale, Cook with 99.7 percent, DuPage 95.3 percent, Kane 87.5 percent, Rock Island 85.7 percent, Winnebago 85.1 percent, Peoria 83.9 percent, and St. Clair 83.2 percent urban are the only counties that exceed the percentage for the state.

The rural population falls into two categories, farm and rural nonfarm. Being an agricultural state, much of the rural population, at least in areas distant from metropolitan centers, is on farms. Generally speaking, the farm population distribution

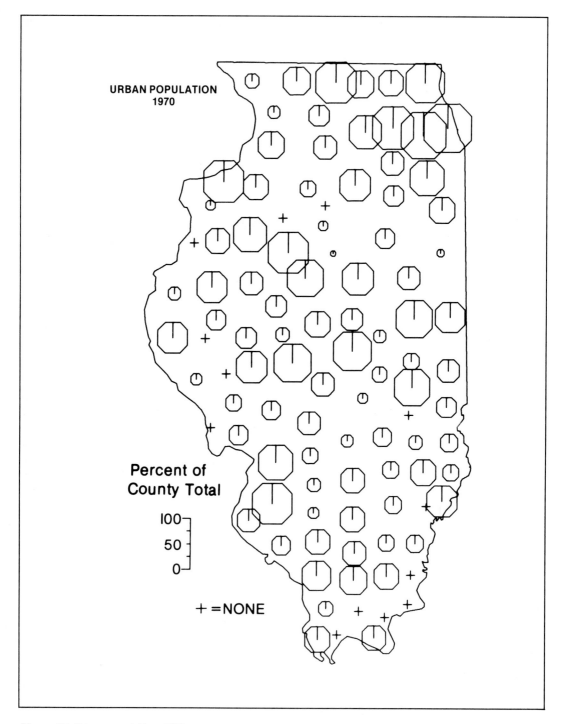

URBAN POPULATION
1970

Percent of
County Total

100
50
0

+ =NONE

Figure 4-9. Urban population, 1970.

complements the manufacturing-urban distribution. As a percent of the total population, farmers are most dominant away from the major transportation diagonal between Chicago and St. Louis in the west-central and southeastern parts of the state (Fig. 4-10). It is important to recognize, however, that several counties have small percentages residing on the farm only because they also contain large nonfarm populations.

The size of the farm population has, of course, declined as machinery has replaced manual labor and farms have become larger in size although fewer in number (Fig. 4-11). In fact, there was a 23.8 percent drop in the Illinois farm population between 1960 and 1970, leaving less than 4 percent of the total population on farms (Table 4-3). The decline in farm population is an almost statewide phenomenon with only two counties, Massac and Kankakee, registering increases. The greatest percentage decreases are in the southern portion of the state, an area long troubled by a decrease in mining jobs, high unemployment rates, and general economic depression.

The large decline of the farm population in Cook and DuPage counties, 71 percent and 62 percent respectively, represents urban pressures on the remaining agricultural enterprises. Other counties in the Chicago SMSA will feel similar pressures in future decades. There are presently 26,584 farm residents in the Chicago SMSA. Although

only approximately 2,500 of these are in Cook and DuPage counties, the average number of farmers for the six counties as a whole is higher than the state average. There is an obvious advantage in proximity to the enormous Chicago market. This attraction will continue to cluster farmers, especially those involved in market gardening, on the urban fringe.

Economic Patterns

The economic vitality of Illinois is based on the state's diversity and geographic location. Containing the center of the United States population (located 5.3 miles east-southeast of Mascoutah in St. Clair County), Illinois enjoys a strategic economic advantage over other states. Numerous national firms have, therefore, chosen Illinois for their base of operations. Chicago is the headquarters for many national corporations, while major manufacturing and processing plants are scattered throughout the state. This industrial base is complemented by rich agricultural resources and energy resources in southern Illinois. This healthy mix of activities has made the state one of the consistent leaders in per capita income. In 1960 it ranked fourth in per capita income and second only to Connecticut in increase in per capita income between 1950 and 1965.[28]

The economic prosperity, however, is not a spatially uniform phenomenon but one which is geographically rather selective. As a generalization, the southern section of the state has not fared as well as the northern areas. Indeed, unemployment rates are highest in the extreme southern counties. The primary economic base of the area, coal mining and farming, has experienced a precipitous decline. As the farmers and coal miners lost their source of income, they bought fewer goods and services. This, in

Table 4-3. Farm, Rural, and Urban Population in Illinois, 1960 and 1970 (population in thousands).

	1960		1970	
Rural		1,941		1,884
Farm	564		428	
Nonfarm	1,376		1,455	
Urban		8,140		9,230
Total		10,081		11,114

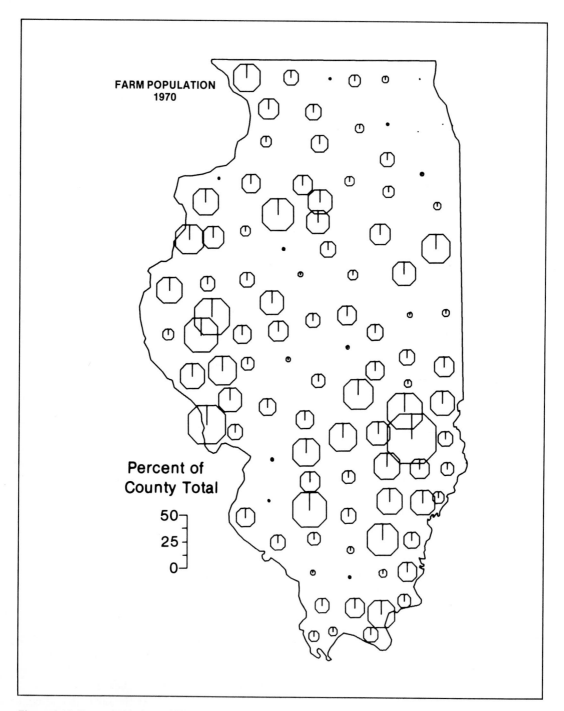

Figure 4-10. Farm population, 1970.

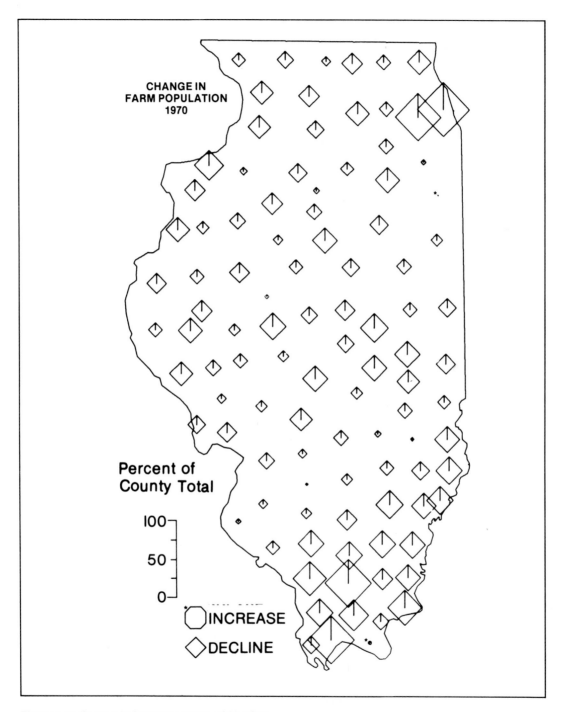

CHANGE IN
FARM POPULATION
1970

Percent of
County Total

100
50
0

◯ INCREASE
◇ DECLINE

Figure 4-11. Change in farm population, 1960–1970.

Figure 4-12. Elderly farmers, in moving to town for their retirement years, have contributed to the decline of farm population. (Courtesy Donald W. Griffin.)

turn, caused unemployment in the retail and service sectors of the economy. Thus the beginnings of a downward spiral have been initiated, and eventually almost all sectors of the economy will be affected, causing a local economic depression and widespread unemployment. The metropolitan St. Louis area is the only major exception to a uniformly high unemployment rate in the southern one-third of the state. Indeed, four of the five counties with the highest rates, Pope (11 percent), Massac (10.5 percent), Alexander (8.3 percent), and Gallatin (8.1 percent), are located at the southern tip of the state. Cumberland (8.2 percent), the exception, is an agricultural county near Effingham and Mattoon. At the other end of the scale, two of the four lowest unemployment rates are among Chicago area counties: Kendall with 1.7 percent and DuPage with 2.1 percent. Generally, unemployment rates are lower in metropolitan areas where economic opportunities are more numerous.

It must be cautioned that these rates are for a specific time and are subject to changes, although often very slowly. For instance, both DuPage and Kendall had 1960 unemployment rates within 0.3 percent of their 1970 rate. But the rates can and do change significantly during a decade. Many of the southern counties had 1970 unemployment rates considerably lower than those of 1960. Examples of the decline are Pulaski, 10.5 to 3.9 percent; Franklin, 12.7 to 6.8 percent; Williamson, 9.4 to 5.8 percent; and Saline, 9.9 to 5.4 percent. Some remained the same (Hardin and White), while several along the Ohio River showed increases (Massac, 7.9 to 10.5 percent and Gallatin, 6.9 to 8.1 percent). During the 1960-70 period the statewide unemployment rate registered a drop from 4.5 to 3.7 percent.

The income pattern resembles the unemployment picture with the southern counties having the greatest percentage of families below the poverty level (Fig. 4-13).

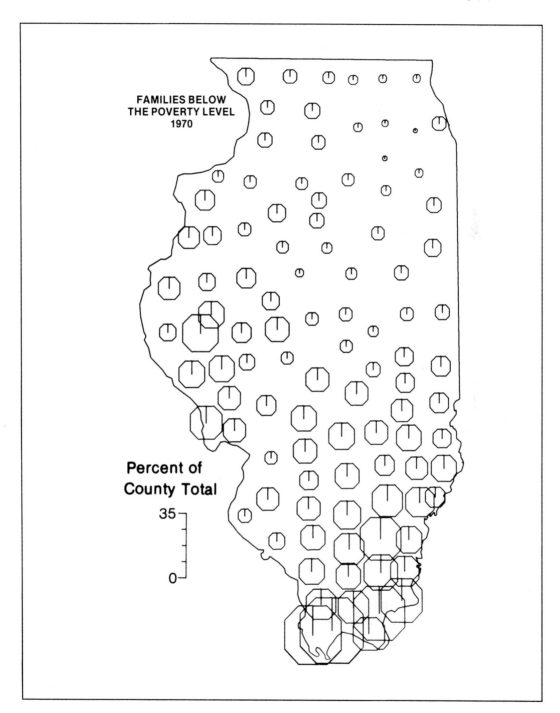

FAMILIES BELOW
THE POVERTY LEVEL
1970

Percent of
County Total

35

0

Figure 4-13. Families below the poverty level, 1970.

Six counties have more than one-fifth of their families with subpoverty incomes; Pulaski (35.7 percent), Alexander (31.8 percent), Pope (29.3 percent), Hardin (23.7 percent), and Hamilton (23.4 percent) lead the list. In contrast, the state average is 7.7 percent.

Cook County, with its large minority populations, has only 7.6 percent of its families with subpoverty incomes and DuPage County has only 2.3 percent, the lowest in the state. These figures indicate that poverty is less common in urban than in rural areas. Because of high density of poor people in some sectors of Chicago, the visual impact of urban poverty is striking. Nevertheless, on a per capita basis the poor rural counties have rates approximately four times those of Cook County, although the latter has the greatest total concentration of impoverished inhabitants. It should be noted that the figures do not refer to a fixed annual income, such as $3,000, but relate to a poverty level based on family size and the cost of living.

Both poverty and unemployment are nearly absent in counties with considerable wealth (Fig. 4-14). The families with 1970 incomes over $25,000, comprising only approximately 6 percent of the total families in the state, are an indication of such wealth. Two suburban counties, Lake and DuPage, with 12.5 and 10.9 percent of their families above that income level, head the list. Cook and McHenry are the only other counties above the state average. These figures indicate the potential for high incomes in the Chicago area, but they also suggest a vivid contrast between the families with high and low incomes.

The level of education achieved is an indicator of at least potential income and tends to regularize incomes. The percent of the population with four or more years of college can be used to show the pattern of educational level in Illinois. Although counties with major universities dominate the pattern, the Chicago metropolitan area is uniformly high, particularly the two suburban counties, DuPage and Lake. On the other hand, the southern one-third of the state—with the exception of the Carbondale area—is characterized by a low percentage of college graduates. This suggests that the educated from this area are drawn away, either to opportunities out of the state or to the industrial and service oriented economies of northern Illinois. It, thus, strengthens the economic disparity between the southern and northern halves of the state. Whether the industrial-education complex, in the long run, sufficiently benefits the areas from which it draws manpower to merit these concentrations is a point of dispute among regional geographers and economists. To be sure, the welfare of the southern counties improves with increased affluence in the urban areas of the north, but whether the income gap increases or decreases hinges on the extent to which the urban areas are dependent upon the southern counties for raw materials, agricultural products, recreational facilities, and other resources. Obviously coal mining has served as an important economic linkage between areas in the south and the north, but in time new dependencies are established.

The economic variations, then, can be summarized as prosperity in many of the urban and rural counties in the north and at least a short-term recession in the southern one-third of the state. Many of the southern counties, however, are displaying signs of recovery from the depression in the mining industry with current reemphasis on coal.

Mobility Status

Economic variations in the state are also reflected in migration patterns, since the

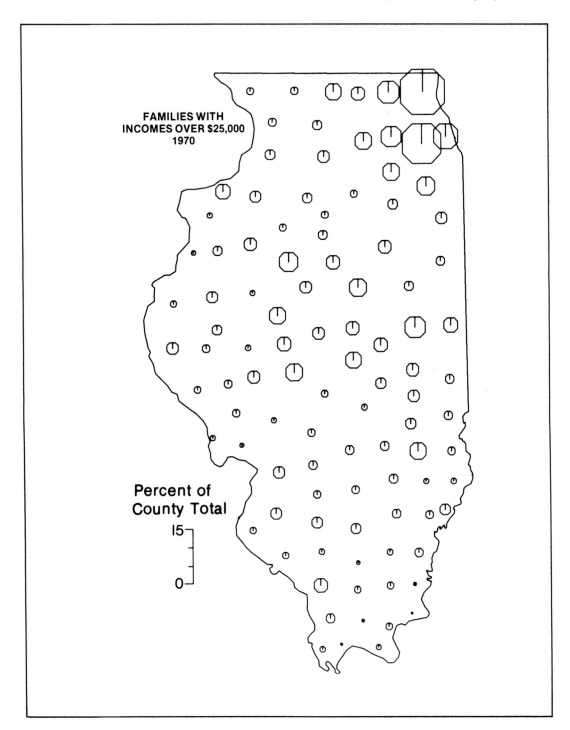

**FAMILIES WITH
INCOMES OVER $25,000
1970**

Percent of
County Total

15

0

Figure 4-14. Families with incomes over $25,000, 1970.

economically viable areas attract migrants from the less prosperous areas. The net migration map (Fig. 4-15) clearly shows that the majority of Illinois counties are experiencing a net outflow of population. Indeed, seven counties lost more than 10 percent of their 1960 population by 1970. (Alexander County headed the list with a loss of 25.5 percent.) On the other hand, a population gain resulting from a net in-migration was recorded by the suburban Chicago counties and urban areas downstate. Outside the northeast, counties with major universities such as Jackson (Southern Illinois University), McLean (Illinois State University), and McDonough (Western Illinois University) had the most pronounced growth from net migration.

In other counties with population growth the gains are attributable strictly to the natural increase in population. In fact, 18 counties with population gains between 1960 and 1970 experienced net migration losses. For instance, more people moved out of Cook County than moved in, but it still had a 7.1 percent population increase—an addition of over 350,000 inhabitants. Likewise, Kankakee County had a 5.6 percent population increase despite a net migration loss of 6.4 percent.

A large segment of the recent migrants to Illinois have come from southern states, although the pattern of inhabitants of southern nativity is notably irregular (Fig. 4-16). For instance, less than 1.5 percent of the residents of Jo Daviess, Calhoun, Jasper, and Schuyler counties were born in the South, whereas in four of the southernmost counties more than 14 percent of the inhabitants are from the South. St. Clair and Champaign counties also have high percentages of southern-born.

Although migration from the South to the North has subsided over the last two decades, the United States population remains an exceedingly mobile one. Over 40 percent of the 1970 Illinois population resided in a different location in 1965, and many of these persons probably moved several times during this period. A willingness to move has enabled many people to improve their economic conditions while providing employers with qualified personnel. The attainment of approximate regional balances in the supply of and demand for labor has significantly strengthened the economy of both Illinois and the United States, although geographic variations in employment rates have not been eliminated.

Ethnic and Racial Characteristics

One of the distinctive features of the Illinois population is its ethnic and racial mix. The state has approximately 1.4 million blacks and 2.2 million inhabitants of foreign stock.[29] The blacks are mainly concentrated in the urban areas; over 90 percent live in the St. Louis and Chicago metropolitan areas. Still other concentrations are found, particularly in Pulaski and Alexander counties which have the highest percentages of blacks, 34 and 28 percent respectively (Fig. 4-17). In terms of absolute numbers, the following counties have more than 10,000 blacks: Champaign, Cook, Kankakee, Lake, Madison, Peoria, St. Clair, Will, and Winnebago. While the number of blacks is increasing in most areas, the southern Illinois counties of Alexander, Massac, Pulaski, and Saline have been experiencing a decline. During 1960-1970 there was a net emigration of over 3,000 blacks from these four counties. This represented a 27 percent decrease

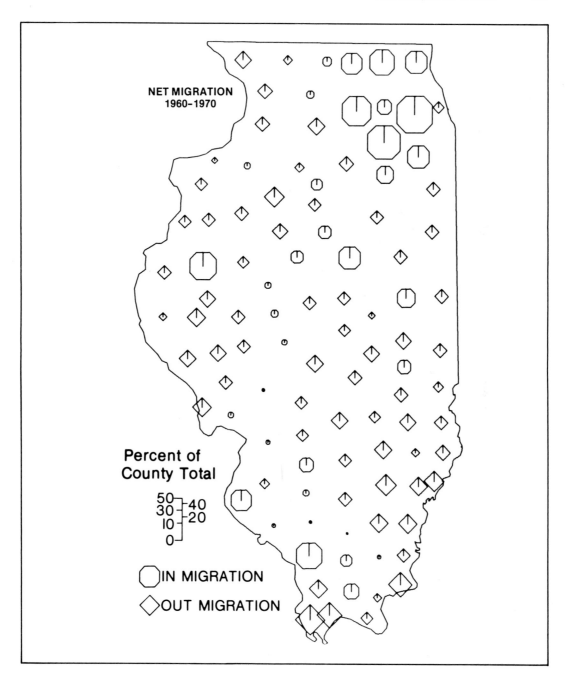

Figure 4-15. Net migration, 1960–1970.

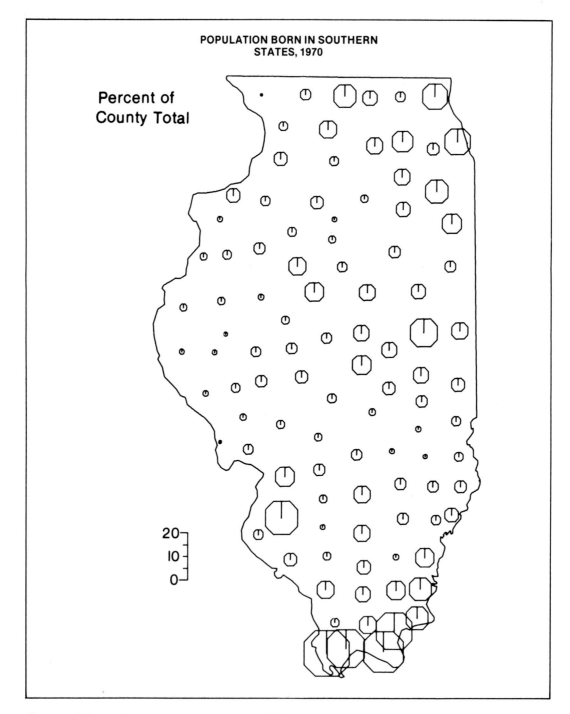

Figure 4-16. Population born in southern states, 1970.

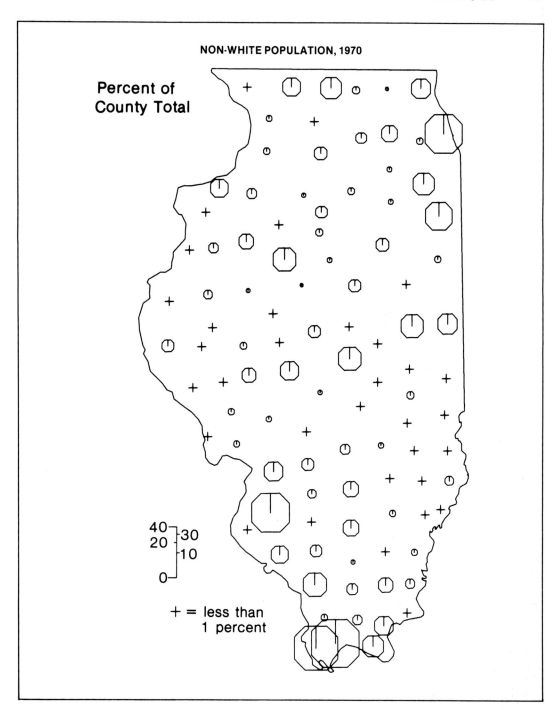

Figure 4-17. Non-white population, 1970.

in their number of blacks while their total population decreased by approximately 10 percent.

Many of the ethnic patterns in Illinois include an even greater degree of clustering (Fig. 4-18). In fact, the Chicago area has a greater relative concentration of foreign-born than blacks. Foreign immigrants to Illinois in most cases have been destined for the Chicago area. Cook County has large ethnic minorities with Poles outnumbering other groups (Fig. 4-19). In most other areas in Illinois, people of German origin clearly outnumber other ethnic populations. Several exceptions, however, break the German dominance. One is a six-county area in the Rock Island-Moline vicinity where over 5,000 first and second generation Swedes represent the dominant ethnic group. Even more Swedes (11,400) are concentrated in Winnebago County (Rockford). Two significant Italian areas are also easily discernible. One is along the Illinois River and includes Bureau, Putnam, Grundy, and Will counties. With approximately 8,500 inhabitants of Italian stock, this area exceeds the southern Illinois concentration of 2,000 Italians in Franklin and Williamson counties. The only other ethnic group which displays territorial prominence is the British. Primarily in McDonough and Fulton counties, they number fewer than 1,000. Nevertheless, people of British stock form the largest ethnic group in this western Illinois area.

In sharp contrast is the Chicago area where over a million first and second generation immigrants reside in the city and another half million in the remainder of Cook County. In the city are approximately 200,000 Poles and 100,000 Germans and Italians. Although the Lithuanian total is not reported separately by the Census, it is one of the largest groups. There are also large numbers (over 50,000) of Swedes, Irish, British, Czechs, Canadians, Mexicans, Puerto Ricans, Austrians, and Yugoslavs. Chicago's Spanish-speaking population is growing rapidly. Approximately three-quarters of the 350,000 persons of Spanish heritage in Illinois live in Cook County. In addition, a sizeable number of American Indians live in the Chicago area. These and other ethnic groups total 28.4 percent of the county's population. DuPage, Lake, and McHenry are the only other counties with foreign stock representing over 19 percent of the total population. The six Chicago metropolitan counties, in fact, are among the leading seven counties in the state in terms of percentage of foreign stock.

In addition to Chicago's distinct ethnic neighborhoods, several suburbs have disproportionately large ethnic populations. For instance, Berwyn (45 percent foreign stock) is characterized by a sizeable Czech population, and neighboring Cicero (36 percent foreign stock) has large groups of Italians, Czechs, and Poles. In addition, Skokie has a large population of Russian extraction among the 44 percent of its inhabitants of foreign stock. These national and racial groups give both the Chicago area and Illinois a population mix of unusual diversity.

Demographic Factors

The profile of the population pyramid of the United States has been changing for several decades. A high birthrate following World War II increased the proportion of the young. Recently, however, birthrates have declined and general population growth rates consequently have decreased substantially. Birthrates within Illinois exhibit no strong spatial patterns (Fig. 4-20). For example, Cook, Kane, and Will counties have birthrates considerably above the state

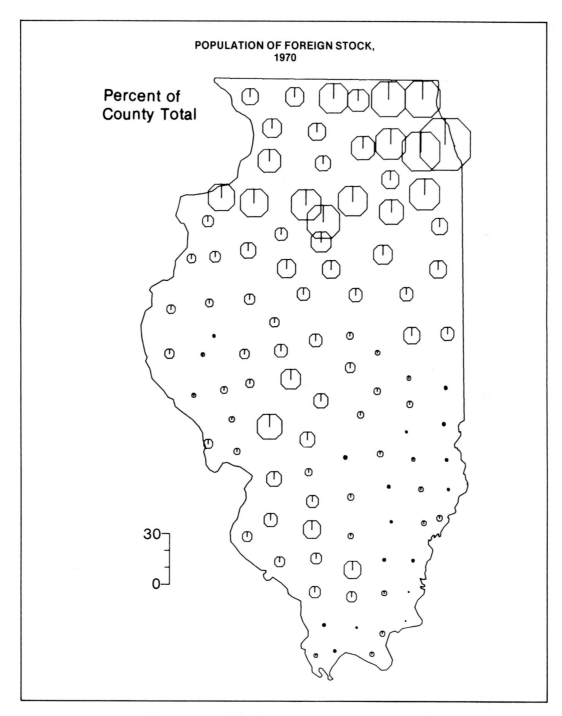

**POPULATION OF FOREIGN STOCK,
1970**

Percent of
County Total

30

0

Figure 4-18. Population of foreign stock, 1970.

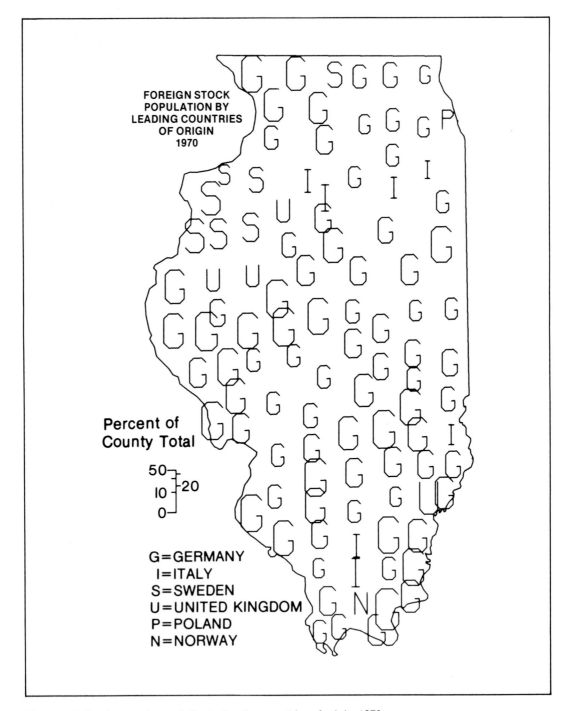

FOREIGN STOCK
POPULATION BY
LEADING COUNTRIES
OF ORIGIN
1970

Percent of
County Total

50
10   20
0

G=GERMANY
I=ITALY
S=SWEDEN
U=UNITED KINGDOM
P=POLAND
N=NORWAY

Figure 4-19. Foreign stock population by leading countries of origin, 1970.

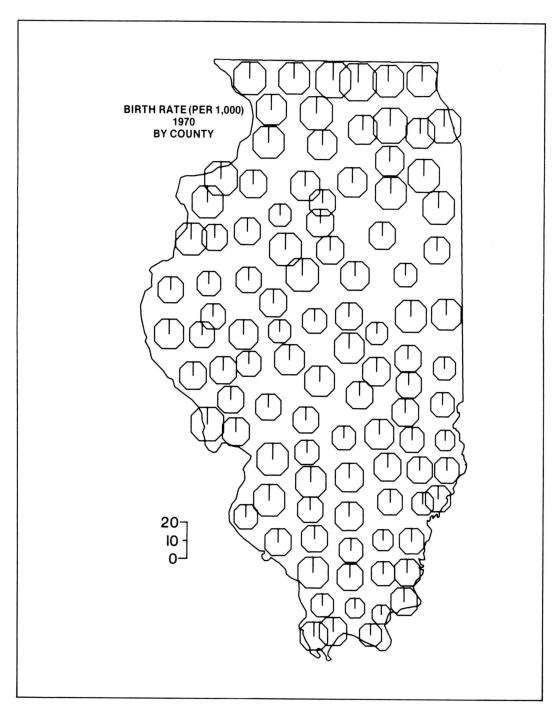

Figure 4-20. Birth rate, 1970 (per 1,000).

average, while other Chicago area counties have rates well below that level. Other counties with relatively high rates are scattered throughout the state; these include Johnson in the south, Calhoun near St. Louis, Tazewell in the interior, and Jo Daviess in the northwest. Boone County, in extreme northern Illinois, has the highest birthrate in the state. The ten counties with the lowest rates are almost all located in the southern half of the state.

The proportion of the population under five years of age, on the other hand, shows a distinct pattern, and only weak spatial correspondence with birthrates. All the suburban Chicago counties have percentages of young children above the state average. In fact, eight of the nine counties with the highest percentages of children under five years of age are Chicago area counties extending from Winnebago to Grundy. Lake County is the only Chicago suburban county not included. Outside of northeastern Illinois, the highest proportion of young children is in Tazewell County, a suburban area of Peoria.

Another significant demographic variable is the female/male ratio. The female population is rapidly becoming more vocal and active in American society. In Illinois, females account for 51.5 percent of the total population. The female majority was first reached during the 1940s and has persisted ever since. Only nine counties have male majorities, and in most cases the numerical superiority of males is very slight. Large male concentrations at the military installations in Lake County and at the universities in Champaign and Carbondale have resulted in clear-cut male majorities in those areas.

An increasingly important variable is families with female heads. Such a situation suggests welfare and low income conditions, although in the future it may reflect greater female decision making in the household.[30] In Illinois approximately 10 percent of the families have female heads. One reason why this figure is so low is the manner in which the census determines who is the head. Generally the male is assumed to be the family head unless otherwise specified. What this implies is that normally the female is identified as the head only when there is no husband present. Regional variations in Illinois families headed by females are highly irregular. Counties with the highest percentages are Alexander (15.9), Pulaski (14.5), Cook (13.5), St. Clair (13.3), Massac (10.8), and Sangamon (10.4). Many of these counties have high in-migration rates, affecting family stability during and after the settlement process.

Summary and Prospects for the Future

Cursory examination of Figure 4-1 suggests that the population redistribution in Illinois since 1830 has been a simple movement toward the industrial northeast. In reality, however, the migration of the population center has been influenced by a complex series of events that have had significant effects on population movements. Economically depressed periods have initiated responses far different than international conflicts or economic prosperity. Despite Illinois' long agricultural heritage, the state has become predominantly urban, with central places thriving in a geometric form not greatly divergent from an hexagonal pattern. These urban centers are competing with each other for dominance and hinterlands, but it is unlikely that any will achieve the status of Chicago or St. Louis. Indeed, Illinois may now have reached a stage of central place and settlement pattern maturity characterized by a near-stationary center of population and growth primarily confined to urban centers already firmly established on the landscape. The 1960-1970 shift in the center was the shortest of any decade, excluding the 1930-1940 southward retreat, and further shifts are likely to be even shorter. Moreover, it is now improbable that there will be major shifts in the hierarchical position of present urban centers, a phenomenon common in previous generations. Illinois' vibrant history of migration and population redistribution will certainly continue but at a much slower pace. The decrease in population growth may indeed preserve many of the gross distributional patterns, but without doubt other characteristics of the population will change.

While forecasting the future is always a speculative proposition, a few more prognostications seem reasonable. For instance, the rural to urban migration will probably continue, but future movements will involve much smaller numbers since the farm population already has reached a low level. Also, the increasing world demand for food products may help keep the farm population stable. There will, however, be a substantial increase in the number of rural nonfarm residents as transportation systems improve, cities decentralize, and urban residents choose to live beyond the city. There also will be a general decrease in mobility associated with a decline in migration from the southern states, although migration to the West can be expected to continue. This decrease in the number of migrants entering the state, together with declining birthrates, suggests a long-term decrease in Illinois' population growth rate. Those born in the post-World War II baby boom are presently in the child bearing age group. By the late 1970s their effect will decline, and the number of newborn consequently will be even lower. Perhaps then total population

will stabilize, subject only to migrational patterns.

Lastly, the ethnic and racial mix will change. Recent immigrants are fewer in number and from different origins than the immigrants of previous decades. The black population, on the other hand, will probably show a slight increase, but the major change should be in a more dispersed distribution. More blacks will find homes in suburban areas of Chicago as well as urban and suburban areas throughout the state.

As a whole the future of Illinois looks bright. There are no imminent trends toward overpopulation, and the strong agricultural and industrial base of the state would appear to insure its future economic viability. While current headlines indicate much racial and ethnic intolerance, it is to be hoped that progress on that front will parallel other healthy trends.

Notes

1. Defined by the U.S. Bureau of the Census as the Chicago Standard Metropolitan Statistical Area.
2. In order of income the cities are Wilmette, Ill. ($21,757); Garden City, N.Y. ($21,198); Highland Park, Ill. ($20,726); Beverly Hills, Calif. ($20,303); and Northbrook, Ill. ($19,992).
3. The U.S. Census draws a distinction between urbanized areas and SMSAs. Urbanized areas are based on density criteria, and SMSAs are county-level regions interacting with the central city in question.
4. Cincinnati and Louisville SMSAs also extend into Indiana, but the populations are only 29,430 and 131,498 respectively in contrast to 633,367 in the Gary, Indiana, SMSA.
5. Robert P. Howard, *Illinois: A History of the Prairie State* (Grand Rapids, Mich.: William B. Eerdmans Publishing Co., 1972), pp. 237-38.
6. Ibid., p. 255.
7. Paul W. Gates, "Disposal of the Public Domain in Illinois." *Journal of Economic*

and Business History 3, no. 2 (February 1931): 216-40.

8. Howard, *Illinois,* p. 304.

9. U.S. Bureau of the Census, *Census of Population, 1880.*

10. Howard, *Illinois,* p. 358.

11. When the population change was less than 50, no symbol was mapped.

12. U.S. Bureau of the Census, *Census of Population, 1880* and *Census of Population, 1890.*

13. Albert Larson and Siim Sööt, "The Use of Population Centers of Gravity in Historical Geographic Analysis: The Nebraska Case." *Iowa Geographer,* Fall 1973.

14. U.S. Bureau of the Census, *Census of Population, 1900.*

15. Howard, *Illinois,* p. 444.

16. Ibid., p. 480.

17. U.S. Bureau of the Census, *Census of Population, 1920; Census of Population, 1930;* and *Census of Population, 1940.*

18. Howard, *Illinois,* p. 507.

19. Ibid., p. 531.

20. Mary Watters, *Illinois in the Second World War,* vol. 2 (Springfield, Ill.: Illinois State Historical Library, 1951-52), pp. 384-85.

21. U.S. Bureau of the Census, *U.S. Census of Manufacturers,* 1939 and 1947.

22. U.S. Bureau of the Census, *U.S. Census of Population,* 1960.

23. U.S. Bureau of the Census, *U.S. Census of Population,* 1950, 1960, and 1970.

24. Ibid., 1970.

25. Ibid.

26. Each of the statistics presented here and on the following pages of this chapter are from one of two readily available U.S. Bureau of the Census sources and are not hereafter cited individually. The data are from the U.S. Bureau of the Census, *Census of Population, 1970, General Population Characteristics,* Final Report PC(1)—B15, Illinois; and *County and City Databook* (Washington, D.C.: U.S. Government Printing Office, 1972).

27. Figure 1-10 provides the names of Illinois counties; thus, it is useful in interpreting other figures in this chapter.

28. Peter Lloyd and P. Dickens, *Location in Space: A Theoretical Approach to Economic Geography* (New York: Harper & Row, 1972), p. 190.

29. The U.S. Census distinguishes between foreign-born and foreign stock. The latter includes the former plus those with at least one parent who was born outside the United States as a foreign national.

30. Many of the other variables in this study are subject to the census methods of information gathering. Also, in filling out census forms, individuals undoubtedly introduce initial errors. The accuracy and reliability of the data vary from variable to variable. Nevertheless, the census is the most comprehensive and authoritative source of information about population aggregates.

Selected References

Allman, John et al. "The Use of Standardized Values in Regionalization: The Example of a Socio-Economic Spatial Structure of Illinois, 1960." *The Professional Geographer,* XVI (May 1964), 5-11.

Altes, Jane. *Population Projections for the State of Illinois and Component Regions to 2010.* Urbana: Bureau of Business and Economic Research, 1967.

Bogart, Ernest Ludlow. "The Movement of Population in Illinois, 1870-1910." *Transactions of the Illinois State Historical Society,* XXIII (1917).

Bogue, Allan G. "Farming in the Prairie Peninsula, 1830-1890." *Journal of Economic History,* XXIII (March 1963), 3-29.

———. *From Prairie to Corn Belt: Farming on the Illinois and Iowa Prairies in the Nineteenth Century.* Chicago: University of Chicago Press, 1963.

Colby, Charles C. *Pilot Study of Southern Illinois.* Carbondale: Southern Illinois University Press, 1956.

Gates, Paul W. "Disposal of the Public Domain in Illinois." *Journal of Economic and Business History,* III (February 1931), 216-40.

Howard, Robert P. *Illinois: A History of the Prairie State.* Grand Rapids, Mich.: William B. Eerdmans Publishing Co., 1972.

Larson, Albert J., and Sööt, Siim. "Centers of Population and the Historical Geography of Illinois." *Bulletin of the Illinois Geographical Society,* XV (December 1973), 34-52.

Lloyd, Peter, and Dickens, P. *Location in Space: A Theoretical Approach to Economic Geography.* New York: Harper & Row, 1972.

Lohmann, Karl. *Cities and Towns of Illinois—A Handbook of Community Facts.* Urbana: University of Illinois Press, 1951.

Mattingly, Paul F. "Population Trends in the Hamlets and Villages of Illinois: 1940-1960." *The Professional Geographer,* XV (November 1963), 17-21.

McDonald, James A. *Population Projections: Economic Growth Prospects.* Springfield: Department of Business and Economic Development, 1967.

Scott, Roy V. *The Agrarian Movement in Illinois, 1880-1896.* Urbana: University of Illinois Press, 1962.

Wakely, Ray E. *Growth and Decline of Towns and Cities in Southern Illinois.* Area Service Bulletin 2. Carbondale: Southern Illinois University Press, 1962.

_____. *Population Changes and Prospects in Southern Illinois.* Area Service Bulletin 1. Carbondale: Southern Illinois University Press, 1962.

Watters, Mary. *Illinois in the Second World War.* 2 vols. Springfield: Illinois State Historical Library, 1951-1952.

Chapter Five

FARMS AND FARMING

Dalias A. Price
Eastern Illinois University

Illinois is one of the leading states in agriculture, ranking fourth in the nation in total farm income after California, Iowa, and Texas. In 1975, Illinois farmers sold almost $5.4 billion worth of agricultural products, an increase of nearly $3 billion over the 1969 total. The amount of sales from crops more than doubled between 1969 and 1974, increasing from $1.3 billion to $3.1 billion. Livestock sales amounted to $1.89 billion in 1975, an increase of about $207 million over the 1969 amount.[1] Obviously agriculture is big business in Illinois and has experienced striking growth in recent years.

Over 80 percent of the state's total land area is in farms, one of the highest percentages in the nation. In 1974 there were 115,059 farms in Illinois, averaging 250 acres each. In fact, 15,001 farms contained 500 or more acres in 1974 and by 1976 there were 2,304 farms larger than 1,000 acres in size. With increasing mechanization, there has been a corresponding growth in the size of Illinois farms over the past several decades. In addition, the value of farmland in the state has increased at a remarkable rate. In 1976 the average value per acre reached $858, but some of the highest quality cropland sold for over $3,500 per acre. The huge amount of capital involved in land, taxes, machinery, and production supplies has made small-scale farming economically marginal and has stimulated a growth in size of farm units.

On their extensive and fertile lands, Illinois farmers produce a variety of crops and livestock. Corn, traditionally raised as a livestock feed, long has been the dominant crop in Illinois; among the states, only Iowa competes with Illinois for the national leadership in corn production. The versatile soybean has become a very close contender to corn in acreage harvested and during recent years has occasionally surpassed corn in cash receipts; Illinois ranks first among the states in soybean acreage and production. Wheat represents only about 2 percent of the state's grain crop, although its production has been stimulated in recent years by growing foreign markets. Illinois also is one of the leading states in pork production. Dairying, while not important enough for Illinois to qualify as America's dairyland, is of significance especially near the large urban markets of St. Louis and Chicago. Beef cattle are less important but still account for some 12 to 14 percent of farm income in Illinois. The persistence of sheep in the agricultural picture of Illinois is mainly a result of their continued production in the southern and western areas of the state.

Illinois is located in the heart of the most productive agricultural region in the world. The mighty Mississippi, the Illinois, the Ohio, and the Wabash rivers long have provided transportation for produce exported from Illinois farms. In addition, roads and highways criss-cross the state, and Lake Michigan provides ocean transportation to far-flung markets throughout the world. Il-

linois leads all other states in the exportation of farm commodities to foreign consumers. Nearby major markets, however, are provided by Chicagoland in the northeast and the St. Louis metropolitan area to the southwest.

Nature's Endowments

The high ranking position of Illinois in the nation's agricultural economy can be attributed to several factors, among which are its superb natural endowments. Climatically, Illinois is characterized by adequate rainfall the year around, and especially significant is the concentration of rain during the growing season. Yearly amounts of rainfall range from 48 inches in southernmost Illinois to 34 inches in the northern part of the state. Droughts occur, but only on rare occasion do they cause severe losses to farmers.

Figure 5-1. Corn has been the leading crop on most Illinois farms since pioneer times. Hybrid varieties with high yielding characteristics are now raised almost exclusively. (Photo by Fred C. Caspall.)

Although winters, especially in central and northern Illinois, tend to be cold, most agricultural pursuits are not unduly handicapped by them. Bitter blizzards, so common to the northern Great Plains, occur only rarely and then in modified form. Heavy snows also are uncommon, yet some snowfall is needed to provide moisture to growing wheat and for early crops in the spring.

The growing season varies a great deal across the state since Illinois extends some 387 miles from north to south. The frost-free period ranges from 210 days in southernmost Illinois, sufficient for growing cotton successfully, to 150 days in the northwestern part of the state. Longer hours of daylight during the summer in the north compensate somewhat for the shorter growing season so that farmers there are able to raise successfully many of the same crops grown in southern Illinois. Occasionally there are problems with early autumn frosts that damage late maturing corn and soybeans, though fortunately not often. In general, climate is kind to the farmers of Illinois and climatic endowments are many. Farmers have learned to take full advantage of them.

Soils also vary a great deal across the state—east-west as well as north-south. Geologic events of the past have provided soil sources of great value and variation. In Pleistocene times ice sheets spread great quantities of soil materials over all of the state except the northwest corner and the Ozarks in the south. The last ice age, called the Wisconsin, spread highly valuable veneers of soil materials over the northern and central parts of Illinois. Later enrichments were brought about by the development of luxurious prairie grasses which helped to impart great fertility to the soils of most of central and northern Illinois. Some of the most productive soils in the world are found in this prairie region. Farmers have

combined science, technology, and hard work to produce crops and raise livestock with great success even in the southern and northwestern areas where natural soil endowments are less generous. Illinois contributes an inordinately large share of the foodstuffs of the nation from its soils.

The Early Years

When explorers and early settlers arrived in Illinois they found a land ready for the ax and the plow. Since they migrated westward mainly by way of the Ohio River, most of the first pioneer farmers entered southern Illinois, a forested land in which they felt comfortable because they had lived earlier in such an environment. They set to work clearing the timber and planting the land with such crops as corn, wheat, and oats. Since they had to be almost self-sufficient, they also grew vegetables and fruit to preserve for use through the winter. In addition, pigs and cattle were essential elements of every farm in those early years.

As these pioneer farmers expanded their tillable land in southern Illinois by clearing the trees, they began to produce surplus foods for which nearby markets were insufficient. They soon realized that they had to find a way of getting their produce transported to growing cities such as Chicago, St. Louis, Memphis, and even far away New Orleans. Some of the first exports of agricultural commodities consisted of hams and other salt meat rafted down the rivers. Wheat and corn, either in the form of grain or as flour and cornmeal, were soon in demand and were eagerly supplied by Illinois farmers to equally eager city consumers.

The Canal Building Era

It soon became obvious to residents of Illinois that means of transportation other than rivers were desperately needed, not only for moving farm surpluses to markets but also to enable pioneer settlers to reach interior areas of the state where navigable rivers were nonexistent or inadequate. Canals were seen as a partial solution to the transportation problem, since the Erie Canal in New York State, finished in 1825, had proven to be a huge success. Later waves of immigrants to Illinois used that link to the West, but more important to Illinois farmers was the fact that it, together with the Great Lakes, provided a water route to ship their produce to the Atlantic Seaboard. The almost immediate success of the Erie Canal convinced Illinoisans to build a canal linking Chicago with the Illinois River and thus the whole Mississippi system. This canal provided a better means of transportation for the farmers who were venturing out onto the prairies of northern Illinois and for them to ship their produce to new markets. The Illinois-Michigan Canal unfortunately was not completed until 1848, which was almost the eve of the railroad building period.

Railroad Construction and the Growth of Cities

The Illinois Legislature in its wisdom decided to further open up the interiors of Illinois by building a railroad north-south from Freeport to Cairo and from Lake Michigan (Chicago) diagonally to connect with the north-south line. When completed in 1856, the two railroads did connect far to the south near Centralia. The Illinois-Michigan Canal was no match for this railroad, the Illinois Central, and for others that quickly followed. By the early 1880s almost every farmer in Illinois had a railroad station within a few miles of his farm. Railroad construction set off an agricultural boom of enormous proportions after the early 1850s.

Land from the public domain was purchased by settlers at land offices scattered over the state where it was sold by the federal government usually for $1.25 per acre. In addition, to help defray construction costs, railroads were given vast acreages of land along their rights-of-way which they sold to prospective settlers as quickly as possible.

Coincident with the rapid settling of the land and railroad building during the nineteenth century was the remarkable growth of cities in Illinois. Chicago began significant growth following the opening of the Erie Canal, and experienced rapid development with the building of the Illinois and Michigan Canal and railroads linking the city with farming areas and other urban centers. Along the new railroads, especially at the intersection of tracks and where they crossed rivers, other cities began to mushroom. Almost all people in these burgeoning urban centers were dependent upon the state's farmers for nearly every calorie of food they consumed, and the farmers were eager, willing, and able to supply the cities' food needs.

Agricultural Development and Mechanization

Land values doubled over and over again during the nineteenth century in Illinois, and farmers became very prosperous, especially those who were able to own the land they tilled.[2] An enormous increase in cultivated land was accomplished during the 1880s with relatively primitive tools and teams of horses, even teams of oxen in early days. The invention of an efficient moldboard plow enabled farmers to cut the thickest, toughest grass sod and turn it over to plant corn, wheat, oats, and other crops in the virgin prairie soil. For a few decades in the early nineteenth century settlers in Illinois avoided

Figure 5-2. Breaking prairie with teams of oxen in Henry County, Illinois, during the mid-nineteenth century, as depicted on a painting by Swedish-American artist Olof Krans. (Courtesy Bishop Hill Heritage Association.)

the prairies. This was understandable, because they were accustomed to living in forest clearings. Forests were valuable assets to pioneer farmers for supplies of nuts, fruit, fuel, and as wood for making such necessities as tools, furniture, houses, and even fencing. Once the prairies were made accessible by railroads, however, settlers began to venture out onto those trackless lands and soon discovered enormous wealth in the black soil beneath the thick, tough sod. Today that very soil provides the backbone of the Illinois farming economy.

As cities continued to grow after the turn of the century, more and more efficient means to provide foodstuffs were acquired by Illinois farmers. Lumbering steam engines, belching great quantities of smoke, were moved from farm to farm to provide stationary power for threshing grain. Steam powered tractors were soon to waddle across fields drawing banks of plowshares, displacing the teams of draft horses that pulled only a single plow or at the most a double shovel affair. The gasoline tractor made its appearance on the agricultural scene and gained wide acceptance after World War I, but horse-drawn equipment persisted on Illinois farms through the Great Depression. Today one still can observe the old ways of cultivation and tractorless farms of the Amish religious sect near Arthur, Illinois; it is a fascinating trip back into the past to see horses still providing true "horsepower" for Amish farmers.

Along with gasoline engines for power, of course, came the "gas buggy"—the Model T Ford—which was superior to the horse and buggy almost from the start. Illinois farmers learned they could drive greater distances to larger towns to exchange their produce for items they no longer had the time or inclination to provide for themselves. The difficulty in negotiating a Model T over mud roads in rainy weather stimulated a demand for paved roads. First constructed during the 1920s, brick and concrete roads were and still are called, understandably, "hard roads" by most Illinoisans. These new all-weather roads were a great boon to Illinois farmers, enabling them to market perishable produce (eggs, butter, milk, etc.) more quickly and to more easily haul bulky products from the farm such as grain and animals by truck. The Model T truly liberated farmers from the rural isolation of earlier years.

During the years between World War I and World War II modern tractors forced horses practically out of existence on Illinois farms. Larger and ever more powerful machines enabled the farmer to cultivate more and more acres with fewer "hired hands." Illinois agriculture experienced a revolution with the acquisition of power tools and equipment by farmers.

Modern Agriculture

Today agriculture is a sophisticated, highly technical, thoroughly mechanized

Figure 5-3. A small gasoline tractor still being used by a farmer in western Illinois. (Courtesy Donald W. Griffin.)

component of the Illinois economy. Much evidence of the technical revolution in farming can be observed as one travels in all parts of the state, even the most remote areas. There are enormous diesel tractors, often with air-conditioned cabs; self-propelled harvesters that can pick and shell corn as well as harvest soybeans and wheat; and ungainly sprayer rigs for the application of such agricultural chemicals as herbicides, pesticides, and fertilizers. The fields of high-yielding crops reflect the development of hybrid seeds since the 1930s. Once harvested, grain crops now are artificially dried and stored in enormous bins on the farmstead. The successful modern farmer must possess expertise in mechanics, economics, chemistry, and a variety of other areas of knowledge. But farming as a "way of life" is in jeopardy. Rarely does the modern Illinois farmer consume directly what he produces on his farm; these days he simply buys his milk, butter, bread, and meat at a nearby supermarket, just as does his city cousin, even though he may actually

Figure 5-4. Modern diesel tractors with enclosed cabs lined up on the sales lot of a farm equipment dealer. (Photo by Ronald E. Nelson.)

produce some of the commodities that he buys back in packaged form.

To illustrate some of the basic characteristics of modern agriculture in Illinois, there follows an overview of three types of farming: (1) production of cash grain crops, (2) speciality cropping such as truck farming and fruit production, and (3) farming operations that center on animals and their products, mainly milk.

Cash Grain Crops

With the development of agricultural mechanization and growth in the market demand for foodstuffs during the early twentieth century, Illinois farming experienced several fundamental changes. For several generations, farmers throughout the state had followed the tradition of diversifying their operations by raising hogs, beef cattle, dairy cattle, and other livestock as well as various field crops. Particularly on the flat prairieland of eastern and central Illinois, this traditional, general farming was replaced by cash grain farming—the production of grain crops for sale rather than for consumption on the farm where they were grown. The exceptionally high natural fertility of the prairies provided high yields of grains, and the flatness of the land facilitated the use of machinery in the fields. Eastern and central Illinois became identified as the Illinois Corn Belt or, more correctly, the Cash Grain Region (Fig. 5-5).

Almost from the beginning of settlement, corn was the dominant crop in the prairie areas of eastern and central Illinois. Although new and strange to nineteenth century European immigrants, it was soon

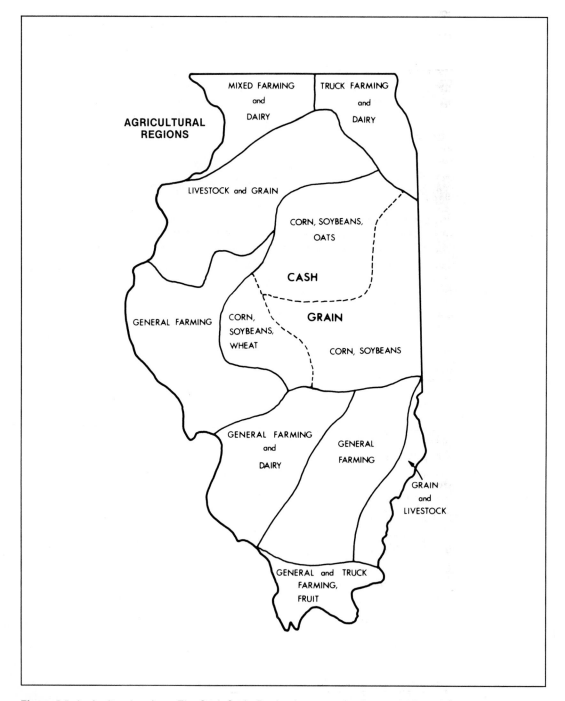

Figure 5-5. Agricultural regions. The Cash Grain Region in eastern and central Illinois is generally the most prosperous farming area in the state. (Adapted from a map in R. C. Ross and H. C. M. Case, *Types of Farming in Illinois,* University of Illinois College of Agriculture, Urbana, 1956.)

adopted by them when they settled in Illinois because the crop was well suited to a pioneer economy. Corn not only gave good yields in a variety of environments, but it also served several functions. It provided feed for farm animals being raised or fattened and served as an important staple for the pioneer farm family in such forms as hominy, cornbread, and "roasting ears." As transportation facilities became more readily available, early farmers in the developing Cash Grain Region discovered that they could sell their corn to the growing market in major cities. In addition to its direct consumption by humans, corn was manufactured into starch and cornflakes, the latter creating a revolution on the breakfast table of Americans, and used for making syrups and, alas, alcoholic beverages. Also, farmers in other parts of the country often encountered

shortages of corn and were anxious buyers of some of the surplus Illinois farmers provided.

During recent years in Illinois, corn has been raised on more than 9 million acres of land—an area greater than that devoted to any other crop (Table 5-1). More than 70 percent of the state's farms are involved in the production of the Illinois corn crop. Corn is grown in every county of the state and, as indicated by Figure 5-7, in most counties in central and northern Illinois it occupies one-third or more of the harvested acreage. Most corn farmers in Illinois now expect a yield of at least 75 bushels per acre and production in excess of 150 bushels per acre in the northern two-thirds of the state is no longer uncommon.[3]

Although Illinois does not possess the environmental endowments for raising wheat

Figure 5-6. A farmer examining the growth progress of his corn crop. Much higher plant populations than were possible in earlier years have contributed to increasing corn yields in Illinois. (Photo by Fred C. Caspall.)

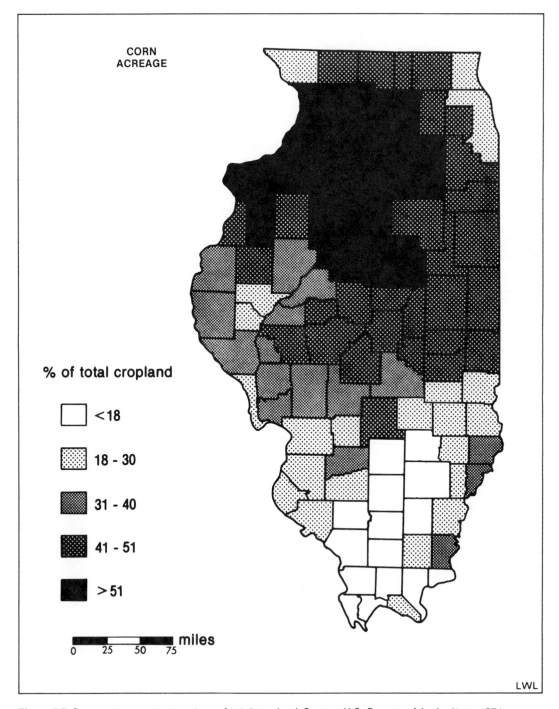

CORN
ACREAGE

% of total cropland

☐ <18

░ 18 - 30

▒ 31 - 40

▓ 41 - 51

█ >51

miles
0   25   50   75

LWL

Figure 5-7. Corn acreage as a percentage of total cropland. Source: U.S. Census of Agriculture, 1974.

equal to that of Kansas, wheat figures significantly in Illinois agriculture. To maintain soil tilth and productivity, generations of farmers have rotated wheat with corn and other crops in Illinois. In 1974, wheat was harvested on 38,000 farms in the state and 1.6 million acres were devoted to its production (Table 5-1). A growing demand for food in the world has stimulated an increase in the acreage planted in wheat during recent years. Yields of approximately 40 bushels per acre now are typical of most wheat-growing areas

Table 5-1. Grain Acreage in Illinois, 1969-74 (in thousands of acres).

Grain	1969	1974
Corn	9,500	9,400
Soybeans	6,400	8,100
Wheat	1,300	1,600
Oats	643	378

in the state. Although it is grown in combination with corn and soybeans in many counties in central and southern Illinois, wheat is particularly concentrated in an area east of St. Louis (Fig. 5-9). This area is involved in dairying and other agricultural pursuits, but wheat is the most important crop here—particularly in Washington County. Nearly all wheat raised in Illinois is winter wheat, a variety that is planted in the fall, has early growth during the winter, and reaches maturity for harvesting in the early summer. Spring wheat is grown on only a very small scale in the northern part of the state.

Oats long have been included in the crop rotation system employed by farmers in Illinois, but they no longer can be regarded as a major crop in the state. Earlier, oats were raised primarily as a feed for horses and served much the same function that diesel fuel and gasoline do for tractors today. With

Figure 5-8. A field of wheat nearly ready for harvesting. (Photo by Fred C. Caspall.)

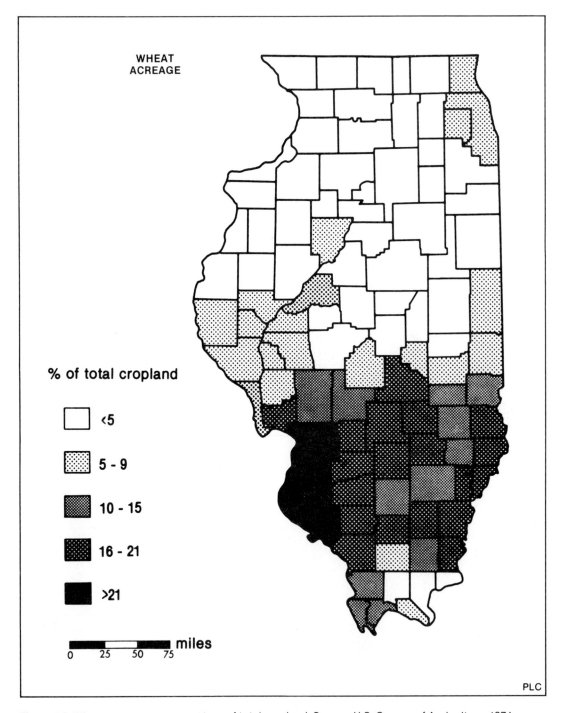

Figure 5-9. Wheat acreage as a percentage of total cropland. Source: U.S. Census of Agriculture, 1974.

the displacement of horses by tractors, however, the acreage devoted to growing oats has declined drastically. The crop was raised on only 17,000 Illinois farms in 1974, and the amount of land planted in oats had decreased to 378,000 acres by that year (Table 5-1). Of course, the demand for oats as animal feed has not been eliminated entirely, and the crop still has minor significance as a source of human food. Most oats raised in Illinois today are concentrated on the cooler northern side of the Cash Grain Region (Fig. 5-5).

Soybeans entered the agricultural scene quite late, initially appearing on farms in the 1920s. This remarkable plant subsequently gained wide acceptance among Illinois farmers, and today it rivals corn as a cash grain. The soybean is an absolute wonder. Not only does it produce well on soils of limited fertility, but it also thrives under a variety of climatic conditions. Yields generally range between 25 and 50 bushels per acre in Illinois. Soybeans serve as a raw material for a variety of industries, including ones involved in making paints, varnishes, plastics, margarine, and cooking oils. In addition, the crop makes an excellent livestock feed, and it is becoming increasingly important as a human food because of its exceptionally high protein content. Some manufacturers recently have developed techniques for converting soybeans into products resembling hamburger, meats, and other foods.

Soybeans are now grown throughout Illinois and the amount of land planted in the crop is rapidly approaching that for corn. The area of most concentrated soybean production is the Cash Grain Region of eastern and central Illinois (Fig. 5-11). As a result of the widespread adoption of soybeans in the

Figure 5-10. A field of young soybeans. When mature and ready for harvesting, the soybean plants will be approximately waist high. Photo by Fred C. Caspall.)

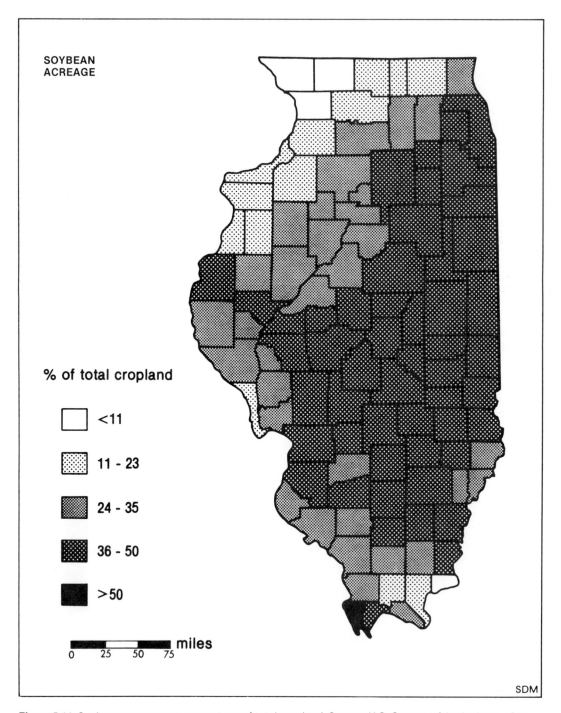

Figure 5-11. Soybean acreage as a percentage of total cropland. Source: U.S. Census of Agriculture, 1974.

state, cash grain farming is more widely practiced than formerly. In 1974 soybeans were harvested on about two-thirds of the state's farms, and the amount of land devoted to the crop had increased to 8.1 million acres (Table 5-1).

Specialty Crops

There is a general tendency for certain areas to develop specialization in agricultural pursuits involving a particular crop or product. The reasons for this are diverse, but one is the tendency of farmers to imitate the practices of their successful neighbors. If one farmer makes a success at raising strawberries, for example, his neighbors, ever on the alert for getting the most from their farms, follow suit. If economic and especially environmental conditions are suitable, the enterprise becomes implanted, and the area acquires a reputation for that specialty.

Strawberry production, in fact, is a good example of areal specialization in Illinois agriculture. Although the strawberry plant can be raised throughout Illinois, the southern part of the state has a climatic advantage because of the earlier arrival of spring. Therefore, southern Illinois growers can market their produce earlier than upstate producers. The first experiment with refrigerated shipment of a perishable crop in the United States involved strawberries from southern Illinois. A man named Parker Earle, living in Cobden, sent a shipment of strawberries to the Chicago market by rail in 1866. The method of refrigeration was very primitive; in fact, the shipment arrived in Chicago a soggy, rotten mess because railroad workmen forgot to replenish the ice supply in the wooden casks containing the strawberries en route. Not being discouraged by this initial failure, Mr. Earle soon perfected a successful technique of shipping perishable fruits and vegetables to the Chicago market in refrigerated railroad cars. As a consequence, there became established a major truck farming and orcharding industry in southern Illinois that persists to this day. The refrigerated car soon revolutionized the distributional characteristics of production of perishable agricultural commodities not only in Illinois but throughout the country.

While most Illinois farmers had fruit trees on their farms in the early days of settlement, certain areas with transportational and environmental advantages took the lead but not until after the railroads provided the necessary "rapid" transportation to city markets. Apple and peach production also illustrates the regional specialization of much of Illinois agriculture. Today the Illinois Ozarks, especially areas around the towns of Anna, Cobden, Villa Ridge, Alto Pass, and Murphysboro, account for the major production of apples and peaches for shipment to the urban areas. Most fruit farmers combine with their orchard enterprises the production of such truck crops as tomatoes, peppers, squash, cucumbers, and beans. This is a happy combination because occasional frosts damage apple and, especially, peach trees. An orchardist can thus sustain a bad season by shifting emphasis to truck farming during such years.

Although not as important as the Illinois Ozarks, there are other areas of significant fruit production in the state. One is Calhoun County, that interesting backbone of land squeezed between the Illinois and the Mississippi rivers just north of St. Louis, where peaches dominate the fruit production, although apples are significant too. This region has capitalized on its proximity to St. Louis for sales and now engages in what is called "U-pick." The urban dweller enjoys driving out to the fruit farm and picking his own fruit; the orchardist and the buyer save labor costs and both are happy.

Other fruit and truck farming regions of lesser significance center on Centralia and Salem. In the past there was greater emphasis on speciality farming here, but most farmers have succumbed to the temptation of government price supports and switched to cash grain production, a somewhat more reliable farming enterprise than orcharding.

In the very southernmost part of the state, primarily Alexander and Pulaski counties, cotton is a residual crop of the once more northerly expanded Cotton Belt. Cotton has suffered materially in the face of competition from soybean and corn production. Cotton gins no longer are located on the Illinois side of the Cotton Belt, and it is economically unfeasible to haul this bulky lightweight fiber to Missouri cotton gins. Thus it appears that cotton is on the way out in Illinois, sad to say.

There is a long list of less important, perhaps more exotic crops produced in Illinois. One is popcorn, a close relative of field corn. Popcorn production is located mainly in the southeastern part of the state, particularly around Ridgeway, which boasts that it is the popcorn capital of the United States. Although Ridgeway's claim is not strictly true, there is considerable local pride in the fact that the area does specialize in commercial popcorn production. Sweet corn is produced in several northern parts of the state. In the Hoopeston area it is a particularly important crop. Most of the corn is processed and canned in nearby communities.

Truck farming and the production of additional specialty crops are found in several other parts of Illinois. Surprisingly, horseradish is a specialty crop grown on the mucklands of the Americans Bottoms in the East St. Louis region. Almost all of the commercial horseradish of the United States is produced by a relatively small number of farmers in this area. Undoubtedly, there are many other parts of the state suitable for horseradish, but local interest and early development of know-how help to explain why there is such a high concentration in this one small area. Watermelon and cantaloupe are grown on the sandy soils in scattered areas of the Wabash bottoms near Crossville in White County and in Mason County adjacent to the Illinois River. Pumpkins for commercial canning are raised in Tazewell County in central Illinois and in Ogle and DeKalb counties in the northern part of the state. Still another odd specialty is the production of cut roses in huge greenhouses at Pana. Early start and abundant fuel in the form of nearby coal help explain why the industry flourishes in that community.

All of the specialty crops combined, we must admit, do not account for a very large percentage of the agricultural income in Illinois. Corn and soybeans are far more important, but regional specialization in minor crops adds to the agricultural diversity and variety of land use in the state.

Animal Production

Illinois farmers who specialize in animal production concentrate mainly on hogs, beef cattle, dairy cattle, and sheep, in that order (Table 5-2). Raising hogs has been common since the first pioneers arrived in Illinois. Hogs were an important element in the subsistence economy prevalent in the early settlement period, but farmers soon realized

Table 5-2. Farm Animals in Illinois, 1969-74 (Inventory in thousands of head).

Animal	1969	1974
Hogs and Pigs	7,000	5,200
Beef Cattle	771	873
Milk Cows	292	237
Sheep	377	223

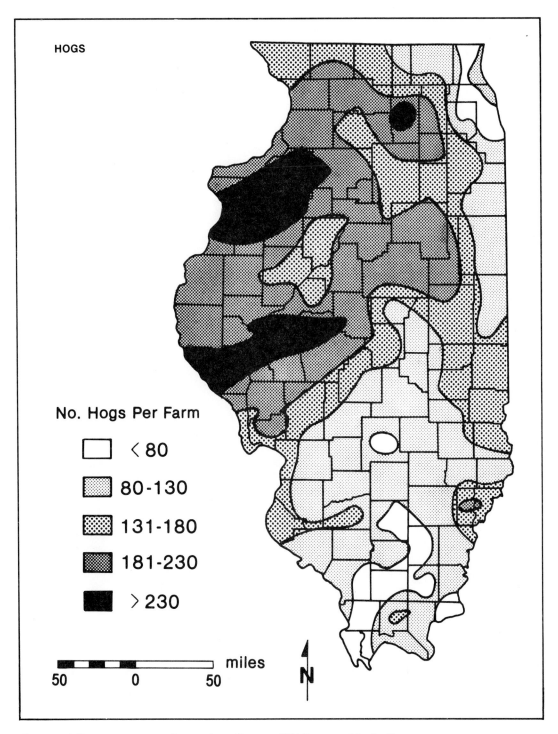

Figure 5-12. Hogs, average number per farm. Source: 1974 Census of Agriculture.

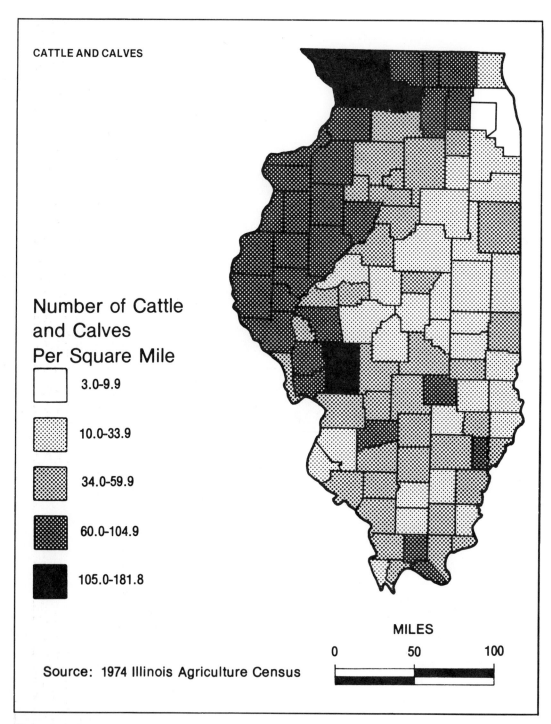

Figure 5-13. Cattle and calves.

that pork in the form of bacon, hams, and lard was in demand by city dwellers. Slaughter houses and butcher shops became common businesses in early towns and villages. As modern transportation facilities developed, however, urban specialization in the meat packing industry evolved. Chicago became the "hog butcher of the world," and other growing cities developed meat packing industries.

Today hogs are raised in most sections of the state but are particularly important in the counties north and west of the Illinois River (Fig. 5-12). In this part of the Corn Belt farmers tend to feed some of their corn crop to livestock rather than sell all of it as grain. Henry County, just east of Rock Island, is the leading hog producer of Illinois. In 1974, hogs were raised on 31,000 Illinois farms—slightly more than one-fourth of all farms in the state. The inventory of hogs and pigs in Illinois during 1974 was 5.2 million animals (Table 5-2).

Beef cattle, like hogs, require great quantities of corn for feed; however, their distribution is not quite the same as that of hogs. The northwestern counties dominate the state in the production of beef cattle and calves, and Ogle County, just south of Rockford, is the leader (Fig. 5-13). Generally beef cattle are both raised and fattened on the same farm in Illinois. While corn is an important element in the feeding of cattle, a great amount of hay and pastureland also are required. This helps explain why the beef and dairy industries are not favored in the Cash Grain Region where the land is so highly productive and expensive that the farmer cannot afford to allow it be used for hay and pasture. The farmer who engages in production of beef cattle has a more diversified enterprise than his counterpart in the Cash Grain Region. The product of his efforts is ultimately a fat animal to be shipped to some urban market for processing. In 1974 the inventory of beef cattle in Illinois was 873,000 head (Table 5-2).

A dairy cow or two was common on every farm in the early days of settlement, but not as a commercial venture. Gradually most Il-

Figure 5-14. A northern Illinois beef cattle farm with feed lots, silos, and a large barn. (Photo by Fred C. Caspall.)

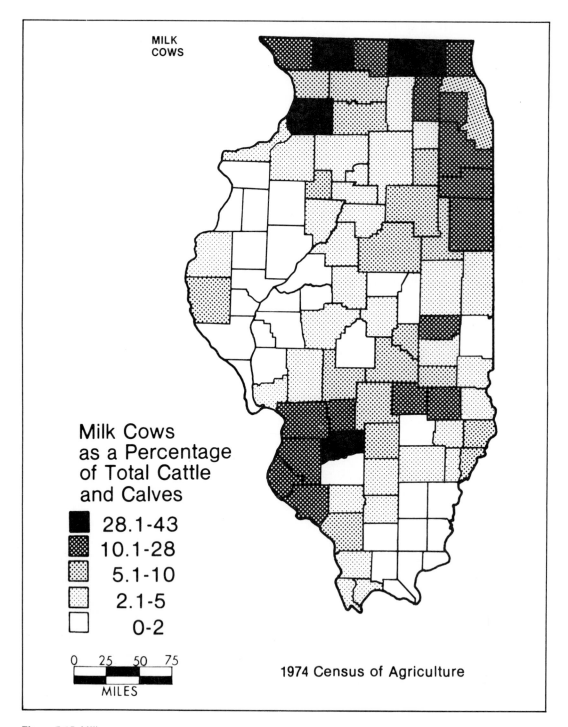

Figure 5-15. Milk cows.

Figure 5-16. A typical dairy farm with silos and a large barn. (Photo by Fred C. Caspall.)

linois farmers gave up dairying and turned to other specialties, while only a relative few expanded their herds to commercial proportions. In metropolitan areas the demand of urban people for milk products increased through the years. The farmers nearest these markets, of course, had a distinct advantage in that their milk could reach the consumer in short time and still be fresh. Those farmers somewhat farther away from the urban markets sold their milk to the producers of cream, cheese, and butter. This pattern now has changed because milk can be shipped hundreds of miles in refrigerated tank trucks. Also, dairying has been affected by technological advances and improved breeds; much more milk now is obtained from one cow than in the past. Consequently, the number of dairy cows and dairy farms has declined. Dairy herds are larger and the dairy farmer has become a highly skilled and trained technician. One farmer alone now can manage a large herd with mechanization

at his disposal, including the ingenious milking machine.

Strong concentrations of dairying in Illinois still remain in the old, city milkshed regions extending from Chicago west and north (eventually into Wisconsin) and from St. Louis east and south—east as far as Effingham County and south as far as Randolph County (Fig. 5-15). These are the significant milk producing regions of the state, although there are minor concentrations of dairying near most larger cities such as Peoria, Decatur, Springfield, Danville, and Carbondale. The inventory of milk cows in Illinois during 1974 was 237,000 head (Table 5-2).

Illinois still persists as a sheep producing state, although certainly not to the extent of some other states. Flocks of sheep are grazed in the hillier sections of the state in the Ozarks and in the northwest; however, the areas west of the Illinois River account for a large share of the sheep produced in Illinois.

There is, in addition, concentration in McLean County and some adjacent areas in the central part of the state. Sheep are raised for their fleece and production of wool and for meat products. The inventory of sheep in Illinois during 1974 was 223,000 animals, a decrease from the 377,000 counted in 1969 (Table 5-2).

Regionalization

From the foregoing descriptions and maps it is apparent that Illinois agriculture varies greatly in character from one part of the state to another. The general regional pattern of agriculture is shown in Figure 5-5, which is adapted from a map in the University of Illinois Experiment Station Bulletin 601 entitled *Types of Farming in Illinois.*[4] While now a bit out of date, this bulletin still provides excellent coverage of types of agricultural pursuits across the state. The largest

and most important agricultural region in Illinois is the Cash Grain Region, which was singled out for attention earlier; it occupies the prairies of the central and eastern parts of the state. Regions of distinctive agricultural characteristics associated with dairying are in northernmost Illinois and in the southwest near the St. Louis urban complex. The regions west and north of the Illinois River and adjacent to the Wabash River in the southeast are distinctive in their mix of crop production and livestock combinations. South of the Cash Grain Region and extending to the northern edge of the Ozarks is a region mainly devoted to general farming in which no particular single enterprise dominates; however, cash grain farming has gained steadily in importance, especially since science has made it possible to produce corn and soybeans for a profit in this area of limited soil resources. In the hill country and stream valleys of southernmost Illinois,

Figure 5-17. A crop and livestock farm in western Illinois. Among the various buildings are machine sheds, silo, barn, and grain bin. (Photo by Ronald E. Nelson.)

truck farming and fruit production are combined with general farming in a final distinctive agricultural region.

The identification of precise reasons for regional specializations is a difficult task. The more obvious reasons, of course, center on variations in soils, terrain, the length of the growing season, the severity or mildness of winters, and the time of the arrival of spring. We cannot overlook, however, the element of judgement by an individual farmer. An assortment of vague reasons, even including personal preferences, may enter into a farmer's adoption of a certain agricultural enterprise. If his experiment proves to be successful, other farmers in the immediate area are likely to follow the example of the initiator.

There are advantages, of course, in concentrating production of certain agricultural commodities in a particular area. Problems common to all farmers can be solved more readily. Dissemination of information and of results of certain farming experiments is easier. Also, there is the matter of marketing in which cooperative efforts are needed to market efficiently products from the farms. A dairy farmer located 50 miles from any other dairy farmer undoubtedly would suffer serious handicaps; no processing plant would send a truck that distance to pick up only one dairyman's daily supply of milk. Regional specialization just makes good sense in Illinois agriculture.

Another significant regional variation in Illinois agriculture involves the ownership of land and farm tenancy. Slightly less than one-half of the farms in the state are now operated exclusively by the owners themselves; the practice of landlords leasing farmland to tenants is widespread and dates from the early days of settlement in Illinois. Undoubtedly most farmers would prefer to own the land they farm, but this is often not feasible or even possible. Because of the

enormous expense involved when a young man chooses agriculture as a career, he is likely to have to rent land for many years before he accumulates enough capital to become the owner of a farm. Furthermore, an increasing number of owner-operators must rent additional land in order to make economical use of all the machinery they must acquire. Today about half of the farmland in Illinois is not owned by the farmers who cultivate it.

The origin of farm tenancy in Illinois is associated with the acquisition of large landholdings by speculators during the period of early settlement. Several people of means acquired vast acreages, particularly in the prairies of central and northern Illinois, by purchases from the federal government as it disposed of the public domain, purchases from the Illinois Central Railroad as it disposed of land granted to it by the government, and other means. The owners of these huge tracts were mostly speculators who were not inclined to settle on the land and cultivate it themselves; therefore, they either hired other people to farm the land or rented it to tenants. Some of these enormous tracts have remained largely intact, a factor which has restricted the amount of land available for purchase to the present time.

Owner-operated farms are concentrated mainly in the southern one-third of the state, in the western Illinois counties bordering the Illinois and Mississippi rivers, and in the tier of counties along the northern border of the state (Fig. 5-18). In general, dairy farmers, livestock farmers, and specialty crop farmers have been primarily owner-operators in the past and continue to be so. With the exception of machinery, investments on such farms are of a decidedly permanent nature. A silo or a milking parlor, for example, cannot be moved from one farm to another. Likewise, fruit trees cannot be moved; they are long term investments, take several years

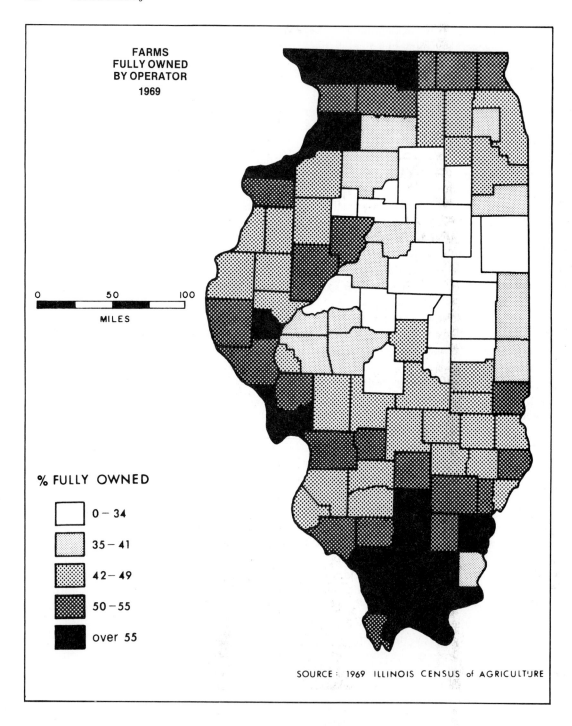

Figure 5-18. Farms fully owned by operator, 1969.

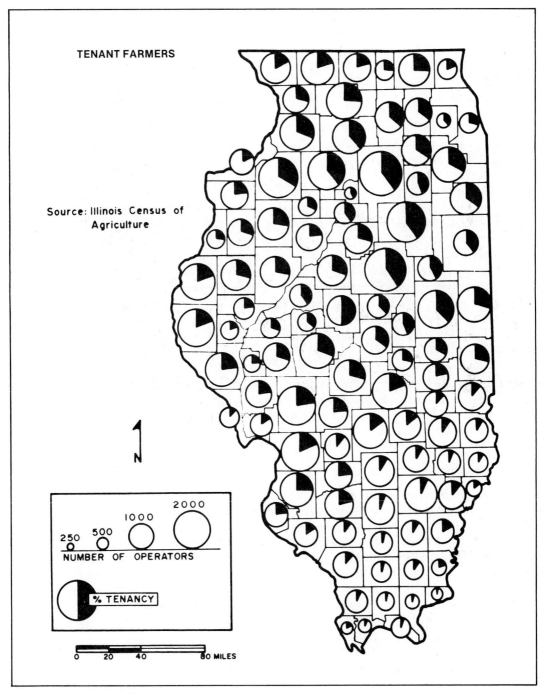

Figure 5-19. Tenant farmers as a percentage of total farm operators, Illinois. Source: Illinois Census of Agriculture.

to begin producing, and require careful attention in order to produce well. Only owners of farms are usually willing to invest in such permanent facilities and trees. Owner-operators have the opportunity to exercise complete control over their farming operations.

The greatest concentration of tenant-operated farms is in the Cash Grain Region of eastern and central Illinois (Fig. 5-19). Most cash grain farmers have heavy investments in huge tractors, combines, cultivators, fertilizing equipment, etc. Such equipment obviously can be moved about from one unit to another, so when a tenant farmer loses his lease or for some other reason moves to another farm there is little difficulty associated with the transfer. The tenant farmer simply moves his equipment to the new farm being leased and avoids loss on his investment. Another reason for the close association of tenancy with the Cash Grain Region is that most landlords prefer the production of cash grain crops on their land because it involves less risk and provides a more dependable and remunerative income than other types of farming.

Farming as a Way of Life

It has long been common to refer to farming as a "way of life," but this characteristic of agriculture in Illinois is rapidly disappearing. Many high officials in government and business now extol the virtues of agriculture as an industry and insist that the nation no longer can afford the relatively small farms on which farmers and their families have earned a livelihood generation after generation. We are told that agriculture must become organized like big business and adopt principles of industry such as automation and mass production.

One cannot deny that agriculture has undergone startling changes during the past

several decades, for better or worse, and in some areas it is already nearly as mechanized and automated as industry. The level of mechanization has reached a point that the farmer himself often is able to do all of the work necessary to operate the farm. There simply no longer is need for additional "hands," including the farmer's children, on many Illinois farms. The children consequently develop a detachment from the land and are forced to seek employment elsewhere. The family thereby becomes scattered and farming as a way of life deteriorates.

The decision by some farmers to move to town rather than live on the land they work also can have an adverse effect on attitudes toward the land. Especially in the Cash Grain Region there are growing numbers of what Walter Kollmorgen called "sidewalk farmers."[5] These are people who live in town but drive out to their farms when necessary to attend to crop production. There also is an increasing number of farms in Illinois operated by what Kollmorgen called "suitcase farmers."[6] These are people who live at such a distance that they carry a suitcase of some sort when they briefly visit their farm to perform such needed work as plowing, planting, cultivating, and harvesting. Suitcase farmers commonly have another occupation in addition to their farming operation.

In 1974 nearly 30 percent of all farms in Illinois were operated by individuals who did not consider farming to be their principal occupation. An increasing number of farmers feel that they are forced to "moonlight" (i.e., work at second jobs) because of the economic uncertainties of farming. Of course, this practice was impossible before farm technology and mechanization reached a high level, but now it is practical for the farmer to work at two jobs. Farming as a way of life may not be eliminated by this practice, but it definitely suffers as farmers devote an increasing amount of attention to their second job.

Some types of farming in Illinois still persist as a way of life. Dairying is the most notable example; it is a year-round operation and requires the farmer's constant attention to his herd. At least twice daily the farmer must attend to the needs of his cows; even with mechanical assistance, he still must work every day. In addition to carrying out the milking, he must keep constant watch on the health of his herd, act as a midwife when calves are born, and make sure that the farm produces as much of the feed for the hungry cattle as possible. The whole family is involved in the many daily duties required to operate a successful dairy farm.

Many farmers are discouraged by the slim profits in dairying, especially when they observe what seems to be a better life enjoyed by their neighbors who engage in cash grain or other types of farming. They often decide to sell their dairy operation and move to a nearby town to find a different job or retire. It has become increasingly difficult to find young men, even the sons of dairymen, to take over when a dairy farmer retires. The younger men prefer jobs that require only 40 hours per week of work time and provide an annual paid vacation.

While dairying is probably the best example of farming as a way of life in Illinois at present, there are others. The raising of hogs and beef cattle and orcharding may not have the demanding daily responsibilities associated with dairying, but they nevertheless require dedication, skill, and almost constant attention on the part of the farmer. Truck farming also is a confining enterprise, although its demands on the farmer are much more seasonal.

A consideration of farming as a way of life in Illinois would not be complete without some attention to the Amish community cen-

Figure 5-20. Amish horses and buggies at a hitching rail in Arthur, Illinois. (Photo by Arlin D. Fentem.)

tered on Arthur in the east-central part of the state.[7] For over a hundred years a settlement of Amish has thrived here in Douglas, Moultrie, and Coles counties. This religious sect feels that modern conveniences such as electricity, automobiles, telephones, and other forms of mechanization are not in keeping with their religious beliefs. Consequently, a visit to the Amish community is like taking a trip 50 years into the past. Common sights are teams of horses pulling plows, cultivators, binders, and wagons through the fields, as the Amish use true horsepower on their farms.

Amish farms have distinctive characteristics that enable an observer to distinguish them from the farms of their neighbors. With tractors, trucks, and other types of mechanized equipment lacking, the farms are necessarily small—generally no more than 80 acres in size—but well cared for and intensively cultivated. The land is divided into many fields, each bordered by a tight fence to contain the large number of livestock. To feed the horses and other animals, oats are raised as a major crop much like they were 50 years ago on most Illinois farms. After the oats and wheat are harvested, strawstacks dot the fields of Amish farms. To increase the income from their small farms, most Amish have dairy herds, chickens, and even large brooder sheds and egg factories. Large barns and other buildings have been constructed to house animals and to store the hay, feed, and other produce of the farms. Commonly two houses stand off the corner from each other on an Amish farmstead; the small one is occupied by the grandparents after they retire. The main house is usually quite large to accommodate

Figure 5-21. An Amish barn and horses in Coles County, Illinois. (Photo by Arlin D. Fentem.)

the many children that are typical of Amish families.

The Amish way of life has a charm, serenity, and single-minded purpose all too rare in Illinois agriculture today. It would be worthwhile for anyone to travel through the Amish country to watch these industrious people at work, to see them riding in their buggies and wagons on the roads, and to buy some of their produce such as honey, eggs, bread, and other bakery goods. They are a peace-loving folk, dedicated to the simple life.

Although agriculture generally has become mechanized, automated, and oriented toward mass production, there are enough hearty souls in Illinois who fortunately love the land and the job of tilling it to prevent a complete disappearance of farming as a way of life. To them, farming is more than simply a means of making a living; it allows greater independence than other types of employment and represents "the good life." They may grumble and complain, as most of us do on occasion, but they continue to stay close to the sod.

Agricultural Trends and Prospects

While prediction is always hazardous, such variables as weather, technological developments, and market conditions make it particularly risky in the case of agriculture. Nevertheless, many trends in Illinois farming are evident, and from them we, perhaps, can make intelligent guesses as to what the future holds.

The tendency toward larger farms continues, although the rate is somewhat slower than in the past. The average size of individual farms in Illinois increased from 242 acres in 1969 to 250 acres in 1974. A continuing increase in the acreage of cash grain farms throughout the state seems likely, with most notable growth to be expected in the

Cash Grain Region where generally large farms are already concentrated (Fig. 5-22). Agricultural experts now recommend that cash grain farmers cultivate at least 600 acres in order to earn a reasonable profit, especially during these times of high inflation rates. With tractors and other equipment increasing in size and efficiency, the individual farmer undoubtedly will have the capability to plow, plant, and cultivate a greater acreage in the future. As a result of the consolidation of smaller farms into larger ones, there is destruction of fences and old farm buildings, wider spacing of remaining farmsteads, and the development of a more open landscape; the Cash Grain Region, in fact, is looking more like rural Kansas each year. Also related to the growth in farm size is the decline in numbers of Illinois farmers, a trend that can be expected to continue into the foreseeable future.

In comparison to cash grain operations, other types of farms in Illinois generally are smaller in size and can be expected to have little or no increase in their future acreages. Among these, beef farms tend to be the largest and dairy farms, hog farms, and orchard farms are relatively moderate in size. The smallest units commonly are truck farms devoted to the production of vegetables and small fruits. Livestock farmers have increasingly turned to the use of feed lots and commercial feeds to increase their production as an alternative to the purchase or rental of additional acreage. The process of confined feeding and fattening of livestock undoubtedly will become even more widespread on Illinois farms in the years ahead.

While cash grain farming continues to expand, other types of farming in Illinois are experiencing stagnation or decline. For example, the number of dairy farms is decreasing and the inventory of milk cows dropped from 292,000 in 1969 to 237,000 in 1974. The

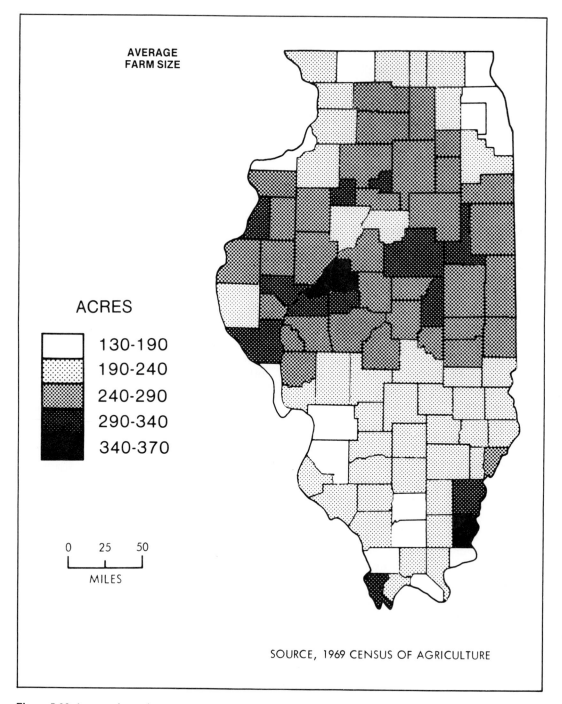

Figure 5-22. Average farm size.

per capita demand for milk and milk products is declining and probably will continue to do so because of competition from soft drinks and other beverages. Specialty cropping is another type of farming in the state that is not experiencing significant growth. Illinois orchardists and small fruit producers are suffering keen competition from growers in western states, especially California. Although Illinois fruit is of equal or superior taste, it cannot compete in appearance with the beautiful western fruit that attracts supermarket shoppers.

The technological and chemical revolution already has significantly changed most aspects of agriculture and its impact may be even greater in the future. The use of chemical fertilizers and weed and pest controls has enabled the farmer to obtain greater crop yields while spending less time operating equipment in the fields. To improve the health and rate of growth of their animals, livestock farmers have adopted scientific breeding techniques and the use of

chemical feed supplements and disease control materials. Growers of soybeans are beginning to benefit from the development of ersatz food products based on that versatile crop; we are promised that soybean hamburger and steak soon will be indistinguishable from the real thing. Artificial bacon is now being marketed on a limited basis, and many other substitute and imitation foodstuffs undoubtedly will soon appear. Fortunately for farmers, most substitute food products must come from the soil. Therefore, the trend toward production of substitute foodstuffs will result in shifts in utilization of Illinois farmland, but the state will continue to be a leader in agricultural output.

An increasingly critical problem in Illinois agriculture, especially for young men starting out in farming, is the burgeoning cost of land, machinery, and other necessities. Land prices have spiraled to the point that the best farmland in the state now sells for more than $4,000 an acre. In the single year of 1976,

Figure 5-23. A combine unloads freshly harvested wheat into an awaiting truck that will transport the crop to a nearby grain elevator. These and other expensive pieces of equipment are necessary for the operation of a modern grain farm. (Photo by Fred C. Caspall.)

land value in Illinois increased by 41 percent. In addition, the cost of machinery and equipment has skyrocketed to a staggering amount. Although different types of farming have different machinery requirements, some combination of tractors, combines, planters, trucks, milking equipment, orchard equipment, and other implements is required. The investment in machinery for even a modest farming operation can easily amount to several tens of thousands of dollars. Because of the enormous capital requirements, farms are being purchased increasingly by professional people and corporations rather than by farmers themselves. The land is then rented to those who actually cultivate it; consequently, farm tenancy continues to expand in Illinois. The young man who hopes to become the owner-operator of a farm faces a difficult and often lengthy struggle. In the face of increasing costs associated with farming, many farmers have taken a second job in a nearby town or city; as indicated earlier, some have become suitcase and sidewalk farmers.

Another serious problem has been the transfer of farmland to urban and industrial uses, especially in the vicinity of larger metropolitan centers. The time has arrived for planners to reserve good farmland in Illinois for agricultural purposes only so that it cannot be diverted from the all-important role of producing foodstuffs. Priorities must be established and restrictions imposed on the conversion of farms into industrial sites, parking lots, shopping malls, and bedroom suburbs.

Summary

Illinois is one of the nation's most important agricultural states; it has played a dominant role in farming for over a century. The state enjoys many advantages for a wide variety of farming types. Nature bestowed fertile soils, gently rolling terrain over most of the state, and the variety of climatic conditions is favorable to many kinds of farming endeavors.

Locational factors also are advantageous for agriculture in Illinois. The state is bordered and crossed by navigable rivers which provide inexpensive transportation linkages. Lake Michigan allows the state to be accessible to ocean-going ships for inexpensive export of Illinois farm products abroad. Major east-west railroad and highway routes cross Illinois and give the state an excellent land transportation network. Many nearby midwestern cities, especially Chicago and St. Louis, provide eager markets for Illinois farm products. The enormous growth of the Chicago area alone has stimulated a corresponding increase in agricultural production in Illinois.

Illinois agriculture has experienced striking development since its humble beginnings. Modern farming is highly mechanized and automated, and it requires great technical and scientific skills on the part of farmers. With mechanization, particularly in the case of cash grain farming, one man now can operate an entire farm single-handedly. There are, however, some types of farming which are more demanding of manpower. Orcharding, dairying, truck farming, and livestock raising are examples of more intensive types of agriculture.

Certain areas in Illinois have developed specialization in a common type of agricultural enterprise. Cash grain farming and dairying represent this tendency, but even small operations producing such crops as horseradish, sweet corn, pumpkin, and popcorn have become concentrated in distinct regions. Regionalization of farming types offers a number of economic advantages.

Agriculture in Illinois has become "big business," and farming is acquiring the characteristics of industry—for better or worse. The trend toward larger sized farms continues, especially in cash grain farming areas. The growth of farm size has been slower in areas of dairying, orcharding, and truck farming, however. Farmers, particularly young men beginning their career, are finding the spiraling cost of land and machinery a difficult problem. Consequently, the practice of tenancy is growing and an increasing number of farmers are working at second jobs in nearby towns. Farming as a way of life is diminishing. The most interesting exception can be found in the Amish settlement near Arthur, where farming continues to be practiced much like it was a half century ago.

Science and technology have become the handmaidens of Illinois farmers. The production of most agricultural commodities has steadily increased as a result of careful plant and animal selection and the use of chemical fertilizers and weed and pest control products. Technology has made possible the conversion of soybeans into artificial beef, bacon, and other foods. New scientific discoveries will likely continue to bring about significant changes in Illinois agriculture.

Farming can be expected to make important contributions to the economic well-being of the state and the nation in the future. Urban expansion and other non-productive inroads upon agricultural lands must be carefully controlled or halted, however, if the nation is to be assured of an adequate supply of foodstuffs in the years ahead.

Notes

1. Recent changes in Illinois agriculture are briefly summarized in Andrew J. Sofranko, "Illinois Agriculture: The Changing Scene," *Illinois Research* 15 (Fall 1973), pp. 3-5, and Michael Bowling and J.C. Van Es, "Changes Over a Decade in Illinois Agriculture," *Illinois Research* 19 (Spring 1977), pp. 14-15.

2. For a detailed study of nineteenth century agriculture in Illinois and neighboring Iowa, see Allen G. Bogue, *From Prairie to Corn Belt: Farming on the Illinois and Iowa Prairies in the Nineteenth Century* (Chicago: University of Chicago Press, 1963).

3. Recent yield variations of the major grain crops in Illinois are reviewed in J.H. Herbst, "Twenty-Year Trends in Crop Yields: Corn, Soybeans, Wheat, and Oats," *Illinois Research* 17 (Summer 1975), pp. 8-9.

4. R.C. Ross and H.C.M. Case, *Types of Farming in Illinois,* Agricultural Experiment Station Bulletin 601 (Urbana: University of Illinois College of Agriculture, 1956).

5. Walter M. Kollmorgen and George F. Jenks, "Sidewalk Farming in Toole County, Montana, and Traill County, North Dakota," *Annals of the Association of American Geographers* 48 (December 1958), pp. 375-97.

6. Walter M. Kollmorgen and George F. Jenks, "Suitcase Farming in Sully County, South Dakota," *Annals of the Association of American Geographers* 48 (March 1958), pp. 27-40.

7. See Lois F. Fleming and Dalias A. Price, "The Old Order Amish Community of Arthur, Illinois, Part I," *Bulletin of the Illinois Geographical Society* VI (June 1964), pp. 4-13, and Lois F. Fleming and Dalias A. Price, "The Old Order Amish Community of Arthur, Illinois, Part II," *Bulletin of the Illinois Geographical Society* VII (June 1965), pp. 4-24.

Selected References

Aldrich, S.R. *Illinois Field Crops and Soils.* Cooperative Extension Service Circular 901. Urbana: University of Illinois, 1965.

Blanchard, W.O. "Agricultural Provinces of Illinois." *Journal of Geography,* 23 (1922), 6-13.

Bogue, Margaret B. *Patterns from the Sod: Land Use and Tenure in the Grand Prairie, 1850-1900.* Vol. XXIV of *Collections of the Illinois State Historical Society.* (Land Series, Vol. I.) Springfield: Illinois State Historical Society, 1959.

Bowling, Michael, and Van Es, J.C. "Changes Over a Decade in Illinois Agriculture." *Illinois Research,* 19 (Spring 1977), 14-15.

Brunn, Stanley D. "The Origin and Movement of Fresh Vegetables to Chicago." *Bulletin of the Illinois Geographical Society,* VII (June 1965), 25-30.

Dovring, Folke. "The Farmland Boom in Illinois." *Illinois Agricultural Economics,* 17 (July 1977), 34-38.

Fleming, Lois F., and Price, Dalias A. "The Old Order Amish Community of Arthur, Illinois, Part I." *Bulletin of the Illinois Geographical Society,* VI (June 1964), 4-13.

———. "The Old Order Amish Community of Arthur, Illinois, Part II." *Bulletin of the Illinois Geographical Society,* VII (June 1965), 4-24.

Hart, John Fraser. "The Middle West." *Annals of the Association of American Geographers,* 62 (June 1972), 258-82.

Herbst, J.H. "Twenty-Year Trends in Crop Yields: Corn, Soybeans, Wheat, and Oats." *Illinois Research,* 17 (Summer 1975), 8-9.

Hoag, Leverett P. "Location Determinants for Cash-Grain Farming in the Corn Belt." *The Professional Geographer,* 14 (May 1962), 1-7.

Kollmorgen, Walter M. "Farms and Farming in the American Midwest." Chapter 7 in Saul B. Cohen (ed.), *Problems and Trends in American Geography.* New York: Basic Books, Inc., 1967.

Price, Dalias A. "Southern Illinois Agriculture." *Bulletin of the Illinois Geographical Society,* I (April 1955), 39-41.

Ross, R.C., and Case, H.C.M. *Types of Farming in Illinois.* Agricultural Experiment Station Bulletin 601. Urbana: University of Illinois College of Agriculture, 1956.

Sofranko, Andrew J. "Illinois Agriculture: The Changing Scene." *Illinois Research,* 15 (Fall 1973), 3-5.

Van Arsdall, Roy N., and Elder, William A. *Economies of Size of Illinois Cash Grain and Hog Farms.* Agricultural Experiment Station Bulletin 733. Urbana: University of Illinois College of Agriculture, 1969.

Weaver, John C. "Changing Patterns of Cropland Use in the Middle West." *Geographical Review,* 44 (1954), 560-72.

———. "Crop Combination Regions in the Middle West." *Geographical Review,* 44 (1954), 175-200.

Weaver, John C. et al. "Livestock Units and Combination Regions in the Middle West." *Economic Geography,* 32 (1956), 237-59.

Chapter Six

MINING
AND MANUFACTURING

Martin W. Reinemann
Northern Illinois University

Mining and manufacturing, the first a primary economic activity and the other a component of the secondary sector, are both actually and relatively important in Illinois. In 1976, the gross state product was nearly 95 billion dollars. Only nine-tenths of 1 percent of this amount was attributable to mining, but manufacturing, the single largest contributor to the gross state product, generated about 28 billion dollars—about 30 percent of the state's total (Table 6-1). Although mining is the least important industry division in the state, Illinois ranked eleventh among all 50 states in 1974 in the value of its mineral production. In addition, the state's mineral output is very significant and necessary to all other industry divisions. Local minerals are used in building and road construction, as raw material in some manufacturing, in producing electricity, and as mineral fertilizers on agricultural land; fur-

Table 6-1. Gross State Product by Industry Division, 1970 and 1976.

	1970	1976[a]
	(figures in millions of $)	
GROSS STATE PRODUCT	60,079	94,957
Private Nonfarm	53,104	82,448
Mining	402	908
Contract Construction	3,025	4,407
Manufacturing	18,891	27,779
Trade	10,506	17,161
Finance, Insurance and Real Estate	7,733	12,380
Transportation, Communication and Utilities	5,234	8,609
Services and Other	7,313	11,564
Government	5,688	8,777
Farm	1,287	3,733

[a]Preliminary.

Source: *Illinois State and Regional Economic Data Book,* 1972 and 1976 Editions, Department of Business and Economic Development, Springfield.

thermore, they constitute the major product hauled by railroads and barges in the state.

In spite of considerable national dispersion of industry and a slight decline in the state's relative share in the nation's manufacturing in recent years, Illinois ranks fourth among all states in value added by manufacture and in number of employees in manufacturing. It is surpassed by New York, California, and Ohio in most measures of manufacturing, but it consistently leads the nation by accounting for over 2 billion dollars (about 8 or 9 percent) of the country's manufacturing exports. Indeed, Illinois has been famous for its manufacturing for a long time.

The State's Mineral Endowment

Illinois has generally ranked high among all states in the value of its mineral production, contributing a little over 2 percent of the nation's minerals by value. Mining as a basis of employment is not very significant, however, as this activity provided jobs for only about 23,700 persons in 1974—about one-half of 1 percent of the state's labor force (Table 6-2).

Even before the state of Illinois was created by the Enabling Act of April 18, 1818, Indian inhabitants made pottery from the native clay, used flint for tools and weapons, procured salt from mineral springs, and carved fluorspar into trinkets.[1] Early explorers reported finds of coal, copper, iron, lead, zinc, silver, building stone, and slate in the Illinois Territory, and most of these minerals were commercially mined as early as the beginning and middle years of the nineteenth century. Other resources such as sand and gravel were not intensively utilized until early in the twentieth century. The degree of development or exploitation of mineral deposits by man is dependent on a number of physical, economic, political, and cultural factors. Some of these are: (1) the

Table 6-2. Illinois and United States Employment by Industry Division—1970.

Industry Division	Illinois		United States	
	Number Employed	Percent	Number Employed	Percent
Agriculture, Forestry, Fishing	121,051	2.6	2,955,775	3.7
Mining	21,531	0.5	655,198	0.8
Construction	245,098	5.4	4,967,387	6.2
Manufacturing	1,393,166	30.4	20,823,873	26.1
Transportation, Communication, and Utilities	205,727	4.5	5,336,480	6.7
Wholesale Trade	190,294	4.2	3,231,801	4.0
Retail Trade	735,627	16.1	12,815,670	16.1
Finance, Insurance, and Real Estate	237,678	5.2	3,918,759	4.9
Service	1,091,959	23.8	20,700,450	26.0
Public Administration	199,415	4.4	4,321,301	5.4
Miscellaneous	137,053	2.9	74,911	0.1
Total	4,578,599	100.0	79,801,605	100.0

Source: *U.S. Census of Population, Detailed Characteristics of the Population: Illinois, United States,* 1970, Tables 183 and 235, respectively.

quantity of the mineral resource; (2) the quality; (3) accessibility; (4) climate; (5) topographic conditions; (6) demand and prices; (7) government policies; and (8) customs, attitudes, and characteristics of the people in the mineralized area.

Mineral deposits are formed by various geologic processes such as igneous intrusions or sedimentary depositions over varying periods of time. In Illinois, as elsewhere in the world's land area, mineral deposits occur in the unconsolidated material between soil and bedrock, as solid matter in the bedrock itself, and in the form of liquids or gases in the spaces of the bedrock. Sand, gravel, and clay are usually found in the first type of location although some clays are mined from bedrock layers. Limestone, dolomite, and sandstone are common types of sedimentary bedrocks used extensively in Illinois. Coal, fluorspar, lead, and zinc are the major solid deposits formed within the bedrock, while crude oil and natural gas constitute fluids and gaseous material found in the pore spaces of bedrock.

Mineral Production and Areal Distribution

Mineral resources may be categorized into three groups: mineral fuels, nonmetallic minerals, and metals. In Illinois, the first group represented about 80 percent and the second group 20 percent of the value of the state's mineral production in 1974 (Table 6-3). The third group, supplying less than 1 percent of the value of all minerals, is relatively insignificant in the state's mining activity. Although only four counties (Cass, Piatt, Morgan, and Putnam) out of the 102 in the state reported no mineral production in 1974, mining in Illinois is highly localized or concentrated, especially by types of minerals. The geographic distribution of mineral

Table 6-3. Illinois Mineral Production, 1974.

Material	Quantity	Value at Plant (in thousands of $)	Percentage of State Total Mineral Values
Coal	58,073,000 tons	580,726	55.84
Crude Oil	27,553,000 bbls.	244,395	23.50
Stone	63,229,000 tons	121,763	11.71
Sand and Gravel	42,705,000 tons	68,566	6.59
Fluorspar	154,000 tons	12,247	1.18
Clays	1,587,000 tons	3,744	.36
Zinc[a]	4,000 tons	2,947	.28
Natural Gas	1,436,000,000 cubic feet	574	.05
Lead[a]	500 tons	222	.02
Other Material[b]	—	4,871	.47
Total		1,040,055	100.00

[a]Recoverable content of ores.

[b]Includes fullers earth, gem stones, natural gas liquids, silver, peat, tripoli, natural bonded molding sand, and stone (dimension).

Source: Ramesh Malhotra and Shirley Halloran, *Illinois Mineral Industry in 1974,* Illinois Mineral Note #66, Illinois State Geological Survey, Urbana, Illinois, February 1977.

production can probably best be analyzed by discussing separately the locations of each of three groups of minerals.

Mineral Fuels

In recent years, Illinois has ranked fourth among the coal-producing states and has supplied about 10 percent of all bituminous coal produced in the United States. The 58.1 million tons produced in 1974 constituted over 55 percent of the state's mineral value (Table 6-3). Coal-bearing, Pennsylvanian age rocks comprise the bedrock beneath the glacial drift for about 65 percent of the state—primarily located south of a line drawn from Rock Island to Joliet. The coal seams of Illinois are said to be one of the largest known bituminous coal reserves reported for any state in the United States.

The latest estimate of reserves compiled by the Illinois State Geological Survey amounts to more than 148 billion tons of coal in seams at least 18 inches thick if less than 150 feet deep (strippable) and at least 28 inches thick if at depths of more than 150 feet. This estimate of the vast quantity represents all of the coal in the ground with thicknesses greater than the specified minimum and does not consider mining conditions, quality, economics, and nonavailability (under towns, highways, and so on). Only those areas heavily drilled for oil and gas were not included in the reserves estimates because of technical mining problems that would be associated with such heavily drilled areas.[2]

Coal production is about equally divided between strip and underground mining methods. At present, there are about 55 operating coal mines located in 22 counties in Illinois (Fig. 6-1). Nearly one-half of the coal production, however, comes from four counties and nearly 75 percent from the following eight counties ranked sequentially according to tonnage produced: Perry, Jefferson, St. Clair, Franklin, Randolph, Williamson, Fulton, and Macoupin.[3] Close examination of Figure 6-1 reveals three regional concentrations: western Illinois, where operations are principally by surface methods; eastern and central Illinois (Douglas, Christian, Macoupin, and Montgomery counties) where there are a small number of underground mines; and southern Illinois, the major coal-producing region, where both mining methods are employed.

Illinois coal is generally found in fairly thick, continuous, and relatively flat-lying beds. Such arrangement of the deposits helps account for the fact that Illinois coal mines are among the most productive in the United States and in the world. The coal is ranked as high-volatile bituminous,[4] averages about 11 percent ash, and has an average total sulfur content of about 3.57 percent, but it ranges from 0.5 percent sulfur to 6 percent.[5] In the past, low-sulfur coal areas (primarily in southern Illinois) have been more intensively mined than other areas. The low-sulfur coal has accounted for about 20-25 percent of total production even though all remaining reserves of low-sulfur coal in southern Illinois have been estimated at only 3 percent of total reserves. Much of the low-sulfur coal is used by steel plants for blending with higher-rank coals to produce metallurgical coke. Present and proposed state and federal regulations on emissions of sulfur dioxide will exclude the use of most Illinois coal unless high percentages of sulfur can be removed before or after combustion. More than three-fourths of all coal used in Illinois is for the purpose of generating electricity. In spite of the tremendous quantities in the state, about one-fifth of all coal used in Il-

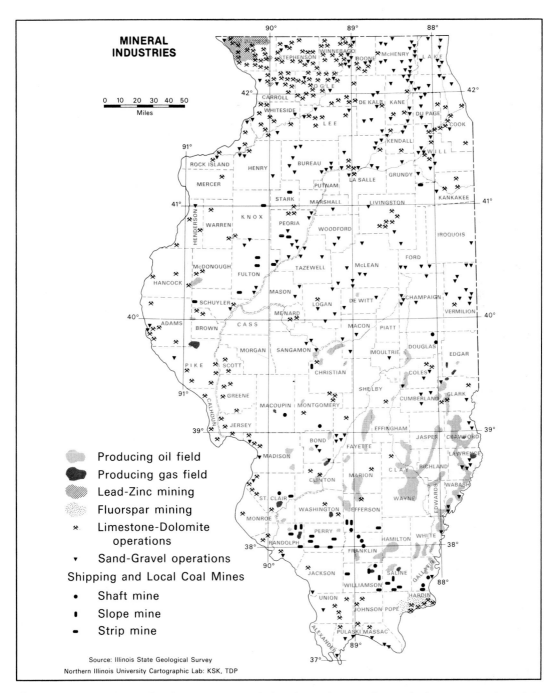

Figure 6-1. Mineral industries. Note that the majority of the sites and fields of mineral production are in northern and southern Illinois.

Figure 6-2. A boring type continuous mining machine in an underground mine in southern Illinois. Such machines as well as the thickness and arrangement of the deposits help make coal mines in Illinois some of the most productive in the world. (Courtesy Illinois Department of Mines and Minerals.)

linois is low-sulfur, western subbituminous purchased by electric generating plants from mines in Wyoming and Montana.

The first commercial oil and gas fields in Illinois were discovered in the late 1880s, but production was meager until new fields were discovered in 1906. Oil and gas zones in the state are associated with Pennsylvanian, Mississippian, Devonian, Silurian, and Ordovician age rocks where structural formations such as anticlines, synclinal basins, and reefs have resulted in oil accumulations.

Most of the oil fields are in southeastern and southern Illinois (Fig. 6-1). Six counties (Lawrence, White, Marion, Wayne, Fayette, and Clay) accounted for 61 percent of the total production in 1975. Oil pools in Mississippian rocks have been the most important, accounting for about three-fourths of the total yield. Pennsylvanian pools or wells have contributed about 16 percent of the total.

Illinois is one of the most important petroleum producing states east of the

Figure 6-3. One of the world's largest strip mining shovels (180 cubic yards) at work mining both #5 and #6 coal veins for the Southwestern Illinois Coal Corporation near Percy in Perry County, Illinois. Such machines help make coal mining in Illinois extremely productive. (Courtesy Illinois Department of Conservation and Illinois Department of Mines and Minerals.)

Mississippi River, but it ranked only tenth among all states and produced less than 1 percent of the nation's crude oil in 1975. With only minor exceptions, crude oil production in Illinois has been declining rapidly since 1941 (Fig. 6-4). New discoveries are not keeping pace with declining old-well production. Nearly three-quarters of all production is already by means of such relatively expensive and low-yielding methods of secondary recovery such as waterflooding.[6] Daily or annual production per well has never been very large in the Illinois oil fields. There were 23,630 producing wells in 1974, and their average annual production per well was about 1,124 barrels, or only about four bar-

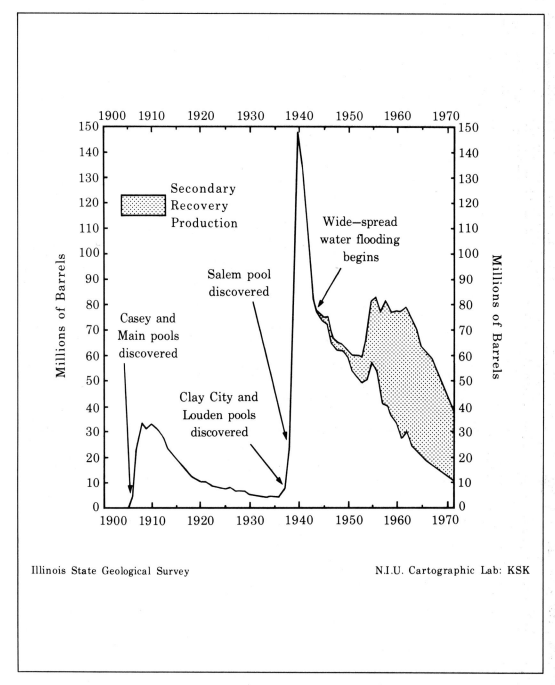

Figure 6-4. Crude oil production in Illinois, 1900 to 1971. Although Illinois is a significant source of crude oil, production has generally declined since the beginning of World War II.

rels per well per day. Declining yields and new discoveries coupled with low financial returns per well would indicate a dismal future for the petroleum industry of the state.

Natural gas discoveries in Illinois occurred about the same time and in the same location as petroleum finds, but Illinois has never been an important producer of this commodity. A considerable amount of solution gas[7] is "produced" (that is, removed from the ground) in association with crude oil production, but the gas is usually flared-off, lost to the atmosphere, or returned underground for storage or for repressuring.

An estimated three billion cubic feet of gas was removed from Illinois wells during 1974, either as solution gas or as gas obtained from separate gas reservoirs, but only about one and one-half billion cubic feet[8] was marketed—all within Illinois (Table 6-3). The marketed production represents a scant 1 percent of the state's total natural gas consumption. There were eight gas fields and 41 producing wells in operation (Fig. 6-1) at the close of 1975, all located in 4 counties (Coles, Williamson, Saline, and Gallatin).

Nonmetallic Minerals

The principal nonmetallic materials mined or quarried in Illinois are limestone, dolomite, clay, shale, common and silica sand, gravel, fluorspar, tripoli (amorphous silica), and peat. It seems incredible that the mine or quarry value of these materials is nearly equal to the total value of crude oil and that about 20 percent of the state's produced mineral value is from this type of product (Table 6-3). Stone, sand, and gravel, especially, are relatively inexpensive materials to mine but costly to transport; consequently, the highest volumes are usually mined near consuming centers. However,

these resources are relatively common and widely distributed so that production points are very dispersed (Fig. 6-1).

There were slightly more than 300 stone quarry operations in existence in Illinois in 1974 (Fig. 6-1) producing crushed and dimension stone for lime, cement, agricultural limestone, concrete and "blacktop" aggregate, ballast, and building stone. Illinois is the most important stone producing state in the nation after Pennsylvania. The largest number of quarries are in the northwest where limestone bedrock is nearly everywhere at, or very near, the surface. Quarry operations tend to be small in this region. The greatest production occurs in the northeastern region from large operations meeting demands of the Chicago Metropolitan Area. The next largest production is in the southwestern region of the state which supplies crushed and dimension stone for the St. Louis Metropolitan Area.

Common sand and gravel operations are largely concentrated (1) in that portion of the state which was covered by the Wisconsin stage of glaciation and (2) in stream valleys where alluvial and glaciofluvial sand and gravel deposits occur (Fig. 6-1). Illinois is the third most important state in sand and gravel production, ranking after California and Michigan. Northeastern Illinois is again the largest producing region in the state; in 1974 it accounted for over 50 percent of the total common sand and gravel tonnage mined.[9] Cook County, the highly urbanized core of the Chicago Standard Metropolitan Statistical Area, has been the leading Illinois county in terms of total value of minerals produced because of the large amount of sand, gravel, stone, cement, and clay produced there.[10]

Silica sand is composed almost exclusively of grains of the mineral quartz (common sand, on the other hand, generally contains a

Figure 6-5. Limestone quarry and crusher in Monroe County, Illinois, south of St. Louis. Limestone and dolomite are the most important stones mined in the state; they were worth about $90 million to the Illinois economy in 1972. (Courtesy Illinois State Geological Survey.)

mixture of quartz and other minerals). Silica sand is used in making glass, as molding sand, and in various grinding and filtration processes. In Illinois, this resource is based on the St. Peter Sandstone which is exposed along the Rock, Fox, and Illinois river valleys because of the upward arching of rock layers (the LaSalle Anticline) in the north-central part of the state. LaSalle and Ogle counties contain the leading producing quarries for this industry which annually mines over 2 million tons of sand valued at nearly 9 million dollars.

Illinois is the nation's leading producer of fluorspar, supplying over 76 percent of domestic shipments in 1974.[11] Because of sizeable imports of this commodity as a result of lower foreign production costs (especially in Mexico), Illinois now accounts for only about 10 percent of all domestic and foreign fluorspar consumed. This calcium fluoride mineral is exclusively produced in the extreme southeastern tip of Illinois in Pope and Hardin counties, primarily from underground mines.[12] The ore frequently contains varying amounts of lead and zinc, leading to some by-product production that is often quite profitable. The major use of fluorspar is for a flux in making steel, but it is also used to make hydrofluoric acid and some enamels, glazes, and certain kinds of glass.

Figure 6-6. A sand and gravel dredging operation in southeastern McHenry County in the Chicago SMSA. (Courtesy Illinois State Geological Survey.)

Commercial clays are found or obtained in Illinois from unhardened glacial and loessial deposits and from bedrock (usually shale) deposits.[13] Clay is used for making such products as pottery, stoneware, drain tile, flue tile, building tile, brick, and special heat-resistant firebrick. The glacial clay deposits are widely scattered throughout Illinois but are used most intensively in and near large urban concentrations, particularly for making brick. The wind-carried loessial deposits have their greatest depth on or near the bluffs of the Mississippi, Illinois, and Ohio rivers. These were once widely used for making tile and brick but their importance has been declining in recent years. Bedrock sources for ceramic materials, the shales and

clays associated with the coal-bearing rocks that underlie much of the state, are the most important sources today. Clay mined in the state was valued at 3.7 million dollars in 1974 (Table 6-3), but the clay products produced by 33 factories scattered in 21 counties were valued at 56.5 million dollars.

Metals

Lead and zinc are the only metallic minerals mined in Illinois, and their value was only one-third of 1 percent of the state's total mineral production in 1974. Deposits are found in Jo Daviess county in northwestern Illinois and in the fluorspar mining area of Pope and Hardin counties in extreme

Figure 6-7. A former sand and gravel strip-mined area near Lincoln, Illinois, now being used for recreation and permanent housing. (Courtesy Illinois Department of Mines and Minerals.)

southeastern Illinois (Fig. 6-1). In the northwest the ore occurs in rocks of Ordovician age, but in the southeast the minerals are found in rocks of Mississippian age. Between 1820 and 1865 the southwestern Wisconsin and northwestern Illinois mining region was the nation's principal producer of lead ore. Recently, production of zinc has increased and that of lead has decreased in this region because the richer ores have been removed and the ores now mined contain less galena (the chief mineral ore for lead) and more sphalerite (the chief ore of zinc).

The Bases for Manufacturing and Industrial Development in Illinois

As has been previously shown (Tables 6-1 and 6-2), the economic activity of manufacturing is the leading contributor to the Gross State Product and it is the single most important industry division in terms of employment. Almost 30 percent of the state's total

in both categories is supplied by manufacturing. This position of primacy among the industry divisions was not achieved until the late 1800s because mining, agriculture, and even commerce were more prominent in earlier periods of the state's development.

Although the word manufacturing is derived from two latin terms (*manus* and *factura*) meaning "making by hand," the activity of manufacturing generally includes processes whereby articles or materials are made by physical labor or by mechanical energy. In this study, all activities designated as manufacturing by the *Census of Manufactures* and included in the *Standard Industrial Classification Manual*[14] under SIC code numbers 20 through 39 will be considered as manufacturing. The term industry is generally broader in meaning and includes such activities as storage, wholesaling, and transport operations as well as manufacturing.

Most manufacturing is not only an urban function but also an extremely important "city-forming" activity because it triggers a multiplier-accelerator process of urban growth. Any expansion of manufacturing in an area can set in motion a chain reaction of further growth in retail trade, services, financial institutions, real estate, insurance, etc. Any regional study of manufacturing, therefore, also becomes a study of urban growth and distribution and initially requires an understanding of historical developments in the region. The remainder of this chapter will provide a brief account of the history of manufacturing in Illinois, followed by an examination of industrial location factors which influenced manufacturing to locate in the state, an analysis of the types of manufacturing present and their patterns of distribution, and a discussion of some trends in manufacturing taking place in the state.

Historical Development of Manufacturing in Illinois

Before the 1860s, the small amount of manufacturing which existed in Illinois was still primarily on a handicraft or home production basis with very little utilization of motive power. Products were usually based on agricultural, forest, and mineral raw materials and were manufactured almost exclusively to meet local demands for shelter, food, drink, transportation, implements, and clothing. Flour and grist mill products, packed meat, lumber, carriages, wagons, printed matter, and agricultural implements were the major items manufactured in Illinois before 1860.[15]

The period 1860-70 was one of considerable industrial expansion and more extensive use of modern-type factories. Local manufacturing was stimulated by demands created by the Civil War, by high war tariffs which were placed on practically all imported manufactured goods, by the general rise of prices which made manufacturing

more profitable, by the development of the West which was enhanced by railroad extensions, and by the increase in market which accompanied a doubling of the population in Illinois between 1850 and 1860 to a total of 170,000 persons. The Civil War and better transportation modes and routes stimulated the state's manufacturers to break into the larger national market and accelerated their shift away from serving only local markets. By 1870 there were approximately 12,597 manufacturing establishments in Illinois employing about 82,979 workers.[16] Although manufacturing was still somewhat dispersed within the state, Chicago was already proceeding toward dominance by producing about 44 percent of all manufactured items. The value of manufactured products produced in Illinois continued to increase and surpassed the value of agricultural products in 1880. This date marks the beginning of manufacturing's supremacy among the state's economic activities.

By 1890 Illinois was the most important manufacturing state west of the Alleghenies and it ranked third in the nation after New York and Pennsylvania. Also by 1890, the Chicago area had achieved second place ranking among the nation's manufacturing centers, a position it has held up to the present. Flour milling had begun to decline in importance as wheat production continued to move westward, but three out of five industries were still closely linked with agriculture. The state led the nation in production of iron and steel, agricultural implements, meat packing, and the manufacture of distilled spirits (from surplus corn) at this time. Manufacturing was much more highly concentrated in 1890 as Chicago contained about 72 percent of all manufacturing in the state.[17] By that year the number of establishments had increased to 20,482 in spite of the general growth in size of many of the state's factories. Manufacturing employment nearly quadrupled in the twenty-year period between 1870 and 1890, reaching a total of 312,000 workers.

At the time of World War I the major types of products manufactured in Illinois had not changed appreciably from those produced earlier. The total number of manufacturing establishments decreased slightly as plants became larger, but manufacturing employment continued to increase rapidly to a new high of 617,927.[18] Peoria was the second most important manufacturing city, followed by Joliet, East St. Louis, and Rockford, respectively.[19] Although the meat packing industry had the highest value of product, both the foundry and machine shop and the printing and publishing industries had higher values added by manufacture.

Between 1914 and the present, manufacturing in Illinois experienced various cycles of growth and decline, both absolutely and relatively. Following a period of decline soon after World War I, the number of

establishments again increased before World War II and continued to grow to slightly over 18,500 by 1967 (Table 6-4). Although the gain in number of establishments during the post-World War II period was not as rapid as in the nation as a whole, the average size of factories in Illinois increased more rapidly and to a greater extent than in the nation.[20] The presence of fewer establishments now than formerly should not be considered a disadvantage for Illinois nor construed as an indicator of manufacturing decline; larger establishments can operate more efficiently by relying upon economies of scale.

Employment in manufacturing in Illinois over the years has been more erratic than number of establishments, probably because of the greater sensitivity of employment to minor changes in the economy. The wartime and postwar booms and the recessions, including the Great Depression of the middle 1930s, are clearly revealed in the employment data shown in Table 6-4. Studies have shown that manufacturing employment

Table 6-4. Manufacturing in Illinois, Selected Years.

	Number of Establishments	Number of Employees	Number of Production Workers	Value Added by Manufacture (in thousands of $)
1900[a]	45,475	446,632	397,919	521,806
1914[b]	18,153	601,221	509,184	905,831
1929[b]	15,333	837,507	691,553	2,930,038
1933[b]	10,740	625,159[d]	420,334	1,200,784
1939[b]	11,983	752,728	590,995	2,187,240
1947[b]	15,988	1,184,820	954,415	6,680,137
1954[b]	17,628	1,177,043	902,967	9,663,848
1958[b]	18,100	1,139,412	835,233	11,664,070
1963[b]	18,593	1,211,200	855,900	14,641,500
1967[b]	18,536	1,397,300	995,100	20,061,500
1971[c]	Not Available	1,282,200	871,200	22,789,800
1974[c]	Not Available	1,372,500	945,400	29,356,700

[a]*U.S. Census of Population,* 1900, Volume VIII. (Includes hand trade and small shops.)

[b]*U.S. Census of Manufactures.*

[c]*Annual Survey of Manufactures,* 1971 and 1973.

[d]1935 data.

growth in Illinois lagged behind the United States average for significant postwar periods, but that in the most recent period studied (1958-1965) the rate of increase was greater in Illinois than in the United States as a whole.[21] However, before analyzing the nature, distribution, and trends of present day manufacturing in Illinois it is advisable to reflect on the general and specific factors which have helped influence manufacturing to locate in Illinois.

Industrial Location Factors

It has been implied that the state of Illinois had some manufacturing activity as soon as there were people living in the area. This is essentially true, but the large concentration of manufacturing here and its continuing national and international importance cannot be explained merely by the presence of a local market.

Why has Illinois become such an important manufacturing area and how has it maintained its position within the rapidly expanding economy of the United States? The conditions or factors which are the bases for industrial development within any region are referred to as industrial location factors. The complex of factors which influence the location of manufacturing can be categorized and studied from various viewpoints. Because manufacturing covers a wide range of activities, the industrial location factors vary greatly from one industry group to another in accordance with different inputs of materials, labor, energy, capital, and location of markets. Manufacturers processing perishable raw materials, or requiring certain types of skilled labor, or producing a bulky product, for example, operate under a different complex of location factors than other manufacturers. Economists, and

others, frequently describe and analyze the characteristics of manufacturing and its locational responses in terms of (1) procurement costs of materials, (2) on-site or processing costs, and (3) distribution costs. Geographers concerned with interpreting the distribution of manufacturing have found it useful to know some of the essentials about the technique of the activity to be studied and something about the activity's historical development and its economic characteristics and requirements.[22] A fourth essential which has been useful for some researchers in appraising reasons for industrial locations and patterns is an understanding of human behavior with respect to noneconomic motives.

Primarily, two separate location theories have been developed to answer the question "Where ought industries to locate?" Weberian theory[23] is directed toward determination of the least cost location. It assumes that demand is constant or unlimited and cannot be influenced by action of individuals. The objective is to identify the factory location as a point where the combined weight movements involved in the assembly and distribution of the product are at a minimum. The market area or profit maximization approach concentrates on the demand aspects of manufacturing and disregards spatial variations in production costs. The major advocate of this approach was August Lösch,[24] who depicted optimal locations as occurring where producers could control or monopolize the largest possible market area, thus maximizing sales and total revenue. No attempt will be made here to explain manufacturing locations in Illinois in accordance with either or both of these theories. Instead, the primary and secondary location factors that help account for manufacturing in general will be considered because significant location factors vary considerably from one manufacturing type or one manufacturing plant to another.

Principal Industrial Location Factors

The major industrial location factors responsible for manufacturing locating and prospering in Illinois were primarily established by 1914. The early nucleus of a large manufacturing economy in the state developed as a result of the favorable combination of such traditional location factors as: (1) available raw materials in the form of agricultural, forest, and mineral products; (2) power and fuel from central and southern Illinois coalfields; (3) a large and relatively prosperous local and regional market; (4) excellent transportation facilities and routes, including cheap river and lake transports as well as extensive railroad and highway networks which facilitated movements of raw materials and manufactured products to and from local, regional, and international points; (5) a large, industrious, productive, and innovative labor supply; and (6) available money capital in the hands of people willing to invest in local manufacturing activities. Equally important for many manufacturers who have chosen to locate in Illinois are the economies achieved by large-scale operations and by locating in a major center of industrial production—a process which may lead to production and distribution advantages referred to as agglomeration economies.[25] Large-scale economies within a single establishment result in savings in fuel and use of equipment, for example. Many or all firms of a single industry located at one place may achieve economies through obtaining specialized services and common pools of labor and by increased total output. Location within an area of industrial concentration can lead to economical linkages with suppliers or customers (especially if they are also manufacturers) and can be beneficial with respect to the economies of management that are obtained by an increase in total size (lower utility and transport costs and better technical advantages are possible, for example). As one of the world's largest industrial markets as well as a very prominent producer of manufactured goods, the Chicago area is the principal location in Illinois where the above types of economies are present.

All of the above industrial location factors are economic or related to economic conditions and need little further explanation. Not as apparent, perhaps, is the fact that they are closely related to Illinois' unparalleled geographic location with respect to physical features, to the concentration of people in the United States, and to the American Manufacturing Belt. Because it has a fortunate combination of good climate, natural vegetation, and soils, Illinois is in the heart of the extremely productive Corn Belt agricultural region and is partly within two others, the Dairy and General Farming regions. These labor-short agricultural regions generated a large demand for agricultural machinery which Illinois manufacturers could readily supply. Another pertinent matter concerning industrial location is that many population concentrations (representing labor and market areas for manufacturers) occur where there are breaks in transportation from one mode to another. Chicago, for example, is located at the break between canal, river, and lake transportation; between lake and railroad or highway; and in fact between different railroad lines. Break in transportation sites encourage the development of both commercial and manufacturing activities. Illinois is also as close to the geographic "center of population" of the United States as is possible; that point has been in southern Illinois for the past three decennial censuses. If one assigns equal weight to each person as a potential customer, Illinois manufacturers have an optimal location with respect to the United States market. The significance of this position is indicated by the fact that nearness to market is considered to be the single most important industrial location factor today by many economists and geographers. Finally, the inclusion of Illinois in the western portion of the so-called American Manufacturing Belt (usually designated as occupying a parallelogram-shaped area between Boston, Milwaukee, St. Louis, and Baltimore) presents Illinois manufacturers with a comparative advantage in supplying various types of consumer markets to the north, west, and south of the state's boundaries.

Secondary Industrial Location Factors

In addition to the role of the major industrial location factors cited, there are many other factors of secondary status which have favored the location of manufacturing in Illinois. Although commonly identified as secondary factors, they are often the most significant reason for a specific manufacturing activity's presence or its site location. Some of these factors are economic, but others are noneconomic in nature. The activity of inventors, for example, in originating and producing new products at a certain place is frequently the paramount reason for subsequent concentration of manufacturing activity at that particular location. The presence of farm machinery factories in Chicago and Moline and a number of machinery and furniture firms in Rockford, for example, is related to the location in those cities of inventors such as McCormick, John Deere, William Deering, William Burson, John Nelson, Marquis Gorham, Robert Bauch, and Howard D. Coleman.[26] George Pullman, inventor of the specialized railroad car for sleeping, was

partially responsible for the concentration of railroad equipment manufacturing in the Chicago area. In addition, he furthered the process of industrial decentralization in the Chicago area by building a complete manufacturing community about a dozen miles south of downtown Chicago in the early 1880s.[27]

Other manufacturers have chosen specific locations in the state because of such secondary location factors as (1) availability of a large supply of surface or ground water; (2) availability of adequate-sized parcels of nearly level land on which to build modern factory complexes and still have space for future expansion; (3) the presence of nearby developmental research facilities; (4) promotional activities of local, state, and regional development agencies or the presence of organized industrial districts;[28] (5) the existence of a local or state tax advantage; (6) the attractive qualities of a particular site or neighborhood; (7) real or imagined cultural amenities;[29] and (8) various governmental roles, functions, or actions. The importance of personal factors in location decisions has been stated and reviewed in many studies;[30] noneconomic attitudes of industrial officials and other influential individuals undoubtedly help explain many factory locations in Illinois as well as in the world. Governmental activities at the state and local level have also influenced many location decisions in Illinois. A major factor, of course, has been zoning regulations. In addition, the building of highways and waterways in or through certain areas, the type and amount of safety and health regulations with accompanying inspections, local building codes, and programs to aid depressed areas have also influenced certain industrial location decisions. It is also undoubtedly true that industrial inertia, most frequently influenced by the high cost of relocating, often causes a manufacturing firm to remain in a specific area or at a specific site even though it may be obvious that another location would be better. Thus the advantages of an early start and other locational attractions of a place may disappear after a period of time, but manufacturing may continue at the original site because of the cost and difficulty involved in overcoming inertia.

Types of Manufacturing in Illinois

The general manufacturing structure of Illinois is revealed and compared to that of the United States in Figure 6-8. In 1973, metal production provided about 60 percent of all manufacturing employment in the state, and in both 1947 and later years this type of manufacture was relatively more important in Illinois than in the nation.[31] Illinois also has lower percentages of employment in textiles, apparel, and wood production but higher proportions in foods, printing, and miscellaneous manufacture (Fig. 6-8).

According to the 1972 *Standard Industrial Classification Manual,* there are 450 different types of manufacturing activities in the United States classified into 143 three-digit and 19 two-digit categories, not including ordinance. Data on employment and value added by manufacture (a Bureau of the Census computation obtained by subtracting the value of material used from the value of product leaving the plant) for all of the major manufacturing categories in Illinois are shown in Table 6-5. The considerable degree of diversity in the composition of manufacturing in the state, an element that has helped Illinois maintain good economic stability, is evident in terms of the number of different types of manufacturing present. There is some employment in all of the two-digit and in as many as 130 three-digit categories,[32] but the manufacture of durable

goods (especially primary metals, fabricated metal products, machinery except electrical, and electrical equipment and supplies) is the most important segment of the Illinois industrial structure. The above four types of manufacture, represented by SIC two-digit categories 33, 34, 35, and 36, have about one-half of the total employment and value added in the state. With the addition of two other types of manufacture, food and kindred products (SIC #20) and printing and publishing (SIC #27), the percentage rises to about two-thirds. Thus, although there is considerable diversity in the type of manufacturing found in Illinois, there is also a very high concentration of employment and value added by manufacture in only six two-digit categories. The concentration of output in a few types of manufacture appears to be the general pattern in most large manufacturing centers in the United States. Chicago, and the rest of Illinois, for example, specialize in machinery and metal products, New York in clothing, Detroit in automobiles, and Los Angeles in aircraft production.

The relative importance of the various two and three-digit categories is also revealed by computing the location quotient for each manufacturing type. The location quotient measures the degree to which a specific region has more or less than its share of any particular industry when compared to total manufacturing. The ratio is calculated by dividing Illinois' share or percent of the national employment in each individual industry by the state's share or percent of the nation's total employment in manufacturing. For example, 112,100 employees in food and kindred products (SIC #20) in Illinois in 1973 represented 7.18 percent of the total employment in that category in the nation. Illinois employment in all manufacturing, 1,276,000, represented 6.76 percent of the

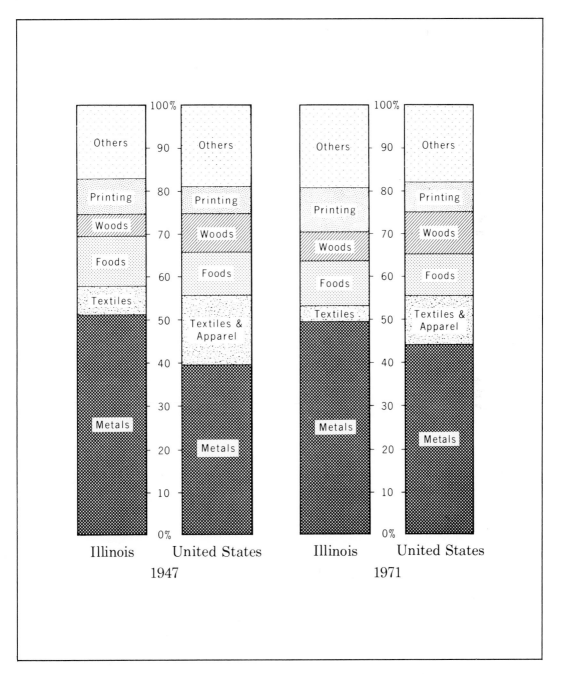

Figure 6-8. Manufacturing structures, 1947 and 1971, based on employment. In recent decades metal production has provided the greatest proportion of manufacturing employment in both Illinois and the nation. Based on Bureau of Census, *Census of Manufacturers, 1947*, and *Annual Survey of Manufacturers, 1971*. N.I.U. Cartographic Lab: KSK

Table 6-5. Manufacturing in Illinois by Selected Industry Groups and Industries, 1967 and 1973.

SIC Industry Description Code		1967		1973		
		All Employees (1,000)	Value Added by Manufacture (million dollars)	All Employees (1,000)	Value Added by Manufacture (million dollars)	Location Quotient[a]
	All Illinois	1,322.7	19,890.0	1,276.0	29,356.7	
20	**Food and Kindred Products**	120.0	2,512.6	112.1	3,236.7	1.06
201	Meat Products	16.3	204.3	15.6	328.3	.77
202	Dairy Products	10.1	189.1	10.5	297.2	.83
203	Preserved Fruit & Vegetable	11.0	196.5	10.2	259.5	.64
204	Grain Mill Products	15.6	484.7	14.9	527.3	1.37
205	Bakery Products	20.7	304.8	18.2	426.0	1.15
206	Confectionary Products	15.6	234.7	16.9	414.5	2.33
208	Beverages	13.4	400.0	12.3	482.0	.89
209	Misc. Foods & Kindred Products	15.3	411.4	8.4	277.1	.89
22	**Textile Mill Products**	5.5	50.5	4.6	83.5	.07
229	Misc. Textile Goods	3.1	30.1	2.1[b]	NA	.43[b]
23	**Apparel & Other Textile Products**	38.4	293.7	30.1	368.7	.32
231	Men's & Boy's Suits & Coats	8.7	72.8	6.0	78.3	.70
232	Men's & Boy's Furnishings	4.1	29.8	3.3[b]	NA	.13
233	Women's & Misses' Outerwear	10.3	80.5	9.4	119.3	.31
234	Women's & Children's Under- garments	2.9	21.3	1.5[b]	NA	.20[b]
238	Misc. Apparel & Accessories	3.5	20.5	3.3[b]	NA	.82[b]
239	Misc. Fabricated Textiles Products	7.4	58.7	8.0	96.6	.62
24	**Lumber and Wood Products**	12.1	112.0	14.0	175.4	.29
242	Sawmills & Planing	1.6	11.0	1.3[b]	NA	.09[b]
243	Millwork, Plywood, & Re- lated Products	3.8	41.0	4.1	43.3	.30
249	Misc. Wood Products	5.6	50.8	6.5	86.7	1.14
25	**Furniture and Fixtures**	25.8	280.9	25.4	431.7	.79
251	Household Furniture	14.1	135.7	12.3	188.3	.56
252	Office Furniture	2.0	27.9	2.1[b]	NA	.73[b]
254	Partitions & Fixtures	5.8	74.9	6.3	108.8	1.59
259	Misc. Furniture & Fixtures	2.9	33.5	3.3	69.0	1.71

*Includes all industry groups and industries with 1,000 or more employees.

[a]See text for definition and methodology. Computations based on *Annual Survey of Manufactures,* 1973 unless otherwise noted.

[b]Data and computations based on statistics in U.S. Department of Commerce, *County Business Patterns (Illinois and U.S. Summary)* 1973.

NA—Detailed information not available from primary sources and/or listed with less than 1,000 employees in *County Business Patterns.*

Sources: 1967 *Census of Manufactures* and 1973 *Annual Survey of Manufactures.*

Table 6-5–*Continued*

SIC Industry Description Code		1967		1973		
		All Employees (1,000)	Value Added by Manufacture (million dollars)	All Employees (1,000)	Value Added by Manufacture (million dollars)	Location Quotient[a]
	All Illinois	1,322.7	19,890.0	1,276.0	29,356.7	
26	**Paper and Allied Products**	40.9	528.8	40.6	861.8	.93
263	Paperboard Mills	2.2	35.3	2.5[b]	NA	.53[b]
264	Misc. Converted Paper Products	16.2	238.4	17.6	413.6	1.31
265	Paperboard Containers and Boxes	20.8	230.2	19.9	373.6	1.32
27	**Printing and Publishing**	107.0	1,600.9	107.0	2,361.7	1.46
271	Newspapers	21.6	271.8	22.9	427.4	.96
272	Periodicals	7.0	151.4	6.9	211.9	1.46
273	Books	9.2	276.9	9.7	398.4	1.41
274	Misc. Publishing	5.3	98.8	4.8	112.5	1.85
275	Commercial Printing	44.7	577.1	45.4	896.8	1.88
276	Manifold Business Forms	3.8	60.1	3.6	90.8	1.30
277	Greeting Card Publishing	1.6	12.8	1.0[b]	NA	.60[b]
278	Blankbooks & Bookbinding	8.2	75.1	3.9	49.0	1.09
279	Printing Trade Services	5.7	77.0	5.1	101.7	1.67
28	**Chemicals and Allied Products**	57.4	1,565.8	54.8	2,408.0	.95
281	Industrial Chemicals	10.1	290.1	6.0	208.8	.89
282	Plastics Materials & Synthetics	2.4	56.9	2.6	147.0	.23
283	Drugs	10.5	283.8	13.4	478.7	1.42
284	Soap, Cleaners, & Toilet Goods	11.1	496.9	13.0	935.7	1.69
285	Paints & Allied Products	9.2	190.1	8.6	240.9	1.84
287	Agricultural Chemicals	NA	NA	1.9[b]	NA	.60[b]
289	Misc. Chemical Products	11.7	214.9	8.0	254.3	1.46
29	**Petroleum and Coal**	11.1	382.7	10.3	660.5	1.12
291	Petroleum Refining	6.5	295.2	6.4	530.9	.97
295	Paving & Roofing Materials	3.6	57.3	2.8	82.2	1.42
299	Misc. Petroleum & Coal Products	1.0	30.2	NA	NA	

*Includes all industry groups and industries with 1,000 or more employees.

[a]See text for definition and methodology. Computations based on *Annual Survey of Manufactures,* 1973 unless otherwise noted.

[b]Data and computations based on statistics in U.S. Department of Commerce, *County Business Patterns (Illinois and U.S. Summary)* 1973.

NA–Detailed information not available from primary sources and/or listed with less than 1,000 employees in *County Business Patterns.*

Sources: 1967 *Census of Manufactures* and 1973 *Annual Survey of Manufactures.*

Table 6-5–*Continued*

SIC Industry Description Code		1967		1973		
		All Employees (1,000)	Value Added by Manufacture (million dollars)	All Employees (1,000)	Value Added by Manufacture (million dollars)	Location Quotient[a]
	All Illinois	1,322.7	19,890.0	1,276.0	29,356.7	
30	**Rubber and Plastic Products N.E.C.**	38.0	474.3	41.1	768.0	.91
301	Tires & Inner Tubes	NA	NA	NA	NA	
302	Rubber & Plastic Footwear	NA	NA	NA	NA	
306	Fabricated Rubber Products N.E.C.	7.9	105.5	3.3	47.0	.45
307	Misc. Plastic Products	26.8	307.9	30.4	519.9	1.17
31	**Leather and Leather Products**	14.0	132.6	6.6	84.3	.37
311	Leather Tanning & Finishing	1.7	23.9	1.4[b]	NA	.88[b]
314	Footwear, except rubber	NA	NA	6.3[b]	NA	
32	**Stone, Clay, and Glass Products**	37.9	553.3	40.3	895.5	.93
321	Flat Glass	NA	NA	1.3[b]	NA	.87[b]
322	Glasses & Glassware	10.2	122.8	10.5[b]	NA	1.27
323	Products of Purchased Glass	2.8	46.2	3.0	85.1	1.20
325	Structural Clay Products	1.9	18.1	1.4	18.3	.40
326	Pottery & Related Products	NA	NA	2.5	34.4	.78
327	Concrete, Gypsum, & Plaster Products	6.7	119.4	8.6	205.4	.65
329	Misc. Nonmetallic Mineral Products	11.6	171.1	13.1	286.4	1.59
33	**Primary Metal Industries**	108.6	1,654.1	101.3	2,314.0	1.23
331	Blast Furnaces, Basic Steel Products	50.5	831.3	51.8	1,286.4	1.29
332	Iron & Steel Foundries	21.1	271.3	20.3	384.9	1.27
334	Secondary Nonferrous Metals	2.7	40.1	2.6	66.1	2.21
335	Nonferrous Rolling & Drawing	15.4	265.0	16.7	380.5	1.23
336	Nonferrous Foundries	9.0	107.8	7.3	139.6	1.24
339	Misc. Primary Metal Products	8.8	127.8	10.1[b]	NA	5.59[b]
34	**Fabricated Metal Products**	144.4	1,971.1	156.4	3,218.1	1.46
341	Metal Cans	10.4	151.9	11.3	267.5	2.07

*Includes all industry groups and industries with 1,000 or more employees.

[a]See text for definition and methodology. Computations based on *Annual Survey of Manufactures,* 1973 unless otherwise noted.

[b]Data and computations based on statistics in U.S. Department of Commerce, *County Business Patterns (Illinois and U.S. Summary)* 1973.

NA–Detailed information not available from primary sources and/or listed with less than 1,000 employees in *County Business Patterns.*

Sources: 1967 *Census of Manufactures* and 1973 *Annual Survey of Manufactures.*

Table 6-5–*Continued*

SIC	Industry Description Code	1967		1973		
		All Employees (1,000)	Value Added by Manufacture (million dollars)	All Employees (1,000)	Value Added by Manufacture (million dollars)	Location Quotient[a]
	All Illinois	1,322.7	19,890.0	1,276.0	29,356.7	
342	Cutlery, Handtools, & Hardware	17.4	229.7	19.2	365.4	1.71
343	Plumbing & Heating, Exc. Elec.	6.0	83.4	6.0	111.9	1.46
344	Fabricated Structural Metal Products	21.2	305.4	22.1	496.6	.78
345	Screw Machine Products, Bolts, etc.	20.0	290.6	20.9	461.1	2.81
346	Metal Forging & Stamping	27.9	393.2	31.2	672.4	1.60
347	Metal Services, N.E.C.	10.4	118.1	10.0	162.7	1.64
248	Misc. Fabricated Wire Products	8.8	86.3	7.5[b]	51.6	.99[b]
349	Misc. Fabricated Metal Products	22.3	312.6	31.0	591.1	1.79
35	**Machinery, Except Electrical**	223.8	3,415.9	216.4	4,911.4	1.61
351	Engines & Turbines	10.6	143.8	11.3[b]	NA	1.35[b]
352	Farm Machinery	31.4	510.9	23.7	526.9	2.42
353	Construction & Related Machinery	63.1	1,022.9	62.4	1,665.1	3.05
354	Metalworking Machinery	38.9	555.9	35.0	692.8	1.75
355	Special Industrial Machinery	17.0	236.9	14.1	326.4	1.02
356	General Industrial Machinery	26.8	412.6	26.2	555.8	1.36
357	Office & Computing Machines	8.9	149.9	9.8	219.4	.66
358	Service Industry Machines	11.9	175.5	15.6	327.6	1.08
359	Misc. Machinery, Except Electrical	15.2	207.6	14.2	259.9	1.05
36	**Electrical Equipment & Supplies**	211.4	2,445.3	180.7	3,590.8	1.49
361	Electrical Distributing Equipment	19.8	226.2	12.6	199.6	1.49
362	Electrical Industrial Appar.	11.9	145.1	12.7	203.2	.89
363	Household Appliances	25.6	313.9	24.2	443.9	2.06
364	Electric Lighting & Wiring Equipment	17.9	242.0	20.8	384.8	1.66

*Includes all industry groups and industries with 1,000 or more employees.

[a]See text for definition and methodology. Computations based on *Annual Survey of Manufactures,* 1973 unless otherwise noted.

[b]Data and computations based on statistics in U.S. Department of Commerce, *County Business Patterns (Illinois and U.S. Summary)* 1973.

NA–Detailed information not available from primary sources and/or listed with less than 1,000 employees in *County Business Patterns.*

Sources: 1967 *Census of Manufactures* and 1973 *Annual Survey of Manufactures.*

Table 6-5—*Continued*

SIC Industry Description Code		1967		1973		
		All Employees (1,000)	Value Added by Manufacture (million dollars)	All Employees (1,000)	Value Added by Manufacture (million dollars)	Location Quotient[a]
	All Illinois	1,322.7	19,890.0	1,276.0	29,356.7	
365	Radio & T.V. Receiving Equipment	38.8	388.8	28.1	812.3	3.70
366	Radio & T.V. Communication Equipment	15.7	190.2	47.3	1,034.7	1.51
367	Electronic Components Accessories	35.8	357.2	28.7	391.2	1.08
369	Misc. Electrical Equipment & Supplies	7.7	101.4	6.2	121.1	.70
37	**Transportation Equipment**	45.2	864.2	50.9	1,253.3	.41
371	Motor Vehicles & Equipment	22.4	425.6	29.1	634.3	.49
372	Aircraft & Parts	7.2	93.1	3.9[b]	NA	.13
374	Railroad Equipment	NA	NA	12.7	436.7	3.56
38	**Instruments and Related Products**	44.0	656.4	45.9	1,030.4	1.40
381	Engineering & Scientific	4.0	58.4	3.9	75.0	1.40
382	Mech. Measuring, Control Devices	15.3	236.3	19.1	416.1	1.68
384	Medical Instruments & Supplies	7.0	132.1	8.4	246.1	1.30
386	Photographic Equipment and Supplies	10.7	153.8	9.7	213.6	1.42
387	Watches, Clocks, & Watchcases	5.3	57.0	3.1	53.4	1.37
39	**Misc. Manufacturing Industries**	37.2	394.9	37.5	612.4	1.24
391	Jewelry, Silverware, Plated Ware	1.5	15.8	1.2[b]	NA	.32[b]
393	Musical Instruments & Parts	6.2	62.5	5.4	73.1	3.10
394	Toys & Sporting Goods	9.0	93.7	10.5	188.3	1.19
395	Pens, Pencils, Office, & Art Goods	3.0	39.7	2.8	51.5	1.25
396	Costume Jewelry & Notions	1.5	169.9	1.2[b]	NA	.35[b]
399	Misc. Manufacturers	16.0	169.9	16.2	242.2	1.58
	Total All Selected 3-Digit Industries	1,233.7	18,211.7	1,247.6	27,554.2	

*Includes all industry groups and industries with 1,000 or more employees.

[a]See text for definition and methodology. Computations based on *Annual Survey of Manufactures,* 1973 unless otherwise noted.

[b]Data and computations based on statistics in U.S. Department of Commerce, *County Business Patterns (Illinois and U.S. Summary)* 1973.

NA—Detailed information not available from primary sources and/or listed with less than 1,000 employees in *County Business Patterns.*

Sources: 1967 *Census of Manufactures* and 1973 *Annual Survey of Manufactures.*

nation's total. Dividing 7.18 by 6.76 produces the location quotient of 1.06. A location quotient of precisely 1.0 would mean that Illinois had neither more nor less of the national industry than its overall volume of manufacturing would indicate. A quotient over 1.0 would indicate a high local concentration of a particular activity, and a quotient less than 1.0 would suggest that an industry is less developed in Illinois than is manufacturing in general. The maximum that a location quotient could be if Illinois had all (100 percent) of a given industry would be 14.8 (100 divided by 6.76); the minimum, of course, would be zero.

Nearly one-half of the two-digit types of manufacture found in Illinois have location quotients over 1.0 (Table 6-5). The order of importance of the major manufacturing groups as indicated by location quotient is:

1. Machinery, except electrical (SIC #35)
2. Electrical equipment and supplies (SIC #36)
3. Fabricated metal products (SIC #34)
4. Printing and publishing (SIC #27)
5. Instruments and related products (SIC #38)
6. Miscellaneous manufacturing industries (SIC #39)
7. Primary metal products (SIC #33)
8. Petroleum and coal products (SIC #29)
9. Food and kindred products (SIC #20)

The above types of manufacture are those in which Illinois has more than its average share of manufacturing employment and which, therefore, are relatively most important on a national basis. However, within Illinois, electrical equipment and supplies is still much more important than instruments because in 1973 it had about 181,000 employees compared with only about 46,000 in instrument manufacture; in addition, it generated over 3.5 billion dollars in value added compared with only about 1 billion dollars in instruments (Table 6-5).

All of the three-digit manufacturing activities in Illinois that had more than 1,000 employees in 1973 are also shown in Table 6-5. They accounted for about 95 percent of the total manufacturing employment in the state. An examination of the data provides very detailed information about the specific types of manufacturing carried on in Illinois. Sixty-two of the 100 three-digit industries for which there are employment data available had location quotients over 1.0. The most important are generally in metal manufacturing with some of the most important specialization occuring in the production of railroad equipment (SIC #374), radio and T.V. receiving equipment (SIC #365), construction and farm machinery (353 and 352), and screw machine products (345). However, Illinois also has a relatively large number of industrial specialties outside of metal manufacture, including such categories as musical instruments (393), confectionary products (207), miscellaneous publishing (274), and commercial printing (275).

Distribution of Manufacturing in Illinois

Manufacturing has always been closely associated with cities and urban development because of its labor and transportation demands and because of its city-forming influences. In Illinois about 86 percent of all manufacturing employment is concentrated in the counties of the nine Standard Metropolitan Statistical Areas (SMSA) defined by the Bureau of the Census. The boundaries between SMSA and non-SMSA counties are shown in Figure 6-9 along with manufacturing employment by counties. It is readily apparent from the map that the largest manufacturing employment concentrations, with

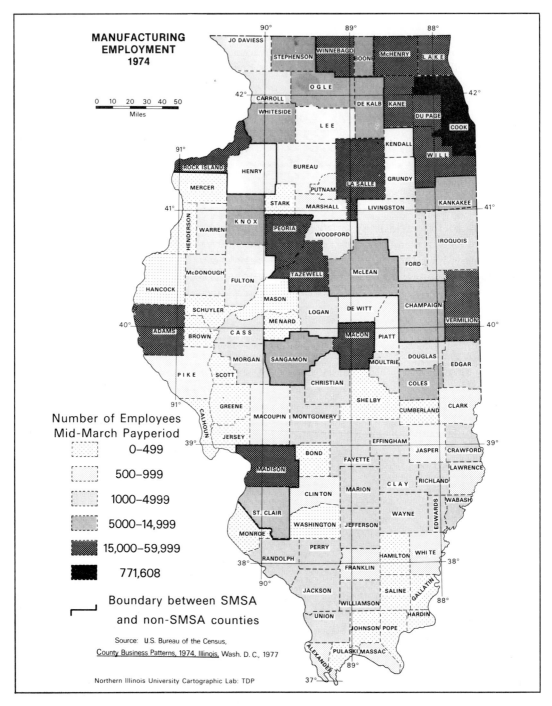

Figure 6-9. Manufacturing employment by counties, 1974. Counties within the nine Standard Metropolitan Statistical Areas of Illinois contain most of the manufacturing employment in the state.

only a few exceptions, are in SMSA counties and in other immediately adjacent counties. Six of the SMSAs are easily discerned on the map, but in the Bloomington-Normal SMSA (McLean County), the Champaign-Urbana SMSA (Champaign County), and the Springfield SMSA (Sangamon County) manufacturing is not as closely related to population because of the large employment in government and educational functions. Another observation regarding manufacturing distribution which is not revealed by the map is that the rank order of manufacturing employment by cities closely approximates the population rank order of cities. Rockford and Peoria, for example, are in second and third positions, respectively, in both categories.

The Chicago Metropolitan Statistical Area (consisting of Cook, DuPage, Kane, Lake, McHenry, and Will counties) has nearly 70 percent and Cook County alone has about 55 percent of all the manufacturing employment in the state. Chicago has about 57 per cent of Cook county's employment in manufacturing, but the city's percentage of all manufacturing employment in the state has steadily decreased to about 32 percent in 1974. The Rockford and Peoria SMSAs and the Illinois portion of the St. Louis SMSA[33] have only 4.1, 3.5, and 3.1 percent, respectively, of the state's manufacturing employment. The Illinois portion of the Davenport-Rock Island-Moline SMSA has about 2.1 percent of the total employment.

Figure 6-9 tends to underscore the fact that there is some manufacturing statewide, but only small pockets of manufacturing activity occur in the southeastern portion of the state where oil and coal mining tend to be dominant activities in low population counties. Additional pockets of minor manufacturing activity occur in some western and central areas of Illinois where agriculture re-

mains most prominent and where cities are primarily trade centers. It is apparent that only about 5 to 10 percent of the manufacturing employment in the state exists south and east of a line roughly connecting St. Louis and Chicago and nearly bisecting the state.

The previous comments regarding employment in manufacturing have been based on absolutes, that is, on the actual number of people in manufacturing within given areas. A somewhat different conception of the spatial distribution can be obtained by observing and analyzing the *relative* importance of manufacturing. Professor Fred Lampe of Southern Illinois University at Edwardsville has recently completed some maps and tables pertaining to the relative importance of manufacturing in Illinois on a county basis.[34] One map (Fig. 6-10) shows county employment in manufacturing as a percent of total county population compared to the state of Illinois as the standard. Such a ratio to ratio comparison produces location quotients similar in meaning to those described earlier in this chapter. This map produces only slightly different patterns than those shown in Figure 6-9 because of the close association of manufacturing with population. A second map (Fig. 6-10) portrays county manufacturing employment as a percent of total county population compared to the United States as a standard. With respect to the two maps, Lampe states:

In Illinois 11.5 percent of the population is in manufacturing whereas in the United States the figure is 9 percent. Since the United States figure is smaller than the one for Illinois, when the division is performed using the same numerator, automatically the ratio for all the counties will be higher when compared to the United States than when compared to Illinois. Some counties therefore, will be in a higher category on Map 2 [Fig. 6-10] than on Map 1 [Fig. 6-10] with the result that the highest

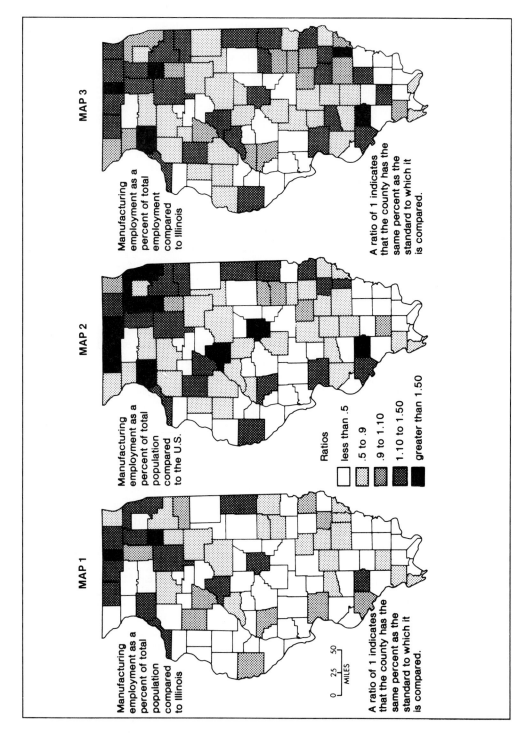

Figure 6-10. Manufacturing employment, 1971. These three maps provide alternative means of showing the relative importance of manufacturing in the counties of Illinois.

category on Map 2 [Fig. 6-10] (compared to Illinois) contains 9 counties while Map 1 (Fig. 6-10) (compared to Illinois) contains only 2. What this means is there are more counties in Illinois where manufacturing is at least one and one-half times more important than in the whole United States when employment is calculated as a percent of the total population than when compared to the state of Illinois.[35]

In general, however, there seems to be only sporadic and minor differences, differences of degree rather than substance, in the employment patterns shown on the two maps. Lampe's third map (Fig. 6-10) produced from ratios relating county manufacturing employment as a percent of total employment to the ratio of the state of Illinois as a standard does produce some noticeably different patterns in the distribution of manufacturing as well as a different perspective.

> On Map 3 [Fig. 6-10] the counties in the highest category of ratios are not, in general, in what we would normally consider the industrial areas of the state, particularly is this true for Perry and Edwards Counties in Southern Illinois. Does this mean that these counties are important manufacturing counties? Well again, it depends on how you define "important." In terms of total employment in manufacturing Edwards County with 705 is not particularly large. Perry County with about 3,000 is larger but certainly manufacturing employment is not as large here absolutely as in many other counties. What the ratio measures and what "importance" means on this map is that of the total employment that does exist in these counties, a large percentage, much larger than the average for Illinois, is employed in manufacturing. That is, there just isn't much else. In the case of Edwards County most of that employment is probably associated with one concern since the figure is given only for the general category and not the specific type. The nondisclosure rule prevents listing employment by specific types where an individual concern could be identified.[36]

Many, if not most, of the counties in southeastern Illinois have location quotients over 1.0 on this third map. This zone of high ratios in the southeastern part of the state is in striking contrast to the lack of concentration shown in Figure 6-9. The differences between Figure 6-9 and this third map can be partly explained by the fact that one or a few fairly large manufacturing plants in a low-population county can bring about a high location quotient. City, county, and state agencies have been actively, and apparently quite successfully, soliciting manufacturers to locate in southern Illinois to help counteract low employment in agriculture and mining and to take advantage of relatively abundant and cheap labor. Manufacturers who have located in this area of the state generally have not been metal fabricators who could benefit best from locations near raw material, skilled workmen, and market. Instead, they are manufacturers of clothing, shoes, and food products, for example, who can especially benefit from inexpensive labor (many of the manufacturing employees are women)[37] and low rental costs and the proximity of supplies of agricultural raw materials. While the third map does reveal the importance of manufacturing employment compared to other types of employment in the counties, the fact remains that total manufacturing employment is very small in most non-SMSA counties and in the southern part of the state. The concentration of large location quotients in northern Illinois results from the spillover of manufacturing activities into counties adjacent to or near major manufacturing counties; it is a part of the trend of many manufacturers to withdraw from the large metropolitan centers and relocate in primarily rural counties to obtain better aesthetic and less congested surroundings, better labor relations, and lower rent and taxes.

Considerable detail about the distribution of certain types of manufacturing in Illinois by two- and three-digit SIC categories on a county basis is included in a series of publications prepared in Springfield by the Department of Business and Economic Development.[38] Statistical tables are presented on a number of establishments according to employment size groupings on labor earnings and hours, on value added by manufacture, and on new capital expenditures. Also included are (1) a map showing the relative importance of each of the 48 states in the two-digit categories, (2) a map showing the locations, by county, of manufacturing establishments in the two-digit category (Fig. 6-11 is an example of this type of map), and (3) maps giving location, by county, of each of the three-digit SIC divisions. These publications are highly recommended for making a detailed analysis of most of the important types of manufacturing found in Illinois.[39]

Trends of Manufacturing in Illinois

Although there have been fluctuations during certain time periods and in some types of production, Illinois has experienced general growth in manufacturing throughout the years. The rate of growth, however, has lagged behind that of many states and regions, and in very recent years there have again been some decreases in manufacturing employment. Between 1967 and 1971, for example, there was a 4.65 percent decrease in manufacturing employment nationally, but in Illinois the decrease was 5.48 percent. There was an absolute growth in value added by manufacturing in Illinois in the same time period, but the increase nationally was about 16.6 percent while that in Illinois was only 12.0 percent. In general, however, manufacturing is still viable and important in the state. Its relatively minor woes appear to accrue from the prevailing uncertainties in national and international economic conditions, from a national trend toward greater dispersal of manufacturing, and from a gradual change occuring in the economic structure of the state and its major metropolitan areas rather than from adverse conditions within the manufacturing sector of Illinois.

A change in the economic structure has been explained by the "changing role theory" which postulates that after manufacturing becomes the preeminent economic activity in an area it can be expected that manufacturing will grow, but at a declining rate, and lose relative significance as the tertiary sector (primarily retail trade and services) overtakes it as an employer and as a producer of G.N.P.[40] Technological improvements also contribute to such a change in roles because more automation in manufacturing has a tendency to create less total demand for manufacturing employees and more demand for people in services. Manufacturing employment decreased 3 percent in the United States between 1950 and 1970, only 2 percent in Illinois, but 5 percent in the Chicago and Rockford SMSAs.[41] In the same time period, employment in the tertiary sector increased 12.9 percent in the United States, 9 percent in Illinois, 8 percent in the Chicago SMSA, and 7 percent in the Rockford SMSA.

The most apparent industrial location trend of this century to affect Illinois, and especially the Chicago SMSA, has been the suburbanization or diffusion of manufacturing plants within or immediately adjacent to major urban areas. In this process the city of Chicago has experienced more change than has the Chicago SMSA. Manufacturing employment decreased steadily in Chicago from over 667,000 in 1947 to 441,000 in 1973 and the city's percentage of the Chicago SMSA's manufacturing employment dropped from 78 percent to 46 percent. The city's share of

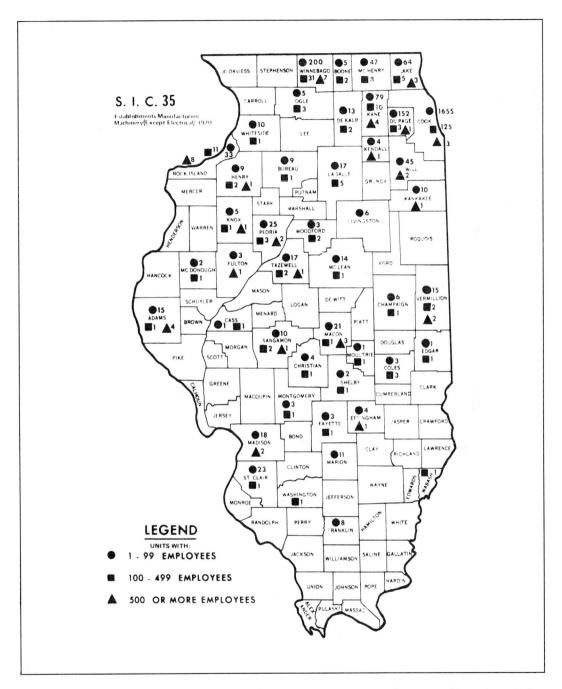

Figure 6-11. S.I.C. 35. Showing the distribution of establishments that manufacture machinery (except electrical), this is an example of maps on the distribution of manufacturing by S.I.C. categories published by the Department of Business and Economic Development.

Figure 6-12. Centex Industrial Park, located immediately northwest of O'Hare International Airport in Elk Grove Village, has developed since 1957 into one of the largest industrial parks (2,250 acres and over 550 firms) in the world. Manufacturing, wholesaling, and commercial establishments here are served by two railroads, have almost immediate access to next-day air freight service to every major city, are near tollways (the Northwest Tollway can be seen in the upper right corner) and other major highways, and can benefit from many agglomeration economies related to labor and material supplies. (Courtesy Bennett and Kahnweiler Associates, Industrial Realtors.)

Figure 6-13. An industrial district of Chicago that has not been affected by the suburbanization trend is the area of heavy industry along the Calumet River south of the city. This area remains the greatest concentration of basic iron and steel industries as well as river and lake port oriented facilities in Illinois. Identified by number on the photo are (1) the Calumet Skyway, (2) Rail-Water Transfer Company, (3) Wisconsin Steel, (4) Valley Mold and Iron Company, (5) Great Lakes Carbon Corporation, (6) Republic Steel Corporation, (7) Ford assembly plant, (8) North Pier Terminal Company, (9) Indiana Grain Cooperative, and (10) the Calumet Expressway. (Courtesy Calumet Area Industrial Development Commission and Chicago South Chamber of Commerce.)

total manufacturing employment in the state declined from 56 to 32 percent in this same time span. In 1947 the Chicago SMSA had about 72 percent of the entire state's manufacturing employment; the proportion decreased to 70 percent in 1973. Also, the Chicago SMSA's share of state manufacturing appears to have remained at a higher level than in other large urban industrial complexes of the United States where the share has held fairly close to 60 percent. Numerous studies have chronicled and analyzed the many types of industrial locations and relocations which have occurred in the Chicago SMSA, but only a few are cited here for reference as the reasons are complex and frequently differ from one industry or region to another.[42]

Attempts to predict or forecast future employment by type of manufacturing or by region are, at best, guesses as the problem is again very complex. The Center for Advanced Computation at the University of Illinois has developed a forecasting model and has presented some preliminary prognostications for Illinois industries up to 1980.[43] According to this source, predicted employment will be greater in all of the two-digit manufacturing activities in 1980 than in 1970 with the exception of food, apparel, petroleum and coal products, and leather and leather products. In some cases (food, lumber, chemicals, and leather) a decline after 1975 is anticipated and in many others the gains in numbers were very small. Most of the commodities manufactured in Illinois are termed high value-added-by-manufacture products which depend on the availability of skilled labor. Such products will probably continue to dominate Illinois manufacturing. Furthermore, it can be expected that they will persist as major elements of the economy because most are marketed outside of Illinois and their sale, therefore, brings money into the state.

Viewed historically, the tendency for manufacturing to continue to concentrate in the SMSAs and adjacent counties (and especially in the Chicago SMSA) seems very apparent. The location of a few large plants in old but minor manufacturing areas will probably continue, but it is unlikely that such moves as the establishment of a Chrysler Corporation plant in Belvidere and a Jones & Laughlin steel mill near Hennepin will lead to any new or large manufacturing concentrations. Nevertheless, a few such moves might accelerate the concentration of manufacturing in certain areas. Because of the advantages of a well-integrated transportation network, nearness to agricultural and mineral raw materials, and the ample high-quality labor found in the area, the upper central portions of the Illinois Valley appear to have the greatest potential for the most rapid growth in manufacturing in the state during the present century.

Notes

1. Hubert E. Risser and Robert L. Major, *History of Illinois Mineral Industries,* Educational Series No. 10 (Urbana: Illinois State Geological Survey, October 1968).
2. M.E. Hopkins, "Coal in Illinois—Key to a Brighter Tomorrow?" *Illinois Business Review* 30, No. 11 (December 1973), p. 6.
3. Ramesh Malhotra and Shirley Hallaron, *Illinois Mineral Industry in 1974,* Illinois Mineral Note #66 (Urbana: Illinois State Geological Survey, February 1977).
4. There is a general increase in coal quality from northeast to southeast within the state.
5. Hopkins, "Coal in Illinois," p. 7.
6. Jacob Van Den Berg and T.F. Lowry, *Petroleum Industry in Illinois in 1975,* Illinois Petroleum No. 110 (Urbana: Illinois State Geological Survey, 1976).
7. Also known as casing-head or wet gas.
8. Van Den Berg and Lowry, *Petroleum Industry,* p. 6.
9. Malhotra and Hallaron, *Illinois Mineral Industry in 1974,* p. 26.

10. Mineral statistics from the Illinois State Geological Survey have included cement and clay products as minerals, although the U.S. Bureau of the Census classes them as manufactured products. If cement and clay products are excluded from mineral production statistics, as they are in Table 6-3, coal and oil producing countries such as Perry, St. Clair, and Franklin would be leading counties.

11. Malhotra and Hallaron, *Illinois Mineral Industry in 1974,* p. 24.

12. J.C. Bradbury, G.C. Finger, and R.L. Major, *Fluorspar in Illinois,* Circular 420 (Urbana: Illinois State Geological Survey, 1968), p. 15.

13. *Atlas of Illinois Resources, Section 2, Mineral Resources* (Springfield: Illinois Division of Industrial Planning and Development, Department of Registration and Education, 1959).

14. Executive Office of the President, Office of Management and Budget, *Standard Industrial Classification Manual* (Washington: U.S. Government Printing Office, 1972).

15. E.L. Bogart and C.M. Thompson, *The Centennial History of Illinois,* Vol. 4, *The Industrial State 1870-1893* (Springfield: Illinois Centennial Commission, 1920), pp. 381-410.

16. Ibid.

17. Keith McClellan, "A History of Chicago's Industrial Development," *Mid-Chicago Economic Development Study,* Vol. 3, prepared for the Mayor's Committee for Economic and Cultural Development by the Center for Urban Studies (Chicago: University of Chicago, February 1966), pp. 1-70.

18. E.L. Bogart and John M. Mathews, *The Centennial History of Illinois,* Vol. 5, *The Modern Commonwealth 1893-1918* (Springfield: Illinois Centennial Commission, 1920) pp. 91-112.

19. Douglas C. Ridgley, *The Geography of Illinois* (Chicago: University of Chicago Press, 1921), p. 223.

20. Jerome D. Fellman and Howard G. Roepke, "The Changing Industrial Structure of Illinois." *Current Economic Comment* 18, No. 4 (November 1956), p. 15.

21. Ibid., pp. 15-17 and Ronald G. Cummings, *Industrial Growth Trends in Illinois* (Springfield: Illinois Department of Business and Economic Development, March 1967).

22. Gunnar Alexandersson, *Geography of Manufacturing* (Englewood Cliffs, N.J.: Prentice-Hall, 1967), p. 6.

23. Alfred Weber, *Alfred Weber's Theory of the Location of Industries,* trans. Carl J. Friedrich (Chicago: University of Chicago Press, 1929).

24. August Lösch, *The Economics of Location,* trans. William H. Woglom and Wolfgang F. Stolper (New Haven, Conn.: Yale University Press, 1954).

25. More detailed accounts of the complexities of agglomeration factors may be found in R.C. Estall and R. Ogilvie Buchanan, *Industrial Activity and Economic Geography* (London: Hutchinson Publishers, 1961), pp. 102-11 and 164-67 and in Richard S. Thoman, Edgar C. Conkling, and Maurice H. Yeates, *The Geography of Economic Activity,* 2nd ed. (New York: McGraw-Hill, 1968), pp. 183-203.

26. For more detailed accounts about these inventors see Alexandersson, *Geography of Manufacturing,* pp. 84-85 and John W. Alexander, "Geography of Manufacturing in the Rock River Valley," *Wisconsin Commerce Papers* 1, No. 2 (August 1949), pp. 149-50.

27. Irving Cutler, *Chicago: Metropolis of the Mid-Continent* (Chicago: Geographic Society of Chicago, 1973), pp. 55-57.

28. Businessmen in the Chicago area have been important leaders in establishing planned or organized industrial districts which provide many valuable and time-consuming services for manufacturers. Many other cities in Illinois also have established industrial districts to help attract and hold manufacturing firms in their communities.

29. Some examples of various types of amenities are pleasant residential surroundings for a factory site, desirable ethnic or cultural characteristics of a community, personal preference for a place established by reason of birth or residence, and favorable business relations established with a particular city or community name.

30. M.L. Greenhut, *Plant Location in Theory and Practice* (Chapel Hill, N.C.: University of North Carolina Press, 1956); D.M. Smith, "A Theoretical Framework for Geographical Studies of Industrial Location." *Economic Geography* 42, No. 2 (April 1966), pp. 95-113; M.I. Logan, "Locational

Behavior of Manufacturing Firms in Urban Areas." *Annals of the Association of American Geographers* 56, No. 3 (September 1966), pp. 451-66; and Michael Eliot Hurst, *A Geography of Economic Behavior* (North Scituate, Mass.: Duxbury Press, 1972), pp. 126-93.

31. Metals include SIC groups 33-37; woods include 24-26; textiles include 22 and 23; and groups 21, 28-32, 38, and 39 are combined in the category called "others."

32. Employment in tobacco manufacture totaled less than 500 in eight establishments in 1967 and thus constitutes a very insignificant industry in the state. Specific data on this industry is usually withheld to avoid disclosures of operations of individual reporting units. Twenty-four of the 130 industry types had less than 1,000 employees each in 1967 and they, too, can be considered relatively insignificant and they are not included in Table 6-5.

33. A recently published article gives a detailed account of manufacturing in the Illinois portion of the St. Louis SMSA. See Robert Koepke, "Manufacturing in Metro East." *Bulletin of the Illinois Geographical Society* 17 (June 1974), pp. 43-55.

34. Fred Lampe, "Just How Important Is This Activity in This Place Anyhow?" mimeographed (Edwardsville, Ill.: Southern Illinois University, 1974).

35. Ibid., p. 4.

36. Ibid.

37. John W. Conoyer, *Geography Through Maps: The St. Louis Gateway,* Special Publication No. 14 (Normal, Ill.: National Council for Geographic Education, 1967).

38. Division of Industrial Development, Department of Business and Economic Development, Springfield, Ill.: *The Food Industry in Illinois, SIC 20, 1973; The Textile Industry in Illinois, SIC 22, 1971; The Apparel Industry in Illinois, SIC 23, 1971; The Lumber and Wood Industry in Illinois, SIC 24, 1971; The Furniture Industry in Illinois, SIC 25, 1971; The Chemical Industry in Illinois, SIC 28, 1973; Rubber Industry in Illinois, SIC 30, 1973; Primary Metal Industries in Illinois, SIC 33, 1973; The Metalworking Industries in Illinois, SIC 34, 1973; The Machinery Industry (Except Electrical) in Illinois, SIC 35, 1972; The Electrical Machinery Industry in Illinois, SIC 36, 1973; and Instrument Industry in Illinois, SIC 38, 1971.*

39. One major omission in the series is the study of the printing and publishing industry, SIC 27, the sixth largest manufacturing employer in the state.

40. John H. Thompson, "Some Theoretical Considerations for Manufacturing Geography." *Economic Geography* 42, No. 4 (October 1966), pp. 356-65.

41. Computed from *Census of Population Statistics.*

42. Northeastern Illinois Planning Commission, *Metropolitan Planning Guidelines, Phase One: Background Documents: Industrial Development* (Chicago, 1965); Martin W. Reinemann, "The Localization and Relocation of Manufacturing within the Chicago Urban Area" (Ph.D. diss., Northwestern University, 1955); Harry P. Hartnett, *A Locational Analysis of Those Manufacturing Firms That Have Located and Relocated within Chicago, 1955-1968* (Chicago: Area Development Division, Continental Illinois National Bank, January 1972); and Mc-Clellan, *Mid-Chicago Economic Development Study.*

43. Michael Babcock and Hugh Folk, "Future Employment in Illinois Industries, 1975 and 1980." *Illinois Business Review* 30, No. 3 (March 1973), pp. 6-8.

Selected References

Alexander, John W. "Geography of Manufacturing in the Rock River Valley." *Wisconsin Commerce Papers* 1 (August 1949), 149-50.

———. "Manufacturing in the Rock River Valley." *Annals of the Association of American Geographers,* 40 (1950), 237-58.

Atlas of Illinois Resources, section 2, *Mineral Resources.* Springfield: Illinois Division of Industrial Planning and Development, Department of Registration and Education, 1959.

Babcock, Michael, and Folk, Hugh. "Future Employment in Illinois Industries, 1975 and 1980." *Illinois Business Review,* 30 (March 1973), 6-8.

Bogart, E.L., and Mathews, John M. *The Centennial History of Illinois,* Vol. 5, *The*

Modern Commonwealth 1893-1918. Springfield: Illinois Centennial Commission, 1920.

————. *The Centennial History of Illinois,* Vol. 4, *The Industrial State 1870-1893.* Springfield: Illinois Centennial Commission, 1920.

Bradbury, J.C.; Finger, G.C.; and Major, R.L. *Fluorspar in Illinois.* Circular 420. Urbana: Illinois State Geological Survey, 1968.

Conoyer, John W. *Geography Through Maps: The St. Louis Gateway.* Special Publication No. 10. Normal, Ill.: National Council for Geographic Education, 1967.

Cummings, Ronald G. *Industrial Growth Trends in Illinois.* Springfield: Illinois Department of Business and Economic Development, 1967.

Cutler, Irving. *Chicago: Metropolis of the Mid-Continent.* 2nd ed. Dubuque, Iowa: Kendall/Hunt Publishing Co., 1976.

Fellman, Jerome D., and Roepke, Howard G. "The Changing Industrial Structure of Illinois." *Current Economic Comment,* 18 (November 1956).

Hartnett, Harry P. *A Locational Analysis of Those Manufacturing Firms That Have Located and Relocated within Chicago, 1955-1968.* Chicago: Continental Illinois National Bank, Area Development Division, January 1972.

Hopkins, M.E. "Coal in Illinois—Key to a Brighter Tomorrow?" *Illinois Business Review,* 30 (December 1973), 6-8.

Koepke, Robert. "Manufacturing in Metro East." *Bulletin of the Illinois Geographical Society,* 17 (June 1974), 43-55.

Malhotra, Ramesh, and Halloran, Shirley. *Illinois Mineral Industry in 1974.* Illinois Mineral Note #66. Urbana: Illinois State Geological Survey, February 1977.

McClellan, Keith, "A History of Chicago's Industrial Development." *Mid-Chicago Economic Development Study.* Vol. 3, Prepared for the Mayor's Committee for Economic and Cultural Development by the Center for Urban Studies. Chicago: University of Chicago, February 1966.

Reinemann, Martin W. "The Localization and Relocation of Manufacturing within the Chicago Urban Area." (Ph.D. dissertation, Northwestern University, 1955).

Ridgley, Douglas C. *The Geography of Illinois.* Chicago: University of Chicago Press, 1921.

Risser, Hubert E., and Major, Robert L. *History of Illinois Mineral Industries.* Educational Series No. 10. Urbana: Illinois State Geological Survey, 1968.

Van Den Berg, Jacob, and Lowry, T.F. *Petroleum Industry in Illinois in 1975.* Illinois Petroleum No. 110. Urbana: Illinois State Geological Survey, 1976.

Chapter Seven

THE METRO EAST AREA

Robert L. Koepke
Southern Illinois University—Edwardsville

Metro East (Fig. 7-1), the Illinois portion of the St. Louis Metropolitan Area and the second most populous area of Illinois, is one of many regions where the struggle with the physical environment continues, although it has been surpassed in importance by the challenge of the cultural environment (including human attitudes, social structures, and institutions). The aborigines and early European inhabitants, who were hunters/gatherers and farmers, were required to deal directly with the physical environment and had limited ability to manipulate it. In contrast, the twentieth-century urban inhabitants of this bicounty area (Madison and St. Clair counties) generally are not directly linked to nature for their livelihood or comforts and possess an enormous ability to manipulate the physical habitat. These modern people, however, do not have the same degree of competence in handling themselves and their world, including the institutions through which they attempt to deal with the physical environment. This chapter is a study of the Metro East area, its physical attributes, and its people and their relationships with their environment in the past, present, and future.

Physical Setting

Surface Features

Metro East is composed of two major and several secondary landform regions.[1] Most of the area of the two counties (Madison and St. Clair) is a loess-covered plain of predominately gentle slopes. Cut into this surface are several noticeable floodplains, including those of the Kaskaskia River, Silver Creek, Cahokia Creek, and Indian Creek. The second major physical region is called the American Bottoms, a lens-shaped major alluvial valley of the Mississippi River of some 175 square miles extending from Alton to Dupo along the western side of Metro

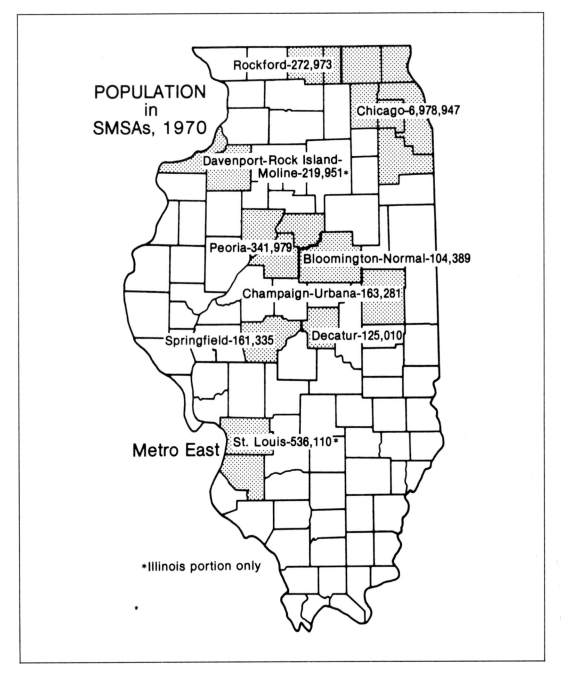

POPULATION
in
SMSAs, 1970

Rockford-272,973

Chicago-6,978,947

Davenport-Rock Island-
Moline-219,951*

Peoria-341,979

Bloomington-Normal-104,389

Champaign-Urbana-163,281

Springfield-161,335

Decatur-125,010

Metro East

St. Louis-536,110*

*Illinois portion only

Figure 7-1. Metro East, the Illinois portion of the St. Louis Metropolitan Statistical Area, contains over one-half million inhabitants in Madison and St. Clair counties. Only the Chicago SMSA has a greater population concentration in the state.

East. Adjacent to the eastern and northern edges of the Bottoms is a strongly dissected portion of the plains region.

Though it is everywhere an alluvial valley, the American Bottoms landform region has some very important internal variations (Fig. 7-2) which can be grouped into seven secondary physical regions. The largest of these is the ridge and swale, an area in the northern part of the Bottoms around Granite City and in the southern part around Cahokia, that has an undulating surface of linear ridges, generally composed of sand, and long narrow swales of clay. The second is the lake region, which contains oxbow lakes, large flat old lake beds, and meander scars. Next is the aggraded cut and fill region, or the Mitchell flats, an area in the northeastern portion of the Bottoms with very little local relief. The surface material of these "flats" is uniformly clay. A fourth component region of the American Bottoms is the East St. Louis rise, a complex area that is generally higher and flatter than the lake region and the ridge and swale topography which nearly surrounds it; the type of soil in this subregion has not been clearly determined. The terrace region, a fifth secondary region in the far northeast section of the American Bottoms, is a high, sandy remnant of an earlier flood plain. The sixth region is an area of alluvial fans, composed of silts washed from the adjacent uplands, along the base of the bluffs on the eastern and northern fringes of the American Bottoms. A tributary meander belt, the final internal region, is adjacent to the bluffs in the north.

Running water is the chief geomorphological agent in the Metro East area. The stream of paramount importance, the Mississippi River, has been flowing through the area for some 200 million years. Encountering some relatively soft rocks (shale and coal), the river removed most of them

and then continued cutting into the harder materials underneath, creating within the previously deposited sedimentary rocks a valley about as wide but deeper than the present one. Since the softer materials did not exist north or south of the American Bottoms at the same elevation because of the nature of the slightly tilted rocks, the Mississippi Valley north of Alton and south of Dupo is consequently narrower. The form of the uplands is also largely the result of running water.

Glaciation also influenced the topography of Metro East. It is not clear if the first two Pleistocene glaciers reached the area, but it is known that the leading edge of the third (Illinoisan) ice sheet covered Metro East. The observable results of this glacial activity are large boulders on the bedrock surface of the Mississippi Valley; the deposition of unsorted and some sorted material on the uplands, such as the ridges around O'Fallon and Belleville; and the creation of a soil, called the Sangamon soil, in the uplands. The fourth, and so far the last, continental glacier (Wisconsin) stopped 75 miles north of the area some 75,000 years ago, but its meltwaters had a marked impact on the present terrain. The valley of the Mississippi, which was a major drainage-way for the heavily laden meltwater, became filled by glacial material to a depth of at least 150 feet. In addition, the uplands to the east and north received fine materials which the wind picked up from the river valley during periods of low water. This material, called loess, which is up to 50 feet thick adjacent to the floodplain, decreases in thickness eastwards.

Following the final disappearance of the glacier, the Mississippi River meandered across the American Bottoms and removed most of the meltwater-deposited materials. Only a few remnants of the earlier flood-

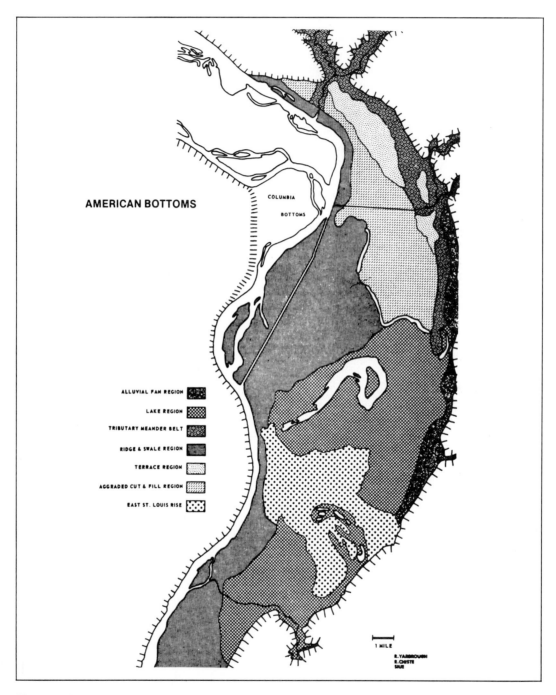

Figure 7-2. The American Bottoms, a wide segment of the Mississippi River floodplain in Metro East, has complex internal physical variations. (From Ronald E. Yarbrough, "The Physiography of Metro East," *Bulletin of the Illinois Geographical Society* XVI [June 1974], p. 18.)

plain remain, the major one being the terrace region in the northeastern portion of the American Bottoms. The upland streams that drained into the Bottoms and the Kaskaskia River also eroded the wind-blown materials, but the amount of loess removed is not known.

Climate

The climate of Metro East is characterized by continental temperatures and sufficient precipitation to produce a humid environment. The January average temperature is 32 °F, while the July average is 79 °F. Severe outbreaks of cold, polar air move through the area every winter and produce minimum temperatures as low as −10 °F. These cold waves are generally of short duration, however, and in three or four days more moderate temperatures, usually above freezing, return. As one would expect at this latitude, winters are noticeably milder than in northern Illinois. In fact, the chief method of removing snow in Metro East is to wait a few days for the sun to melt it. The 80-year average precipitation is 35.4 inches, with June being the wettest month. Thunderstorms produce much of the summer rain. Although snow may occur on any day from early November through April, most of the winter precipitation is in the form of rain. The average annual snowfall of around 17 inches is substantially less than that of upstate Illinois.

Early Occupancy

Aborigines

People have been living in the Metro East area for at least 10,000 years, but it was only during the last 1,700 years that their activities had a significant and permanent impact.[2] Paleoindian (possibly), Archaic, and Early and Middle Woodland people lived in the area but left no enduring imprint on the landscape, whereas there is evidence of the effect upon the area of the Late Woodland and especially the Mississippian people. Beginning around 300 A.D. both the bluffs and the American Bottoms were heavily utilized by Late Woodland people. During the Mississippian period, from 900 A.D. to 1250 A.D., the Bottoms contained a number of major settlements, including a community of possibly 40,000 people at Cahokia Mounds (a Mississippian settlement built on the present-day East St. Louis rise region near the geographical center of the Bottoms). These people probably farmed most of the surrounding arable land. They also cut trees in the nearby bottomland and upland areas to construct enormous defense palisades. The palisade on the eastern side of Monks Mound (the largest mound in the Cahokia Mounds site) was nearly a mile long and contained about 4,500 logs (Fig. 7-3). It was reconstructed at least four times. Beginning around 1250 A.D. the power and influence of the Mississippian "city" of Cahokia declined rapidly. In fact, the decline was so rapid and so complete that when Marquette and Jolliet came into the area some 400 years later, they were unaware of the existence of the mounds at Cahokia.

Since our study of aboriginal people in the Metro East area is still in its infancy, very little is known about them or about their struggle with the physical environment. We know that their settlements were built on high ground and near water, but we have little information about their life-style or social organization. The reflections of a local professional archeologist on the possible reasons for the decline of the Mississippian communities offer some insight into the struggles of these people.

The decline of Cahokia may well be the result of many factors. The apparent abandonment of villages and farmsteads in the period

Figure 7-3. Monks Mound, the largest of the Cahokia Mounds and the largest prehistoric man-made structure north of central Mexico. The dimensions of the mound are 1,000 feet north-south, 800 feet east-west,
and 100 feet from the base to the highest point. The volume is 21,690,000 cubic feet. The mound contains
four terraces, some of which are visible in this photograph. A portion of the reconstructed palisade (east of
the mound, not on it) can be seen in the upper center. (Photo courtesy of the Illinois Department of Conservation.)

after 1050 A.D. and the accompanying concentration of population in the city of Cahokia itself could indicate pressure from hostile Late Woodland groups. The building of palisades at this time might reflect the same kinds of pressures. The resulting concentration of population at Cahokia and the abandonment of supporting farming villages could have overburdened the economic system and led to collapse. Another possibility, however, could have been a minor climatic shift which led to crop failure and thus to the collapse of the economy. A third alternative explanation of the collapse . . . involves the hypothesis that Cahokia was a major center of trade and that its wealth and power are reflective of its virtual monopoly of the mechanisms and raw materials of trade. The hostility of Late Woodland peoples could have disrupted the trade networks and contributed to the decline. Finally, it is quite possible that the decline of Cahokia is the result of the exhaustion of natural resources in the immediate area. The destruction of the natural habitat due to the enormous use of wood seen in the construction of palisades, temples and houses may well have deforested much of the bottoms. Deer would have been chased out of the area due to hunting pressure and the reduction of habitat, and it is even possible that the populations of fish and waterfowl which constituted important supplements to the diet at Cahokia may have been adversely affected. Additionally, the continued use of agricultural fields near the city could have led to the exhaustion of the soils. All of these factors working together might have led to starvation and a mass movement of Mississippian peoples out of the American Bottoms.

Clearly the present state of knowledge does not allow us to choose between these hypotheses and answers must wait on further research.[3]

French

The year 1699 marks the beginning of the European settlement period in Metro East. In that year, following the assignment of the governor of Quebec, the Seminary of Foreign Missions founded a mission to the Tamoroa Indians in the southern portion of the American Bottoms. In addition to serving as a religious center, the mission, called Cahokia (but located some ten miles southwest of the Mississippian Cahokia Mounds site), was also an agricultural village and a center for commercial activities. Cahokia became in time one of a series of French communities established southward along the Mississippi River through Ft. Chartres and Kaskaskia to Ste. Genevieve. With the demise of some earlier French midwestern settlements, Cahokia became the site of the longest continuous European settlement in the Midwest. Unfortunately, little has been written about the organization and administration of this early French settlement, but the founding of the mission itself is indicative of the importance of the societal element in the establishment and operation of French Cahokia. Even less is known about the struggle of the people with the physical environment, but one can surmise from the establishment of St. Louis in 1764 on a portion of high ground on the west bank of the Mississippi River, overlooking, but not in, the American Bottoms, that settlers were forced to deal with the problem of flooding.

The French who settled Cahokia left a distinctive mark on the present-day landscape of Metro East. The French long lot system of land division (Fig. 7-4) has had a permanent effect on the shape of agricultural fields in western St. Clair County, the direction of major roads in this portion of Metro East (such as Illinois Route 15), and the orientation of some later settlements, such as East St. Louis, Alorton, and Centreville.[4] At least three buildings from this first European settlement period also remain in the Village of Cahokia; however, they have not received the public attention they deserve.

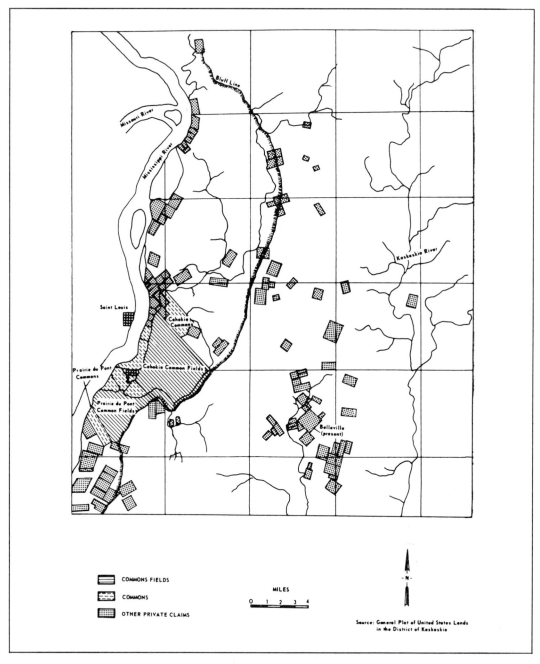

Figure 7-4. Private land claims in the vicinity of Cahokia, ca. 1810–1813. The French community of Cahokia is southwest of the Cahokia common fields. The common fields are oriented as shown on the map, but the width of the lots is not drawn to scale. (From William Baker, "Land Claims as Indicators of Settlement in Southwestern Illinois, circa 1809–13," *Bulletin of the Illinois Geographical Society* XVI [June 1974], p. 38.)

British

The impact of the British on Metro East was as limited as their tenure. In 1763, the area was part of the land ceded to the British by the French, and just 15 years later George Rogers Clark occupied the village of Kaskaskia for the United States. The period of American occupation had begun.

American Occupancy

It is this last cultural group, the Americans, who are responsible for the current Metro East landscape. They built the cities in which a half million people live today, the railroads and roads which traverse and tie the area together, and a levee system to hold back Mississippi River water during all but excessively high river stages. The Americans also established institutions and produced a social system to manage the area.

Early Period

For the first 75 years of American occupancy, the history of Metro East primarily involved the expansion of agriculture, the establishment of retail/governmental centers, and the beginning of coal mining. Subsistence farming probably was common in the area, but it is likely that many farmers also found a ready market for their agricultural goods in the growing city of St. Louis. In order to transport the commodities of these and other farmers in southwestern Illinois to St. Louis, a ferry across the Mississippi River was established. In 1817, Illinoistown, the first permanent settlement at the Illinois end of the ferry, was laid out. Illinoistown (later renamed East St. Louis) did not experience immediate growth, however, for even as late as 1837 the Reverend John Mason Peck still referred to it as a small village. In the same year a young Corps of Engineers lieutenant by the name of Robert E. Lee completed a plan to improve the harbor of St. Louis, which was also to have a lasting impact on the Illinois side of the river. Basically, Lee's plan involved the building of structures that would narrow the river. Not only did this help to maintain St. Louis as a riverport (rather than Illinoistown, perhaps), but it also aided the development of a large flat expanse of land between today's downtown East St. Louis and the Mississippi riverfront. Also in 1837, a small coal railroad was built across the Bottoms, generally following the relatively high ground found in the East St. Louis rise region. Beginning at the bluffs near Belleville (founded in the early 1800s), the line extended to Illinoistown. In addition to the cities noted, this early period of settlement saw the establishment of Edwardsville in Madison County and Alton on the bluffs at the north end of the American Bottoms.

Railroad Period

The beginning of construction on the Ohio and Mississippi Railroad from Illinoistown in 1852, rather than establishment of the Belleville-Illinoistown coal line, marks the beginning of the railroad era in Metro East. By 1857, Metro East was connected to Vincennes, Indiana, by the Ohio and Mississippi, and soon thereafter to Baltimore by what is today the B & O/C & O Railroad. Other rail lines were constructed in Metro East, and by 1875 ten railroads traversed the area, most of them focusing on East St. Louis. Because the Mississippi represented an early obstacle, these rail lines from the east terminated in Illinois and the railroad cars were ferried across the river. Although the opening of the first bridge (Eads Bridge) across the Mississippi at St. Louis in the 1870s eliminated the need to ferry all of the cars, the freight yards remained on the East St. Louis side of the river. The citizens of the area, and especially of East St. Louis, have been trying for years to originate and implement a plan whereby this now underutilized space of the railyards (much of which was created by the actions of Lt. Lee) can be rejuvenated.

Urban/Industrial Period

The activities during the early and railroad periods of American occupancy left their mark on the present landscape of Metro East, but most of what exists in the area today is a result of developments over the last 80 years. During this most recent period manufacturing became the paramount economic activity in the area, stimulating not only a substantial growth in the pre-1890 cities but the creation of other, completely new, urban centers as well (e.g., Granite City and Wood River). Interurban lines and major highways were built to connect these urban complexes. Also, flood protection levees and internal drainage facilities were constructed during this period.

The settlement pattern resulting from the urban growth during the American period is dominated by five moderate-sized urban communities scattered throughout the two counties and generally separated from each other by agricultural land (Fig. 7-5). The community areas, none containing more than 130,000 people are Alton-Wood River on the north; the Tri-Cities of Granite City, Madison, and Venice in the center; East St. Louis-Cahokia on the south; and Collinsville-Edwardsville and Belleville-Fairview Heights-O'Fallon on the east. The smaller towns, all in the eastern, primarily rural portion of Metro East, include Hamel, Marine, Troy, Mascoutah, and Lebanon.

Population growth during the urban/industrial period occurred in different portions of Metro East at different times. During the 40 years from 1890 to 1930, most of the population increase took place in the American Bottoms in the communities of East St. Louis-Cahokia; the Tri-Cities of Granite City, Madison, and Venice; and the Wood River-Roxana segment of the Alton-Wood River area. During the last 40 years (1930-1970), increases have occurred over a much wider area. A large part of the total increase took place in the upland communities of Belleville-Fairview Heights-O'Fallon and Alton-Wood River, with substantial increases still occurring in the bottomland centers of East St. Louis-Cahokia and the Tri-Cities. Most of the future growth in population is expected to occur in the uplands bordering the American Bottoms.

The scattered urban settlement pattern found in Metro East is not characteristic of the entire St. Louis region or other metropolitan areas similar in size to the St. Louis Metropolitan Area (Fig. 7-6). In St. Louis City and St. Louis County, Missouri, which are the major elements in the western portion of the St. Louis SMSA, most of the people live in one large urban complex. Similarly, in Chicago most of the people are concentrated in a single urban cluster. When the six United States metropolitan areas with a 1970 population of between two and three million are studied, it becomes clear that four areas have a primarily compact settlement pattern (Washington, D.C.; Pittsburgh; Baltimore; and Cleveland), while just two, Boston and St. Louis, have a large number of separate suburban centers along with a compact segment. The Boston area exhibits a "shotgun" pattern, in which the separate population concentrations are found scattered around the urban core. By

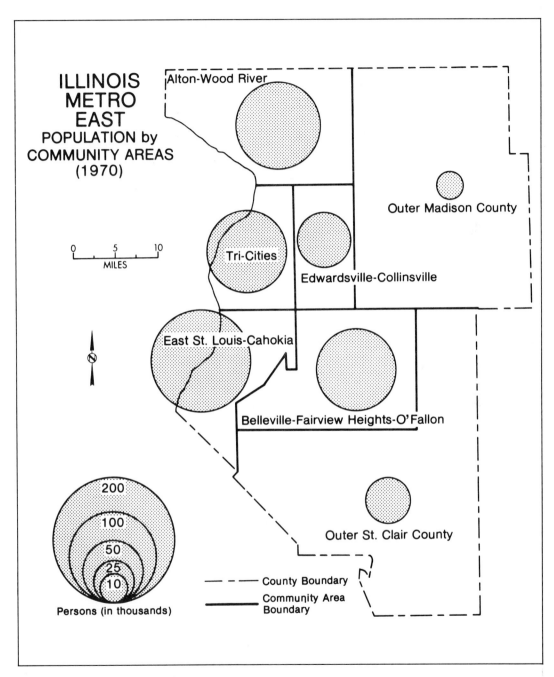

Figure 7-5. The community areas of Metro East. The most populous community areas are in the American Bottoms.

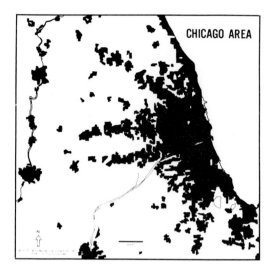

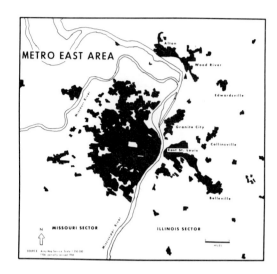

Figure 7-6. General urban patterns of the two major Illinois metropolitan areas. The separate urban nuclei in the St. Louis area are relatively widely scattered and mostly on the Illinois side of the Mississippi River.

contrast, the separate urban nuclei of the St. Louis area are found primarily in one part of the area—Metro East Illinois.

Life in these moderate-sized Metro East communities is similar to that in nearly any American community of comparable size. Generally, comfortable older residences, some from the 1890-1920 era, and new structures in the small subdivisions on the edge of the community are characteristic of the Metro East urban centers. Much of the commerce revolves around the ever-present, community central business district, which contains the town's banks, savings and loans, movie theaters, and numerous specialty retail shops. The development of discount stores, new unplanned shopping areas, and a regional shopping center in Fairview Heights are beginning to have a noticeable impact on the shopping habits of residents, however. Unfortunately, few of the downtown businessmen have realized the implications to them of these new shopping patterns, and even fewer have responded to the competi-

tion. Children in the towns of Metro East attend schools of local community school districts and participate in strongly-supported high school sports. Many people work in industrial and commercial establishments in their own communities, although commuting to jobs in other parts of Metro East, as well as to the Missouri portion of the urban area, is common.

A strong feeling of community identity prevails in the cities of Metro East. People from Alton think of themselves as Altonians, Belleville residents as Bellevillites, and those from Granite City as Granite Citians. The schools and central business districts, acting as focal points for individual and community thoughts and activities, help to develop and maintain this sense of local identity. The residents of these cities are kept informed about their towns by locally-oriented newspapers which maintain the cohesiveness of the communities.

This sense of belonging also comes from the proud and, in several instances, extensive history of the communities in Metro East. Cahokia, of course, is the oldest permanent European settlement in the Midwest, predating St. Louis by more than 50 years. Alton was an early rival of St. Louis, and Belleville and Edwardsville were developing communities when most of St. Louis was still farmland. The continuity of life—some would call it "roots"—is part of the life of residents of Metro East.

To most people today, however, the "good life" means more than just living in a small town. It also includes access to professional sports, major recreational facilities, first-class medical services, and the variety of goods offered in large, urban shopping centers. Normally, the availability of such urban services is dependent upon living in a large, urban complex. Most people must choose between the advantages of living in either a small town or a metropolis. The residents of Metro East, however, can enjoy the benefits of both. The assets of the major urban area of the region in St. Louis City and St. Louis County, Missouri, are accessible to most area residents in less than 30 minutes. Because of the short distance and good road transportation, much of it new interstate highways, Metro East residents are able to enjoy professional football or baseball in Busch Stadium and hockey in the Arena near Forest Park. Shopping in the large department stores of downtown St. Louis or in the major outlying shopping centers, such as River Roads, Northland, Northwest, Jamestown, and South County, is convenient for most residents of Metro East. Forest Park, with its zoo, art museum, and Municipal Opera, is handy, as are the medical facilities in that area.

In most instances, the scattered, small-town character of the Metro East population nodes is a significant, positive feature. Such a settlement pattern, however, also causes some problems, the major one being a weak-to-nonexistent identification with the entire bicounty Metro East area. Partly because they too seldom come in contact with people from other parts of Metro East, most residents do not feel that they are part of an area larger than their hometown. They may be part of the same physical region, but they are not part of the same "mental" region. With such an orientation, the development and completion of projects necessary for the betterment of the entire Metro East area is difficult at best. People are interested in local needs, not area-wide ones, if they are interested at all. The political clout of the more than 500,000 people also suffers at state and federal levels because of this lack of unity. Too few people in the area realize that allegiance to an area is in addition to, and not in place of, allegiance to a town.

The dispersed town pattern in Metro East will continue for at least another decade. Considerable population increase can be accommodated in and around the existing urban centers before they begin to coalesce. While the trend is toward a merging of the population concentrations, it need not continue nor produce a future settlement pattern which citizens of the area find unattractive. The people have the option of determining the type of Metro East they wish to have in the future and implementing measures to make it happen.

Manufacturing

One of the most important economic functions of Metro East is manufacturing, which, as was pointed out earlier, has played a key role in the growth and establishment of the area's cities.[5] Manufacturing plants employing hundreds of people and occupy-

Figure 7-7. The Granite City Steel works of the National Steel Corporation (looking to the southeast). The computerized rolling mill is in the long building in the foreground, the basic oxygen furnace is in the tall building in the center, and the two blast furnaces and nearby coke ovens are near the top of the photograph. Granite City Steel is the only integrated iron and steel plant in the St. Louis Metropolitan Area and the only one in downstate Illinois. (Photograph by T. Mike Fletcher. Courtesy of Granite City Steel, Division of National Steel Corporation.)

ing extensive sites are prominent features of the landscape in and around these cities. The manufacturing in Metro East is best characterized by the word *concentrated*—i.e., concentrated in location within the bicounty area, in a few types of industries, in a few large plants, and in the time period during which the plants were established.

Manufacturing in Metro East is comprised of a few major industries. Primary metals (mainly iron and steel production; grey iron and steel foundries; and rolling, drawing, and extruding of nonferrous metals) accounted for over 18,000 of the area's ap-

proximately 53,000 employees in manufacturing as of 1969 (the most recent year for which detailed statistics are available). Another 5,400 were employed in the food industry (primarily meat packing, wet corn milling, and malt liquors); 5,300 in stone-clay-glass products (nearly all manufacture glass containers); 5,000 in chemicals; and 4,300 in petroleum refining. Together these five industries employ over 70 percent of the total Metro East manufacturing labor force.

The large plants of a few firms account for most of the manufacturing employment in Metro East. Twenty-one firms in the same number of plants employ nearly 37,000 people or 70 percent of the total number of workers in manufacturing. Just seven of the largest plants, each employing over 2,000 people, have a total employment of more than 25,000, or nearly half of the Metro East area's total manufacturing workers in 1969.

Most of the larger plants—those with a current employment of at least 5,000 people—have been established in the area during the last 80 years. Five plants employing over 17,000 were established before 1900. Eight plants began operations in the area between 1900 and 1920, and today they employ nearly 12,000. Five of the large plants, with an employment of 3,700, are more recent, having been erected between 1940 and 1960. No existing large plants were located in the area between 1920 and 1940 or after 1960. The 13 plants that began opera-

tion in Metro East before 1920 today employ nearly 30,000 people or 54 percent of the total manufacturing labor force.

The period 1890-1919 has been designated by Robert Harper in his study *Metro East: Heavy Industry in the St. Louis Metropolitan Area* as the "golden era" for manufacturing.[6] Harper notes that in addition to being the period when many of the area's large plants were established, this was the time when the employment growth in Metro East was nearly equal to that of the larger St. Louis, Missouri, area. Between 1890 and 1919, the employment in manufacturing in Metro East grew by 20,972, while the increase in St. Louis was 25,247. During these 30 years the location of manufacturing also expanded; before 1890, manufacturing was localized in and around the cities of Alton, East St. Louis, and Belleville. By 1919 it was

Figure 7-8. The Wood River refinery of the Shell Oil Company is one of the two largest of this corporation, with a capacity of 300,000 barrels of petroleum per day. The refinery, which originated in 1918, today covers 2,000 acres in the northern end of the American Bottoms. (Courtesy of Shell Oil Company.)

well established in the Tri-Cities and on the floodplain terrace in Wood River-Roxana.

Our knowledge of the reasons for the development of manufacturing in these two counties is not complete, but what is known is mainly the result of work by Lewis Thomas and Robert Harper. Both conclude that manufacturing in Metro East is a result of the availability of low-cost, flood-protected land; the large number of railroads, which made possible the rapid receipt of material and shipment of products; the availability of cooling and process water from either the river or the floodplain aquifer; and the considerably lower freight costs on coal, an important industrial material around the turn of the century, in comparison to the costs in the city of St. Louis. Because the Mississippi River is on the west side of its valley in most of the St. Louis area, the floodplain and its associated extensive level sites are nearly all in Illinois. According to Thomas, land costs in 1927 in the American Bottoms, such as in the Tri-Cities area, ranged from 5 to 35 cents per square foot, while those in the Mill Creek Valley in central St. Louis were one to five dollars per square foot. The cost of delivering one ton of coal to East St. Louis in 1913, Thomas notes, was 32 cents, while it was 52 cents to transport a like amount to St. Louis. The difference was in part because the interstate transportation of coal from Illinois into Missouri came under the jurisdiction of the Interstate Commerce Commission, while the Illinois Public Service Commission set the intrastate rates from the Illinois mines to East St. Louis.

Within the last 20 years, Metro East has lost several of its large manufacturing plants, most of them in one of the area's oldest centers of manufacturing, East St. Louis. The now underutilized buildings and sites once occupied by Alcoa, Armour, American Zinc, Emerson Electric, and

Mobil Oil that ring East St. Louis are reminders of the growth and decline which are part of all aspects of life, including manufacturing. With changing conditions, some plants survive at their older sites, while others meet the challenge by changing their method of production or their location.

The people of Metro East are beginning to cope with this loss of manufacturing and especially with the type and locational pattern of manufacturing they wish to have in the future. Many in the area are now thinking that light industry in addition to the existing or additional heavy manufacturing would be desirable. Thought has also been given to where this manufacturing ought to be located (Fig. 7-9). Work is now underway to convert some of the empty agricultural land into sites that will be of interest to industry.

This last phase of the current industrial development program is the most difficult. First of all, it takes money to buy property, build roads, and extend utilities. Secondly, not enough people (especially investors) understand the true character of the Metro East area. To many, Metro East is just a heavy industrial area that contains only working class people of limited skills and hard-core, unemployed blacks, who live in towns with corrupt governments and heavy air pollution. This, of course, is an inaccurate description of the area, but it is one that too many hold and act upon. The attitude of people towards this area, be it correct or not, is now far more important in influencing the type and location of growth than are physical factors such as topography, soil, or water.

Drainage and Flood Control

Control of the water which has formed and influenced the American Bottoms portion of Metro East has been necessary in

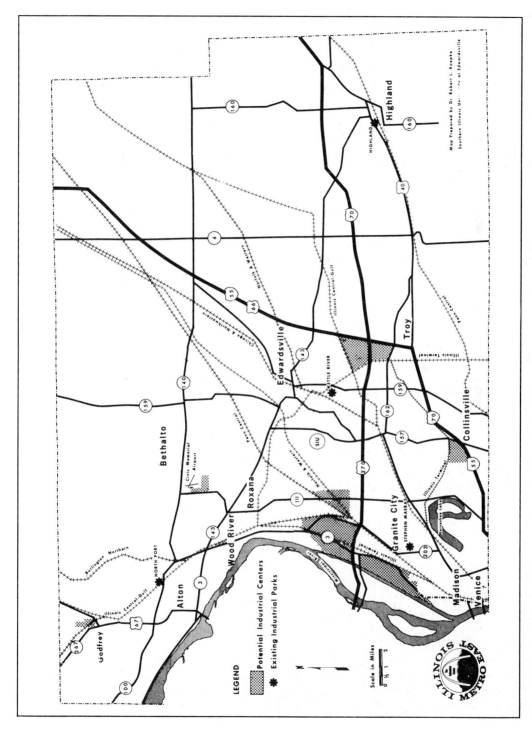

Figure 7-9. Potential industrial centers, Madison County, Illinois. The map also shows the sites of existing industrial parks.

order to make the area habitable and a satisfactory location for homes and businesses. Before significant modifications by man, the Mississippi River floodplain in Metro East was a wet land. Around the turn of the century the Bottoms contained several lakes—Cahokia Lake, Pittsburg Lake, Spring Lake, Horseshoe Lake, Indian Lake, and Grassy Lake—and many streams. The American Bottoms also received the overflow of the Mississippi River itself, such as the 1844 record flood during which steamboats traveled directly to the bluffs, according to local histories. The Bottoms also received the water of other streams, many with large upland tributary areas. Cahokia Creek, for example, has a tributary area of 290 square miles, most of it on the uplands. Water falling on the Bottoms itself often ponded because of the slight gradients and numerous low areas, some without outlets, that were produced by the complex actions of the Mississippi River in the formation of the surface of the Bottoms.

While high river water and runoff from the uplands affected the American Bottoms for centuries, it was not until 1907, in response to the flood of 1903, that the East Side Levee and Sanitary District was formed to provide a major levee system for protection from the river, diversion of upland streams, and drainage ditches for interior flood control. Whereas some levee districts had been formed earlier and some levees had been constructed locally, the East Side Levee and Sanitary District was the first to plan for flooding in nearly the entire Bottoms and to construct facilities to protect and to drain the Bottoms.

One of the first accomplishments of the district was the construction of the Mississippi River levee during the period 1911-15. This system consists of a riverfront levee along the east bank of the Mississippi River and flank levees on the north along the Cahokia Diversion Channel and on the south along the Prairie du Pont floodway. The flood control act of 1936 authorized the U.S. Army Corps of Engineers to strengthen these levees; this federal project was essentially complete in 1968. Today most of the American Bottoms is protected with a 200-year levee (i.e., the probability of it being overtopped is 0.5 during any one year).

The East Side Levee and Sanitary District also tackled the water problem produced by the upland tributary streams that empty into the floodplain. In fact, the first action of the district was the construction in 1910 of a diversion across the floodplain to the Mississippi River. One of the previously noted flank levees was constructed to prevent flooding from Mississippi River water backing up into this diversion channel. In 1917 the district began a similar project on the south end of the Bottoms by building a floodway with flank levees for Prairie du Pont Creek. A year earlier, in 1916, improvements consisting largely of straightening and deepening were begun on the portion of Cahokia Creek still remaining within the Bottoms. In 1920 construction began on Canal No. 1, which was to go along the base of the bluffs from Prairie du Pont floodway and cut off all the streams before they traveled through much of the Bottoms. The canal was never completed and now receives the water from just one upland stream, Powermill Creek, and a small area around the canal.

Hence, within two decades after the flood of 1903, the East Side Levee and Sanitary District had a system to protect the American Bottoms from the Mississippi River and to some extent from the major upland tributary streams. Additional laterals to the major ditches have since been constructed, such as Goose Lake Ditch; some streams have been relocated, such as the portion of Cahokia Creek through East St. Louis; and as has been noted, the levees have been raised. But by and large the flood protection and drainage system established by the district during its initial years is the system that exists today.

Because of the accomplishments of the early engineers, the East Side Levee and Sanitary District, and assistance by the Army Corps of Engineers, some sections of this system have been quite effective. The protection offered by the levees has so far been complete, with the levees never having been overtopped, even during the flood of 1973. The Cahokia Diversion Channel and the Prairie du Pont floodway have also worked effectively since their installation. Unfortunately, the same cannot be said for the remainder of the interior drainage system. By and large, the upland streams still deposit more water than the bottomland canals, lakes, and ditches can hold, and heavy rains still cause damage by ponding in farm fields and in some urban areas. The hillside drainage problem exists today not because of a lack of knowledge—the engineering studies are numerous—but rather because the information has not been used to solve the problem. The struggle is not with the physical environment, but rather with the cultural environment. The original studies of the East Side Levee and Sanitary District indicated how the problem could be solved from an engineering point of view. Other studies with similar conclusions have been made by the City of East St. Louis in 1946, the State of Illinois in 1950, the Corps of Engineers in 1962, and the Southwestern Illinois Metropolitan and Regional Planning Commission in 1975. If plans could do the job, the problem would have been solved long ago. Plans, however, must be implemented in order to be effective. This im-

plementation in turn requires agreements by all interested parties on goals and plans and then the expenditure of money by some of them. Such agreements have not been obtained to date in the American Bottoms.

The difficulties are well illustrated in the Blue Waters segment of the American Bottoms (located in the southern end of the Bottoms around the Village of Cahokia). In their 1962 report the Corps of Engineers estimated that some 1,400 acres and a number of residences in the Blue Waters area were susceptible to surface interior water damage. In November, 1962, the trustees of the East Side Levee and Sanitary District stated their willingness and legal authority to act as the required local sponsor for the Corps plan to reduce or remove the water damage. Finally, the U.S. Congress through the Flood Control Act of 1965 authorized a system of structural improvements. By 1974 the Corps had basically completed the necessary detailed engineering in the Blue Waters area. In the years since the authorization of the project, the local people and institutions have "dropped the ball." For several years the local sponsor, the ESLSD, languished in its support and the project stalled. Lack of money was one element, but ineffective internal management was probably another. In an effort to get the project going, the state of Illinois agreed to act as the local sponsor in lieu of the levee district and also indicated a great interest in some completed solutions to the problems. But before the Corps plans could be implemented, a new state administration with different ideas on how to handle the water problem was installed in Springfield. The state's desire now was to minimize their involvement, especially in the expenditure of funds. Unfortunately, the solution proposed by the state under their objectives is different from that proposed by the Corps with their objectives. To date, the institutional impasse has not been resolved and the internal flood hazard remains.

The Future

Illinois Metro East has an intriguing present and a proud past, but the future should be more important to the citizens, institutions, and researchers of the area. Of course, it is necessary to understand the past and the present, for they are the foundations upon which the future will be built; but the people of today can only study, not influence, the activities and patterns in either of these time periods. It is only the future over which people have some degree of control. What is, is here now; what was, is gone; what will be, is all that remains.

Unfortunately, the future is a period about which little information is available. Researchers in Metro East, as elsewhere, have not pushed enough of their investigations into what tomorrow may be or should be like. Local citizens have generally been so busy with the present (or so disinterested) that the future has been almost ignored. The governmental sector is also oriented towards handling today's problems today and leaving tomorrow's needs for tomorrow.

If Metro East is to be a good place to live in the future, the local people must make three major commitments. One is to dedicate themselves to work toward a better tomorrow. Without this dedication there will be little attention given to the future and without this attention the future will be left to take care of itself. As noted earlier, the settlement pattern, the quantity and location of manufacturing, and the solution of environmental problems such as drainage are features of the area over which people have some control, *if* they will simply "put their hands on the plow." A second commitment is to work toward answering the following series of questions about themselves and their area: What is the area like? How did it get this way? What can it be in the future and what do the people of the area want it to be? The third commitment is to develop a system or procedure whereby people can effectively transform this area from its present to its ideal condition.

While the building of a better tomorrow is not a high priority item in the area today, the seed of "what about tomorrow?" is beginning to sprout. Growth, development, and planning are not major topics of citizen discussions, but the local press is pointing out more and more the potential, need, and problems of growth and the need for management. The professional planners are gathering information on the present character of the area and its future potential. Reports are also coming out of Southern Illinois University at Edwardsville, especially from the faculty and graduate students in the Department of Earth Science, Geography and Planning. Adequate local planning budgets, however, are not yet on the scene or even on the horizon.

In addition to recognizing the need for dealing with tomorrow today and the consideration of a series of questions about what tomorrow can and should be like, the people of Metro East need to come to grips with the system whereby the area can be changed. So far, this important element has received the least amount of attention by both laymen and professionals. How much of the management of an area should be at local, regional, state, and federal levels? How does the need and desire of local people to manage their own activities mesh with the advent of regional, state, and perhaps even federal planning and the appearance on the scene of the federal Environmental Protection Agency? Who should make the decisions at these various levels—citizens, politicians, elected public officials, appointed officials, local technocrats, or regional or state technocrats? In other words, what form should an important element of today's cultural environment take?

The struggle of people in Illinois Metro East to make a home for themselves goes on. For previous inhabitants a large part of the struggle was with the physical environment. Today people seem reasonably well equipped to handle the physical environment, but less well equipped to struggle effectively with their cultural environment. Yet the character and patterns existing in this part of Illinois when the 300th anniversary of the founding of the United States is celebrated will depend to a considerable degree upon the outcome of the people's attempts (if any) to form their own future through their cultural environment.

Notes

1. For a more detailed description of the landforms of Metro East, see Ronald E. Yarbrough, "The Physiography of Metro East." *Bulletin of the Illinois Geographical Society* XVI (June 1974), pp. 12-28.
2. See Harry B. Kircher, "The Sequent Occupance of Metro East." *Bulletin of the Illinois Geographical Society* XVI (June 1974), pp. 3-11 for an account of the progression of human groups (Indian, French, English, and American) that have occupied the area.
3. Sidney Denny, "Cultural Elements-Archaeology." Section XIV, Environmental Inventory Report Part A (St. Louis: U.S. Army Corps of Engineers, St. Louis District, August 1973), pp. XIV-3, XIV-4.
4. William Baker, "Land Claims as Indicators of Settlement in Southwestern Illinois, circa 1809-13." *Bulletin of the Illinois Geographical Society* XVI (June 1974), pp. 32-34.
5. Robert Koepke, "Manufacturing in Metro East." *Bulletin of the Illinois Geographical Society* XVI (June 1974), pp. 43-55.
6. Robert A. Harper, *Metro East: Heavy Industry in the St. Louis Metropolitan Area* (Carbondale, Ill.: Southern Illinois University, 1958).

Selected References

Altes, Jane. *East St. Louis: The End of a Decade.* RUD Report No. 3. Edwardsville, Ill.: Southern Illinois University, Regional and Urban Studies and Services, January 1970.

Baker, William. "Land Claims as Indicators of Settlement in Southwestern Illinois, Circa 1809-13." *Bulletin of the Illinois Geographical Society,* XVI (June 1974), 29-42.

Bond, John. *The East St. Louis, Illinois Waterfront: Historical Background.* Washington: U.S. Department of the Interior, Division of History, 1969.

Conyer, John W. *Geography Through Maps: The Saint Louis Gateway.* Special Publication No. 14. Normal, Ill.: National Council for Geographic Education, 1967.

Harper, Robert A. *Metro East: Heavy Industry in the St. Louis Metropolitan Area.* Carbondale, Ill.: Southern Illinois University, 1958.

Kircher, Harry B. "The Sequent Occupance of Metro East." *Bulletin of the Illinois Geographic Society,* XVI (June 1974), 3-11.

Koepke, Robert L. "Manufacturing in Metro East." *Bulletin of the Illinois Geographical Society,* XVI (June 1974), 43-55.

Koepke, Robert L., and Creed, Sara. *Directory of Manufacturers, Illinois Metro East Area.* Metro East Resources Report No. 3. Edwardsville, Ill.: Illinois Metro East Corporation, April, 1969.

Megee, Mary. "The American Bottoms: The Vacant Land and the Areal Image." *The Professional Geographer,* Vol. XIII (November 1961), 5-9.

Werner, Carol A. "Agriculture and Urban Change: The Case of Metro East." *Bulletin of the Illinois Geographical Society,* XV (June 1973), 29-40.

Yarbrough, Ronald E. "The Physiography of Metro East." *Bulletin of the Illinois Geographical Society,* XVI (June 1974), 12-28.

Chapter Eight

THE CHICAGO METROPOLITAN AREA[1]

Irving Cutler
Chicago State University

Geographic Attributes

Only a century and a half ago the Chicago area was a wilderness of flat, poorly drained land blanketed with prairie grass, clusters of trees, and foul-smelling marshes. Occasionally Indians would pass through the area in quest of game. Today, with a population of 3,369,359, Chicago ranks second in the United States and twentieth among the great cities of the world. Moreover, the population of its burgeoning suburban area is now even greater than that of the city itself. The six counties of northeastern Illinois which constitute the Chicago Standard Metropolitan Statistical Area, although occupying only 6.6 percent of the area of Illinois, contain 6,981,347 people, or 62 percent of the state's 11,113,976 inhabitants.

Despite the area's inauspicious setting, the essentials for its rapid growth were present when the first settlers arrived. These essentials included:

1. Location near the geographic center of the vast and fertile plains between the Appalachian Mountains to the east and the Rocky Mountains to the west. Chicago's situation enabled it to become the center of the most productive agricultural hinterland in the world. The flat terrain permitted easy access to this rich tributary empire and allowed the city itself to expand unimpeded.

2. Conveniently located and economically accessible, important natural resources—the forests of the North, the iron ore of Minnesota and Wisconsin, the coal of Illinois and nearby states, and an unlimited supply of fresh water.

3. Location at the southwesternmost tip of the world's greatest lake system. This made possible exceptionally low transportation costs and a great range of domestic and overseas connections. In addition, Chicago's location is at a natural point of convergence for land

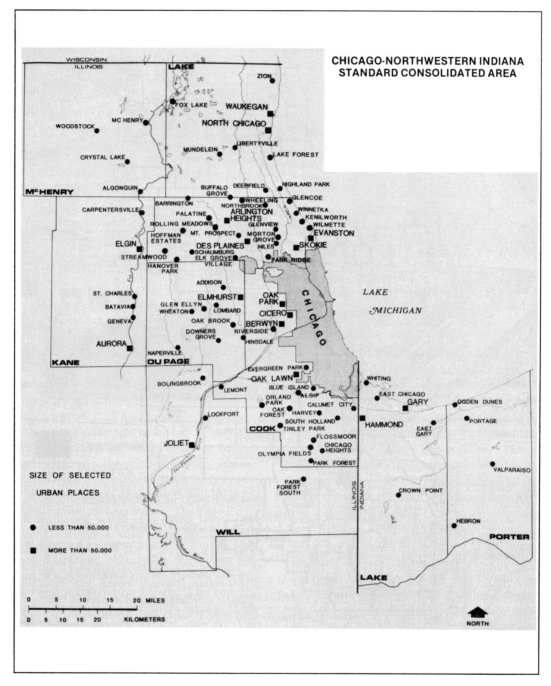

Figure 8-1. Chicago-Northwestern Indiana Standard Consolidated Area. The six counties of northeastern Illinois in the Chicago Standard Metropolitan Statistical Area contain about 7 million people, by far the greatest population concentration in the state.

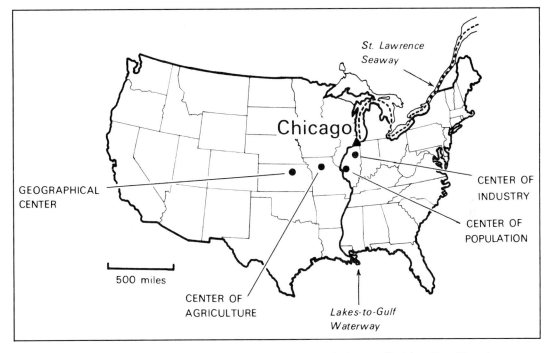

St. Lawrence
Seaway

Chicago

GEOGRAPHICAL
CENTER

CENTER OF
INDUSTRY

CENTER OF
POPULATION

500 miles

CENTER OF
AGRICULTURE

Lakes-to-Gulf
Waterway

Figure 8-2. The situation of Chicago. A major asset of Chicago is its excellent location. (Based on a map from Chicago Association of Commerce and Industry.)

traffic between the East and Northwest that had to find its way around the southern tip of Lake Michigan. Long before the coming of the white man, numerous Indian trails joined at Chicago.

4. The short natural waterways of Chicago, which eventually were modified to provide the only all-water connecting link between the Great Lakes-St. Lawrence Seaway and the rich Mississippi Valley.

The Natural Setting

The topography of the Chicago region is the result of millions of years of geologic action. The limestone bedrock, which underlies the area and occasionally can be seen in quarries, road cuts, and river channels, is largely the compressed remains of the limy skeletons and shells of countless creatures that lived in the tropical sea that covered the midcontinent millions of years ago. This limestone provides basic building material and also solidly anchors Chicago's giant skyscrapers.

The glaciers, which once covered the Chicago area, ground down elevations, polished rough surfaces, gouged and deepened such areas as the basin of Lake Michigan, and left behind a covering of glacial drift averaging between 50 and 60 feet in depth over the limestone bedrock. In the Chicago region, the last glacier receded about 13,500 years ago, having sculptured the basic landscape surface. Chicago now occupies a lake plain which is hemmed in by the Valparaiso Moraine, a ridge of glacial drift parallel to the shoreline of Lake Michigan. This crescent-

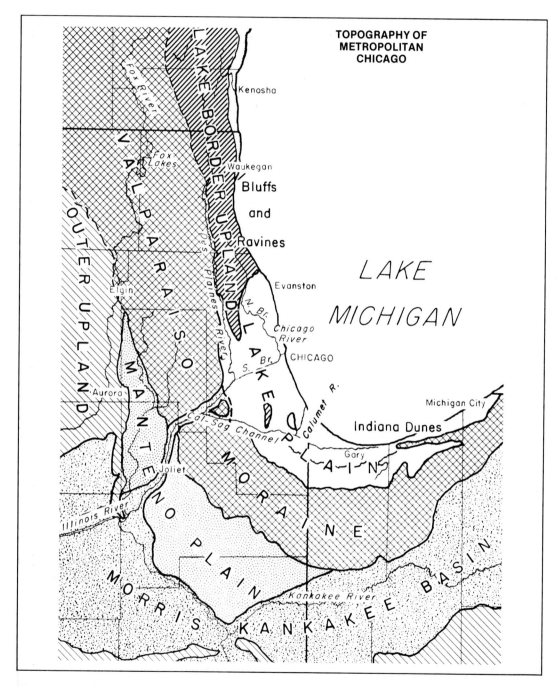

Figure 8-3. Topography of metropolitan Chicago. (Reproduced by permission from Rutherford H. Platt, *Open Land in Urban Illinois,* Northern Illinois University Press, 1971. Based on F. M. Fryxell, *The Physiography of the Region of Chicago.*)

shaped moraine averages 15 miles in width, ranges from less than 100 to over 500 feet above the level of the lake, and is significant especially in regard to the drainage pattern. It stretches from southeastern Wisconsin to southwestern Michigan; its inner edge is followed approximately by the Tri-State Tollway some dozen or so miles from Lake Michigan. The northern part of the Valparaiso Moraine is characterized by rounded hills and undrained depressions. In Lake County, Illinois, and crossing into Wisconsin, many of these depressions are occupied by about 100 small lakes and ponds. This inland lake region is an important recreational and residential area, with sizeable settlements around such larger water bodies as Fox Lake, Pistakee Lake, Round Lake, Long Lake, Grays Lake, and Lake Zurich.

On the lakeside of the northern part of the Valparaiso Moraine is the much smaller Lake Border Upland, an elongated belt of nearly north-south ridges with a width of 5 to 15 miles. The main segment extends northward from about Des Plaines and Winnetka, with a narrow extension south into the Lake Plain as far as Oak Park. Some ridges rise to about 200 feet above the lake level and are interspersed by gentle sags occupied by small streams and an occasional marsh, such as the Skokie Lagoons. Lakeward of the Valparaiso Upland and the Lake Border Upland spreads the flat Lake Plain on which Chicago is situated.

The Lake Plain

Since water drainage to the north was blocked by ice when the last glacier retreated, glacier meltwater filled the depression between the receding ice front and the Valparaiso Moraine. This created a lake that at its highest elevation rose about 60 feet above the present surface of Lake Michigan.

This enlarged Lake Michigan, geologically known as Lake Chicago, covered the entire area of the present city of Chicago. The boundary line of the lake reached from about what is now Winnetka through the present communities of Maywood, La Grange, and Homewood, crossing the state line at Dyer and continuing eastward beyond Chesterton, Indiana. The accumulated water receded in stages, finding its way into the Illinois-Mississippi River drainage system by enlarging two outlets through the Valparaiso Moraine drainage divide. One of these outlets, which now holds the Calumet Sag Channel, was through the Sag Valley south and southwest of the city; the other, to the southwest, sometimes known as the Chicago Portage, contained first the Illinois-Michigan Canal and later the Chicago Sanitary and Ship Canal as well as other important transportation arteries.

The lake bottom of Lake Chicago left the Chicago area remarkably flat—a lake plain—except for a few small islands that had existed in the lake, such as Mount Forest Island, Blue Island, and Stony Island, and some spits, sandbars, and crescent-shaped beach ridges that emerged as the water receded in three distinct stages. These ridges stand about 60 feet, 40 feet, and 20 feet higher than the approximately 580 feet height above sea level of present Lake Michigan. Driving away from the lake on an east-west street, such as Devon Avenue or 111th Street, will take one over each of the beach ridges of Lake Chicago within a distance of 10 to 15 miles. Because they were often the best-drained ground in an otherwise marshy area, some of the sandy spits, bars, and beaches of the Chicago area became Indian trails, and some are now parts of main roads. The good drainage also made these areas attractive locations for cemeteries and golf courses. Both Graceland

and Rosehill spits have had their names adopted for the large cemeteries established there.

Three small lakes near the Chicago-Hammond portion of the state line are isolated remnants of the glacial Lake Chicago. In recent decades these lakes have declined in size because of marginal filling and drainage alterations. Lake George, on the Indiana side, has virtually disappeared; Wolf Lake is a recreational area; and Lake Calumet is being developed as the major port of Chicago. Beach ridges separate the three lakes from Lake Michigan. A series of such ridges has hampered drainage in the Calumet district.

The basic topography of the Chicago area resulted from the superimposition on the limestone bedrock of an uneven layer of glacial drift and of Lake Chicago's deposits. Since the Ice Age, a number of limited topographic changes have occurred. Through weathering, wind and water deposition, and vegetative growth, the present soils have been formed on the surface of the deposits of the glacial period. The soil is generally of rich, fine quality, and very productive agricultureally except where there are major drainage problems or where extensive sand deposits have accumulated, such as along parts of the shore at the head of Lake Michigan.

Another noteworthy postglacial change has been the development of the scenic bluffs and ravines along the lake between Winnetka and Waukegan by shoreline erosion. Some of the bluffs are almost 100 feet high, and many of the more than 20 major ravines extend a mile or so inland. The effect of lakeshore erosion in this area is dramatically illustrated by the following report:

> In 1845 and for about ten years following there was a village located in the southeast corner of what is now the Fort Sheridan grounds. This village was known as St. Johns. The chief industry was brick making, the yards employing as many as eighty men. . . . North of the clay pit remnants of a foundation and of an orchard are at the very margin of the lake cliff. Reports differ as to the amount of land that has been cut away at this point, but all agree that it was more than 100 feet. Some old settlers insist that 300 to 400 feet have been removed, and that the cliff and even overhanging are reported by some to have been in the yard to the west of the westernmost house in the village. If this is true, the entire side of the village of St. Johns is east of the present shore line.[2]

Today even these meager traces of the village have vanished, prey to the attacking waves and currents.

Rivers and Drainage

The Chicago River is the outstanding topographic feature of the rather featureless Lake Plain that contains the city of Chicago. Though short and sluggish (the important South Branch is only about half-a-dozen miles in length), the river has been a major factor in the city's establishment and growth. It was the early connecting route between the East and the commercial wealth of the Middle Prairie. Early Chicago centered upon the river and in the period of its greatest use the river handled huge cargoes of grain, lumber, and manufactured goods.

The river's main channel with its two branches forms a *Y,* with the junction near the Merchandise Mart. This configuration has, by tradition, divided Chicago into three broad sections—the North, South, and West sides. The North Branch originates in Lake County, Illinois, as three small streams flowing southward in the sags of the moraines of the Lake Border Upland. The streams join in northern Cook County and flow southeastward toward the junction with the main channel. The South Branch was usually navigable only as far west as the present Leavitt Avenue (2200 West). Often, however, during spring high water it was possible to push canoes across the marshy divide all the way to the Des Plaines River (near 49th Street and Harlem Avenue) by using seasonal Mud Lake, which bridged most of the six-mile portage between the two rivers.

The Chicago River has been greatly modified since it was navigated by the early explorers. It has been straightened and widened. The sandbar, which blocked its mouth and caused it to bend southward and flow into the lake opposite the foot of Madison Street, has been removed. An artificial island, Goose Island, was created and a sharp bend bypassed by the construction of the mile-long North Branch Canal. Most important, the portage was eliminated, and the South Branch of the river was connected with the Illinois-Mississippi River system, first by the Illinois and Michigan Canal and later by the Chicago Sanitary and Ship Canal. The flow of the Chicago River was reversed into these connecting waterways.

At the southeastern end of the city is Chicago's other important river—the Calumet. Unlike the Chicago River, the Calumet played an insignificant role in Chicago's early history. Today, however, it traverses one of the most industrialized areas in the world—"the Ruhr of America." The early settlers found the Calumet to be an erratic, meandering stream that had formed an elongated loop parallel to the lake. Later, man also altered this river to suit his purposes. It was reversed to flow away from Lake Michigan into the Calumet Sag Channel near Riverdale, and thus drain the Lake Plain of southern Chicago and northwestern Indiana westward into the Chicago Sanitary and Ship

Canal, and so eventually into the Illinois-Mississippi system.

The reversal of the Chicago and Calumet rivers altered the unusual drainage pattern of the Chicago region. In creating moraines parallel to Lake Michigan, glacial action also caused a divide parallel to the lake and relatively close to it. Water on one side of the divide flows into the St. Lawrence River system; on the other side, into the Gulf of Mexico. The divide is less than four miles from the lake in the Waukegan area, and at its farthest point, south of Hammond, Indiana, only about 20 miles from the lake. A few short rivers on the eastern side of the divide such as the Chicago and Calumet broke through sandbars to reach Lake Michigan, but the major rivers, such as the Fox, Des Plaines, and Kankakee, never penetrated the moraines. They flow into the Mississippi Basin. In places, the divide is less than 100 feet above Lake Michigan and at its lowest point, the Chicago outlet at Summit, Illinois, it is a barely discernible 15 feet above the lake.

Because the land is flat, the rivers are generally sluggish and drainage poor. Furthermore, layers of impermeable clay left by the glaciers hampered the drainage of surface waters, created a high water table, and helped make early Chicago a virtual sea of mud for at least part of the year. To get adequate gradient for storm and sanitary sewers, the Metropolitan Sanitary District of Greater Chicago has had to provide more than a dozen pumping stations to enhance the flow to the extensive drainage canal system.

Historical Development

In 1673, Louis Jolliet and Père Jacques Marquette, while returning to Canada after exploring the Mississippi Valley, became the first whites to pass through the Chicago area. In the ensuing decades, French explorers, trappers, and fur traders occasionally traversed the area mainly because of its excellent geographical location and short portage between the Chicago and Des Plaines rivers. Indians, mainly Potawatomi, traded furs and sometimes camped in the area they called "Checagou," evidently referring to the wild onion smell which permeated the air.

The area was ruled by the British from 1763 until their evacuation was finally procured by the Jay Treaty of 1794. During the late 1770s, Jean Baptiste Point du Sable established what was probably Chicago's first permanent dwelling on the north bank of the Chicago River near the present Tribune Tower. From this base, du Sable carried on trade with the Indians for about two decades.

In 1803 the United States Army erected Fort Dearborn at an elevated point in the bend near the mouth of the Chicago River to secure the area and protect the important waterway linkage, which became even more important with the Louisiana Purchase the same year. Despite the fort, settlement in the area remained very sparse, due mainly to the hostility of the Indians who were angered by the continued takeover of their lands. This hostility was brutally manifested in the War of 1812 when the Indians ambushed and killed 53 settlers and soldiers and burned the fort to the ground. The fort was reestablished in 1816. A few settlers, tradesmen, and agents were attracted to its vicinity, but large-scale settlement did not begin until the conclusion of the Black Hawk War in 1832. The treaty with the Indians provided for their relocation west of the Mississippi River in return for certain payments in cash and goods.

In 1832, the Indians assembled in Chicago for their final payments. Also present were a motley collection of wayfarers—horse dealers and horse stealers, peddlers, grog sellers, and "rogues of every description, white, black, brown, and red—half-breeds, quarter-breeds, and men of no breed at all." By ruse, whiskey, and thievery, they managed to separate the Indians from a good part of their money and goods. About 800 Indians joined in a last defiant dance of farewell before crossing the bridge over the South Branch of the Chicago River and heading westward until Chicago saw them no more.

Town and City

No longer impeded by fear of the Indians, and aided by improved transportation, such as the Erie Canal-Great Lakes route, the trickle of newcomers to the little military and trading outpost grew into a stream. Men were drawn to Chicago by cheap land, jobs, and a speculative fervor stimulated by plans for a canal that would connect Lake Michigan with the Mississippi River.

Incorporated in 1833, the new town covered a 3/4-square mile area centered upon the main channel of the Chicago River. In the same year, it was described by the Scottish traveler Patrick Shirreff:

Chicago consists of about 150 wood houses, placed irregularly on both sides of the river, over which there is a bridge. This is already a place of considerable trade, supplying salt, tea, coffee, sugar, and clothing to a large tract of country to the north and west; and when connected with the navigable point of the river Illinois, by a canal or railway, cannot fail of rising to importance. Almost every person I met regarded Chicago as the germ of an immense city, and speculators have already bought up, at high prices, all the building-ground in the neighborhood.[3]

Chicago's rapid growth can be shown in a number of ways. In 1833, only four lake steamers entered its harbor; by 1836, the number had increased to 450. A parcel of land at South Water and Clark streets purchased for $100 in 1832 was sold for $15,000 in 1835. And by 1837, when Chicago was incorporated as a city, its population exceeded 4,000 and it encompassed some ten square miles.

The author John Lewis Peyton portrayed the burgeoning Chicago of 1848 as follows:

> The city is situated on both sides of the Chicago River, a sluggish, slimy stream, too lazy to clean itself, and on both sides of its north and south branches, upon a level piece of ground, half dry and half wet, resembling a salt marsh, and contained a population of 20,000. There was no pavement, no macadamized streets, no drainage, and the three thousand houses in which the people lived, were almost entirely small timber buildings, painted white, and this white much defaced by mud. . . .
>
> Chicago was already becoming a place of considerable importance for manufacturers. Steam mills were busy in every part of the city preparing lumber for buildings which were contracted to be erected by the thousand the next season. Large establishments were engaged in manufacturing agricultural implements of every description for the farmers who flocked to the country every spring. A single establishment, that of McCormick employed several hundred hands, and during each season completed from fifteen hundred to two thousand grain-reapers and grass-mowers. Blacksmith, wagon and coachmaker's shops were busy preparing for a spring demand, which with all their energy, they could not supply. Brickmakers had discovered on the lake shore near the city and a short distance in the interior, excellent beds of clay, and were manufacturing, even at this time, millions of brick by a patent process, which the frost did not hinder, or delay. Hundreds of workmen were also engaged in quarrying stone and marble on the banks of the projected canal; and the Illinois Central Railway employed large bodies of men in driving piles, and constructing a track and depot on the beach. Real estate agents were mapping out the surrounding territory for ten and fifteen miles in the interior, giving fancy names to the future avenues, streets, squares, and parks. A brisk traffic existed in the sale of corner lots, and men with nothing but their wits, had been known to succeed in a single season in making a fortune— sometimes, certainly, it was only on paper.[4]

By 1850, Chicago's population had grown to about 30,000 and its future role as a great transportation and industrial center was already clearly evident. The 97-mile-long Illinois and Michigan Canal opened in 1848, connecting the Great Lakes with the Mississippi Valley. Shortly thereafter, a period of vigorous railroad building brought railroad tracks to Chicago from almost every direction. By 1855, Chicago was already the focus of ten trunk lines.

Chicago's location and its excellent transportation connections with the rich agricultural hinterland helped forge strong bonds of interdependence between the city and the farmers of the Midwest. The farmers funneled their produce to Chicago; the city provided stockyards, food processing, and grain elevators, as well as ships and trains to deliver the farm commodities eastward. From Chicago the farmers were shipped clothing, processed foods, household items, lumber, and farm equipment. Much of the farm equipment was manufactured by the McCormick Reaper factory, which had been established in 1847 on the north branch of the Chicago River at the site of the former du Sable cabin. Cyrus McCormick was among the first of a long line of commercial and industrial entrepreneurs who, together with their employees, were to help make Chicago "Hog Butcher for the World, Tool Maker, Stacker of Wheat, Player with Railroads, and the Nation's Freight Handler."

Figure 8-4. Chicago in the 1860s. Prominent features of the city are the rectangular grid street pattern and the great activity on the lake and river. (Lithograph, Rufus Blanchard, Chicago. Courtesy Chicago Historical Society.)

On the whole, political and economic dominance was held initially by men from the eastern United States. With remarkable combinations of thrift, shrewdness, and drive, they acknowledged no barriers to the successful expansion of a wide range of enterprises. In their climbing to the top, they often had little regard for others, but perhaps they did what had to be done to raise a city out of a swamp. Among these pioneer leaders was William B. Ogden of New York, who was elected the city's first mayor in 1837. One of the earliest of many Chicagoans to promote railroad building, he later became the first president of the Union Pacific. Potter Palmer, who arrived in 1852, made a fortune in dry goods and cotton speculation and added to his wealth by developing State Street. In 1867 Marshall Field, who came from Massachusetts, became a part owner in the firm that later bore his name. Two farm youths from the East, Philip D. Armour and Gustavus Swift, helped make Chicago the meat packer of the nation. A new era in railroad travel began in 1864 when George Pullman invented the sleeping car. Later his shops for building passenger and freight cars spread over 3,500 acres near Lake Calumet. Julius Rosenwald, a native of Springfield, Illinois, learned the clothing business, went to work for Sears, Roebuck and Company, and eventually became its president and board chairman as well as one of the nation's great philanthropists. Sears's major competitor was founded shortly after the Chicago Fire of 1871 by A. Montgomery Ward, who had lost everything in the conflagration but $65 and the clothes he wore. He later earned the nickname "watchdog of the lakefront" for his long, but successful struggle to save the Grant Park area from being commercialized.

Mudhole of the Prairies

The land survey provisions of the Federal Ordinance of 1785 imparted to early Chicago a basic, functional pattern of land subdivision and roads. Using a rectangular grid system, the survey divided the land into square-mile sections. The section lines were a mile apart and ran either north-south or east-west. They became main traffic thoroughfares, major routes of public transportation, and ribbons of commercial development that ultimately became overextensive and inefficient. Major shopping areas often developed at the intersections of these primary arterials. Superimposed on the rectilinear street system were a number of diagonal streets, some of which began as Indian trails.

Mud was the main problem of the early Chicago streets. In 1848, Chicago

> could boast of no sewers nor were there any sidewalks except a few planks here and there, nor paved streets. The streets were merely graded to the middle, like country roads, and in bad weather, were impassable. A mud hole deeper than usual would be marked by signboards with the significant notice thereon, "No bottom here, the shortest road to China."[5]

The difficulty arose because Chicago was flat and low, being only about two feet above the river level. Moreover, the sewage that did drain off into the Chicago River flowed into Lake Michigan, the city's source of drinking water. The resulting epidemics of cholera, typhoid, and other diseases were not finally curtailed until the flow of the river was reversed in 1900. Before that, Chicago tried to lift itself from the quagmire by raising the elevation of the city. Fill—sometimes obtained from the dredgings of

Figure 8-5. State Street in the late 1860s after it had already replaced Lake Street as the main commercial thoroughfare. Chicago's first mass transportation line—the horse drawn street railway car—was established on State Street in 1859. View is looking south from Lake Street. (Courtesy Chicago Historical Society.)

Figure 8-6. The forks of the Chicago River looking north from Randolph Street before the fire of 1871. The North Branch flows from the top left and the South Branch from the lower right to form the main stem of the river. Two of the major activities along the river are evident here: lumber yards and grain elevators. The open bridge on the right is at Lake Street; in the right background are Illinois and Michigan Canal barges tied up near Wolf Point on the north side of the main stem of the river. (Courtesy Chicago Historical Society.)

the waterways—was used to raise street levels. For a time, however, Chicago exhibited a confusing pattern of disjointed sidewalks, some up and some down, depending on whether the owner had raised his property or not. And even today, especially in the inner city, one can find yards and homes below the raised street level, some with stairs leading down to the first floor.

The Fire and Its Aftermath

Despite such problems, Chicago continued to grow and prosper. It was buoyed by the opening of the Illinois and Michigan Canal, the coming of the railroads, the development of substantial industry (stimulated somewhat by the Civil War), the further settling of its rich hinterland, and the accelerating influx of newcomers. Between 1850 and 1870 the population increased tenfold, from 30,000 to about 300,000.

The disastrous Chicago Fire of 1871, however, cast a temporary pall on the city. Chicago in 1871 was a city of wood— wooden houses, wooden roofs, even wooden sidewalks. After an unusually long period of drought, the city became tinder dry. The stage was set for the fire that broke out on October 8 in Mrs. O'Leary's barn (at the site of the present Chicago Fire Academy). Fanned by a southwest wind, the fire spread rapidly. When it finally subsided two days later, it had thoroughly gutted about four square miles of the city including the entire downtown area. The fire took more than 250 lives, destroyed some 17,000 buildings, and left almost 100,000 people homeless.

The determined Chicagoans, who had already created a city on marshland, immediately turned to the task of rebuilding it. By 1875 little evidence of the catastrophe remained. The fire accelerated the movement

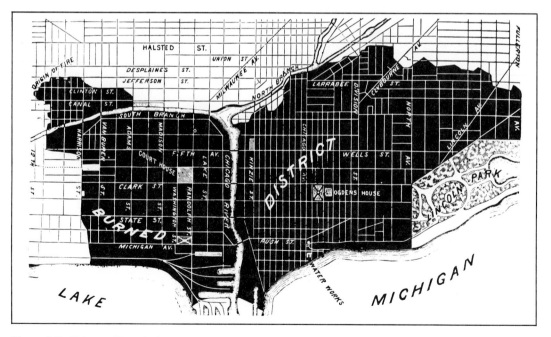

Figure 8-7. Chicago Fire of 1871. The area destroyed by the fire is indicated in black. (Courtesy Chicago Historical Society.)

of residential homes from the central business district. The new buildings in the downtown area were larger and higher, and they conformed to a new city ordinance that outlawed wooden buildings there. In other parts of the city thousands of homes were going up, many of brownstone and brick. The rebuilding activities attracted to Chicago thousands of laborers and numerous architects, many of whom helped construct the first skyscrapers using the innovative steel skeleton, elevators, and the floating foundation.

Despite the fire, depressions, and such sporadic, violent labor strife as the Haymarket Riot, Chicago continued to grow rapidly. Besides its commercial and transportation importance as a major handler of grain, cattle, and lumber, the city was becoming increasingly a major center of diversified manufacturing. The annexation by Chicago in 1889 of four sizeable, but relatively sparsely populated communities— the towns of Jefferson and Lake, the city of Lake View, and the Village of Hyde Park— increased its size from 43 square miles to 168 square miles, and by 1890 the city had a population of 1,099,850. In the preceding decade the output of many of its major industries had more than doubled.

From Fair to Fair

In 1893, just 22 years after the fire had leveled the heart of the city, Chicago again attracted worldwide attention, this time with its dazzling, classically styled World's Columbian Exposition. With its customary audacity, the city built the Exposition on an apparently impossible sandy site along the lakefront eight miles south of the river. The Exposition sparked a real estate boom on the South Side, especially in the Hyde Park-Woodlawn area around its grounds. As a legacy to the city, it left Jackson Park, the

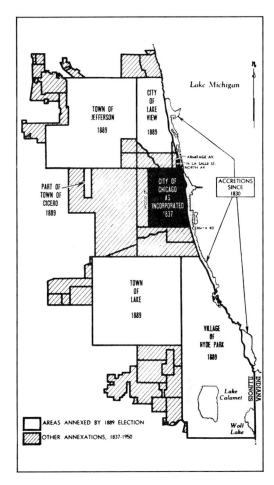

Figure 8-8. Growth of Chicago, 1837–1950. In one year, 1889, Chicago increased its size about fourfold through a series of annexations. Since 1950 Chicago has annexed about 15 additional square miles accounted for largely by the land of O'Hare International Airport plus a few small pieces of land on the northwestern and southwestern fringes of the city. (From *Chicago*, Chicago Board of Education, 1951.)

Midway, and the Museum of Science and Industry (the Fine Arts building of the Exposition).

The many facets of Chicago life in the 1890s were depicted by George W. Steevens, an English journalist, in this vigorous portrayal:

Chicago! Chicago!, queen and guttersnipe of cities, cynosure and cesspool of the world! Not if I had a hundred tongues, every one shouting a different language in a different key, could I do justice to her splendid chaos. The most beautiful and the most squalid, girdled with a twofold zone of parks and slums; where the keen air from lake and prairie is ever in the nostrils, and the stench of foul smoke is never out of the throat; the great port a thousand miles from the sea; the great mart which gathers up with one hand the corn and cattle of the West and deals out with the other the merchandise of the East; widely and generously planned with streets of twenty miles, where it is not safe to walk at night; where women ride straddlewise, and millionaires dine at midday on the Sabbath; the chosen seat of public spirit and municipal boodle, of cut-throat commerce and munificent patronage of art; the most American of American cities, and yet the most mongrel; the second American city of the globe, . . . the first and only veritable Babel of the age; all of which twenty-five years ago next Friday was a heap of smoking ashes. Where in all the world can words be found for this miracle of paradox and incongruity?[6]

In the first three decades of this century the growth of Chicago continued unabated despite periodic depressions, the curtailment of European immigration during and after

World War I, and the gangster era of the prohibition years, which created an image of lawlessness that the city's many accomplishments failed to overcome. During this period the population almost doubled, increasing from 1,698,575 in 1900 to 3,376,808 in 1930. By 1930 the entire city area, except for some small patches mainly on its fringes, had been occupied. In addition, especially after World War I, population was flowing increasingly into the suburbs.

Chicago's Century of Progress Exposition of 1933-34 celebrated a century of remarkable growth. The structures of the World's Fair were erected on artificially created land along the lakeshore from Roosevelt Road to 39th Street. Although the Fair was held in the depths of the Great Depression, it attracted over 39 million people and proved an unqualified financial success. More important, it showed the world how far the little muddy portage-town had come in 100 years.

The Burnham and Subsequent Plans

Some of Chicago's finest features are the result of its pioneering efforts in city plan-

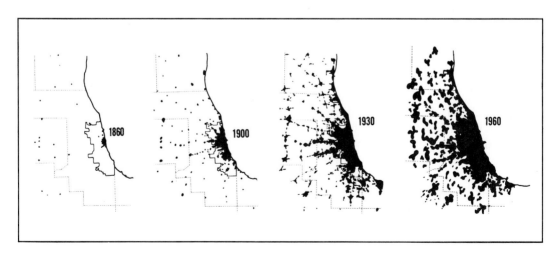

Figure 8-9. Metropolitan growth, 1860–1960. (From Pierre DeVise, *Chicago's People, Jobs, and Homes,* Vol. 1, Department of Geography, DePaul University, 1964.)

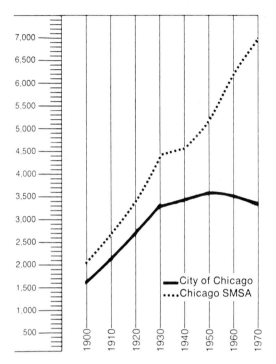

POPULATION CHANGE 1900 - 1970
(IN THOUSANDS)

■City of Chicago
•••Chicago SMSA

Figure 8-10. Chicago's population of 3,369,359 in 1970 was slightly less than the 1930 population of 3,376,438. During the same interim the population of the SMSA, excluding Chicago, more than tripled from 1,073,208 in 1930 to 3,611,988 in 1970.

ning. In 1869 Frederick Law Olmsted developed the basic park and connecting boulevard system which has served Chicago so well for a century. In 1893 the World's Columbian Exposition gave Chicago a glimpse of the advantages of urban design that incorporated an orderly arrangement of structure and space. And in 1909 the renowned architect Daniel H. Burnham, who had presided over the construction of the World's Columbian Exposition, proposed a monumental long-range *Plan of Chicago* which introduced comprehensive city planning to Chicago and the nation.

Although Burnham's plan did not ade-

quately foresee such problems as housing and the effect of the automobile, it was bold in conception, metropolitan in scope, and comprehensive in its incorporation of the advanced concepts of the time. It stressed the "city beautiful" trend with broad avenues, parks, and civic centers. Officially adopted by the city, it has guided public improvements for many years. Although not all of Burnham's specific suggestions have been implemented, some outstanding features of present-day Chicago were either proposed or advanced by the plan, and more than a half billion dollars have been expended in its implementation. Major recommendations and achievements of the Burnham Plan included:

1. The widening of major thoroughfares, the double-decking of Wacker Drive and part of Michigan Avenue, and most important, the creation of a regional highway system extending up to 60 miles beyond the city—a metropolitan approach which has been at least partially implemented by the expressway system.

2. The consolidation of railway terminals, still not fully achieved but anticipated in the near future. The Union Station was built as the plan suggested.

3. The construction of new docks and navigation facilities. In accordance with the plan, Navy Pier was built, Lake Calumet developed, the South Branch of the Chicago River straightened, and a number of bridges constructed.

4. The development of a continuous lakefront park. Twenty of the city's 25 miles of lakeshore are now devoted to recreational and cultural facilities. Only one of the string of contemplated offshore islands has been completed.

5. The extension of outlying forest preserves.

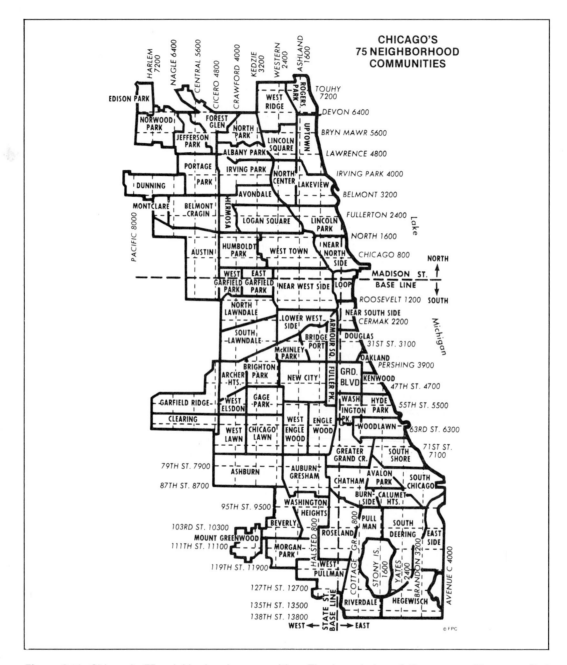

Figure 8-11. Chicago's 75 neighborhood communities. The boundaries of the communities were first delineated over 40 years ago through the work of the Social Science Research Committee of the University of Chicago. Since then only minimum boundary refinements have been made, although a 76th community, O'Hare, was created out of the land annexed in the 1950s for the airport. (Reproduced by permission from M. S. Ratz and C. H. Wilson, *Exploring Chicago,* Follett Publishing Company, 1958.)

An incidental, but far-reaching result of the Burnham Plan was the provision for planning on a permanent basis. The plan stimulated the development of two organizations, one for the city's planning, the other for planning on a more regional scale. From these earlier agencies have evolved the city's present policy-making Chicago Plan Commission and its administrative arm, the Department of Planning, City and Community Development. Serving the six counties of the northeastern part of the state is the Northeastern Illinois Planning Commission.

Subsequently, other measures were taken to ensure the orderly development of Chicago, but none of these has as yet matched the effects of the Burnham Plan. In 1966 the city proposed the Comprehensive Plan of Chicago, which was later supplemented by detailed plans for each of 16 geographic areas of Chicago, including the central area. Comprehensive plans for Chicago's lakefront and for the downtown riverfront were also published. The recent plans have emphasized the human element—raising the quality of family life and the environment, expanding economic opportunities for the disadvantaged, and improving transportation and land use. No proposals, however, have dealt with the problem of racial segregation.

The recent plans have recommended high-density communities along the lakefront, in the downtown area, and along mass transportation routes; low-density housing in the outlying parts of the city; medium density in between; and a "mix" of housing densities in some areas. Major development projects for the downtown area include those over the Illinois Central land near the lakefront, the "South Loop New Town" on the railroad land south of the Loop, additional new construction in the area east of North Michigan Avenue and north of the river, and scattered development in the Loop itself. The all-encompassing Chicago 21 Plan, sponsored by a nonprofit organization composed mainly of business and real estate people, deals with the future development of most of the central area. Recommendations for major new transportation facilities include the proposed Crosstown Expressway and a new downtown subway. Some of these proposals are being independently implemented, but progress in adopting and fulfilling the major components of the most recent comprehensive city plan has been slow.

People and Settlement Patterns

Chicago's unprecedented growth from a marshy wilderness to a city of well over three million people in less than a century and a half resulted largely from an almost constant flow of settlers attracted by its economic opportunities. The major points of origin of the settlers changed with the passing decades. The first arrivals came mainly from the eastern United States. (Unlike southern Illinois, very few of Chicago's early settlers came from the South.) Then, starting around the 1840s, large numbers began to arrive first from northwestern Europe, later from eastern and southern Europe, and most recently from the United States South and the Caribbean area. In all, Chicago is an amalgam of over 40 identifiable ethnic and racial strains.

European Immigrants

By 1890, over three-fourths of Chicago's one million people were either European immigrants or the children of European immigrants, with Germans, Scandinavians, and Irish, in that order, being the three largest foreign-born groups. The flow of Europeans to Chicago continued unabated until the outbreak of World War I, but the geographic sources of immigration began to shift markedly about 1880. From 1880 until 1927, when national immigration quotas went into effect, the majority of immigrants came from eastern and southern Europe, with Poles, Italians, eastern European Jews, Bohemians, Lithuanians, Russians, Greeks, Serbians, and Hungarians among the largest groups. At the peak of immigration, Chicago was the world's largest Lithuanian city, second-largest Bohemian city, and third-largest Irish, Swedish, Polish, and Jewish city.

When immigration was sharply curtailed in 1927, foreign-born whites constituted about 27 percent of Chicago's total population. This figure had fallen to 20 percent by 1940, 15 percent by 1950, and 11 percent by 1970. The number of foreign-born in Chicago in 1920 and in 1970 by major country of origin is shown in Table 8-1. These figures show that the number of foreign-born is now comparatively small; the proportion from northwest Europe has also declined markedly.

The median age of the foreign-born is 62, foreshadowing a further decline of the group which at one time constituted a majority of Chicago's people. Their decrease also marks the decline of one of Chicago's most colorful eras—a period when much of the city was a microcosm of various European cultures. The city was filled with the sounds of dozens of languages, exotic dress, and myriad ethnic shops, schools, churches, synagogues, cafes, coffeehouses, and newspapers. At that time the immigrants cherished the security of their own institutions in their own neighborhoods as they worked their way upward economically and socially despite occasional hostility encountered from "native Americans," many of whom were themselves the children or grandchildren of immigrants.

The Ethnic Checkerboard

The new immigrant groups usually sought housing in the congested, low-rent areas around the Loop, especially on the near west side, in areas abandoned by earlier immigrant groups who had moved upward economically and outward geographically. The old ghetto area on the near west side has been home for a succession of ethnic groups—Irish, Bohemians, Jews, and now blacks.

The desire of the immigrants to be close to their countrymen and to establish in their

Table 8-1. Foreign-born in Chicago.

Native Country	1920	1970
Poland	137,611	55,711
Italy	59,215	32,539
Germany	112,288	31,430
U.S.S.R.	102,095	22,640
Ireland	56,786	13,766
Lithuania	18,923	12,130
United Kingdom	37,932	10,867
Austria	30,491	9,559
Czechoslovakia	50,392	8,329
Sweden	58,568	7,005

new land the institutions they had cherished in their birthplaces led to the formation of numerous ethnic neighborhoods. Some of these neighborhoods such as the Venetian, Neapolitan, and Sicilian were even established on the basis of ethnic subgroups. Going southward down Halsted Street a half century ago one would pass successively through Swedish, German, Polish, Italian, Greek, Jewish, Bohemian, Lithuanian, and Irish neighborhoods.

On Halsted Street was Jane Addams's Hull House, which catered to immigrants who were often needy, poorly educated, and bewildered by the unfamiliar setting. Jane Addams described the conditions of the immigrant groups as follows:

> Between Halsted Street and the river live about ten thousand Italians. To the south on Twelfth Street are many Germans, and side streets are given over almost entirely to Polish and Russian Jews. Still farther south, these Jewish colonies merge into a huge Bohemian colony. To the northwest are many Canadian-French and to the north are Irish and first-generation Americans. The streets are inexpressibly dirty, the number of schools inadequate, sanitary legislation unenforced, the street lighting bad, the paving miserable and altogether lacking in the alleys and smaller streets, and the stables foul beyond description. The older and richer inhabitants seem anxious to move away as rapidly as they can afford it. They make room for newly arrived immigrants who are densely ignorant of civic duties. Meanwhile, the wretched conditions persist until at least two generations of children have been born and reared in them.[7]

In time, with some acculturation and economic success, the immigrant groups and

Figure 8-12. Vendors about 1300 South Halsted Street in the Maxwell Street area, circa 1906—a type of old world activity transplanted to America. The market still exists, but on a much smaller scale, the victim of redevelopment, expressway construction, a changing neighborhood, and changing shopping patterns. (Courtesy Chicago Historical Society.)

especially their offspring moved outward from their crowded islands near the downtown area, often migrating in an axial pattern. Thus, many of the Germans moved outward along Lincoln Avenue and the Poles along Milwaukee Avenue. From their congested Pilsen colony in the Halsted-Ashland area south of 16th Street, the Bohemians moved westward into South Lawndale, and later into Cicero and Berwyn. Each

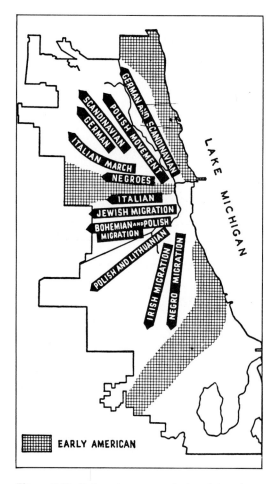

EARLY AMERICAN

Figure 8-13. Outward movement of racial and nationality groups in Chicago. (From Samuel C. Kincheloe, *The American City and Its Churches.* Friendship Press, New York, 1938.)

migration outward was usually accompanied by a further loosening of old world ties as each new generation became more assimilated, more geographically dispersed, and more active in the city's civic and economic affairs.

Recent Population Trends

The 1970 U.S. Census figures for Chicago indicated a population of 3,369,359, down substantially from the 1950 peak of 3,620,962. This decline resulted largely from the sizeable exodus of white families to the suburbs and a lower population density in the city caused by considerable redevelopment, including housing and expressway construction. (Chicago's population density declined from a peak of 17,011 per square mile in 1950 to 14,816 per square mile in 1970.)

The 1970 census data also showed that substantial changes had taken place in the composition of Chicago's population. In 1970, native whites of native parentage comprised about 1,400,000 people, or only a little more than 40 percent of the population; native whites of foreign or mixed parentage comprised less than 20 percent; foreign-born, 11 percent; and blacks numbered about 1,100,000, or nearly a third of the population. The population of Latin American origin had also risen rapidly to about a quarter of a million, or 7.3 percent of the city's total population. About 106,000 of the Latin Americans were of Mexican descent; 79,000 of Puerto Rican descent; and 14,000 of Cuban descent. The Latin American population more than doubled between 1960 and 1970, with the major residential concentrations of Puerto Ricans and Cubans radiating north and northwest of the central area of Chicago, and the major concentration of Mexicans southwest of

Figure 8-14. Division Street near Damen Avenue looking eastward, 1975. The street is one of the main business thoroughfares of the growing Puerto Rican community on the northwest side of Chicago. In the background is the San Juan Theatre featuring Spanish language films. The population of the community formerly was predominately of Polish descent. (Photograph by Irving Cutler.)

downtown and a smaller concentration in the Calumet area on the southeast side. The Japanese, Chinese, and Filipinos each numbered around 10,000; the city's American Indian population totaled about 7,000.

This changing composition of Chicago's population results from the fact that the most recent wave of migration to the city has been not from Europe but mainly from the southern states and, to a lesser extent, from Mexico, Puerto Rico, and, more recently, Cuba. The new migration was spurred by the continuing demand for labor, especially during World War I, World War II, and the boom years that followed the end of the conflict in 1945.

Blacks have lived in Chicago since its earliest days. Chicago was a terminus of the underground railroad, and by the time of the Civil War there were several hundred blacks in the city. However, the percentage of blacks remained relatively small until the World War I period. In 1910 blacks constituted only 2 percent of the population. This figure rose to 4 percent in 1920, 7 percent in 1930, 8 percent in 1940, 14 percent in 1950, 23 percent in 1960, and 32 percent in 1970. Today Chicago is the second-largest black city in the world, exceeded only by New York.

When the number of Chicago blacks was small they were widely scattered. As the blacks grew in number they became increasingly concentrated in older, deteriorated neighborhoods of the inner city that earlier immigrant groups had abandoned. The major axis of black settlement was on the near south side, between State Street and South Parkway (Dr. Martin Luther King, Jr., Drive), with smaller black settlements on the near west side and near north side. As the black population increased during World War I, the black neighborhoods became grossly overcrowded, with all the resulting social ills. The consequences were poor

housing, higher rents, school segregation, loss of employment opportunities because of difficult accessibility to available jobs, and racial tension. Attempts to enlarge the ghetto were often stymied by hostility and sometimes by violence. Prejudice and restrictive real estate practices combined to confine the blacks within certain boundaries.

The large black migration to Chicago during and after World War II built up a strong housing demand. The ghetto boundaries—Cottage Grove Avenue, Stony Island Avenue, Ashland Avenue, etc.—began to give way, and on a map the black residential areas resembled an inverted *L* with the main segment pushing southward toward the city limits and another segment pushing westward toward the city limits. The expansion of the black ghetto has been on a block-by-block basis and has almost always been confined to the periphery of the established ghetto. Sizeable parts of Chicago still have no black residents, and the city remains highly segregated.

Like the immigrant groups that preceded them, the blacks began by taking over the worst jobs and residential areas; but, unlike the earlier immigrant groups, the second and third generation blacks could not readily escape from the ghetto even when they could afford to—and an increasing number could. Even blacks with wealth and education were for the most part confined to the ghetto. They usually moved into adjacent neighborhoods whose white population had fled to the city's periphery or into the suburbs. Thus, like the white settlement patterns, black residential areas in the city reflect an economic stratification. The quality of neighborhoods, homes, education level, job status, etc., generally improves as one proceeds outward from the inner city.

Although most of the suburbs have enacted open-housing laws, the percentage of suburban blacks has increased only slight-

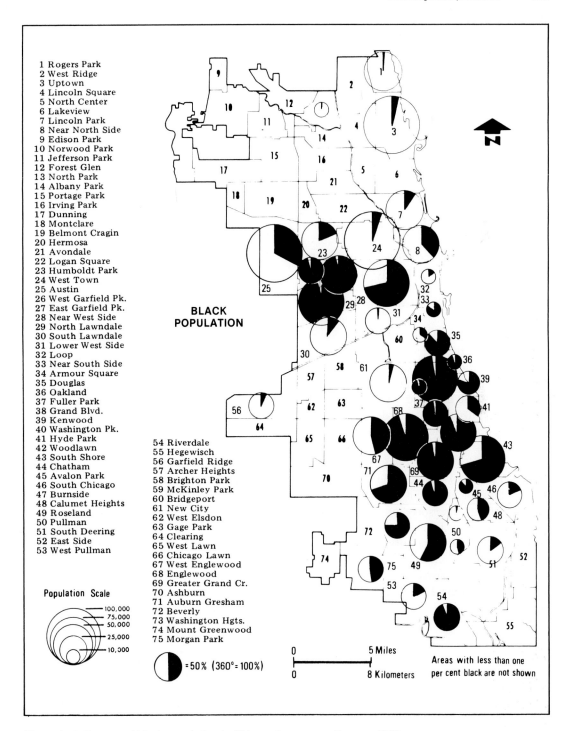

1 Rogers Park
2 West Ridge
3 Uptown
4 Lincoln Square
5 North Center
6 Lakeview
7 Lincoln Park
8 Near North Side
9 Edison Park
10 Norwood Park
11 Jefferson Park
12 Forest Glen
13 North Park
14 Albany Park
15 Portage Park
16 Irving Park
17 Dunning
18 Montclare
19 Belmont Cragin
20 Hermosa
21 Avondale
22 Logan Square
23 Humboldt Park
24 West Town
25 Austin
26 West Garfield Pk.
27 East Garfield Pk.
28 Near West Side
29 North Lawndale
30 South Lawndale
31 Lower West Side
32 Loop
33 Near South Side
34 Armour Square
35 Douglas
36 Oakland
37 Fuller Park
38 Grand Blvd.
39 Kenwood
40 Washington Pk.
41 Hyde Park
42 Woodlawn
43 South Shore
44 Chatham
45 Avalon Park
46 South Chicago
47 Burnside
48 Calumet Heights
49 Roseland
50 Pullman
51 South Deering
52 East Side
53 West Pullman

54 Riverdale
55 Hegewisch
56 Garfield Ridge
57 Archer Heights
58 Brighton Park
59 McKinley Park
60 Bridgeport
61 New City
62 West Elsdon
63 Gage Park
64 Clearing
65 West Lawn
66 Chicago Lawn
67 West Englewood
68 Englewood
69 Greater Grand Cr.
70 Ashburn
71 Auburn Gresham
72 Beverly
73 Washington Hgts.
74 Mount Greenwood
75 Morgan Park

BLACK
POPULATION

Population Scale

—— 100,000
—— 75,000
—— 50,000
—— 25,000
—— 10,000

◐ = 50% (360° = 100%)

0 ———— 5 Miles
0 ———— 8 Kilometers

Areas with less than one
per cent black are not shown

Figure 8-15. Percent of black population in Chicago by community area–1970.

ly. About 90 percent of the blacks of the metropolitan area still live in Chicago. Many of the suburbs still house no blacks at all, and a few have merely token integration. Fairly sizeable black populations in predominantly white suburbs are found in only a few communities, such as Evanston, Glencoe, Summit, Markham, Harvey, Oak Park, and Maywood. Two-thirds of the suburban blacks still live in industrial satellites such as Gary, Chicago Heights, Waukegan-North Chicago, and Joliet, or in black-ghetto suburbs such as Robbins, Phoenix, and East Chicago Heights.

In recent years, partly because of the impact of the civil rights movement, increasing opportunities for blacks in Chicago have been made available in education, employment, and politics. Declining birthrates and dwindling migration from the South, coupled with the continued expansion of black population into former white neighborhoods, have taken part of the pressure off some of the crowded black ghettos. By the early 1970s over a third of Chicago's nonwhite population had achieved "middle class" status, often because there was more than one breadwinner in the family. Increasingly, such blacks were able to find improved housing, some in neighborhoods at the ghetto borders, some on a nondiscriminatory basis in such urban redevelopment or renewal areas as Sandburg Village, Lake Meadows, Prairie Shores, South Commons, and Hyde Park-Kenwood and in such south suburban areas as Park Forest and Park Forest South.

Socioecononic Patterns

The Chicago Metropolitan Area consists of several hundred communities, of which 75 are recognized neighborhood community areas in Chicago and the remainder are suburban municipalities. The communities of the area are characterized by a great range of socioeconomic diversity. This range is indicative of the diverse racial, ethnic, and educational backgrounds of the people and of the wide variation in the opportunities available to them. Estimated median family income in the Chicago Metropolitan Area ranges from about $7,000 annually in some inner city communities of Chicago to about $43,000 annually in several affluent suburbs. In general, the lowest income levels are found in the overcrowded, inner city black areas on the south and west sides. Family income increases concentrically as one proceeds outward toward the more recently occupied periphery of the city—with the highest income in the peripheral Chicago communities of Forest Glen ($20,000) and Beverly ($19,000)—and reaches its peak in the suburbs.

Both the communities of Chicago and the suburban communities vary markedly in economic status. Of the 25 wealthiest suburbs, 15 are to the north, while only seven are to the west, and three are to the south. In addition to such physical amenities as the lake and interesting topography, wealthy North Shore suburbs have the attraction of good commuter transportation to the Loop and extensive areas free of polluting industries. The poorest suburbs are virtually all to the south of the city, with the largely black suburb of Robbins having the lowest income.

Many of the economic elite of early Chicago lived close to the center of the city along such once fashionable streets and boulevards as Washington, Jackson, Ashland, Michigan, Wabash, Prairie, Indiana, and Calumet. With the spread of industry and immigrant groups into these areas, some

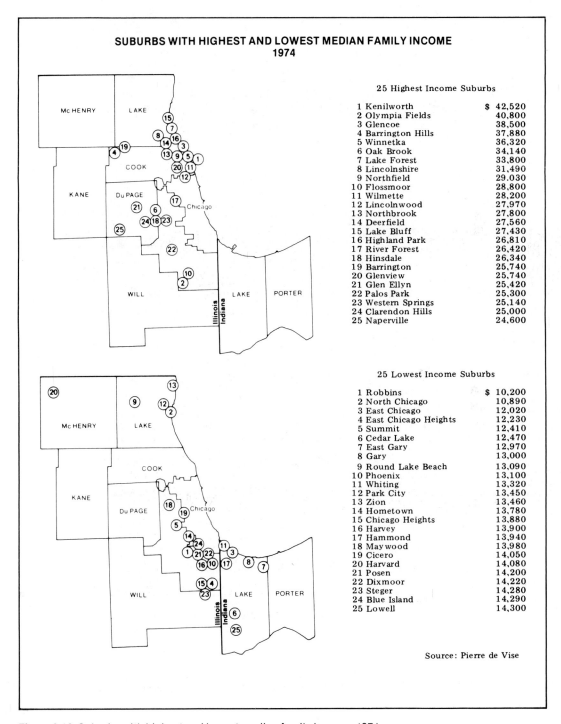

SUBURBS WITH HIGHEST AND LOWEST MEDIAN FAMILY INCOME
1974

25 Highest Income Suburbs

1	Kenilworth	$ 42,520
2	Olympia Fields	40,800
3	Glencoe	38,500
4	Barrington Hills	37,880
5	Winnetka	36,320
6	Oak Brook	34,140
7	Lake Forest	33,800
8	Lincolnshire	31,490
9	Northfield	29,030
10	Flossmoor	28,800
11	Wilmette	28,200
12	Lincolnwood	27,970
13	Northbrook	27,800
14	Deerfield	27,560
15	Lake Bluff	27,430
16	Highland Park	26,810
17	River Forest	26,420
18	Hinsdale	26,340
19	Barrington	25,740
20	Glenview	25,740
21	Glen Ellyn	25,420
22	Palos Park	25,300
23	Western Springs	25,140
24	Clarendon Hills	25,000
25	Naperville	24,600

25 Lowest Income Suburbs

1	Robbins	$ 10,200
2	North Chicago	10,890
3	East Chicago	12,020
4	East Chicago Heights	12,230
5	Summit	12,410
6	Cedar Lake	12,470
7	East Gary	12,970
8	Gary	13,000
9	Round Lake Beach	13,090
10	Phoenix	13,100
11	Whiting	13,320
12	Park City	13,450
13	Zion	13,460
14	Hometown	13,780
15	Chicago Heights	13,880
16	Harvey	13,900
17	Hammond	13,940
18	Maywood	13,980
19	Cicero	14,050
20	Harvard	14,080
21	Posen	14,200
22	Dixmoor	14,220
23	Steger	14,280
24	Blue Island	14,290
25	Lowell	14,300

Source: Pierre de Vise

Figure 8-16. Suburbs with highest and lowest median family income–1974.

Figure 8-17. View eastward from the Ogden Avenue viaduct north of Division Street, 1954, showing part of the near north side area that Harvey Zorbaugh discussed in 1929 in his book entitled *The Gold Coast and the Slums.* The Gold Coast consists of the luxury high-rise apartment buildings along the lakefront, visible in the background. (Photograph by Lillian Ettinger. Courtesy Chicago Historical Society.)

of the wealthy moved farther out along north Lake Shore Drive or into Kenwood, Hyde Park, and South Shore, and some moved into the suburbs.

In time, former high-income areas in Chicago deteriorated into the city's worst slums, as the vacated mansions of the rich were subdivided to accommodate the poorer migrants. However, in the post-World War II period some of these areas experienced massive redevelopment, again emerging as highly desirable locations, such as Lake Meadows, Prairie Shores, and South Commons south of the Loop and the Sandburg Village area to the north. Urban redevelopment, generally radiating outward from the downtown area, has been uplifting inner city areas with more expensive high-rise housing. At the same time, however, the poor who lived in these areas before redevelopment

Figure 8-18. Aerial view of Lake Meadows apartment community looking northwest from south of 35th Street with the Illinois Central Gulf Railroad tracks at the lower right. The integrated community was developed under the urban renewal program by the New York Life Insurance Company on what had been one of the worst slum areas of the city. The development contains a shopping center, elementary school, public park, community center, and an office building. The high-rise apartment complex in the right background is the adjoining Prairie Shores apartment development, also integrated. More than a century ago much of this land was owned by Senator Stephen A. Douglas who lies buried in the small park just west of the tracks with a tall pillar topped by his statue capping his tomb. (Courtesy Department of Urban Renewal, City of Chicago.)

have been pushed out. Once again they have crowded into what were once stable neighborhoods, creating new slums.

Commerce and Industry

Chicago started as a small trading and military post. Buoyed by its excellent location in a growing area, it soon evolved into a bustling lake and river port, then into a canal terminal and railroad center, and finally into a major commercial and distribution center. Developing more slowly at first, but generally paralleling its commercial development, Chicago's small-scale manufacturing of a century ago expanded until the city became the second-largest industrial center in the nation. Today, it is the nation's leading producer of a variety of items ranging from snuff to steel. Moreover, about 40 percent of the nation's manufacturing and over 30 percent of its wholesale and retail trade are concentrated within a 500-mile radius of the Loop.

Early Industry

The earliest industries of Chicago—milling, meat-packing, tanning, and woodworking—were closely related to the products of the surrounding fields and forests. Other industries arose in response to the need of the area's growing population for printed matter, household utensils, clothing, wagons, boat supplies, building materials, and quarry products.

Chicago early developed a lucrative symbiotic relationship with its rich hinterland. It received, processed, and distributed the products of the farm, and it produced and sent back to the farms clothing, furniture, and agricultural machinery and implements. One of Chicago's earliest major industries was the farm machinery company (the forerunner of International Harvester) established by Cyrus McCormick on the north bank of the Chicago River.

In 1856 the largest group of related firms in Chicago—86—were in food processing, meat-packing, and industries using animal by-products such as leather. The printing industry ranked second with 65 firms, and next, with more than 50 firms each, were the textile-garment-millinery and the building trades industries. The latter included brickyards, planing mills, lumberyards, and door and sash factories.

Certain industrial location patterns were already apparent. The area north of the river contained the fewest factories. These included the McCormick Reaper and Mower Works and a number of breweries which clustered in the area because of its large German population. The present downtown area, south and east of the river, contained the printing industry and numerous handicraft industries, such as dressmaking, shoemaking, tailoring, and cigar manufacturing. West of the river, on the near west side, were numerous metal-using and metal-manufacturing firms.

Many early industries congregated along transportation routes—first along the waterways, later along the railroads. Lumber, grain, and tannery facilities were concentrated along the Chicago River. More than 500 acres of land between Halsted Street and Western Avenue along the river's south branch became the largest lumber distribution center in the world. The lumberyards, stocked from the Wisconsin, Michigan, and Canadian forests, supplied the booming home building and furniture industries of the city and the needs of the prairie farmers. Today a residual maze of tracks and lumber slips still occupy the area, but there are few lumberyards. However, Chicago retains its preeminence as a furniture mart.

In 1867 manufacturing in the Chicago area was described as follows:

At first Chicago began to make on a small scale the rough and heavy implements of husbandry. That great factory, for example, which now produces the excellent farm wagon every seven minutes of every working day, was founded twenty-three years ago by its proprietor investing all his capital in the slow construction of one wagon. At the present time, almost every article of much bulk used upon railroads, in farming, in warming houses, in building houses, or in cooking, is made in Chicago. Three thousand persons are now employed there in manufacturing coarse boots and shoes. The prairie world is mowed and reaped by machines made in Chicago, whose people are feeling their way, too, into making woolen and cotton goods. Four or five miles out on the prairie, where until last May the ground had never been broken since the creation, there now stands the village of Austin, which consists of three large factory buildings, forty or fifty nice cottages for workmen and two thousand young trees. This is the seat of the Chicago Clock Factory. . . . A few miles farther back on the prairies, at Elgin, there is the establishment of the National Watch Company, which expects soon to produce fifty watches a day. . . . They are beginning to make pianos at Chicago, besides selling a hundred a week of those made in the East; and the great music house of Root and Cady are now engraving and printing all the music they publish. Melodeons are made in Chicago on a great scale.[8]

Until the 1860s Chicago industry produced mainly for the local market and the market of the surrounding farm area. The requirements of the Civil War, however, helped to propel Chicago industry into the national market. After the Civil War, the city's industrial expansion continued unabated through an era of great technological advances and industrial consolidation. Manufacturing rapidly surpassed commerce in importance and became the dominant source of employment in Chicago.

Two of the largest industrial concentrations in Chicago in the latter half of the nineteenth century were the Union Stock Yards and the Pullman Palace Car Company. A consortium of railroad and packing interests established the former in 1865 as a replacement for the city's numerous, small, scattered stockyards. The yards were located on land which was originally outside of the city limits. Eventually, they occupied about a square mile. For about a century they were the largest and busiest stockyards in the world. A peak was reached soon after World War I, when the yards employed over 30,000 people and received nearly 19,000,000 head of livestock annually.

The stockyards declined rapidly after World War II. By then, they were in the congested, highly taxed, geographic center of Chicago. There were labor problems, and a trend toward decentralization was taking place in the nation's meat-packing industry. Furthermore, the yard's facilities had become obsolete, since they had been designed to be served by railroads and most animals were now being shipped by truck. In 1971, after 106 years of service, the Union Stock Yards closed. On the land formerly occupied by the yards are dozens of new, small plants, virtually none of which are engaged in activities related to meat-packing.

The Pullman Palace Car Company was the foremost of the numerous railroad equipment manufacturers established in the Chicago area. It was founded by George Pullman, the inventor of the sleeping car. The Chicago area was a desirable site for the company because of the city's position as the railroad hub of the nation, its central location, its growing steel industry, and the availability of a vast tract of vacant land to the south of the city on the west shore of Lake Calumet. The company's operations were unique, not only in size, but in being

Figure 8-19. The Union Stock Yards about 1910, looking southwest from the pens toward "Packingtown" where the animals were slaughtered and the meat processed. The area contained such meat packing giants as Armour, Swift, Wilson, Cudahy, and Libby, McNeil & Libby. Visible are ramps for moving the animals and the Stockyards branch of the South Side Elevated for the transportation of workers, although many lived within walking distance of the yards. After more than a century of operation, the yards closed in 1971. (Courtesy Chicago Historical Society.)

centered in a privately constructed, planned, company-owned "total community" with separate residential, industrial, recreational, and commercial areas. The community, erected in the early 1880s, prospered until the prolonged and violent Pullman strike of 1894. Thereafter, under court mandate, its private character disappeared rapidly. However, the basic pattern and the homes of the almost century-old, sturdily-built community are still largely intact. Although the Pullman Company's operations have been drastically curtailed and many of its facilities are utilized by other firms, some famous landmarks remain and should continue to remain for a long time, as Pullman was recently declared a National Historic Landmark.

Present Industry

In the twentieth century the Chicago area's industrial growth has been so rapid that it now ranks second among United States metropolitan areas in the number of manufacturing employees. Of the area's 3.25 million workers, more than one million are engaged in industry; 625,000 in trade and transportation; 450,000 in service; 170,000 in finance, insurance, and real estate; and the remainder in a great variety of other occupations. During this century the location, facilities, and products of Chicago's industry have changed greatly. The leading products of the pre-World War I period—meat-packing, men's clothing, furniture, agricultural implements, and railway equipment—have declined in relative importance. At the same time, Chicago's industrial base has undergone widespread diversification. In addition, numerous large concerns representing a diversity of industries are headquartered in Chicago.

Chicago's largest industrial employer is the mass production, consumer-oriented electrical goods industry. The city is the nation's leading producer of radios, television sets, telephone equipment, electrical machinery, and household appliances. Ranking, in descending order of employment, behind the electrical products industry are primary metals (mainly steel), nonelectrical machinery (farm equipment), industrial machinery, fabricated metals (cans, auto parts), foods, printing and publishing, chemicals and related products (oils, drugs, cosmetics, soap, paints), and transportation equipment. Chicago is usually the nation's leading producer in many of these fields, including steel, metal wares, confectionary products, surgical appliances, railroad engines and equipment, soap, paint, cosmetics, cans, industrial machinery, commercial printing, and sports goods. To supply these industries, millions of tons of iron ore, coal, chemicals, petroleum, lumber, paper, and farm products are brought into the area annually.

Traditionally, manufacturing in the Chicago area was concentrated along the rivers and railroads, but in recent years there has been increasing industrial development near expressways and in organized industrial districts. A growing proportion of the area's industrial establishments, including numerous concerns once situated in the inner city, is now found outside of the city proper.

More than one-third of the approximately 15,000 manufacturers and over half of the industrial jobs in the metropolitan area are now located outside the city limits of Chicago. Some suburban industries were established well before the turn of the century, but most are of post-World War II vintage. The shift of industry to the suburbs is due to such factors as limited acreage and high land costs in Chicago as well as to the general problems which plague most large cities today—congestion, plant obsolescence, high tax and insurance rates, crime, poor schools,

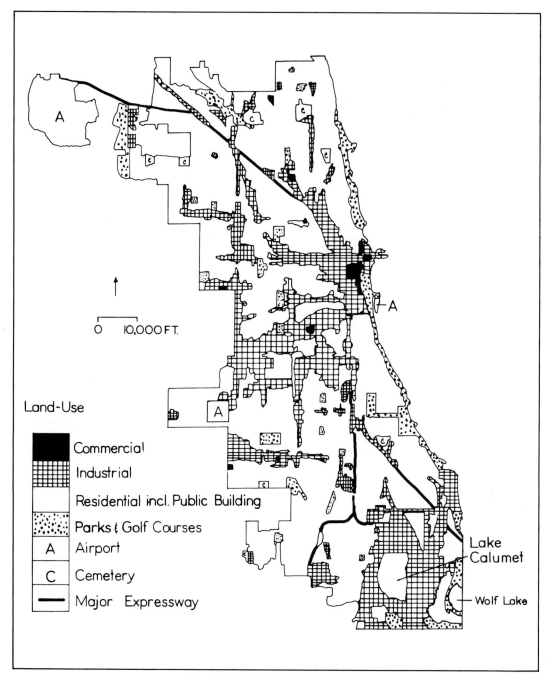

Figure 8-20. Land use in Chicago, 1960. Residential areas also include commercial streets. (From Ying Cheng Kiang, *Chicago,* Adams Press, Chicago, 1968.)

racial conflict, labor problems, and pollution. Although the suburbs are not free from these difficulties, the problems are usually less severe. Furthermore, many suburban areas can still offer large tracts of vacant land at relatively reasonable cost—land that meets modern industry's demand for expansive one-story plants and acres of parking and landscaping. Railroad and water sites, in which Chicago excels, are not as essential to increasingly truck-oriented industry.

Chicago-area communities employing large numbers of industrial workers include Cicero, Bedford Park, Waukegan, North Chicago, Aurora, Melrose Park, Joliet, Skokie, Chicago Heights, and La Grange in Illinois and Gary, Hammond, East Chicago, and Whiting in adjacent northwestern Indiana. In the post-World War II period there was a strong movement of industry to the north, northwest, and west suburban areas, based probably on good transportation, desirable environmental factors, and minimal racial problems. More recently, lower-priced and sizeable tracts of land and improving transportation of the south and southwest suburban areas have been attracting increasing numbers of industrial plants.

The industrial migration out of the city has reduced Chicago's economic base and increased unemployment among the poorly educated and the unskilled, especially the blacks. These groups find it difficult to take on jobs in the suburban areas far from their residences in the inner city.

Wholesale and Retail Trade

Chicago's wholesale trade equals its manufacturing industries in dollar volume—around $60 billion annually. Chicago is a principal market for grain, machine tools, produce, fish, and flowers. Its giant Merchandise Mart and American Mart make it the furniture marketing center of the nation. The Chicago Board of Trade and the Chicago Mercantile Exchange are among the world's largest commodity markets. The area's advantages as a distribution center have also helped to make it the home headquarters of the nation's four largest mail order concerns: Sears, Ward, Spiegel, and Aldens.

Because of its huge wholesale trade, its accessibility, and its accommodations, Chicago has long ranked as the nation's convention capital. About 1,500 conventions, trade shows, and expositions are held annually. To accommodate the annual influx of well over 2 million conventioneers and buyers, Chicago offers 1,400 hotels and motels with 135,000 rooms, over 5,000 restaurants, and numerous exhibition facilities (including the giant McCormick Place). Chicago also has many museums, theaters, sporting events, nightclubs, and other features of interest to visitors.

Organized Industrial Districts

Chicago has been a leader in the development of organized industrial districts. The accelerating growth of such districts has countered the previous tendency of often locating industry indiscriminately throughout residential areas, which often resulted in blight.

Chicago's Union Stock Yards and Pullman were pioneering forerunners of organized industrial districts. One of the largest, the Central Manufacturing District, was begun in 1902 to develop a tract of land immediately north of the Union Stock Yards. This development proved so successful that half a dozen others, containing a total of more than 500 industrial plants, have been established by the company in the Chicago Metropolitan Area. The Clearing Industrial

Figure 8-21. South Water Market looking east on 15th Street from Aberdeen Avenue, 1941. This is the major wholesale fruit and vegetable market in the city with annual sales of about $400 million. It opened in 1925 to replace the South Water Street market in downtown Chicago. The market consists essentially of six long buildings containing 166 virtually identical units. The advent of the long trailer truck has severely congested the market streets and brought periodic proposals for the construction of a new market. (Courtesy Chicago Historical Society.)

District was established by the railroads in 1909 in Bedford Park, just south of today's Midway Airport. It now operates ten separate industrial tracts containing over 275 plants in the southern and western fringes of the city and in some suburbs.

Today the Chicago area has over 150 industrial districts. The largest is the Centex Industrial Park begun in 1956 northwest of O'Hare Airport in an area that in recent years has experienced great industrial, commercial, and residential growth. Unlike earlier industrial districts, Centex is part of a larger complex, Elk Grove Village, which includes planned residential and commercial areas as well as industrial sections. Here more than 200 plants conform to the modern trend of well-landscaped one-story buildings with adequate parking facilities for the automobile-oriented workers. As in other districts, the industries are mainly of a light manufacturing or service nature.

The Calumet Industrial Complex

The heavy industry of the Chicago area is confined largely to the extreme southeastern part of the city and eastward around the southern end of Lake Michigan beyond Gary to the new Burns Harbor development. In Chicago the six miles along the Calumet River from its mouth to Lake Calumet contain one of the greatest industrial complexes in the world. The river is lined with a maze of steel plants, grain elevators, shipyards, chemical plants, and other facilities.

Industry began to develop in the Calumet area about a century ago. Here were large tracts of vacant, swampy, and sandy land, near plenty of fresh water, available at low cost, and strategically located near a great and growing market but outside the urban areas. The lake, rivers, and railroads offered virtually unexcelled transportation. A variety of heavy industries came to be located in the area. Oil refineries concentrated around Whiting, Indiana, making it one of the largest inland refinery centers in the world. Major producers of railway equipment were scattered throughout the area. Huge soap, paint, chemical, and cement plants were constructed. Some of these plants are related to the Calumet area's main industry—steel. The Calumet Industrial Complex is the nation's leading steel-producing area and one of the greatest steel centers of the world. Its production of about 30,000,000 tons annually is greater than that of Britain, France, or the Ruhr district of Germany.

Chicago's steel industry was originally located on Goose Island in the Chicago River. Later it moved to South Chicago, where it grew along both the Lake Michigan shore and the Calumet River. The industry subsequently expanded into the sand dune and swamp area of adjacent Lake County, Indiana, and, in the 1960s, further eastward along the lake into Porter County, Indiana, where two new steel plants were recently built. The area's accessibility by low-cost water transportation to the Lake Superior iron ore ranges has been particularly beneficial. Today there are ten steel plants in the area owned by eight companies. Three of these plants are among the largest in the nation.

Despite the construction of new steel plants and the expansion of most of the older ones, the Chicago area requires more steel than it produces. Its steel mills are unable to meet fully the demands of the 15,000 manufacturing plants in the Chicago area and the thousands more in the city's hinterland.

The steel industry has been a major employer in the Chicago area, and its presence

Figure 8-22. Aerial view looking northward from about 92nd Street and the Calumet River, 1936. The area shown is mainly the community of South Chicago. Along the lake from the Calumet River to 79th Street is the South Works of the United States Steel Corporation. Northwest of the plant, in the upper left, is the neighboring community of South Shore. (Courtesy Chicago Historical Society.)

Figure 8-23. Aerial view of Interlake's Riverdale, Illinois, steel making facility in the bend of the Little Calumet River. The river separates Riverdale from Chicago. Hot metal is shipped to the Riverdale plant in torpedo cars from another company plant about five miles away in Chicago. (Courtesy Interlake, Inc.)

has undoubtedly aided the establishment of many other industries. But the older steel mills have also brought appalling air and water pollution; dirt and grime and congestion have blighted the areas surrounding them. Only in recent years, under public pressure, have strenuous efforts been made to improve these conditions.

The Changing Central Business District

Downtown Chicago, where the city began, is now the heart of a great metropolitan area, but its structure and functions are changing rapidly. Until recent years it was relatively compact, circumscribed by physical barriers—to the east the lake, to the north and west the river, and to the south a maze of railroad facilities. Enhancing the area's importance was its position as the hub of one of the nation's greatest concentrations of rail, waterway, and road transportation. It was also the focal point of the highly developed internal transit system of the city.

Lake Street, just south of the river and its wholesaling activity, was the main commercial street of early Chicago. By the late 1860s, however, the principal focus of retail activity had shifted to what is still the city's main retail street—State Street. Although State Street was completely gutted by the Chicago fire, it was quickly rebuilt on an even grander scale to become that "great street." The postfire building boom helped to develop the modern skyscraper and the world-famous innovative Chicago School of Architecture which included Louis Sullivan, Dankmar Adler, William Le Baron Jenny, Henry Hobson Richardson, and, more recently, Frank Lloyd Wright and Ludwig Mies van der Rohe. Another incidental result of the fire occurred because some of its debris was dumped into the lake along the

original shoreline east of Michigan Avenue. Eventually it formed the impressive facade of downtown Chicago—Grant Park.

The commercial and manufacturing activities of the downtown area grew with the expansion of the city's population from a half million in 1880 to well over 3 million a half century later. The growth in the activities of the downtown area was accompanied by specialization of functions. What was probably the world's most concentrated shopping district stretched for almost a mile along State Street; the wholesale produce area was situated along the main stem of the river; LaSalle Street became a major financial center; Market Street was the heart of the garment district; entertainment facilities were spread along Randolph Street; and smaller enclaves contained concentrations of millinery, florist, furniture, music, and other specialty establishments. Multistory buildings used for light manufacturing were located to the west and, to a lesser extent, to the north of the downtown area.

Historically, retail expansion had been slow to develop north of the river. However, the opening of the Michigan Avenue bridge in 1920 sparked a major breakout from the relatively compact downtown area. This started the development of the "Magnificent Mile" of luxury shops, hotels, and office buildings north of the Loop, a development that coincided with a major downtown building boom in the 1920s. However, from the coming of the Depression until the end of World War II, virtually all major construction was brought to a standstill.

After almost a quarter century of stagnation, the completion in 1957 of the 41-story Prudential Building on the air rights over the Illinois Central tracks launched the greatest era of construction that downtown Chicago

Figure 8-24. State and Madison Street about 1905. The Louis Sullivan designed Carson Pirie Scott store is on the right and the Mandel Brothers (Wieboldt's) store is on the opposite side of Madison Street. Vehicular traffic includes the horse and buggy, cable car, electric streetcar, and the automobile. (Courtesy Chicago Historical Society.)

Figure 8-25. Aerial view of downtown Chicago and adjacent areas in 1975, looking northeast from approximately Harrison Street. In the lower right is the Eisenhower Expressway. The Chicago River curves from the foreground north and then eastward toward the lake. The five tallest buildings in the city are Sears Tower (110 stories) in the center foreground, the First National Bank Building (60 stories) behind it and slightly to the right, the Standard Oil Building (80 stories) in the upper right, John Hancock Center (100 stories) in the upper left, and Water Tower Place (74 stories) just in front of it. In the far upper right beyond the Standard Oil Building on the lakefront from left to right are the Central District Filtration Plant, Navy Pier, and the lock of the Chicago River Controlling Works. (Photograph by Kee T. Chang. Courtesy Chicago Association of Commerce and Industry.)

has yet experienced. The John Hancock Center soars 100 stories tall. The Sears Tower complex rose to 110 stories, to become the world's tallest building, dwarfing such erstwhile Chicago giants as the First National Bank building (60 stories), Marina City (61 stories), Lake Point Tower (70 stories), Water Tower Place (74 stories), and the Standard Oil building (80 stories). Chicago now contains three of the five tallest buildings in the world.

The building boom is expanding, especially to the north and, to a lesser extent, west across the river. Major multistructure skyscraper complexes have been proposed west of the river, over the Illinois Central air rights in an 83-acre area from Randolph Street north to the river, and to the south in the McCormick Place area. Most of the new developments provide for well-landscaped open plazas, and a promenade area is planned for part of the riverfront. However, expansion to the south of the downtown area has been blocked by the facilities of the railroads.

The functions of the downtown area have been changing significantly. Manufacturing and wholesale activities have declined drastically. The structures in which these activities were conducted are being replaced by office buildings and, increasingly, by tall apartment buildings on the fringe of the Loop. Some buildings, such as the John Hancock Center and Water Tower Place, combine residential, retail, and office functions. The entertainment function of the downtown area (largely a nighttime activity) has also been declining, spreading into the Old Town and New Town areas to the north and into the suburbs.

Retail growth in the downtown area has been adversely affected by the dispersal of many of the higher income families to the suburbs and by the proliferation of large, modern shopping centers. It has also been hurt by the concentration of low-income, minority groups around the downtown area and by congestion and parking problems. Nevertheless, commerce in the downtown area has almost held its own. The area serves some 800,000 people daily and sells almost $1 billion worth of merchandise annually, many times as much as the largest shopping center.

As the core of an ever larger metropolitan area, downtown Chicago is by far the front runner in many other important categories. It still has the highest concentration of daytime population within the metropolitan area, the highest land values, the greatest building density, and the largest array of services. The downtown has the best accessibility for shoppers and employees, with commuter railroads and the CTA now being augmented by a series of expressways which focus on the area from most parts of the city and suburbs. And the wave of redevelopment pushing outward from the downtown area should ultimately improve the environment of the surrounding area and provide better educated employees and higher income customers.

If implemented, the recently released Chicago 21 Plan will provide innovative guidance and coordination for the development of downtown and the adjacent community areas into the twenty-first century. It proposes to stabilize and improved the central area and includes plans for substantial new residential development such as the "South Loop New Town" in the present railroad area south of the Loop. A major aim of the plan is to have more people—including members of nonminority groups—live, shop, work, and be entertained in the central area.

Figure 8-26. Sears Tower, the world's tallest building, rises to a height of 110 stories (1,454 feet). It consists of nine nodular tubes of varying heights. The building contains over 16,000 employees. (Courtesy Chicago Convention and Tourism Bureau.)

Figure 8-27. The vision of the future of the central area of Chicago, showing new planned developments including South Loop New Town, Illinois Center-Ogden Slip, and others along the lakefront and riverfront. (From the *Chicago 21 Plan,* Department of Development and Planning, City of Chicago, 1973.)

Figure 8-28. Aerial view of Chicago's lakefront and downtown area looking northward from approximately 1900 South, 1974. Toward the center is the recreational-cultural complex of Soldier's Field, Field Museum of Natural History, the Shedd Aquarium, and the Grant Park Music Shell. At the left are the facilities of the Illinois Central Gulf Railroad and at the right is South Lake Shore Drive. The tallest buildings in the background from left to right are Sears Tower, First National Bank Building, Standard Oil Building, and the John Hancock Center. (Photograph by Kee T. Chang. Courtesy Chicago Association of Commerce and Industry.)

The Transportation Network

Transportation has been of prime importance in the settlement and growth of the Chicago region and has provided for the spread and movement of people and goods within the area and for linkages with other areas throughout the world. At first by water and wagon, then by rail and motor highway and through the air, the circulation tentacles of the growing metropolis have branched out to weave agriculture, commerce, and industry into a viable economic unit.

Chicago contains one of the greatest multilayered transportation networks in the world. In addition to being a major passenger center (which includes the world's busiest airport), it contains an array of facilities geared to handle the millions of tons of raw materials needed by the nation's largest steel industry as well as the millions of packages shipped annually by its unrivaled complex of mail order houses. The area's transportation network handles an estimated 86 tons of goods per capita annually compared to 54 tons per capita for the nation.

Water Transportation

The relative importance of the various modes of transportation has changed through the years. Water transportation dominated the early era; it has been said that Chicago was a port before it was a city. Chicago was blessed with natural waterway routes that were improved and supplemented to take advantage of its location at the junction of the major water routes. The Illinois and Michigan Canal was completed in 1848, the Chicago Sanitary and and Ship Canal in 1900, and the Calumet Sag Channel in 1922. In 1959 the St. Lawrence Seaway was opened.

During the 1880s when canal and port traffic reached a peak, the arrivals and clearances of over 26,000 vessels were recorded annually for a number of seasons. For the next half century, water traffic decreased, chiefly because of competition from the railroads. The once flourishing canal barges and the package freight and passenger ships on Lake Michigan largely disappeared, although on the whole the bulk industrial water traffic in iron ore, coal, and limestone for the steel mills continued to increase.

Water traffic began to revive with the completion of the Illinois Waterway in 1933. This made possible barge traffic of a nine-foot draft all the way from Chicago to the Gulf via the Illinois and Mississippi rivers as well as into a number of the Mississippi's tributaries. And although smaller ships had been operating through the old St. Lawrence Seaway for more than a century, the opening of its modern version in 1959 was an event that was to make Chicago a major world port.

The ports of the Chicago area usually handle over 80,000,000 tons annually, making it one of the world's largest water transportation centers in tonnage. About a third of the tonnage consists of barge traffic on the inland waterways. Much of the tonnage is bulk cargo destined for the numerous steel mills in the Calumet area; some is coal for the utilities, building materials, chemicals, and grain; and a small but growing amount is in general cargo to and from overseas ports.

The Port of Chicago accounts for about a third of the value of Great Lakes overseas trade. It is served by 42 steamship lines sailing to 121 ports in 63 countries. Annually it has received between 200 and 800 calls by vessels engaged in overseas trade, with the smallest number of calls prevailing in recent years. These vessels unload autos, steel, fish, whiskey, beer, wine, olives, and furniture

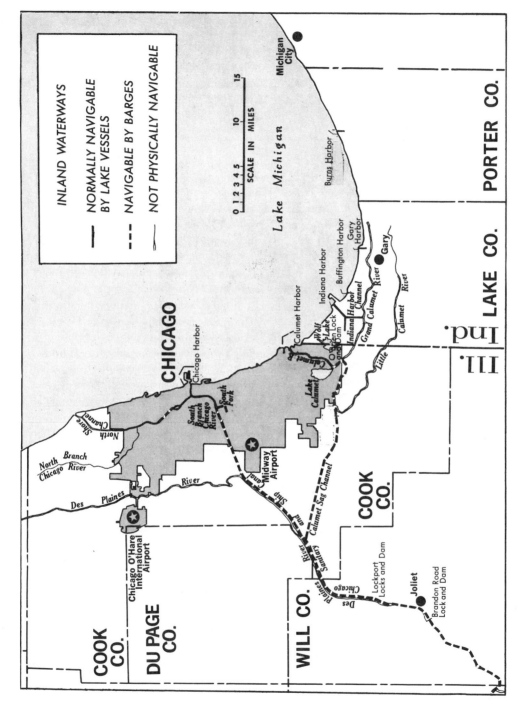

Figure 8-29. Harbors and Waterways of the Chicago Area. (Updated from *Mid-Chicago Economic Development Study*, Mayor's Committee for Economic and Cultural Development of Chicago, 1966.)

Figure 8-30. The Chicago Sanitary and Ship Canal at Summit, Illinois, 1961, showing oil storage tanks and an inbound tow carrying coal for the Commonwealth Edison Company in Chicago. The leading commodities handled by the area's inland waterways are coal and oil. (Photograph by Larry E. Hemenway. Courtesy Chicago Historical Society.)

and load up scrap metal, machinery, farm equipment, animal and vegetable oils, hides, lumber, and a variety of food products, especially grain. Chicago's numerous waterside grain elevators store the produce of the rich hinterland and can always supply grain to complete the "topping off" of an overseas vessel.

The Port of Chicago now consists of numerous harbors. Chicago Harbor includes Navy Pier, which handles a declining percentage of general overseas cargo, and the main stem of the Chicago River. The latter was once Chicago's major port, but the river is now mainly a handler of newsprint for the newspaper plants along its north bank. The future of these facilities is very limited because of neighboring land congestion and high land values. The South Branch of the Chicago River has some facilities for handling bulk barge cargoes and is a link in the Lakes-to-Gulf Waterway. The North Branch

has a 21-foot channel to North Avenue and a 9-foot channel to the Commonwealth Edison Company plant near Addison Street; however, it has relatively little water traffic because it dead-ends in the north.

The main water traffic of the Chicago area has become concentrated in the Calumet area. The heavily industrialized six-mile stretch of the Calumet River from Lake Michigan to Lake Calumet handles more tonnage than any other Chicago waterway. This consists of great quantities of raw materials for the numerous steel plants along its banks as well as grain, chemicals, coal, and general cargo.

The recently developed Lake Calumet Harbor contains the most complete array of port services and facilities in the Chicago area. Located about a dozen miles from downtown, it is the area's major overseas port. Here the Chicago Regional Port District is developing the largest Great Lakes

Figure 8-31. Chicago Harbor. In the foreground is the Lake Shore Drive Bridge over the Chicago River. In the background to the right is the lock of the Chicago River Controlling Works and to the left is Navy Pier. (Courtesy *Chicago Tribune.*)

facility for the handling of ocean, lake, and inland-barge shipping. Grain elevators, transit sheds and warehouses, tank farm, scrap facilities, and a variety of transportation facilities enable Lake Calumet Harbor to handle 17 ocean freighters at one time. In addition, the harbor handles barge traffic from the Illinois waterway and is a strategic point of interchange with Great Lakes overseas traffic. The harbor's major handicaps— inadequate depth and obstructive bridge approaches—have been largely eliminated. Lake Calumet Harbor is the core of the new Port of Chicago.

Two canals—the 16-mile Calumet Sag Channel and the 28-mile Chicago Sanitary and Ship Canal—are vital links in the Lakes-to-Gulf Waterway. The Calumet Sag Channel links the Calumet area waterways with the Chicago Sanitary and Ship Canal; the Chicago Sanitary and Ship Canal links the South Branch of the Chicago River with the Illinois and Mississippi rivers. The canals handle barges carrying bulk cargo and provide scattered facilities for oil, building materials, and other products. Both were originally designed primarily to provide sewage-diversion facilities and to reverse the

Figure 8-32. The Chicago Regional Port District terminal at the south end of Lake Calumet, looking north-west. At the upper left are two 6.5 million bushel grain elevators. Just beyond the lower right of the photo Lake Calumet joins the Calumet River. (Courtesy Chicago Regional Port District.)

flow of polluted water away from Lake Michigan—Chicago's source of plentiful, low-cost fresh water. The canals and other facilities of the Metropolitan Sanitary District of Greater Chicago have helped to protect both the city's water supply and its lakefront beaches from the type of pollution that has plagued other Great Lakes urban centers.

To the east of Chicago in Indiana are the ports of Indiana Harbor, Buffington, Gary, and the new Burns Harbor (in the Indiana Dunes area). Their tonnage is almost wholly bulk cargo destined for the steel mills, although they also service chemical and cement plants and oil refineries.

The Port of Chicago has been handi-capped by a nine-month shipping season, labor problems, a shortage of various facilities (including those used to handle containers), lack of adequate promotion, and the absence of a unified port authority between Illinois and Indiana, and until recently, within the city of Chicago. Despite these current obstacles, the Port of Chicago has continued to grow in importance and now ranks as one of the greatest inland ports in the world.

Land Transportation

The first railroad to Chicago was built in 1848, the year in which the Illinois and Michigan Canal was completed. At first the railroads were regarded as supplemental to the waterways, and many of Chicago's railroads terminated at or near the waterways of the downtown area. However, the railroads quickly surpassed and even supplanted waterway traffic. Soon railroads led into the city from 27 radiating routes, and Chicago earned the title "Player with Railroads and the Nation's Freight Handler." Today the city is served by railroad companies representing about one-half of the total railroad mileage in the country, and on an average day about 35,000 freight cars—more than the combined New York-St. Louis total—are loaded and unloaded in Chicago. To facilitate distribution and interchange among its numerous industries and railroads, the Chicago area developed a web of a dozen intersecting belt, switching, and industrial railroads.

The railroads strongly affected Chicago's growth and national role as well as local land use and settlement patterns. First, they brought great numbers of laborers to build the roads; thereafter they brought the per-

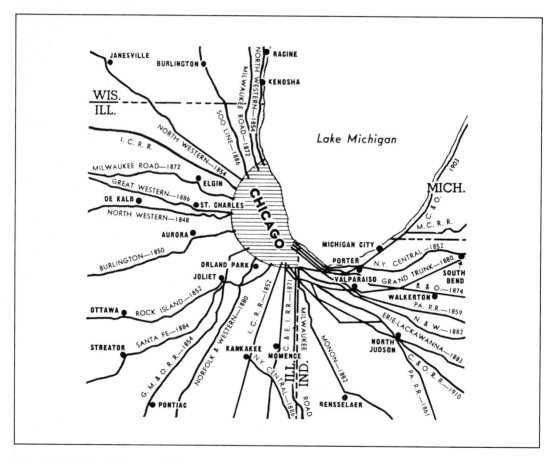

Figure 8-33. Historical map of Chicago's railroad network. Dates mark arrival of railroads to Chicago. (Courtesy *Chicago Tribune.*)

manent settlers who opened up the land. The railroads employed thousands directly, while many more worked in the manufacturing of railroad equipment. By making transportation cheaper, more reliable, and more accessible and by offering service to virtually all parts of the country, the railroads stimulated the growth of agriculture, manufacturing, and commerce in the Chicago area. (Many railroads directly fostered industrial development.) The railroads also made possible the dispersal of population along the commuter routes into the outlying parts of the city and into the suburbs. They continue to aid the viability of Chicago's downtown by making it readily accessible to commuters from most parts of the growing metropolitan area.

Although benefiting the city in many ways, the railroads also cut it up like a pie. This created neighborhood and traffic barriers and noise and pollution problems. In addition, the facilities of the railroads have blocked the expansion of the downtown area to the south and preempted long stretches of choice lakefront land.

Despite such technological innovations as piggybacking and the unit train, the railroads' share of intercity freight tonnage has declined to about 50 percent in recent decades, and the once bustling intercity passenger service has virtually disappeared except for the Amtrak service. As a result, rail employment has declined sharply and many of the railroad facilities—especially the older yards, stations, and auxiliary facilities toward the inner part of the metropolitan area—are outmoded, underutilized, and available for consolidation or redevelopment. More modern and less congested rail facilities have been developed in the suburban areas.

Much of the railroads' losses has been due to competition by the automobile and the truck. Chicago has become the nation's largest trucking center, with daily scheduled service to more than 54,000 communities. Trucks now handle about one-fourth of the intercity freight tonnage.

The trucking industry has exhibited a greater locational flexibility than have other modes of transportation. Its terminal complexes have been moving generally outward, especially to the southwest, away from the former close ties with rail and water freight facilities and from congested inner city areas with their small, poorly located facilities. The new truck terminals are usually in areas with ready access to the expressway and tollway system of over 500 miles that was superimposed in the 1950s and 1960s on the Chicago area's basic road pattern. Expressways now radiate from the center of the city in most directions. Connecting into and combining with the expressway system are new interstate highways in greater number than in any other city.

Like the railroads in earlier years, the automobile and highways are playing a major role in the location and dispersal of population and economic activities, especially in suburban areas. Settlement need no longer be aligned along railroad routes. The automobile has made huge new areas accessible for residential, commercial, and industrial uses. The expressway system, in particular, has altered area traffic patterns and affected other modes of transportation, especially mass transit.

An extensive multimodal mass transit system, consisting of commuter railroads, suburban bus lines, and the giant Chicago Transit Authority with its elevated, subway, and bus lines, has long been instrumental in establishing the urban form of the Chicago area and, by its central-area focus, in pre-

Figure 8-34. Lake Shore Drive, one of the earliest prototypes of the expressway, looking south toward downtown from Lincoln Park, 1974. In the foreground is Belmont Harbor; some of Chicago's numerous beaches are visible along the lake shore. (Courtesy Chicago Association of Commerce and Industry.)

Figure 8-35. Chicago's traffic problems are not new. View, about 1910, south on Dearborn Street from Randolph Street. (Courtesy Chicago Historical Society.)

serving the viability of the downtown area. In recent decades, the growing use of the automobile, the establishment of an expensive expressway network, the dispersal of the population into areas of lower population density, and rising costs have resulted in rapidly declining ridership and financial difficulties for the mass transit system. However, the energy and pollution crisis, renewed government interest in mass transportation because of its relatively low cost and efficiency, and the creation in 1974 of the Regional Transportation Authority for the six counties of Northeastern Illinois are all

Figure 8-36. A double-decker Chicago and North Western Railway commuter train leaving the downtown area during the afternoon rush-hour. To the right is the clogged Kennedy Expressway. (Courtesy Chicago and North Western Railway.)

examples of measures which hold promise of reversing or at least stabilizing the steady decline of mass transportation in the area.

Expansion of the Chicago Metropolitan Area

The greater Chicago Metropolitan Area is a mosaic of eight counties and hundreds of fiercely independent, highly competitive, and immensely variegated communities (although often centerless), stretching ap-

proximately from the Wisconsin state line into northwestern Indiana. The area has a total population of almost eight million, with the city of Chicago containing fewer than half of this number. And while Chicago continues to lose population, the sprawling suburban "Outer City" now has more people, more jobs, rising political power, and an immensely greater growth potential than the struggling, but still powerful, metropolis.

The 1970 census showed that while the city of Chicago had a net loss of 183,447 people, or 5.2 percent of its population, between 1960 and 1970, the remainder of the Chicago-Northwestern Indiana Standard Consolidated Area (which includes the Illinois counties of Du Page, Kane, Lake, McHenry, and Will, as well as Cook County outside of Chicago and the Indiana counties of Lake and Porter) had a net gain of 1,001,300 people, or about 31 percent. Similar trends were evident between 1950 and 1960, when Chicago experienced a 1.9 percent decrease in population, whereas the population of the remainder of the area increased about 70 percent. During that decade one-fifth of Chicago's people, most of them white families with school-age children, moved to the suburbs. The movement from the suburbs to the city was comparatively small; it consisted mainly of young adults without families and older adults whose children were grown.

Although a few suburbs are almost as old as Chicago, rapid suburban growth around the city is largely a phenomenon of the post-World War I period. Chicago itself is, in fact, largely an amalgamation of suburbs that in years past found it advantageous to be annexed to the city which could more readily supply needed services. Suburbs annexed by Chicago make up a sizeable part of its communities: Lake View, Hyde Park, Jefferson Park, Washington Heights, West Roseland, Rogers Park, West Ridge, Norwood Park, Austin, Edison Park, Morgan Park, Clearing, Mt. Greenwood, etc. In the last half century, however, annexation of suburban areas by Chicago has been minimal, as the remaining suburbs have preferred not to become politically attached to the big city with its growing problems.

The growth of Chicago's suburbs has been closely related to the development of transportation facilities. Some early communities were established along the water-

ways; later, ribbons of suburbs developed along the railroads; and more recently, with the advent of the motor vehicle, suburban settlement has become extremely diffuse.

Before the coming of the railroads, there were a few water-oriented communities and a number of small farm-service villages outside of Chicago. The railroads enabled people for the first time to live some distance from downtown Chicago and still commute there to work. As the railroads radiated out from downtown, they located stops every few miles around which homes and often a few shops were built and the nucleus of a suburb developed. More than a century ago, settlements resembling widely spaced beads on a string had been established along the main commuter railroads. Along the present Northwest Line of the Chicago and North Western Railway were the communities of Des Plaines, Palatine, and Barrington; along the North Line of the Chicago and North Western Railway were the communities of Evanston, Wilmette, Winnetka, Glencoe, Highland Park, and Lake Forest. These communities usually numbered only a few hundred people since the inhabitants had to live close to the local railroad station.

The increasing use of the automobile resulted in a rapid increase in suburban growth, especially after World War I. The growth rate was substantially slowed during the Depression of the 1930s and the World War II period, but thereafter it rose to an unprecedented rate. At first, the automobile chiefly allowed people to reside further from the commuter railroad stations; later, following improvements in roads, it allowed them to commute to work independently of the railroads. The result was a surge of population outward from the city into the areas between the railroad radials.

There are numerous examples of rapid suburban growth. To the north of Chicago,

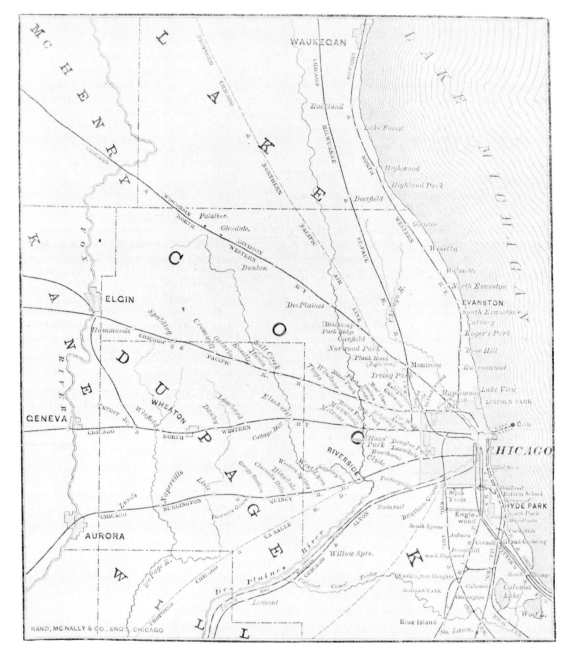

Figure 8-37. Chicago and vicinity, 1873. (From a suburban real estate promotion map. Courtesy Chicago Historical Society.)

Skokie was a small village of 783 people in 1920 with a truck-farming economy serving the Chicago market. The general exodus to the suburbs and improved transportation—especially the opening of Edens Expressway—resulted in an increase of its population to about 70,000 today. To the south of Chicago, the planned community of Park Forest, which was farmland until the late 1940s, now has a population of more than 30,000. Similarly, Oak Lawn, to the southwest, increased from 3,483 in 1940 to over 62,000 today, and Addison, to the west, increased from 819 in 1940 to over 25,000 at present.

There are many reasons for the population decline in Chicago and the growth in the number of suburban inhabitants, a pattern which is common across the nation. The central city has no space for further growth; indeed, recent expressway construction and slum clearance have slightly decreased the population density of Chicago. In addition, many inhabitants of the central city move to the suburbs to escape its negative aspects—racial conflict, slums, crime, high taxes and high land values, congestion, pollution, poor schools, and other problems.

The 1950s and 1960s were, on the whole, decades of prosperity. Automobiles, highways, and homes were built at an unprecedented rate. The "open space, good life" attractions of the suburbs, some real and some imaginary, held strong appeal for young and growing families. Improved transportation, higher standards of living, increased leisure, industrial decentralization, government financial aid, and mass construction of homes all helped accelerate the movement to the suburbs.

In some instances, migration to the suburbs is undoubtedly a response by whites to the approach of blacks; in other cases, it is a flight of the wealthier classes from the poorer classes or of the more "Americanized" from ethnic groups. The smallness of most suburbs makes possible a more homogeneous grouping of people with their own "kind" than would be possible in the big city. Even housing may take the form of look-alike structures put up by a single developer in a single effort.

Largely urbanized stretches now radiate outward from the Loop, especially along the commuter rail lines. In some directions the built-up areas extend about 40 miles to the vicinity of Waukegan, Barrington, the Fox River Valley cities, Joliet, and slightly beyond Chicago Heights and Gary. Between the railroad radials, urbanization has been filling in rapidly; there, however, the distance from Chicago of urbanized areas is usually not as great and the movement outward is often discontinuous. Patches of open space occur because of "leapfrogging" by developers who decide to acquire more distant land because it is more readily available and/or has certain amenities and cost advantages.

Suburban Characteristics

The suburbs of Chicago are far from uniform. They may differ from each other as much as do individual communities within the city. In fact, parts of Chicago are more suburban in character than some suburbs, and some suburbs are more densely populated than the average Chicago community. Chicago's suburbs are rich and poor, new and old, planned and unplanned, white- and blue-collar, industrial and dormitory, close-in and far-out, populated by young and old, successful and unsuccessful, with and without previous community tradition, homogeneous or heterogeneous in population—and everything in between. They usually differ markedly in race, religion, and ethnic backgrounds as well as in education and vocational level. In economic level, they range from Kenilworth, which had an estimated median family income in 1974 of almost $43,000, to Robbins, whose median family income was about $10,000.

Despite their differences, the suburbs exhibit certain general patterns and trends.

1. Their population density is lower than that of Chicago, as suburban homes generally occupy larger acreage. Chicago's population density is about 15,000 per square mile

(declining toward the periphery); in the suburbs it averages about 5,000 per square mile, although there is a substantial variation due to differences in zoning laws and their enforcement. A community's zoning laws control residential density and reflect the attitudes and socioeconomic status of its inhabitants, the transportation facilities, and—an increasingly important consideration—the availability and cost of land.

2. The population density of the suburbs generally increases as their distance from Chicago decreases. Some of the older, larger, close-in suburbs, built largely in an

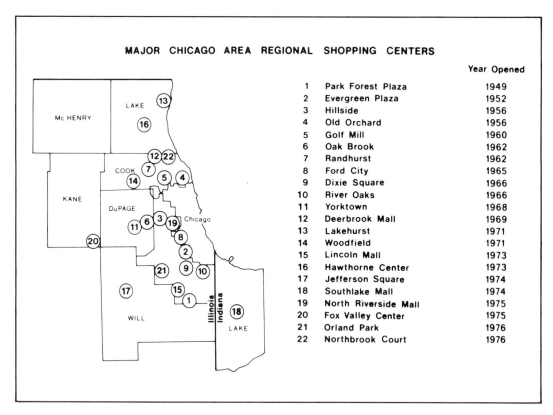

MAJOR CHICAGO AREA REGIONAL SHOPPING CENTERS

		Year Opened
1	Park Forest Plaza	1949
2	Evergreen Plaza	1952
3	Hillside	1956
4	Old Orchard	1956
5	Golf Mill	1960
6	Oak Brook	1962
7	Randhurst	1962
8	Ford City	1965
9	Dixie Square	1966
10	River Oaks	1966
11	Yorktown	1968
12	Deerbrook Mall	1969
13	Lakehurst	1971
14	Woodfield	1971
15	Lincoln Mall	1973
16	Hawthorne Center	1973
17	Jefferson Square	1974
18	Southlake Mall	1974
19	North Riverside Mall	1975
20	Fox Valley Center	1975
21	Orland Park	1976
22	Northbrook Court	1976

Figure 8-38. Major Chicago area regional shopping centers. (Source: Compiled from *Directory of Shopping Centers in the United States and Canada.* 16th edition, 1975, The National Research Bureau, Inc., Burlington, Iowa.)

earlier period and with good rapid transit connections to Chicago—Evanston, Oak Park, and Cicero, for example—have a relatively high population density of between 10,000 and 13,000 per square mile. Some of these mature suburbs, like Chicago itself, are deteriorating around their commercial cores. In a way, such suburbs are simply extensions of the city, with population density decreasing outward from the city.

3. There is an accelerating trend toward building multiple-dwelling units in some suburban areas. In the 1960s some 150,000 such units were constructed. Such construction helps to circumvent high land costs, adds to local tax revenue, and better meets the needs of some families. The rapidly rising cost of single-family homes has priced them out of the range of many families.

4. Another trend is the development of planned, more self-sufficient communities embodying separate, compatible locations for residential, commercial, industrial, and recreational functions. Elk Grove Village near O'Hare Field is a prime example. Other suburbs are reserving areas for industrial and commercial use in order to broaden their tax base. Some smaller planned developments are being built around recreational facilities, including artificial lakes.

5. The decentralization of industry and commerce is enabling larger numbers of suburbanites to work in the suburbs. The proportion varies somewhat with income and occupation. Thus, the suburbs with the highest proportion of rail commuters to Chicago are high-income, white-collar, residential communities such as Winnetka, Glencoe, Western Springs, Hinsdale, and Homewood. Conversely, industrial communities which are large consumers of labor, such as Whiting, Melrose Park, Northlake, Bedford Park, and the more distant Aurora,

Elgin, Joliet, North Chicago, and Waukegan, supply few commuters.

6. Much more than Chicago, the suburban area is strongly oriented toward the automobile. The growing expressway network, in particular, has extended and opened areas for residential, commercial, and industrial development while sometimes reducing commuting time. There is very little effective public transportation for the newer commuting patterns of diffuse intersuburban movement and reverse commuting from Chicago to the suburbs as compared to the old, traditional journey from the suburb to Chicago's center. The recently established Regional Transit Authority for the six counties of northeastern Illinois may bring about some of the public transportation needed to cope with the new patterns.

7. In general, the suburbs have a substantially higher median income and higher educational and professional job levels than the city of Chicago. The suburbs have a much smaller foreign-born and black population. Chicago's black population has increased rapidly in recent decades, until it now comprises about one-third of the city's population; during the same period, the number of blacks in the suburban area has held constant at around 5 percent of the total suburban population. Another developing socioeconomic characteristic is that the newer, more distant suburbs have a younger population than the older, closer suburbs.

8. The growth trends in the suburban areas vary widely, as is shown in Table 8-2.

9. While suburban living offers many advantages, it may also have certain drawbacks. These may include poor public transportation, long commuting distances, and inadequate facilities, such as for sewage and water, especially if the suburb is new or has grown rapidly. There may also be a short-

Table 8-2. County Population, 1950-70.

County	Population			Increase 1960-70	Percentage Increase 1960-70
	1950	1960	1970		
Cook	4,508,792	5,129,725	5,492,369	362,644	7.1
Du Page	154,599	313,459	491,882	178,423	56.9
Kane	150,388	208,246	251,005	42,759	20.5
Lake	179,097	293,656	382,638	88,982	30.3
McHenry	50,656	84,210	111,555	27,345	32.5
Will	134,336	191,617	249,498	57,881	30.2
Lake (Ind.)	368,152	513,269	546,253	32,984	6.4
Porter (Ind.)	40,076	60,279	87,114	26,835	44.5
Suburban Cook	887,790	1,579,029	2,125,412	546,091	34.6

age of schools, churches, and shopping facilities. School taxes may be heavy since the suburbs, particularly the newer ones, usually contain a high proportion of young married couples with growing families. As the children grow up and leave for college, take jobs elsewhere, and settle in newer communities farther out from Chicago, the suburb may decline in population and be saddled with an overabundance of deteriorating facilities.

10. Although suburbia still has fairly large areas of open land, especially toward the fringes, the supply is decreasing steadily. The Northeastern Illinois Planning Commission had approved the "finger plan" to guide future development and preserve some open space in its six-county area. This plan called for the orderly development of the area along the major transportation routes, or "fingers," radiating out of Chicago. Under the plan, communities would concentrate industrial, commercial, educational, medical, and other service facilities, as well as high-density residential areas, including skyscraper complexes, along the corridors of the main transportation routes. More sparse-ly populated residential areas would be placed farther out, although close enough to transportation facilities. In the wedges between the corridors would be open space and recreational facilities which would also serve to absorb pollution. The plan was designed to maximize the use of land and transportation facilities and to prevent chaotic, congested, and polluted urbanization. It would enhance accessibility by centralizing transportation facilities in the corridor. Due to various economic and political pressures, however, the plan has not been implemented, nor does effective large-scale implementation seem likely in the foreseeable future.

11. The suburban areas of Chicago can be divided broadly into north, west, and south sectors. These sectors differ in their rate of growth, economic and social status, and industrial development. Within each sector, too, there are noticeable, though usually less pronounced, differences.

North Suburban Growth Patterns

The north suburban area has grown more rapidly since World War II and also ranks

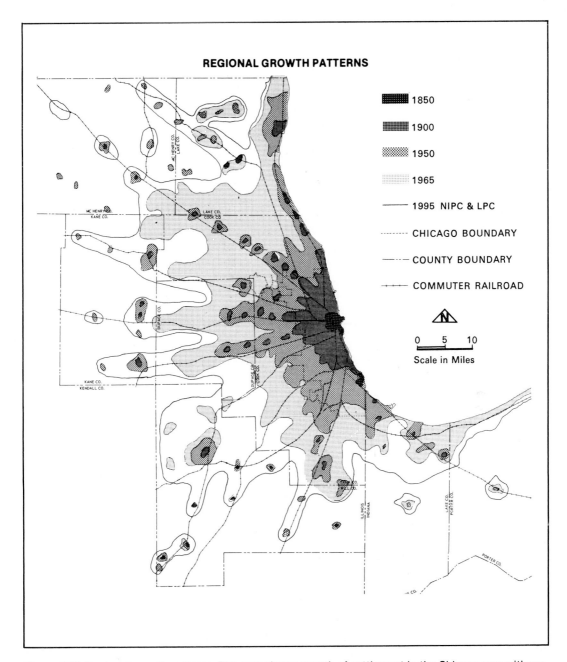

REGIONAL GROWTH PATTERNS

1850
1900
1950
1965
1995 NIPC & LPC
CHICAGO BOUNDARY
COUNTY BOUNDARY
COMMUTER RAILROAD

0   5   10
Scale in Miles

Figure 8-39. Regional growth patterns. The map shows growth of settlement in the Chicago area with projections to 1995, based on data provided by the Northeastern Illinois Planning Commission and the Lake-Porter Regional Transportation and Planning Commission. (Courtesy Regional Transportation Planning Board, 1973)

higher economically, socially, and educationally than either the western or southern areas. It contains 15 of the 25 communities with the highest income in the Chicago area. North of Chicago there are very few lower income suburbs to supply the blue-collar workers who are badly needed by local industry. The very small black population is concentrated largely in Evanston, Glencoe, and Waukegan-North Chicago; the other northern communities have few or no blacks.

Population has long been aligned along the three commuter railroads in the area with a recent, rapid buildup between the railroad lines. In addition to well-established transportation facilities, the northern sector has such aesthetic attractions as (1) the numerous small lakes and ponds of the inland lake area to the northwest, which developed first as a recreational area and later as the site of permanent homes; (2) rolling topography, such as that to the northwest around Barrington; and (3) most important, the Lake Michigan shoreline, which is further enhanced by the picturesque North Shore Ravines from Winnetka to Waukegan. This long-settled lakeshore area, with its attractive physical features, good rail transportation, and freedom from obnoxious industry, contains more high-income suburbs than any other sector of the Chicago area, including four of the top five—Kenilworth, Glencoe, Barrington Hills, and Winnetka.

The lakeshore suburbs—some in existence for more than a century—have now largely achieved maturity, and their prospects for population growth are very limited. But the suburbs just to the west of the lakeshore suburbs, such as Skokie, Glenview, Northfield, Northbrook, and Deerfield, have grown very rapidly in recent years because of the availability of land, the opening of the

Edens Expressway, and their proximity to the prestigious shoreline suburbs.

Aligned northwest in the corridor of the Chicago North Western Railway is another group of long-established suburbs—Park Ridge, Des Plaines, Mt. Prospect, Arlington Heights, Palatine, Barrington, Crystal Lake—populated by families of a generally more modest income than that of the North Shore families. These suburbs have experienced rapid growth in recent years. The growth of northwestern communities near O'Hare Field such as Schaumburg, Elk Grove Village, Streamwood, Hoffman Estates, and Hanover Park has been especially rapid.

Light industry has expanded rapidly in the northern area, often having moved from Chicago. Much of this industry is in the growing fields of electronics, chemicals, and pharmaceuticals. Research and office facilities also are increasing rapidly. There is virtually no heavy industry in the northern sector. The major north suburban centers of employment are Evanston, North Chicago-Waukegan, Skokie, Niles, Morton Grove, Des Plaines, and Elk Grove Village.

Urbanization to the north has now pushed deeply, but by no means solidly, into Lake County. Much of the northern third of the county to the Wisconsin line is still largely rural, but here and there new developments are appearing.

West Suburban Growth Patterns

The suburbs west of Chicago are more heterogeneous than those to the north and northwest. Because of Chicago's narrow east-west width, this area includes the suburbs closest to the Loop (in some places only about six miles away), such as Cicero, Berwyn, and Oak Park. These are old, sizeable, mature suburbs that have had very little room for growth in recent decades. While Berwyn and Oak Park are mainly residential, Cicero is the largest industrial employer of the western area. Oak Park, somewhat like Evanston to the north, is a community that shares characteristics of both the big city and suburbia, and also like Evanston, it has a large number of apartment buildings.

At the far west, almost 40 miles from the Loop, are a string of satellite communities aligned along the Fox River in extreme eastern Kane County. The larger of these communities (from north to south) include Carpentersville, Elgin, St. Charles, Geneva, Batavia, and Aurora. These old residential-industrial communities were originally estab-

lished largely because of their location along the river. Their sizeable industrial base, especially that of Elgin and Aurora, combined with their distance from Chicago, has traditionally made for self-sufficiency in employment and, thus, relatively little commuting to Chicago. Only in recent years has the frontier of urban expansion from Chicago reached into the Fox Valley area.

Between the suburbs on the periphery of Chicago and the Fox Valley suburbs is an area that has grown rapidly in the post-World War II period—western Cook county and Du Page county. Western Cook County is almost entirely urbanized. It contains a number of industrial-residential com-

Figure 8-40. The Oak Brook Shopping Center is located in Oak Brook, Illinois, near the intersection of the East-West and Tri-State Tollways. It ranks second in sales among the area's 22 regional shopping centers. Its opening in 1962 stimulated rapid growth of office buildings, industry, hotels, and residential development in the area. (Photograph by Hedrich-Blessing. Courtesy Draper and Kramer, Inc.)

munities with very large industrial employment such as Melrose Park, La Grange, Bedford Park, Franklin Park, Bellwood, and Maywood. River Forest, Western Springs, and Riverside are attractive high income suburbs. Riverside was one of the nation's first planned communities, having been laid out in 1866 by Frederick Law Olmsted. Of the suburbs in western Cook County, only Maywood has a substantial black population. (About 42 percent of its residents are black.) However, Oak Park's black population, spilling over from the West Side of Chicago has increased substantially in the last few years.

Du Page County, due west of Chicago, is rapidly urbanizing. In 1950 far more than half of its land was still devoted to agriculture and it had a population of just 154,599. Today the extent of its agricultural land is rapidly shrinking and its population exceeds half a million. Between 1960 and 1970 the population of Du Page County rose 56.9 percent, by far the largest percentage increase of any county in the Chicago Metropolitan Area.

Du Page County is largely residential, with a relatively high income status. Median family income, the value of homes, and median school years completed are higher in Du Page County than in any other county of the Chicago Metropolitan Area. Du Page County has no sizeable industrial communities but a number of its communities engage in some manufacturing; Naperville, West Chicago, and Addison are the largest, though relatively small industrial employers. The new National Accelerator Laboratory Area is in the southwestern corner of the county. Two giant regional shopping centers, Oak Brook and Yorktown, have been developed in the eastern part of the county near the East-West Tollway.

The population is still predominantly aligned along the two major railroads, although beginning to diffuse throughout the county. Blacks constitute a small fraction of 1 percent of the county's population. This may be traceable to early restrictive practices, high value of homes, and the paucity of industrial employment opportunities.

South Suburban Growth Patterns

The southern sector of suburbs forms a large arc stretching from Will County in the southwest, through southern Cook County in the south, into Lake and Porter counties, Indiana, in the southeast. Although the very size of this sector allows for great diversity, in general it contains the suburbs with the lowest value of homes, the lowest levels of schooling, the greatest proportion of blacks, and the greatest amount of heavy industry. It also has a greater growth potential than the other sectors.

The area southwest of Chicago's border to Joliet in Will County was at one time one of the slowest growing suburban segments of the metropolitan area. It was handicapped both by its distance from the Loop and by what is probably the poorest transportation to downtown Chicago of any sector. The recent opening of several expressways plus the existence of one of the few remaining suburban areas with plentiful supplies of relatively cheap land (Will County, for example, was still almost three-fourths in farmland in 1970) has helped it become one of the fastest growing areas around Chicago. The area also has the advantages of aesthetically attractive topographic and moraine features such as in the Mount Forest-Palos area, location along the Calumet-Sag Channel and the Chicago Sanitary and Ship Canal, and good employment opportunities at such nearby industrial centers as those located in the Clearing Industrial District, Joliet, and Alsip. Because homes are relatively moderate in price, a large number of blue-collar workers have moved in, many having left the south side of Chicago after blacks moved into their neighborhoods. As yet, relatively few blacks live in the southwest suburbs.

Due south of Chicago in southern Cook County, spilling over into Will County in an area served by the Illinois Central Gulf and Rock Island Railroads, are a large number of small and medium-sized communities. Most are older, mature suburbs, but a number developed after World War II. A few communities, such as Blue Island, Riverdale, and especially Harvey and Chicago Heights, are highly industrialized. Many combine industrial and residential properties and contain populations with a low-to-moderate income range and educational level. The suburbs of Robbins, East Chicago Heights, Phoenix, Dixmoor, and Posen, for example, are among the poorest in the Chicago area. However, there are a few notable exceptions, especially the residential suburbs of Flossmoor and Olympia Fields. In income, these two commuter communities along the Illinois Central Gulf Railroad rank among the top ten suburbs in the Chicago area. Among the other high-ranking suburbs from a socioeconomic viewpoint is the planned community of Park Forest. Adjoining it is an even newer planned community partially completed—Park Forest South in Will County.

After a long period of slow growth, this area has also been developing more rapidly because of construction of new expressways, the availability of cheap land, and the mitigation of some drainage problems in the eastern section. Its growth has also been due to an influx of blacks as part of their southward movement from the heart of Chicago. Many have been attracted by jobs in heavy industry, especially in the numerous steel plants nearby. Despite the fact that the south suburban area probably contains the largest percentage of blacks of any suburban

sector around Chicago, most of its communities have few, if any, blacks. On the other hand, a few communities contain very large percentages of black residents, such as East Chicago Heights, Phoenix, and Robbins.

Across the state line in adjacent Lake County, Indiana, the area exhibits characteristics quite different from those in other sectors around Chicago. This is an area of very heavy industry, steel in particular and oil refining and chemicals to a lesser extent. The area fronts on Lake Michigan and contains part of the Indiana Dunes. Surface drainage is poor and severe pollution problems have been precipitated by the heavy industry of the area. Northern Lake County contains a number of good-sized industrial cities—Hammond, Whiting, East Chicago, Gary—some large enough to be considered metropolitan areas. Gary, with a population of 175,415 in 1970, and Hammond, with a population of 107,790, are the second and third largest cities of the eight-county metropolitan area.

Unlike more rural southern Lake County, this is an area of industrial stagnation and, in some instances, of declining population brought on at least partially by the conditions created by industry and its expansion. All four of the latter cities lost population in the 1960-70 decade. As a whole, the area ranks low in median income, value of homes, and educational levels. There are very large black communities in Gary and East Chicago; in Gary slightly more than half of the population is now black. A substantial Latin American population also lives in northern Lake County.

Farther east is still sparsely populated Porter County, Indiana. In 1970 it had 87,114 people as compared to Lake County's 546,253. It contains only small cities. Its growth, however, has been accelerating largely as a result of the construction within the last decade of two huge steel mills and Burns Harbor on the lakeshore east of Gary. Porter County contains Indiana Dunes State Park. In addition, after years of bitter conflict ending in the enactment of compromise federal legislation, a national dunes park has been established there. In this struggle the conservationists, who wished to preserve more of the scenic dunes for the benefit of the burgeoning population of the area, were opposed by commercial and industrial interests desirous of stimulating economic growth by taking advantage of the area's excellent location for industry.

The Rural-Urban Fringe

The farm acreage around Chicago continues to decline as urbanization progresses outward from the central city. The once productive truck and dairy farms of Cook County have largely disappeared. The same process is accelerating in the adjoining counties, although most of them still have 40 percent or more of their land in farms. In fact, in Kane and McHenry counties more than 80 percent of the land is in farms.

The change of an area from rural to urban generally follows a pattern with accompanying problems. First there is an influx of non-farm rural residents.

They come to the countryside for cheaper land and lower taxes, sunshine and open spaces, room to relax and enjoy outdoor living, a safe and healthy environment in which to raise their children, a place to grow a garden and perhaps a few chickens, a refuge during misfortune, and a home in their declining years.

The change in the rural scene often begins when a farmer sells off a front lot or two or perhaps a front tract or an acre or so. The price the farmer received was high compared with the value per acre of his farm as a whole. Because of this, other farmers are induced to sell off their frontages. More houses follow. Later, entire farms are broken up into tracts and subdivided. The change continues and as

the years go by, country roads begin to look like residential streets. As the non-farm population grows, land is bought for gas stations and roadside stores and shops, then for other business and industrial uses.[9]

If the area is unincorporated and without adequate government regulation, new construction may be substandard, a honky-tonk may be created, and the natural environment may be defaced.

This intrusion of non-farm rural residents often creates problems that virtually force farmers to sell out. Whereas an eighty acre farm may contain one family, an eighty acre subdivision may hold 120 families. Without adequate advance planning and zoning, the farmers may find their schools suddenly crowded, new problems of water, sewage disposal and drainage, increased traffic and higher taxes. Often there is a time lag before the subdivision assumes its full tax load, and the farmer may be assessed at land values similar to those of the subdivisions. Highway relocations may divide his farm. There may be zoning disputes.

The aggressive farmer may feel himself hemmed in as far as expansion is concerned. He may even have to put up fencing against trespassers. He may have to use his land more intensively in order to pay the higher taxes. Necessary farm services are often curtailed as an area becomes more urbanized, and a farmer so isolated may encounter difficulty, for example, in arranging for a truck to collect his milk. The result of these problems, plus the attraction of high land prices, is that the farmer sells his land.[10]

In this way distant "exurbia" becomes ultimately suburbia, and another tier of suburbs develops around Chicago.

Chicago-Suburban Interaction

More disruptive than the limited rural-urban conflict is that between Chicago and its surrounding suburbs, despite the fact that both have problems that neither can solve alone. Rainwater falling in one community may create flood problems for others; traffic in the heart of the central city may cause expressway backups all the way out into the suburbs; disease, pollution, and crime cannot be hemmed in by political boundaries. The major obstacle to solving such problems is that, although the Chicago Metropolitan area has a certain economic unity, it is a fragmented, overlapping, disorganized political structure—often offering inadequate, conflicting, and uncoordinated solutions at the local level. The "real Chicago" crosses state lines and encompasses more than 1,500 governmental units, ranging from counties to mosquito abatement districts. This multiplicity of governments has led to an absence of coordination in road construction, the use of open space, water control, mass transit development, air pollution control, and refuse disposal. It has also resulted in increased costs because each community, regardless of size, must usually provide its own services: police, fire, garbage, school, etc.

Chicago provides employment and a variety of services for suburban commuters who do not share proportionately in their cost. The suburbs, on their part, generally refuse to become enmeshed in the many problems and burdens of the central city. Political rivalry has often widened the gap between Chicago and surrounding areas; in recent decades Chicago has consistently voted Democratic while the suburbs generally have tended to vote Republican. Racial, religious, and economic differences between Chicago and the suburbs have also been divisive.

Fortunately, there has been a growing trend toward cooperation among the numerous governmental units of the Chicago area. Chicago supplies water to 84 other communities and the Metropolitan Sanitary District of Greater Chicago handles the sewage of 110 cities and villages. The Comprehensive Plan of Chicago recommends principles of development for the metropolitan area. The Northeastern Illinois Planning Commission has become increasingly influential in the general planning of the six counties in its area. The new Regional Transportation Authority is designed to coordinate and improve transit facilities for the same six counties. In addition, groups of suburbs have concluded cooperative pacts dealing with such services as police, fire, water, health, and street construction and maintenance.

Midwest Megalopolis

Future planning will have to encompass a much greater area and population. By about the turn of the twentieth century, the population of the suburbs alone may exceed the total metropolitan population of 1960, and the suburbs of Chicago will have merged with those of Milwaukee and other large communities to form a giant urbanized area whose basic framework is already evident.

Chicago is already the nucleus of a developing conurbation—a Midwest Megalopolis—that stretches almost 300 miles between approximately Elkhart, Indiana, and Green Bay, Wisconsin. This urbanizing area encompasses about six thousand square miles and arches roughly around the southern and southwestern shores of Lake Michigan through such cities as South Bend, Gary, East Chicago, Hammond, Chicago, and its suburbs; it continues northward through Waukegan, Kenosha, Racine, Milwaukee, and beyond. This area of developing urban coalescence, with its hundreds of large and small communities, already contains more than 10 million people, about two-thirds of whom live in Chicago and its surrounding metropolitan area. The orderly, harmonious, and efficient development of the emerging megalopolis is one of the most crucial current problems of the Chicago area.

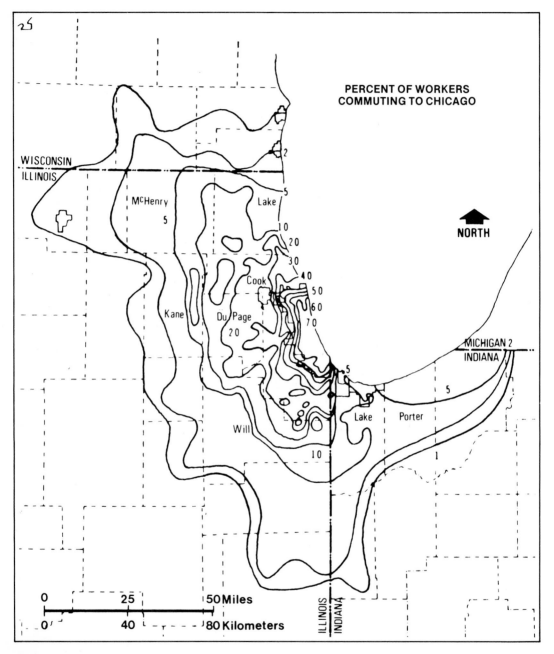

Figure 8-41. Percent of workers commuting to Chicago, 1970. The percent of workers from the area in and around Chicago who work in the city is indicated on the isolines connecting points of equal value. The range on the map is from 1 percent in areas as far away as 100 miles in southeastern Wisconsin to 70 percent in Chicago itself. (Courtesy Brian J. L. Berry, ed., *Chicago: Transformation of an Urban System,* Ballinger Publishing Company, 1976.)

Notes

1. Adapted from Irving Cutler, *Chicago: Metropolis of the Mid-Continent,* (Dubuque: Geographic Society of Chicago and Kendall/Hunt Publishing Company, 1976).
2. Wallace W. Atwood and James Goldthwait, *Physical Geography of the Evanston Waukegan Region,* Bulletin No. 7 (Urbana: Illinois State Geological Survey, 1908), p. 4.
3. Patrick Shirreff, *A Tour Through North America; Together with a Comprehensive View of the Canada and the United States* (Edinburgh: Oliver and Boyd, 1835), p. 226.
4. John Lewis Peyton, *Over the Alleghenies and Across the Prairies: Personal Recollections of the Far West One and Twenty Years Ago (1848)* (London: Simpkin, Marshall & Co., 1869), pp. 325-29.
5. Joseph Kirkland and John Moses, *History of Chicago,* vol. 1 (Chicago: Munsell and Company, 1895), p. 119.
6. George W. Steevens, *The Land of the Dollar* (New York: Dodd, Mead, and Company, 1897), p. 144.
7. Jane Addams, *Twenty Years at Hull House* (New York: Macmillan, 1910), pp. 81-82.
8. James Parton, "Chicago." *Atlantic Monthly* 19 (March 1867), pp. 325-45.
9. U.S. Department of Agriculture, *The Why and How of Rural Zoning,* Agriculture Information Bulletin No. 196 (Washington, D.C.: Government Printing Office, 1958), p. 1.
10. Irving Cutler, *The Chicago-Milwaukee Corridor: A Geographic Study of Intermetropolitan Coalescence,* Studies in Geography No. 9 (Evanston, Ill.: Northwestern University, 1965), pp. 126-27.

Selected References

Abbott, Edith. *The Tenements of Chicago, 1908-1935.* Chicago: University of Chicago Press, 1936.

Addams, Jane. *Twenty Years at Hull House.* New York: Macmillan, 1910.

Ahmed, G. Munir. *Manufacturing Structure and Patterns of Waukegan-North Chicago.* Research Paper No. 46. Chicago: University of Chicago Department of Geography, 1957.

Andreas, Alfred T. *History of Chicago.* 3 Vols. Chicago: A.T. Andreas, 1884-86.

Appleton, John B. *The Iron and Steel Industry of the Calumet District.* University of Illinois Studies in the Social Sciences, Vol. 13, No. 2 Urbana: University of Illinois, 1925.

Atwood, Wallace W., and Goldthwait, James. *Physical Geography of the Evanston-Waukegan Region.* Urbana: Illinois State Geological Survey, Bulletin No. 7, 1908.

Bach, Ira J. *Chicago on Foot—Walking Tours of Chicago's Architecture.* Chicago: Rand McNally and Company, 1977.

Berry, Brian J. L., ed. *Chicago: Transformation of an Urban System.* Cambridge: Ballinger Publishing Company, 1976.

_____. *Commercial Structure and Commercial Blight.* Research Paper No. 85. Chicago: University of Chicago, Department of Geography, 1963.

Breese, Gerald W. *The Daytime Population of the Central Business District of Chicago.* Chicago: University of Chicago Press, 1949.

Bretz, J. Harlen. *Geology of the Chicago Region.* Urbana: Illinois State Geological Survey, Bulletin No. 65. Part I, Geology of the Chicago Region, 1939; Part II, the Pleistocene, 1955.

Buder, Stanley. *Pullman: An Experiment in Industrial Order and Community Planning 1880-1930.* New York: Oxford University Press, 1967.

Burnham, Daniel H., and Bennett, Edward H. *Plan of Chicago.* Chicago: The Commercial Club, 1909.

Burnham, Daniel H., and Kingery, Robert. *Planning the Region of Chicago.* Chicago: Chicago Regional Planning Association, 1956.

Campbell, Edna Fay; Smith, Fanny R; and Jones, Clarence F. *Our City—Chicago.* New York: Charles Scribner's Sons, 1930.

Chicago Area Transportation Study, *Final Report,* 3 Vols. Chicago, 1959, 1960, and 1962.

Chicago Guide, eds. *The Chicago Guidebook.* Chicago: Henry Regnery Company, 1972.

Chicago Land Use Survey. Vol. I: *Residential Chicago.* Vol. II: *Land Use in Chicago.* Chicago: Chicago Plan Commission, 1942, 1943.

Chicago Plan Commission. *Forty-four Cities in the City of Chicago.* Chicago: 1942.

_____. *Master Plan of Residential Land Use of Chicago.* Chicago, 1943.

City of Chicago Department of Development and Planning. *Chicago 21: A Plan for the Central Area Communities.* Chicago: 1973.

_____. *The Comprehensive Plan of Chicago.* Chicago: 1966.

_____. *Historic City: The Settlement of Chicago.* Chicago: 1976.

City of Chicago, Department of Public Works. *Chicago Public Works: A History.* Chicago: Rand McNally and Company, 1973.

Condit, Carl W. *Chicago 1910-29: Building, Planning, and Urban Technology.* Chicago: University of Chicago Press, 1973.

_____. *Chicago 1930-70: Building, Planning, and Urban Technology.* Chicago: University of Chicago Press, 1974.

_____. *The Chicago School of Architecture: A History of Commercial and Public Building in the Chicago Area, 1875-1925.* Chicago: University of Chicago Press, 1964.

Cowles, Henry C. *The Plant Societies of Chicago and Vicinity.* Chicago: Geographic Society of Chicago, Bulletin No. 2, 1901.

Cox, Henry J., and Armington, John H. *The Weather and Climate of Chicago.* Chicago: Geographic Society of Chicago, Bulletin No. 4, 1914.

Cramer, Robert E. *Manufacturing Structure of the Cicero District, Metropolitan Chicago.* Research Paper No. 27. Chicago: University of Chicago Department of Geography, 1952.

Cromie, Robert. *The Great Chicago Fire:* New York: McGraw-Hill, 1958.

Cutler, Irving. *Chicago: Metropolis of the Mid-Continent.* Dubuque: Geographic Society of Chicago and Kendall/Hunt Publishing Company, 1976.

_____. *The Chicago Metropolitan Area: Selected Geographic Readings.* New York: Simon and Schuster, 1970.

_____. *The Chicago-Milwaukee Corridor: A Geographic Study of Intermetropolitan Coalescence.* Northwestern University Studies in Geography No. 9. Evanston: Northwestern University Department of Geography, 1965.

Davis, James L. *The Elevated System and the Growth of Northern Chicago.* Northwestern University Studies in Geography No. 10. Evanston: Northwestern University Department of Geography, 1965.

Dedmon, Emmett. *Fabulous Chicago.* Chicago: Random House, 1953.

De Meirleir, Marcel J. *Manufactural Occupance in the West Central Area of Chicago.* Research Paper No. 11. Chicago: University of Chicago Department of Geography, 1950.

De Vise, Pierre. *Chicago's People, Jobs and Homes—the Human Geography of the City and Metro Area.* 2 Vols. Chicago: De Paul University, 1964.

_____. *Chicago's Widening Color Gap.* Chicago: Interuniversity Social Research Committee, 1967.

Draine, Edwin H. *Import Traffic of Chicago and Its Hinterland.* Research Paper No. 81. Chicago: University of Chicago Department of Geography, 1963.

Drake, St. Clair, and Cayton, Horace R. *Black Metropolis.* 2 Vols. New York: Harcourt, Brace & World, Inc., 1970.

Duddy, Edward A. *Agriculture in the Chicago Region.* Chicago: University of Chicago Press, 1929.

Duis, Perry. *Chicago: Creating New Traditions.* Chicago: Chicago Historical Society, 1976.

Duncan, Otis Dudley, and Duncan, Beverly. *The Negro Population of Chicago: A Study of Residential Succession.* Chicago: University of Chicago Press, 1957.

Farr, Finis. *Chicago: A Personal History of America's Most American City.* New Rochelle: Arlington House, 1973.

Federal Writers Project. *Illinois, A Descriptive and Historical Guide,* 2nd ed. Chicago: A.A. McClurg & Co., 1947.

Fellman, Jerome D. *Truck Transportation Patterns of Chicago.* Research Paper No. 12. Chicago: University of Chicago Department of Geography, 1950.

Frazier, E. Franklin. *The Negro Family in Chicago.* Chicago: University of Chicago Press, 1932.

Fryxell, F.M. *The Physiography of the Region of Chicago.* Chicago: University of Chicago Press, 1927.

Goode, J. Paul. *The Geographic Background of Chicago.* Chicago: University of Chicago Press, 1926.

Graham, Jory. *Chicago—An Extraordinary Guide.* Chicago: Rand McNally & Company, 1968.

Hansen, Harry. *The Chicago.* Rivers of America Series. New York: Farrar & Rinehart, Inc., 1942.

Harper, Robert A. *Recreational Occupance of the Moraine Lake Region of Northeastern Illinois and Southeastern Wisconsin.* Research Paper No. 14. Chicago: University of Chicago Department of Geography, 1950.

Helvig, Magne. *Chicago's External Truck Movements.* Research Paper No. 90. Chicago: University of Chicago Department of Geography, 1964.

Hillman, Arthur, and Casey, Robert J. *Tomorrow's Chicago.* Chicago: University of Chicago Press, 1953.

Hoyt, Homer. *One Hundred Years of Land Values in Chicago, 1830-1933.* Chicago: University of Chicago Press, 1933.

Illinois Sesquicentennial Commission. *Illinois Guide and Gazetteer.* Chicago: Rand McNally and Company, 1969.

Jensen, George Peter. *Historic Chicago Sites.* Chicago: Creative Enterprises, 1953.

Johnson, Charles B. *Growth of Cook County.* Vol. 1. Chicago: Board of Commissioners of Cook County, Illinois, 1960.

Karlen, Harvey. *The Governments of Chicago.* Chicago: Courier Publishing Company, 1958.

Kenyon, James B. *The Industrialization of the Skokie Area.* Research Paper No. 33. Chicago: University of Chicago Department of Geography, 1954.

Kiang, Ying Cheng. *Chicago.* Chicago: Adams Press, 1968.

Kirkland, Joseph. *The Story of Chicago.* 3 Vols. Chicago: Dibble Publishing Company, 1892-1894.

Kitagawa, Evelyn M., and Taeuber, Karl E. eds. *Local Community Fact Book: Chicago Metropolitan Area, 1960.* Chicago: Chicago Community Inventory, University of Chicago, 1963.

Klove, Robert C. *The Park Ridge—Barrington Area: A Study of Residential Land Patterns and Problems in Suburban Chicago.* Chicago: University of Chicago Department of Geography, 1942.

Kogan, Herman, and Kogan, Rick. *Yesterday's Chicago.* Miami: E. A. Seemann Publishing, Inc., 1976.

Kogan, Herman, and Wendt, Lloyd. *Chicago: A Pictorial History.* New York: Bonanza Books, 1958.

Lewis, Lloyd, and Smith, Henry Justin. *Chicago, the History of Its Reputation.* New York: Harcourt, Brace and Company, 1929.

Lind, Alan. *Chicago Surface Lines: An Illustrated History.* Park Forest: Transport History Press, 1974.

Longstreet, Stephen. *Chicago 1860-1919.* New York: David McKay Company, 1973.

Lowe, David. *Lost Chicago.* Boston: Houghton Mifflin Company, 1975.

Mayer, Harold M. *Chicago: City of Decisions.* Papers on Chicago, No. 1. Chicago: Geographic Society of Chicago, 1955.

_____. *The Port of Chicago and the St. Lawrence Seaway.* Research Paper No. 49. Chicago: University of Chicago Press, 1957.

_____. *The Railway Pattern of Metropolitan Chicago.* Chicago: University of Chicago Department of Geography, 1943.

Mayer, Harold M., and Wade, Richard C. *Chicago: Growth of a Metropolis.* Chicago: University of Chicago Press, 1969.

Miller, John J. *Open Land in Metropolitan Chicago.* Chicago: Midwest Open Land Association, 1962.

Nelli, Humbert S. *The Italians in Chicago, 1880-1930: A Study in Ethnic Mobility.* New York: Oxford University Press, 1970.

Northeastern Illinois Metropolitan Area Local Governmental Services Commission. *Governmental Problems in the Chicago Metropolitan Area.* Edited by Leverett S. Lyon. Chicago: University of Chicago Press, 1957.

Northeastern Illinois Planning Commission. *The Comprehensive Plan for the Development of the Northeastern Illinois Counties Area.* Chicago, 1968.

_____. *Open Space in Northeastern Illinois, Technical Report No. 2.* Chicago, 1962.

_____. *A Social Geography of Metropolitan Chicago.* Chicago, 1960.

_____. *Suburban Factbook.* Chicago, 1971.

Olson, Ernst W. *History of the Swedes of Illinois.* 2 Vols. Chicago: The Engberg-Holmberg Publishing Company, 1908.

Pierce, Bessie Louise. *A History of Chicago.* 3 Vols. New York: A.A. Knopf, 1937-57.

_____. *As Others See Chicago—Impressions of Visitors, 1673-1933.* Chicago: University of Chicago Press, 1933.

Platt, Rutherford H. *Open Land in Urban Illinois.* De Kalb: Northern Illinois University Press, 1971.

Poles of Chicago, 1837-1937. Chicago: Polish Pageant, Inc., 1937.

Poole, Ernest. *Giants Gone—Men Who Made Chicago.* New York: McGraw-Hill Book Company, Inc., 1943.

Quaife, Milo M. *Checagou: From Indian Wigwam to Modern City, 1673-1835.* Chicago: University of Chicago Press, 1933.

_____. *Chicago and the Old Northwest, 1673-1835*. Chicago: University of Chicago Press, 1913.

_____. *Chicago's Highways Old and New: From Indian Trails to Motor Road*. Chicago: D.F. Keller & Company, 1923.

Randall, Frank A. *History of the Development of Building Construction in Chicago*. Urbana: University of Illinois Press, 1949.

Rossi, Peter H., and Dentler, Robert A. *The Politics of Urban Renewal: The Chicago Findings*. New York: The Free Press of Glencoe, 1961.

Salisbury, Rollin D., and Alden, William C. *The Geography of Chicago and Its Environs*. Chicago: Geographic Society of Chicago, Bulletin No. 1, 1899.

The Sentinel's History of Chicago Jewry, 1911-1961. Chicago: Sentinel Publishing Company, 1961.

Siegel, Arthur, ed. *Chicago's Famous Buildings*. Chicago: University of Chicago Press, 1970.

Sinclair, Upton. *The Jungle*. New York: Doubleday Page and Co., 1906.

Smith, Henry Justin. *Chicago's Great Century, 1833-1933*. Chicago: Consolidated Publishers, 1933.

Solomon, Ezra, and Bilbija, Zarko G. *Metropolitan Chicago: An Economic Analysis*. Glencoe: The Free Press, 1959.

Solzman, David M. *Waterway Industrial Sites, A Chicago Case Study*. Research Paper No. 107. Chicago: University of Chicago Department of Geography, 1966.

Taaffe, Edward J. *The Air Passenger Hinterland of Chicago*. Research Paper No. 24. Chicago: University of Chicago Department of Geography, 1952.

Townsend, Andrew J. "The Germans of Chicago." Ph.D. dissertation, University of Chicago, 1927.

University of Chicago Center for Urban Studies. *Mid-Chicago Economic Development Study*. 3 Vols. Chicago Mayor's Committee for Economic and Cultural Development, 1966.

Wendt, Lloyd, and Kogan, Herman. *Lords of the Levee: The Story of Bathhouse John and Hinky Dink*. Indianapolis: Bobbs-Merrill Company, 1943.

Willman, H.B. *Summary of the Geology of the Chicago Area*. Urbana: Illinois State Geological Survey, Circular 460, 1971.

Wirth, Louis. *The Ghetto*. Chicago: University of Chicago Press, 1928.

Zorbaugh, Harvey W. *The Gold Coast and the Slum*. Chicago: University of Chicago Press, 1929.

Appendix

THE SWEEP OF GEOGRAPHICAL HISTORY: EVENTS IN THE GROWTH OF ILLINOIS

Alden Cutshall

ca. 11,500 B.C.	Last glacier receded from modern Illinois.
ca. 10,000 B.C.	Glacial Lake Chicago broke through its confining moraines to drain southwest into the Illinois and Mississippi rivers.
ca. 8,000 B.C.	Archaic Indian culture existed in the Illinois area (evidence found in Modoc rock shelter near Prairie du Rocher).
ca. 6,000 B.C.	Oldest of the twelve successive Indian settlements at Kampsville as unearthed in recent archeological discoveries.
ca. 700	Site of Cahokia Mounds first inhabited, later expanded to cover about six square miles and may have had a peak population between 30 and 40 thousand.
ca. 1,500	Cahokia site abandoned; reasons for abandonment unclear.
1673	Marquette and Joliet were the first Europeans to reach Illinois country.
1680	La Salle visited Illinois; Fort Creve Coeur established on the bluffs above the Illinois River near Peoria.
1696	Father Francois Pinet's mission established at what is now Chicago.
1699	Cahokia, oldest permanent settlement in modern Illinois, founded.
1703	Jesuits established Kaskaskia.
1717	Illinois country became part of French colony of Louisiana; formerly it had been administratively a part of Quebec.

1717	First Negro slaves brought to Illinois from Santo Domingo to a location near Fort de Chartres.
1720	First Fort de Chartres completed.
1723	Prairie du Rocher in present Monroe County was settled.
ca. 1737	Ancient log house now known as Cahokia Courthouse was built; it is probably the oldest private dwelling in the Midwest.
1756	Fort de Chartres, considered the most formidable on the continent, was rebuilt.
1763	Illinois country ceded to Britain by France.
1778-79	George Rogers Clark secured Illinois country for Virginia; Virginia created the county of Illinois.
ca. 1779	Jean Baptiste Point du Sable established a trading post at Chicago.
1787	Northwest Ordinance established government for Illinois as part of Northwest Territory.
1796	du Sable sold trading post to Le Mai.
1800	Illinois became part of Indiana Territory.
1802	Pierre Menard House was built overlooking the little Kaskaskia settlement at its feet.
1803	Fort Dearborn established at present site of Michigan Avenue and Wacker Drive in Chicago.
1804	John Kinzie bought trading post from Le Mai at what is now Chicago; government land offices opened at Kaskaskia and Vincennes.
1806	Shawneetown settled.
1809	Illinois Territory established by Congress with Kaskaskia as its capital. Shawneetown, the oldest permanent English settlement in the state and once described as having more business activity than any place west of Pittsburgh, was reestablished.
1810	Flatboats of coal shipped down the Big Muddy (southwestern Illinois) and Mississippi rivers to New Orleans.
1811	First steamboat on Ohio. Great Earthquake. First post office in Illinois established at Shawneetown.
1812	Fort Dearborn destroyed by Potawatomi Indians. Gallatin, Johnson, and Madison counties formed; only Randolph and St. Clair were in existence prior to this date.
1814	Government land office established at Shawneetown; Alton founded; first newspaper published in Illinois.
1815	Shawneetown's population estimated at 350.
1816	Fort Dearborn rebuilt; first bank in Illinois, The Bank of Illinois in Shawneetown, approved; Fort Armstrong begun, which initiated the Rock Island settlement.
1818	Illinois became 21st state; Albion founded; Lawrenceville, Vienna, and Fairfield were new communities.
1819	Mt. Vernon and Belleville founded.
1820	Capital moved from Kaskaskia to Vandalia, then a mere hamlet;

	government land office established at Palestine in Crawford County; price of land was $1.25 an acre.
1821	Springfield founded. Permanent occupation of Galena was well underway; lead had been mined there for many years by Indians and seasonal migrants from southern Illinois.
1822	Quincy and Urbana settled.
1823	Salem founded as the halfway station on the Vincennes-St. Louis stage-coach route. First permanent settlement in LaSalle County at modern Ottawa.
1825	New counties created were Adams, Calhoun, Clay, Hancock, McDonough, and Warren; Paris settled; first law school in Illinois was opened.
1826	First ferry across the Illinois River, the Dixon Ferry.
1827	Danville started, first settlement at the salt spring four miles west of the present city.
1828	First steamboat reached Peoria; McKendree College created at Lebanon.
1829	Decatur settled; Illinois College founded at Jacksonville; first wagonload of lead from Galena to Chicago via modern Dixon, Plainfield, and Naperville; according to popular legend, four men on horseback rode from Chicago to Shawneetown in an unsuccessful attempt to borrow $10,000 for use in developing their village on Lake Michigan; Shawneetown referred to as the financial capital of the state.
1830	Abraham Lincoln moved to Illinois; German refugees from Revolution of 1830 established a colony in St. Clair County, the beginning of extensive German settlement in that part of the state.
1831	Cook County formed; Joliet founded. Legislature organized LaSalle County; formerly it was a part of Peoria County.
1833	Champaign County organized; formerly it was part of the then large Vermilion County. Chicago organized as a town. Oak Park settled.
1834	Aurora settled; Rockford established; State legislature made Hubbard's Trace a state road, marked with milestones and terminating in downtown Chicago, where it became State Street; first Norwegian settlement in the United States, in LaSalle County.
1835	Elgin settled; Waukegan's modern settlement began; Freeport founded.
1836	Winnetka settled on old Green Bay Road.
1837	Legislative action made Springfield the state capital; Chicago incorporated as a city. Cairo settled. John Deere designed an effective steel plow at Grand Detour. Lincoln, then called Pottsville, settled; renamed in 1857 to honor the man who had earlier surveyed townsite. Severe depression in the country.
1838	First railroad in operation in Morgan County between Meredosia and Morgan City.
1839	The original Illinois iron furnace was built near Elizabethtown, now in Shawnee National Forest; rebuilt and enlarged prior to the Civil War, it was operated until 1883. Mormons settled in Nauvoo; capital moved to Spring-

field; Rockford incorporated; Du Page County, the 75th county in Illinois, formed; new bank building constructed in Shawneetown; Abraham Lincoln House in Springfield was built.

1840	Four largest cities were Chicago (4,470), Springfield (2,574), Alton (2,340), and Quincy (2,319).
1841	Olney incorporated.
1843	Bloomingtom founded; Elmhurst settled.
1845	Nauvoo the largest city in Illinois, population 20,000.
1847	McCormick reaper plant built in Chicago; *Chicago Tribune* began publication.
1848	New state constitution prohibited slavery; Illinois and Michigan Canal opened; Chicago Board of Trade established; Galena and Chicago Union Railroad completed from Chicago to the Des Plaines River, its first cargo a load of wheat from its western terminus to downtown Chicago.
1850	Chicago's population was 30,000; Chicago raised the grade on many downtown streets.
1851	Illinois Wesleyan University began instruction.
1852	First train on Illinois Central from Calumet (Kensington) to downtown Chicago station.
1853	First state fair; Illinois Central extended to Randolph Street, tracks laid on a trestle in the Lake.
1854	Evanston founded; cholera epidemic in the Chicago area.
1855	Kankakee begun; Northwestern University founded.
1856	Chicago Historical Society, the oldest cultural society in Illinois, was organized.
1857	Illinois State Normal School, the first state-supported college in Illinois, was established just outside Bloomington.
1861	East St. Louis incorporated.
1865	Chicago's Union Stockyards established; first commercial rolling of steel rails in America took place at North Chicago Rolling Mill Company.
1867	Cicero founded; University of Illinois established by legislative action (opened in 1869 at Urbana-Champaign).
1870	Third Illinois Constitution adopted.
1871	Great Chicago fire.
1874	Joseph Glidden of DeKalb obtained a patent on barbed wire; segregation forbidden in Illinois public schools.
1875	Swift and Armour packing companies began operation in Chicago.
1888	State capitol completed.
1889	Jane Addams opened Hull House; Chicago Opera Company formed.
1890	University of Chicago chartered.
1891	Chicago Symphony Orchestra formed.
1892	Armour Institute, now Illinois Institute of Technology, established. Granite City established.

1893	World's Columbian Exposition with first Ferris wheel and first pay toilets; severe depression in the United States.
1895	The General Assembly approved the establishment of three regional normal schools, later built at Charleston, Macomb, and DeKalb.
1897	Chicago Loop created by new elevated train lines; first movie made in Chicago.
1898	Geographic Society of Chicago organized.
1899	Dowie established Zion, a religious community, in Lake County.
1900	Chicago Sanitary and Ship Canal completed; Chicago River made to flow backwards.
1903	Iroquois Theatre fire in Chicago; Millikin University founded in Decatur. First effective child labor law in Illinois.
1904	First oil well in Illinois, in Clark County; the beginning of the first oil boom (Clark, Crawford, Lawrence, and Wabash counties).
1905	Illinois and Mississippi Canal, then called Hennepin Canal, completed.
1910	Beginning of civil service in some state jobs.
1914	First paved roads in Cook County outside of Chicago.
1916	In Chicago, Navy Pier, then called Municipal Pier, completed. Edgewater Beach Hotel built.
1918	State centennial celebration.
1921	Cahokia Mounds scientifically studied for the first time.
1924	Rev. Preston Bradley began a radio ministry in Chicago that was to continue without interruption for 51 years.
1927	World's largest hotel (until the 1970s), now Conrad Hilton, completed in Chicago.
1929	Palmolive Building, now home of Playboy enterprises, completed.
1930	Adler Planetarium opened; lowest temperature recorded in Illinois, $-35°$, on January 22 at Mt. Carroll.
1931	First dramatic television program broadcast from Chicago.
1933	Illinois waterway opened; Century of Progress opened.
1934	Brookfield Zoo completed; construction had begun in 1926. The hottest day in Chicago, $105°$, on July 24.
1936	Highest temperature recorded in Illinois, $115°$, at Greenville.
1937	Disastrous flood at Shawneetown; oil discovered in Clay County; start of new southern Illinois oil boom.
1940	United States center of population shifted westward into Illinois to northern Richland County; Park Forest, the first entirely planned suburban community in the state, was incorporated.
1942	Stevens Hotel, now Conrad Hilton, used as a naval training station; first self-sustaining atomic reaction at the University of Chicago Stagg Field laboratory.
1948	O'Hare Airport officially opened, but most traffic continued to use Midway Airport until 1955.
1950	Illinois Geographical Society formed; it was formerly the Illinois Chapter of the National Council of Geography Teachers.

1958	Congress Expressway (Eisenhower) completed in Chicago.
1959	St. Lawrence Seaway opened; Chicago became a deep water port.
1960	Dresden nuclear power plant began operation; McCormick Place opened in Chicago.
1965	University of Illinois at Chicago Circle, the only university ever named for a traffic interchange, opened.
1967	Record snowfall paralyzed Chicago; Weston chosen for nuclear accelerator; National Council for Geographic Education opened a central office in Chicago.
1968	Illinois celebrated its sesquicentennial.
1970	Fourth Illinois Constitution.
1971	Chicago Union Stockyards closed.
1973	Sears Tower, tallest building in the world, topped out in Chicago.
1974	Regional Transit Authority created in Chicago area counties.
1975	In Chicago, Mayor Richard J. Daley reelected for an unprecedented sixth term; students at Senn High School represented 54 countries and 40 different languages.
1976	The nation's bicentennial sparked the writing and publication of many local histories in the state.
1977	The coldest January on record at most recording stations in Illinois, 14 degrees below normal at Chicago.
1978	Chicago Daily News, begun in late 1875 and one of the few remaining major evening papers in the country, ceased publication.

Index